A COUNSELOR'S GUIDE TO CAREER ASSESSMENT INSTRUMENTS

Second Edition

EDITED BY:

Jerome T. Kapes
Texas A & M University
and
Marjorie Moran Mastie
Washtenaw Intermediate School District, Michigan

The National Career Development Association
1988

A Publication of The National Career Development Association

Copyright 1988 by The National Career Development Association, A Division of
The American Association for Counseling and Development

ISBN 1-55620-040-4 (hardcover) 1-55620-050-1 (softcover)

Copies may be ordered from
  Publication Sales
  The American Association for Counseling and Development
  5999 Stevenson Avenue
  Alexandria, Virginia 22041
(Order 72212 hardcover; 72204 paper cover)

About the Editors

Jerome T. Kapes is Professor of Vocational Education and Educational Psychology at Texas A&M University where he teaches courses in vocational guidance, measurement, evaluation and research. His professional experience includes faculty positions at Penn State and Lehigh University before coming to Texas A&M in 1978. He is a graduate of Penn State with a B.S. and Ph.D. in Vocational-Industrial Education and M.Ed. in Counselor Education. Dr. Kapes has been a member of AACD (APGA) since 1967 with divisional membership in NCDA and AMECD. He is a Nationally Certified Counselor (NCC) and a Nationally Certified Career Counselor (NCCC). Additionally he holds membership in the American Vocational Association (AVA), the American Educational Research Association (AERA), the American Vocational Education Research Association (AVERA), and the National Association for Industrial and Technical Teacher Educators (NAITTE). He is an author or co-author of over 50 articles, books and monographs, and has presented papers at over 40 national and state professional association meetings. Much of his research and publication activity has been in the area of career development and related measurement topics.

Marjorie M. Mastie is the Consultant in Measurements and Guidance at Washtenaw Intermediate School District in Ann Arbor, Michigan. Her extensive experience in career guidance measurement has included positions as Assistant to the Director at the National Assessment of Educational Progress, in which she guided the preparations for NAEP's Career and Occupational Development Assessment; as developer of Michigan's Career Development Assessment; and as a nationally recognized consultant in assessment and career guidance. She has taught at both Eastern Michigan University and The University of Michigan, from which she holds a B.A. and M.A. and is a candidate for the Ph.D. in Guidance and Counseling with specialization in the measurement of career develoment. A member of AACD since 1961, AVA and AERA, Mrs. Mastie is President of Michigan CDA and has been a Presidential candidate, Trustee, and Newsletter Editor of NCDA, Secretary of AMECD, and a Director of NCME. She is author or co-author of five books and dozens of chapters and articles focusing on vocational assessment, assessment as a counseling tool, and appropriate uses of measurement in career guidance.

Table of Contents

ACKNOWLEDGMENTS

Even though in tackling this second edition of the *Counselor's Guide*, the editors benefited from the experiences gained from the first edition, the task was no less demanding. As editors we want our readers to know about the many individuals who worked with us and in other ways made the project possible.

Those closest to the project were members of our advisory committee, whose continuous efforts are described in Chapter I. Several of these individuals were with us for the first edition and unselfishly agreed to serve again even with the knowledge of the work involved. These faithful colleagues include Chris Borman, Dave Jepsen, Dale Prediger and Bert Westbrook. Joining the group were George Grisdale, Joe Kandor and Frank Womer from AMECD and Karl Botterbusch, Linda Parrish and Michael Peterson who were particularly helpful with the special populations sections.

The most important staff function was carried out by the project assistant, Nanciann Frazier, who completed her Master's Degree in Counseling at Texas A&M University while working 50% time on the *Counselor's Guide*. She was responsible for production and mailing of all forms and correspondence, much of the library research that went into discovering instruments and reviews and the extensive chapter of brief descriptions of additional instruments. If anyone was indispensable to the project it was Nanciann. A second staff person who contributed from the central office was Niel Carey, NCDA Executive Director. Niel handled all matters requiring NCDA input and regularly communicated with both editors offering advice and support. A third staff position which we requested and received from NCDA was our Production Editor, Ed Whitfield. Ed was responsible for the production editing for the first edition as Chair of the Publications Committee and graciously consented to convert our many pieces of manuscripts into a polished finished product. Other members of NCDA who supported the project in many ways associated with their roles included three consecutive presidents, Sunny Hansen, Linda Pfister, and Duane Brown; Media Committee Chair, Roger Aubrey, and NCDA Trustee, Dennis Engels. Also important to the creation of the *Counselor's Guide* were the Buros Institute and especially James Mitchell, Director, and the Test Corporation of America in the persons of Clark Smith, Chief Executive Officer, and Jane Guthrie, Senior Editor.

The institutions that employ us have also provided much support. At Texas A&M we are especially indebted to Daniel Houscholder, Head of the Department of Industrial, Vocational and Technical Education, where the project was housed, and Michael Ash, Head of the Department of Educational Psychology. Departmental secretaries Sally Lesher, who handled our bookkeeping and Carla Heinchon who typed much of our correspondence have also helped greatly. Also, Educational Psychology graduate students Timothy Vansickle and Charlotte Kimmel donated much time to the project with nothing in return but good experiences.

At Wastenaw Intermediate School District we are grateful to Michael Emlaw, Superintendent, and John Bowen, Deputy Superintendent, for their support of the project, and to several secretaries in the Instruction Department for their assistance.

There were, of course, many others who contributed and without whom there would be no *Counselor's Guide*. These include the many reviewers, authors and publishers who contributed directly by writing reviews, chapters or other sections of the *Guide*. While they have the pleasure of an important job well done, our readers may want to thank them directly when the occasion arises.

While so many have given so much to make this second edition of the *Counselor's Guide* a reality, we are particularly grateful to our families from whom we borrowed the time to devote to this task. To Evelyn, Becky, David, Scott, Lynn and Andy, we dedicate this book and promise to be home in time for supper.

JTK
MMM

Preface

When *A Counselor's Guide to Vocational Guidance Instruments* was first published in 1982, the Board of Directors of the National Vocational Guidance Association (NVGA) and the editors, Jerome Kapes and Marjorie Mastie, believed the handbook would be an invaluable tool to counselors in a wide range of settings. They were right—as has been evidenced by the large number of copies distributed since that time.

The needs met by this demand, as well as the changes that have occurred in assessment practices, led to the decision to publish a second edition. The astute observer will notice that the names of both the publisher and the volume are different. NVGA has become the National Career Development Association (NCDA) and the publication has been retitled *A Counselor's Guide to Career Assessment Instruments*. These are not the only differences; this edition has been expanded to include new instruments and additional text material.

The NCDA Board deeply appreciates the willingness and enthusiasm (and hard work) that Jerome Kapes and Marjorie Mastie have exerted to make this second edition a reality. Our thanks also to the many individuals who contributed as authors and reviewers.

Linda A. Pfister, Past President
Duane Brown, President
National Career Development Association

CHAPTER I

The Counselor's Guide
Why, What and How

The Counselor's Guide: Why, What and How

Jerome T. Kapes
Texas A&M University

Marjorie M. Mastie
Washtenaw ISD, Ann Arbor

WHY THIS BOOK CAME TO BE

If you didn't want the world beating a path to your door, you shouldn't have built that mousetrap!

In its simplest form, this is the message that has come through during the five years that the first edition of the *Counselor's Guide* has been available. And although we hadn't expected the reaction, we have been soundly gratified by it, for we had undertaken the first volume on sheer faith. Our introduction to the first edition had read:

"The urgent need for a volume such as this was the compelling force from the beginning. What was surfacing in the field was a state of real desperation."

We had seen the desperation personally, among our colleagues, students, and fellow practitioners, but we had only our personal belief that the *Counselor's Guide* would be the answer. Now the data are in—

- Three printings (6000 copies) have been sold.
- The book has been widely adopted as a supplemental text in measurement courses.
- Numerous local, state, and regional workshops based on the book have been held, with a copy for each participant.
- Libraries stock it as a standard reference work.
- The catalogues of some publishers of tests and guidance materials now list the book.
- Individual practitioners in schools, colleges, agencies, and businesses nationwide have their own dog-eared personal copies on their desks.

Just as we began to relax and enjoy the success of our book, however, the clamoring for a second edition began. New instruments continued to be issued regularly, as did major revisions of existing instruments. Practitioners doing career counseling with adults wanted a new section on the personality/style/personal type measures they find so useful. The Carl Perkins Act mandate required that school personnel remain current on the very latest available instruments. Users of the volume rightfully urged addition of a chapter on interpreting the results of assessment. Excellent new reviews appeared in the literature. Publishers moved. Instruments went out of print. Prices changed. The world kept spinning—and it was time to return to the task.

Two early decisions were inescapable. First, the title of the volume needed to be changed to reflect current terminology. Just as the National Vocational Guidance Association (NVGA) has become the National Career Development Association (NCDA), so had "vocational guidance" instruments become instruments used in "career guidance," "career counseling," and/or "career development" programs. New usage is appearing that generalizes all of these to "career assessment" instruments, so our new title was born.

Second, we considered for a time whether the new *Counselor's Guide* would replace or supplement the original: whether we would include all former material plus new instruments and revisions, or whether we would include primarily reviews of new instruments and recent revisions. Sheer bulk convinced us that the editions would have to be viewed as cumulative, with each supplementing and updating what had gone before. Users are, thus, encouraged to build a set of *Counselor's Guides* so as to have access to all-inclusive information.

With these decisions made—and the editors convinced by the "world beating a path to our doors" that what we had thought was a one-time contribution was to be an ongoing responsibility—the work could begin again.

SECOND EDITION CONSIDERATIONS

What to change

Our first task as editors was to assemble an advisory committee, which included many of the same members who served on the first committee with several additions. Many decisions about format and content again needed to be made. Among the more noticeable changes that were decided upon are: adding several introductory chapters that make the *Guide* more comprehensive for use as a course text, moving some instruments to the additional instruments chapter, identifying and adding new instruments to the review chapter, increasing the length of the reviews, adding a section on personality measures, greatly expanding the additional instruments chapter (from70 to 126 instruments), expanding and adding annotations to the Sources of Information about Tests and Testing appendix, and adding a users' matrix.

The reviews address 21 new instruments along with 22 instruments from the first edition. For those instruments retained from the first edition, an entirely new review by a different reviewer has been provided.

Reviews and Reviewers

The decision as to what instruments to include in the second edition was based on the several studies reported in the next section of this chapter as well as the best professional judgment of our advisory committee. The principles underlying the decisions were:

a) Include all major instruments as identified by a consensus of studies.
b) Include instruments that have undergone major change.
c) Include new instruments that appear to have promise.
d) Include prominent personality measures in a new section.
e) Include selected special population instruments other than work samples. (Botterbusch, 1987 has dealt with work samples extensively—see Appendix A for further information.)
f) Exclude computerized instruments except as they may be referenced as versions of standard instruments.

The decision as to what to do with computerized instruments was particularly difficult since so many existing instruments are being computerized and many new computer-based instruments are being developed. In the opinion of the advisory committee, it was difficult to do justice to the new computerized measures while covering the traditional instruments. Also, research on these instruments and available knowledgeable reviewers are scarce. The decision to exclude computerized measures was made easier with the emergence of two other sources which are, or will soon be, available to the profession. The first of these is *Psychware Sourcebook: A Reference Guide to Computer-Based Products for Assessment in Psychology, Education, and Business* published by Test Corporation of America. (See Apendix A for further information.) The second source will be the product of an AACD Media Committee project undertaken as part of a new Counseling Software Review Board (CSRB). This document, which is expected to be completed by December, 1988, will review approximately 400 computer-based counseling tools including career assessment instruments.

The process of selecting instrument reviewers was similar to that followed for the first edition, except that more sources of reviewers were available. While the Buros Institute again agreed to allow the *Counselor's Guide* to use reviewers from its *Mental Measurements Yearbooks*, the newly created Test Corporation of America, publishers of *Test Critiques*, also joined in the project. Although a majority of reviewers came from these two sources, many others were selected from reviews published in professional journals, with some needing to be recruited for instruments for which no previous review existed.

All reviews and other sections of the *Guide* were subjected to external evaluation. However, the opinions expressed by the various authors and reviewers are their own.

CONTEXT INFORMATION FOR USERS

Before deciding to employ psychometric instruments for career assessment there is contextual prerequisite information the user needs to possess. This includes a knowledge of what instruments are available for the particular intended use, access to sources of good information about the available instruments, and awareness of the various legal, ethical and social considerations that impact the career assessment process. A brief discussion of each of these context considerations follows.

Instrument Availability and Use

Just as each user must discover what is available for use in career counseling, the editors and advisory committee for the *Counselor's Guide* needed a good source of information about what instruments were being currently used. We had as starting information the Zytowski and Warman (1982) study, *The Changing Use of Tests in Counseling* and the Engen, Lamb and Prediger (1982) study, *Are Secondary Schools Still Using Standardized Tests?* We also had the content of the *Counselor's Guide* first edition. A review of the literature failed to turn up any new studies on the frequency of use of particular tests in career counseling settings, so the advisory group undertook its own study.

The sample for this study was 100 persons who were selected from the 611 AACD members who held joint membership in both NCDA and AMECD. Of this group, 59 were selected because they were identified as holding leadership positions in the area of career assessment. The additional 41 persons were selected at random from those remaining on the list. The questionnaire consisted of three sections with instructions. The respondents were first asked to respond "yes, no or ?" to the list of instruments reviewed in the main section of the first edition of the *Counselor's Guide*. Additionally, the respondents were asked to nominate other instruments to include and to recommend other changes in content or format for the second edition. The response to this survey was somewhat disappointing, with the return rate being only 32%. In general, the respondents selected the best known instruments most frequently and seldom responded with a "no" vote. The special populations instruments received fewer responses than other categories (with a number of respondents indicating a lack of knowledge in this area). Conversely, the most nominated instruments not in the first edition were from the special populations and personality areas. A cross-section of other instruments was also nominated with almost no recommendations for changes in the content or format from the first edition. Table 1 provides a ranked listing of the most frequently cited instruments from each of the three sources of information available on the use of career assessment instruments.

From the information available in the table, the most preferred or used instruments are evident, but some observed problems suggest caution in interpreting the meaning of the lists. In both the *Counselor's Guide* survey and the Zytowski and Warman study, one instrument each (i.e. Career Development Inventory-Kuder and California Occupational Interest Inventory) was selected which is no longer available. This probably occurred because the old name was confused with an instrument with a similar well known name (i.e. Career Development Inventory and California Occupational Preference Survey). Secondly, only the best known instruments used in the mainstream are likely to be ranked high on any list, leaving many specialized or new instruments with few nominations. Lastly, return rates in all studies of this type are much less than would be needed in order to be sure the population of users has been adequately sampled. Therefore, while these studies confirm the popularity of the well known instruments, they do little to shed light on what else might be available that may be useful for a particular need.

Sources of Information about Available Instruments

When the first edition of the *Counselor's Guide* was published in 1982, there was only one comprehensive source available to those needing information about

TABLE 1: RANKED LISTS OF PREFERENCE FOR OR USE OF CAREER ASSESSMENT INSTRUMENTS FROM THREE STUDIES[a]

Counselor's Guide Survey (1986)[b]	Zytowski & Warman (1982)	Engen, Lamb & Prediger (1982)
Self Directed Search	(Aptitude only)	Armed Services Vocational Aptitude Battery
Kuder Occupational Interest Inventory	Differential Aptitude Tests	Differential Aptitude Tests
Strong-Campbell Interest Inventory	Bennett Mechanical	General Aptitude Test Battery
Differential Aptitude Tests	Minnesota Clerical	Kuder Occupational Interest Survey
Career Development Inventory	(Interest & Related)	Strong Vocational Interest Blank
Career Maturity Inventory	Strong-Campbell Interest Inventory	Strong-Campbell Interest Inventory
Harrington-O'Shea Career Decision Making System	Kuder Occupational Interest Inventory	Kuder General Interest Survey
Kuder General Interest Survey	Self Directed Search	Ohio Vocational Interest Survey
Career Assessment Inventory	Kuder General Interest Survey	Self Directed Search
Work Values Inventory	Career Assessment Inventory	California Occupational Preference Survey
Ohio Vocational Interest Survey II	Study of Values	Judgment of Occupational Behavior-Orientation
Armed Services Vocational Aptitude Battery	California Occupational Interest Inventory	Vocational Interest, Experience and Skill Assessment
Career Development Inventory-Kuder		State Career Information System Instruments
General Aptitude Test Battery		Local Instruments
Career Awareness Inventory		Career Maturity Inventory
California Occupational Preference Survey		Career Planning Program
Hall Occupational Orientation Inventory		Harrington-O'Shea Career Decision-Making System
Jackson Vocational Interest Survey		Hall Occupational Orientation Inventory
Minnesota Importance Questionnaire		Interest Determination, Exploration and Assessment System
World of Work Inventory		Picture Interest Exploration Survey

Notes: a) Brackets indicate tied ranks.
b) Top 20 in *Counselor's Guide* survey—selected on half or more returns.

7

career assessment instruments. That source was the Buros Institute publication *Test in Print II* and its companion set of reviews, the *Eighth Mental Measurements Yearbook* (MMY), which was published in 1978. Since that time, the Buros Institute, relocated at the University of Nebraska, has released *Tests in Print III* (1983) and the *Ninth Mental Measurements Yearbook* (1985) and has established an on-line data base through Bibliographic Retrieval Service (BRS) which makes reviews for subsequent yearbooks available as they are received.

A second major source of test information and reviews became available in 1983 when Test Corporation of America released its first volume of *Tests* and subsequently published five volumes of *Test Critiques* (TC) between 1984 and 1987. The reviews in TC differ somewhat from those provided by the MMY in that more coverage is given to a description of the test, and information in addition to the traditional technical evaluation covered by the Buros reviews is provided. However, the MMY usually provides reviews from more than one reviewer, while TC publishes only one review of each test. Also, each edition of the MMY is comprehensive over most published tests in the U.S. and other English-speaking countries, while TC is selective and cumulative, and includes the most-used instruments in psychology, education and business.

In addition to these two major providers of test information and reviews, there are other more limited sources of information which the career counselor may find useful. Included among these are the publications of the Stout Vocational Rehabilitation Institute—Materials Development Center at the University of Wisconsin-Stout which specializes in the assessment of handicapped and disabled persons. A second source of this nature is VOC-AIM in Starkville, Mississippi, which publishes vocational assessment materials specifically for use with special students in school settings. The professional journals continue to publish recent reviews; those likely to contain reviews or articles about the use of career assessment instruments are the *Journal of Counseling and Development*, the *Career Development Quarterly* and the *Measurement and Evaluation in Counseling and Development Journal*. Also, the Committee to Screen Career Counseling Instruments which is sponsored by the Association for Measurement and Evaluation in Counseling and Development (AMECD) publishes test reviews, many on recently developed instruments, in the organization newsletter, AMECD *Newsnotes*.

Those desiring additional information about the sources described here as well as other sources of information about tests and testing are encouraged to consult Appendix A, which contains an annotated bibliography of available sources.

Legal, Ethical and Social Considerations

Today's user of career assessment instruments needs to consider many more external factors than did those who pioneered the field. Very few laws existed forty years ago when the post World War II expansion of the use of tests in career counseling began. Since that time, both state and federal laws have been passed which either govern the use of tests or promote and sometimes even require their use.

Federal legislation that has promoted the use of tests for career counseling programs can be traced back to 1958 when the *National Defense Education Act* was passed with its emphasis on counseling and guidance in the public schls. This law was followed by *The Elementary and Secondary Education Act of 1965* and its later amendments that continued to promote public school guidance and counseling activities, including testing and assessment.

A second stream of federal legislation that at first promoted vocational or career guidance and eventually required the use of tests in the public schools began with the *Vocational Education Act of 1963* and was expanded by its subsequent amendments in 1968 and 1976. The 1984 *Carl D. Perkins Vocational Education Act*, which requires that expenditures for guidance and counseling be no less than under previous acts, also includes in section 204 (c) a specific requirement for handicapped and disadvantaged students that states:

> Each student who enrolls in a vocational education program and to whom subsection (b) applies shall receive - (1) assessment of interests, abilities, and special needs of such student with respect to completing successfully the vocational education program,
> . . .

Operating alongside the last two federal vocational education acts has been *The Education of All Handicapped Children Act* of 1975 and its subsequent amendments. This legislation requires the use of tests and other assessment devices as input to constructing Individualized Education Plans (IEP's) for all handicapped children through age 21 in the public schools. Since many handicapped students in the public secondary schools are served in vocational education programs, tests targeted to this group have expanded greatly in number, if not in quality.

Emerging over somewhat the same time period as vocational education and handicapped legislation, the career education movement also contributed to the use of tests in career guidance and counseling. Beginning in 1971 and promoted by separate legislation in 1974, 1976 and 1977, this movement has been largely integrated into the public schools. At the present, its major impact in assessment is probably the downward movement of the use of career assessment instruments into the elementary and middle schools.

While the above described legislation promoted the use of assessment as part of the career guidance and counseling function of the schools, other legislation was passed that regulated its use. In 1979 the Department of HEW's Office of Civil Rights issued federal *Vocational Education Programs Guidelines for Eliminating Discrimination and Denial of Services on the Basis of Race, Color, National Origin, Sex and Handicap*. These guidelines, based on three pieces of previous civil rights legislation (Civil Rights Act of 1964, Title IX of the Education Amendments of 1972 and section 504 of the Rehabilitation Act of 1973), prohibit the use of tests in ways that would limit a person's options to pursue training in vocational education programs. Other federal legislation or guidelines that restrict or govern the use of tests include the 1974 *Family Educational Rights and Privacy Act* (The Buckley Amendment) and the National Institute of Education (NIE) (1978) *Guidelines for Assessment of Sex Bias and Sex Fairness in Career Interest Inventories*.

The professional associations have also provided guidance for the use of tests in career counseling as well as in other areas. *The Standards for Educational and Psychological Tests* (1985) published by the American Psychological Association (APA) on behalf of a joint committee of APA, the American Educational Research Association (AERA) and the National Council for Measurement in Education (NCME) has a separate section for Test Use in Counseling. The recently published supplement to these standards provides *Guidelines for Computer-Based Tests and Interpretations* (1986). The National Board for Certified Counselors (NBCC) as well as its specialty sub-group the National Board for Certified Career Counselors (NBCCC) have also produced a code of ethics that includes a section on Measurement and Evaluation. In 1980 the American Personnel and Guidance Association (APGA now AACD) published its policy statement *Responsibilities of Users of Standardized Tests* (RUST). This document, which is currently under revision, was included as Appendix B of the first edition of the *Counselor's Guide*. An abbreviated checklist based on the RUST document as well as the other guidelines described above is included as Chapter V in this edition.

HOW TO USE THIS BOOK

Clearly, as evidenced by the success of the first edition, the *Counselor's Guide* is an invaluable tool. In order to capitalize on its value, however, each reader must become familiar with the overall contents of the book and with the specific information that is available in each section so as to be able to access it quickly when needed. To that end, the component parts are described here.

- Ed Herr's chapter defining the counselor's role in assessment (Chapter II) does a masterful job of putting measurement into perspective as one of the tools of the counselor.
- Frank Womer's practical summary of the principles of choosing an appropriate test (Chapter III) could well serve as a basic reference in an introductory measurement class and will most certainly be a much-appreciated review for those whose graduate work is a distant memory.
- The chapter by Howard Tinsley and Richard Bradley on interpreting results (Chapter IV) responds with sensitivity and precision to practitioner requests for a sound statement of guidelines for using test data with clients.
- Dale Prediger and Nancy Garfield's checklist of testing competencies and responsibilities (Chapter V) may be used as an informal self-evaluation device and belongs in the hands of every professional.
- Forty-three individual test entries comprise the heart of this volume (Chapter VI). These are divided into seven categories to facilitate perusal and selection of an appropriate instrument for a given use: Multiple Aptitude Batteries, Interest Inventories, Measures of Work Values, Career Development/Maturity Instruments, Combined Assessment Programs, Personality Measures, and Instruments for Special Populations.

Reviews begin with descriptive information in a standardized format for easy comparison, followed by a brief critical review of the instrument's strengths and weaknesses by a professional of acknowledged expertise. Users will find in these entries the answers to daily factual questions:

For what ages is this test appropriate? Who publishes it? What is the date of this inventory? Is there a new edition yet? Can this be given within one of our class periods? Can it be hand-scored? How expensive would it be for me to test the entire ninth grade with this? What kinds of scores would we get from this instrument?

Beyond these factual answers, users will find here the kind of practical information and critique that they need for evaluating instruments for potential use:

10

Are there reasons to believe this instrument may not be appropriate for the use I have in mind? Does this test really measure what we want to measure? What other instruments of this type are there for me to consider? Is there an entire category of measures we have overlooked?

- Nanciann Frazier's extensive compilation of 126 tests and inventories selected for review (Chapter VII) offers users a number of other instruments for their consideration in particular circumstances.
- Robert Jordan and David Jepsen's annotated bibliography (Appendix A) suggests a manageable number of the best current reference sources in testing and career assessment should users find themselves with areas of weakness that need "beefing up."
- Publishers' full addresses follow (Appendix B) to simplify requests for specimen sets or other assistance and to facilitate ordering.
- A user's matrix has been created (Appendix C) to aid the reader in identifying appropriate instruments to consider for a given use.
- Finally, the complete index offers easy access to the desired information of the moment, for it has been central to all plans for this document that it will be useful, usable, and used.

Once the reader has an overall picture of what is available here, thoughtful consideration should be given to *perspective*. Fairness and balance in the treatment of reviewed instruments drove all deliberations by the editors, advisory committee and writers: we have made this reference as dependably honest and accurate as it was in our power to achieve. Nevertheless, limitations of length, of technical documentation, and of occasional divided professional opinion suggest that serious readers will need to undertake additional investigation, using the technical manuals and the sources referenced. This guide can neither teach a measurement course nor make a selection decision for a busy practitioner. The user must assume his or her own responsibility to achieve full professional competency through ongoing professional development programs and a great deal of experience with the instruments described here.

With this perspective in mind, however, we are pleased to offer this tool to assist in clarifying and making manageable a complex and demanding body of knowledge required of today's professional counselor.

REFERENCES

American Personnel and Guidance Association (APGA). (1980). *Responsibilities of users of standardized tests* (APGA Policy Statement). Falls Church, VA: Author.

American Psychological Association. (1985). *Standards for educational and psychological tests*. Washington, D.C.: Author.

American Psychological Association. (1986). *Guidelines for computer-based tests and interpretations*. Washington, D.C.: Author.

Department of HEW, Office of Civil Rights. (1979, March 21). *Vocational education programs guidelines for eliminating discrimination and denial of services on the basis of race, color, national origin, sex and handicap*. Washington, D.C.: Federal Register, 44 (6).

Engen, H.B., Lamb, R.R. & Prediger, D.J. (1982). Are secondary schools still using standardized tests? *Personnel and Guidance Journal, 60, 287–290.*

Zytowski, D.G. & Warman, R.E. (1982). *The changing use of tests in counseling. Measurement and Evaluation in Guidance, 15(2), 147–152.*

CHAPTER II

The Counselor's Role In Career Assessment

The Counselor's Role in Career Assessment

Edwin L. Herr
Professor and Head
Division of Counseling and Educational Psychology
and Career Studies
The Pennsylvania State University

Whether one considers the historical roots of career guidance or its more contemporary models, the counselor's role and assessment have always been interactive. Career assessment whatever its form—tests, inventories, observational schedules, performance centers—has been a fundamental tool of the counselor engaged in vocational or career guidance. The most recent statement of competencies in vocational/career counseling, adopted by the Board of Directors of the National Vocational Guidance Association (now the National Career Development Association) in 1981 advocates that the counselor should demonstrate competencies in six areas: general counseling, information, management/administration, implementation, consultation, and in individual/group assessment. Among the sub-sets of knowledge and skill subsumed by the broader competency in individual and group assessment are seven emphases:

1. Knowledge of appraisal techniques and measures of aptitude, achievement, interest, values, and personality.
2. Knowledge of strategies used in the evaluation of job performance, individual effectiveness, and program effectiveness.
3. Ability to identify appraisal resources appropriate for specific situations and populations.
4. Ability to evaluate appraisal resources and techniques in terms of their validity, reliability, and relationships to race, sex, age, and ethnicity.
5. Ability to demonstrate the proper administration of appraisal techniques.
6. Ability to interpret appraisal data to clients and other appropriate individuals or groups of people.
7. Ability to assist clients in appraising quality of life and working environments (National Vocational Guidance Association, 1981).

THE ROOTS OF CAREER ASSESSMENT

These competencies in assessment and others that might be cited suggest that from the turn of this century, the time of Frank Parsons, the person so frequently called the Father of Vocational Guidance, to the current time, the needs for assessment as well as its forms have grown and broadened. Some 80 years ago as Parsons was preparing his major work, *Choosing A Vocation*, posthumously published in 1909, the architecture of the trait-and-factor approach was outlined. This rudimentary process of vocational guidance or "true reasoning" as Parsons named it, consisted of three steps:

> First, a clear understanding of yourself, aptitudes, abilities, interests, resources, limitations, and other qualities. Second, a knowledge of the requirements and conditions of success, advantages and disadvantages, compensation, opportunities, and prospectives in different lines of work. Third, true reasoning on the relations of these two groups of facts (Parsons, 1909, p. 5).

This brilliantly conceived paradigm has inspired many of the perspectives on assessment, the counselor's role, and the processes comprising vocational guidance for much of our history, certainly at a minimum into the 1950s. The three steps of Parsons' model embrace several seminal notions which in our more sophisticated day still have fundamental importance to us. Essentially the notions are that an individual can be described as possessing certain characteristics (traits, interests, skills, aptitudes, etc.) that can be measured, that different occupations or educational alternatives can be analyzed and described in terms of the amounts and configurations of such traits they require, and that when individual characteristics and the requirements of occupations or educational options are matched and evaluated through a procedure which he called True Reasoning, and we call decision-making, an effective choice can occur. Finally, this entire process can be enhanced if the client engages in it with an experienced advisor or counselor.

In Parsons' day, a time of major immigration of persons from abroad and from the rural areas to the cities of this nation in quest of jobs and freedom, the heterogeneity of such populations and the literal explosion of industrial diversity in America fueled the use of assessment as a vital mechanism to identify talents and to distribute them throughout the burgeoning occupational structure. In so doing, Parsons' model added spark to the psychometric momentum that was under way in Europe and just beginning to be transplanted to these shores by Binet and others as they brought intelligence tests and additional rudimentary forms of measurement to adapt to the needs of this dynamic country. World War I intensified the need for assessment devices that could discriminate among the aptitudes of persons capable of implementing the increasingly bureaucratic organization and technological weapons systems of the armed forces of the day.

The early years of assessment in vocational guidance were largely periods in which classifying, identifying and "creaming talent" spurred the search for better and fuller information about individual differences, the importance of such differences, and how they could be measured. In the ensuing decades research efforts in vocational guidance and, more recently, in career guidance have focused the empirical spotlight on how occupational activity differs and the meaning of such differences for person-job fit, for job satisfaction, employee satisfactoriness and for individual adjustment and success. The resulting insights have

16

modified assessment strategies to include not only assessment of workers but also measurement of environments and their mutual typologies. And, in our most recent decades, research has turned from individual differences in ability to cope with work tasks or job requirements or performance potential to issues of readiness to choose, to planfulness, to adaptability.

THE CHANGING DEFINITIONS OF VOCATIONAL AND CAREER GUIDANCE

In 1951, Super (1951) recommended that the definition of vocational guidance adopted in 1937 by the National Vocational Guidance Association be revised. The Association concurred. Therefore, the earlier view of vocational guidance as "the process of assisting the individual to choose an occupation, prepare for it, enter upon it, and progress in it" was changed to "the process of helping the person to develop and accept an integrated and adequate picture of himself and of his role in the world of work, to test this concept against reality, and to convert it into a reality, with satisfaction to himself and to society" (Super, 1951). With acknowledgement that the language of the time was male-dominated, the essential thrust of the 1951 redefinition of vocational guidance was to move the focus of research and practice in assessment from a primary emphasis on what is to be chosen (the content of choice, the specific job or occupation at issue) to the chooser (the readiness, the independence, the skills of the person doing the choosing). Within such a context, our initial concerns about assessing the traits and factors making up the content of individual choices—e.g., aptitudes, interests, job requirements—however important they continue to be, have been complemented, augmented, or replaced by assessments primarily concerned with the "process of choice": how ready is the individual to choose; how planful, how knowledgeable about the choice process, how able is this person to define the choice problem immediately ahead, to collect pertinent information and weigh its personal value? In pursuing such understanding, psychometricians and researchers have turned their attention to identifying the importance in mediating how one's career behavior unfolds of undecidedness and indecisiveness, of work salience, of different decision-making styles, of perceptions of self-efficacy, of the acquisition of task approach skills, of the presence of irrational beliefs about work and personal capacity.

Clearly, we can still use Parsons' original three step design to suggest that each of these steps has stimulated different approaches to assessment of individual differences, occupational requirements, and choice-making styles. It is also apparent that, looked at in very broad terms, they also describe research eras across time and reinforce the likelihood that research about the use of career assessment will be faced with many challenges ahead.

THE ASSESSMENT CHALLENGES OF COMPREHENSIVE CAREER GUIDANCE

One of the major trends of the past quarter century is the growing comprehensiveness of career guidance (Herr and Cramer, 1984). As the major providers of vocational and career guidance have changed from schools and employment services to include business and industry, private practice, and the armed forces the term "comprehensive career guidance" has taken on new and different meanings in theory and in practice. Comprehensive sometimes means that career guidance is delivered in a programmed, preplanned or systematic manner. In other contexts, comprehensive has been used as interchangeable with longitudinal; the provision of career guidance in an articulated fashion over an extended period of time—kindergarten to grade twelve in the public schools, the four years of college or university, the months spent in a corrections facility or a rehabilitation program, or the period of one's tenure within a particular firm, business or government agency. At other times, comprehensive has referred to a developmental content designed to equip the recipients of career guidance—children, youth, adults, those with a long history of employability skills starting a new career, those with relatively minimal vocational knowledge and skills who are involuntarily displaced from work, those who are exploring an occupational structure in dynamic flux, those about to retire from work or decelerate in relation to it—with the attitudes, knowledge, and skills by which they can anticipate, plan, and act on a variety of career-related tasks. The term comprehensive has also been used to reflect the reality that career guidance can no longer be seen as a one-time event in life; rather it must be conceived as a life-long process which persons enter and leave at different transition points. And, finally, comprehensive means that it is an inclusive process, not an exclusive one. It has importance to all groups in the society as their career development unfolds and as the political and social contexts shift in which their self-identity, work salience, family roles, needs for learning and re-learning, and occupational mobility are played out.

THE CLASSIFICATION OF CAREER ASSESSMENT

As the impact of the growing comprehensiveness of career guidance has unfolded, the repertoire of interventions represented has broadened and become more discriminating as applied to a larger number of populations and settings. So it is with assessment. The uses of tests and inventories in support of the broadening purposes of career guidance has broadened in turn. These uses of career assessment can be classified in many ways and various observers have their own schemes or categorical system to do so. Earlier in this chapter, assessment has been differentiated in terms of its uses in providing insight into individual status with regard to factors important to the content of choice or to the process of choice. In differentiating assessment purposes in this way, we have learned more and more about what individual characteristics are "fixed effects" and which are modifiable, under what conditions and with what interventions. For some purposes, we have learned to "teach the test" in individual and group activities designed to educate people about the components of choice, rather than assuming that unwise or uninformed choice-making was somehow related to one's gene pool instead of education or experience.

Classification of career assessment has taken other forms as well. One of these structures assigns four major uses to tests or other assessment procedures (Herr & Cramer, 1984). These include prediction, discrimination, monitoring and evaluation. Respectively, the purposes of each of these uses of assessment emphasize, first, using assessment to forecast the odds, the probabilities of individual success in educational, occupational, or other types of career options. In such circumstances, counselors use assessments to help persons consider how

18

competitive they might be in terms of vertical mobility, how high they can reach, what kind of performance they are capable of achieving, in what areas they may experience ceilings on their performance in specific aptitudes which can be circumvented or strengthened.

The second use of assessment, discrimination, is concerned not with performance per se, but rather with the resemblance or similarity between a given individual's values, interests and preferences and those which characterize persons in the occupational or educational environments being considered. In such instances, the question for assessment is not how competitive in learning or performing specific work tasks can this person be but how compatible with the dominant modes of interpersonal behaviors, values, and expectations—the affective dimensions of different work cultures—is this person likely to be. Put somewhat differently, the discrimination function in assessment helps persons identify the occupational and educational groups they most resemble and the types of supervision and time structures they work within most effectively. Such assessment insights help persons understand that an effective work choice is not only a function of how well one performs the work content but, as well, how positively one adapts to or feels congruent with the work environment. Together the uses of tests for prediction and for discrimination encompass much of the information pertinent to the "content of choices."

A third use of assessment is monitoring individual readiness to choose, the status of one's decision-making orientation, the level of career maturity, the availability and quality of the attitudinal and cognitive variables comprising an individual's ability to choose. These insights represent the diagnostic ingredients which undergird decisions about educating individuals to choose, "teaching them the test," providing them decision-making models, helping them cope with independence-dependence, indecisiveness and indecision, and other elements which relate to the "process of choice."

A fourth use of assessment is in the evaluation of career guidance. Evaluation, however simple or sophisticated it may be, is essentially a series of activities or processes designed to determine how well the goals of career guidance have been achieved. Evaluation may be employed to compare the efficacy of different interventions, or the summative results of a developmental career guidance program, or the pre-post-intervention changes in attitude, knowledge or skill of individuals who have been engaged in career guidance. Assessment devices provide the mechanisms to examine relationships between career guidance processes or programs and the behavioral outcomes achieved by individuals or groups. Assessment provides feedback about individual achievement given different counselee characteristics, situational conditions, or intervention strategies. In a sense, assessment devices are both objects of research and evelation and the vehicles by which to carry out such activity. Their use in gathering information about groups of persons has advanced our knowledge of career behavior and the types of interactions most likely to be effective in facilitating such behavior. In individual terms, the use of assessment devices has converted vague abstractions about opportunities for action into probabilities (odds) that persons can consider within their own value systems and risk-taking styles.

While other terms can be used to identify the purposes of assessment just cited, it is likely that the underlying purposes of prediction, discrimination, monitoring, and evaluation will continue to shape counselor's roles in assessment for the foreseeable future. What will change are the applications of these purposes or the social metaphors that assessment will serve. In addition, there will continue to be new theoretical and research insights into the importance and the use of career assessment.

CAREER ASSESSMENT AND DECISION MAKING

One major stream of thought which has implications for assessment is that which rests in theoretical perspectives on decision making. Current perspectives hold that decision making is fueled by information. Choice making is not impulsive; it is a sequential narrowing and specifying of choice options as one translates various psychological and occupational information, whether accurate or not, into a self concept system and a set of images of how certain educational and occupational alternatives will permit one to implement the self concept (Super, 1980). In preparing for and executing decision making, Gelatt (1962) for example, talks about the need for a predictive system (aptitude information, information about alternatives available), a valuing system (interests, values, information about the importance of different alternatives to oneself) and a decision system (ways of converting the information obtained in a predictive and valuing system into a plan of action) as being essential ingredients for choice.

A second paradigm of relevance is that which has come to be labeled self-efficacy theory. Antecedents to such theoretical perspectives were earlier labeled as expectancy x value theories of motivation. In overly simplified terms, according to expectancy x value approaches, personal choice behavior or motivation depends upon the expectancy that the act will be followed by a given consequence (or outcome) and on the value or attactiveness of that consequence (or outcome) to the person contemplating a particular action. From such a view there are two types of expectancies about which people are concerned. The first E→P) has to do with the person's estimate of the probability that he or she can accomplish the intended performance (such as perform the required tasks, meet rigid deadlines, etc.) in the particular situation. The second expectancy (P→O) has to do with subjective probability estimates that if a particular performance is achieved it will lead to certain outcomes (a pay raise, promotion, some other reward). Self-efficacy theory (Bandura, 1977) extends this line of thinking by emphasizing that behavior changes and decisions made are mediated by expectations of self efficacy: expectations or beliefs that one can perform a given behavior.

Inherent in self-efficacy theory or expectancy-value theory is the affirmation that people choose or perform depending upon how they understand a situation or how they view themselves. If they see themselves as a loser, however that is defined for them, they will choose those things which are less challenging with immediate gratifications and little requirement for commitment. On the other hand, if they see themselves as a winner they will choose in accordance with the confidence and expectancies associated with such a view. To put it in the terms of the great philosopher Alfred North Whitehead, people create their own realities by what they choose and by what they avoid choosing.

To be somewhat redundant, understanding of self and of opportunities is based upon experience and information. Neither of these forms of input is necessarily accurate; therefore people make wrong estimates of their chances of success, avoid opportunities in which they could succceed, settle for less than they could achieve because the information which feeds their decision making or self-efficacy is faulty. Some faulty input occurs because developmental experiences in the home and community provide inconsistent, inaccurate or limited information. The school or the workplace striving to create conditions for personal excellence can neutralize such faulty information by providing personal information which is objective, which is comprehensive, and which is competently interpreted to the end that persons are encouraged to pursue personal excellence in whatever areas of strength or talent they have. The school or workplace seeking personal excellence will also provide assessments which reinforce challenges, not cause them to be avoided.

THE COUNSELOR'S ROLE IN ASSESSMENT

While much more might be said about career assessment, its various purposes, and its role in facilitating personal excellence, it may be useful to complete this chapter by returning to the counselor's role in career assessment.

The counselor's role in career assessment is a complex one. In the first instance, it requires the counselor to continually learn about the emerging use of career assessment and the instruments available for different populations and different purposes. As career guidance has become more comprehensive in the consumer groups served and the settings in which it is employed, there has been a major expansion in the number and complexity of the types of tests and measurements available. Older instruments are constantly being revised and their technical properties and administration procedures altered. Such growth challenges the counselor and the researcher to stay abreast of such developments and to effectively incorporate their meaning into practice.

Counselors using career assessments are also being challenged to be technologists. The number of aptitude, interest, decision making and other forms of career appraisals which are programmed for microcomputer use and reporting is rapidly growing. As this occurs, changes arise in the counselor's relationships with clients, the types of information used, as well as the ethical responsibilities involved. NCDA, AACD, NBCC and other professional groups are increasing their attention to defining the competencies needed by counselors in using computer-assisted career guidance systems. As they do, they are redefining their ethical codes and incorporating into them the direct and the subtle implications for counselor practice which result. The Association of Computer-Based Systems for Career Information (Bloch, 1987) has recently advocated that ethical statements for certified counselors include their accountability that the computer application and any career information it contains is appropriate for the respective needs of clients and that it is non-discriminatory. In addition, it requires that counselors understand and can use all aspects of the computer user system employed and that they must insure that all career information, presumably including assessment data, contained in computer systems be bias-free, valid, current, accurate and locally relevant. More could be said about these matters. Suffice it to say, however, that while computer systems and other advanced technology applied to career assessment may extend counselor capabilities to score and report individual data and facilitate client decision-making they also add to the counselor's need for knowledge and skill in using such technology.

In engaging in career assessment, counselors must remember that many critics object to the influence which any form of testing exerts in this society. In part, this criticism evolves from observations that some counselors and other test users attribute an inappropriate amount of confidence to the results of testing as "objective" markers from which decisions can be made. Further, by the content included and the criteria of success established, tests tend to shape goals, define what is relevant to decisions, and, indeed, affect the structure of social institutions dependent upon test results. Counselors engaged in career assessment must be able to address such criticisms in general and as they affect particular subpopulations. Much recent controversy has been focused on whether it is appropriate to use standardized tests and test content conceived by and validated on predominantly middle class white populations with Black or other minority groups whose developmental and educational experiences, economic conditions, and language systems have been different from those groups on whom the assessment was originally developed. This concern is present not only with regard to standardized tests, but pervades all forms of assessment. Each counselor must come to grips with his or her response to these matters. Part of this response necessarily incorporates attention to what populations make up the norm groups and the nature of the research which describes the use of assessment with different subpopulations.

Each counselor engaged in career assessment must, at minimum, be concerned about two sets of characteristics: the technical or scientific aspects of a particular instrument and the social functions of the assessment. Test bias can lie in either side of this equation through overinterpretation, sexism, content, differential validity, the selection model, the wrong criterion, the testing atmosphere (Flaugher, 1978) among other matters. Cronbach (1980), has recently reminded us that it is important to differentiate between the technical aspects of test bias and the questions of proposed use of tests which are really ethical or policy questions of bias. The latter raises questions, not about predictive validity, but whether tests should be used to select or facilitate access to opportunity, for whom and under what conditions?

For the counselor engaged in career assessment, the role is a critical one in a historical period where knowledge is power in an Information Society. The counselor plays a role as a switching mechanism between personal characteristics and opportunities. Career assessment becomes a linking strategy to help individuals conceptualize themselves and their options with accuracy and with insight. However, any career assessment device has social validities beyond those technically defined: It can be used to enable the counselor to maximize opportunity or to be a gate-keeper, to exclude or to include persons, to constrain or to liberate. Each counselor must deliberate seriously about what career assessment means to him or to her with regard to such possibilities.

REFERENCES

Bandura, A. (1977). Self-efficacy: Toward a unifying theory of behavior change. *Psychological Review*, 84, 191, 215.

Bloch, D. (1987). Personal correspondence.

Cronbach, L.J. (1980). Validity on parole: How can we go straight? In W. B. Schroder (Ed.), *New Directions for Testing and Measurement: No. 5 Measuring Achievement Progress over a decade*. San Francisco: Jossey-Bass.

Flaugher, R. L. (1978). The many definitions of test bias. *American Psychologist*, 33(7), 671-679.

Gelatt, H. B. (1961). Decison-making: A conceptual frame of reference for counseling. *Journal of Counseling Psychology*, 9, 240-245.

Herr, E. L. and Cramer, S. H. (1984). *Career Guidance and Counseling Through the Life Span: Systematic Approaches (2nd Edition).* Boston: Little, Brown & Company.

National Vocational Guidance Association (1981, September). Vocational/Career Counseling Competencies Approved by the Board of Directors. Falls Church, VA.

Parsons, F. (1909). *Choosing a Vocation.* Boston; Houghton-Mifflin.

Super, D. E. (1951). Vocational Adjustment: Implementing a Self-Concept. *Occupations,* 30, 88-92.

Super, D. E. (1980). A life-span, life space approach to career development. *Journal of Vocational Behavior.* 16(3), 282-298.

NOTE: Significant portions of this chapter were abridged from the author's original address at the AACD Professional Development Institute ''Using Assessment in Career Development,'' New Orleans, April 20, 1987.

CHAPTER III

Selecting An Instrument: Chore or Challenge

Selecting an Instrument: Chore or Challenge?

Frank B. Womer
Emeritus Professor of Education
The University of Michigan

Instrument selection requires some minimum understanding of tests and test development. It also requires a lot of common sense in judging how well the fixed characteristics of an instrument relate to your own counseling needs for the type of information that a specific test or inventory provides. Using the "Testing Competencies and Responsibilities Checklist" (Chapter V) is one way of deciding if you have the requisite competencies. Since you already have secured this book and are studying it, you probably meet the second suggested criterion.

There certainly is no one "best" aptitude test or interest inventory for everyone who wants to measure either one, nor is there one "best" instrument for any of our categories of tests. There always will be and should be some elements of personal judgment. At the same time, there are standards against which published instruments can and should be checked. A screening process should be used to eliminate all test instruments that do not meet reasonable standards. From one point of view, test selection is a process of sequential test elimination, leading up to a final selection. Also, in most cases, the task is to find a good, usable instrument rather than to find the best possible instrument. Establishing criteria for "best" can be an elusive process.

The following procedure is suggested as a practical guide for instrument selection:

1. Identify those instruments that by reputation and/or use *seem* to measure what you want to measure.
2. From those instruments identified in step one, identify those instruments that *also* are designed to meet your own informational needs.
3. Then identify those instruments that *also* fit within the practical limitations under which you must function.
4. Next identify those instruments that *also* meet acceptable standards of technical development and quality.

5. Then identify those instruments that *also* meet your own personal and professional judgments of validity.
6. Finally, select the instrument(s) that best survive(s) this sequential process.

Readers of this book already have in their hands one reference for an initial screening of the many tests that are considered to be vocational guidance instruments. Forty-three instruments have survived that screening. Survival, in this context, can best be described as having met a test of time; these instruments are being used by enough different people that they might be considered acceptable for a first-cut approach.

This type of initial screening has advantages. It means that you do not have to create your own initial list. It also has the further advantage of having classified the 43 instruments reviewed in seven categories. If you are looking for an interest inventory you would begin by considering the thirteen instruments reviewed under that category. To that list you can consider adding those included in the Interest Inventory category in the "Additional Career Assessment Instruments" chapter of this book.

The editors of this book, however, may not have included some good instruments for one reason or another, or perhaps something good has just been published. You must go beyond any one single listing of available instruments. A search of current catalogs of test publishers and/or flyers about new test instruments may turn up additional names. A knowledgeable counselor, director of guidance, professor, or consultant whom you know may have a suggestion or two to add to your initial list. Appendix A of this book, "Sources of Information About Tests and Testing," can also be used to lead you to information about additional instruments.

The purpose of the initial screening is to include *all* reasonable possibilities.

PURPOSE/INTENDED USE

For each instrument that is a "reasonable possibility," you need to relate the specific purposes and/or suggested uses to your own desires/needs for specific information. If you are looking for an interest inventory to be used primarily as an instructional tool in a unit on career awareness, you have different test needs than a counselor who is looking for an interest inventory that will pinpoint how a student's interests relate to on-the-job workers. Similarly, one counselor may want an instrument that covers knowledge of the world of work and another counselor may prefer to use non-test information to assess that characteristic.

Each test author has specific goals and objectives which his/her instrument is trying to assess. When you want the type of information that a test author is trying to produce, there is the possibility that instrument will be useful for you. But you may be looking for information that a specific test is not designed to provide. If so, you should move on to an examination of other instruments or to some other data-gathering device or methodology.

The test descriptions in this publication include statements of purpose. For instruments not covered here, you should look in the test manual for such a statement. A match between stated purpose of an instrument and client needs is a necessary condition for test selection, but is not itself a guarantee that the match really exists.

PRACTICAL LIMITATIONS

An instrument requiring administration by someone with special training, if you do not have and cannot easily acquire that training, presents a problem. An instrument requiring 40 minutes of continuous testing time to be used in a situation when 30 minutes is the maximum time available presents a problem. A testing situation that requires frequent retesting calls for a test with multiple forms. The appropriateness of an instrument in terms of age or grade placement or in terms of the reading level of the questions needs to be considered. These are examples of practical considerations that testers cannot avoid. Because of time considerations, cost considerations, special equipment needed, special training needed, types of derived scores available, scoring ease, etc., some instruments are more practical to use in your situation than others.

Such considerations cannot be ignored even though in some Utopian setting it would be nice to be able to select instruments solely on their relevance to your own needs and their high technical qualities. Fortunately, many tests fall within a broad range of relative ease of usability. It is hoped that only occasionally will an instrument have to be ruled out of contention on the basis of some practical concern.

It is recommended that you put the instruments you are considering in a rough rank order according to usability, but at this stage of test selection you eliminate a test from consideration only when there is some aspect of practical utilization that clearly rules out that instrument.

A danger to guard against when ranking tests on various aspects of practicality is the possibility of selecting a test *because* it is the shortest or the cheapest or the easiest to administer. Quality information comes from quality instruments. Practicality becomes most important *after* you identify several different tests that all meet high quality standards. You use the standard of practicality here only to eliminate the obviously impossible choices.

TECHNICAL QUALITY

Instruments that provide high quality information must be valid, must be reliable, must have good norms, and must have minimal item bias. The best reviews of tests, and the best personal and professional judgments of test quality will attend primarily to these attributes. Appendix A in this book provides appropriate references for technical considerations.

Validity

Validity judgments deal with the quality of the inferences that can be made from test scores. Does a career awareness instrument really assess career awareness? Does an aptitude battery predict future performance well enough to make its results useful? Are the differences between scores on an interest inventory real differences rather than random occurrences? Unless you can answer yes to important questions like these, which should be posed for every such instrument, you should not seriously consider the use of a test—not even if that test is free, takes only ten minutes to administer, and provides 25 different scores. Acquiring data of questionable quality may be much more dangerous than using no test-generated information at all.

Validity may be assessed by the expert judgment of professional reviewers (see the reviews in this book), by personally examining the results of statistical studies, and by your own personal and professional judgments of an instrument itself. When reading professional reviews of instruments, be sure to be on the lookout for statements that describe precisely the types of inferences that are deemed to be reasonable for the test being reviewed, as well as the types of inferences that are deemed to be unreasonable or invalid.

When looking at correlation coefficients that indicate that Test A (being reviewed) relates closely to Test X (a widely used test), be sure that you accept this as evidence of validity *only* if you accept Test X itself as a valid measuring device. When looking at correlation coefficients that indicate that selected scores on Test B (being reviewed) correlate with success in the freshman year in eight different engineering programs, interpret that evidence as an indication that Test B may be valid for predicting successful *preparation* for an engineering career. (Successful completion of an academic program of professional preparation is a necessary, but not sufficient, condition for success in a profession.) When making inferences that different scores on Test C (being reviewed) do represent interest patterns, look for evidence outside the test scores that people with different score patterns truly have different interests and/or have made different career choices.

In attempting to judge the validity of various instruments, you should not overlook the fact that continuous successful use of an instrument by large numbers of dedicated, well-trained counselors may be indirect evidence of the validity of that instrument in a great variety of settings. While you should *not* choose to use Test D just because you know that it is being used in several neighboring school districts, the fact that the instrument is being used by others may be enough evidence to warrant a close examination of its particular qualities—both strengths and weaknesses. You must be convinced that an instrument you are using with your counselees does provide valid scores from which reasonable inferences can be made.

Reliability

Sometimes validity and reliability are considered to be the twins of test evaluation—a test must be valid and it must be reliable. But since an unreliable test cannot be a valid test, there may be a temptation to assume that gathering evidence of test validity automatically produces evidence of test reliability. This inference is satisfactory *if* you are dealing solely with correlational evidence of the validity of a given test in relationship to other criteria. Test E cannot correlate highly with grades in college unless both Test E and the college grade point average are fairly reliable. But since many evaluations of test validity are judgmental in nature, you dare not assume that test reliability is an established fact whenever such judgments are made.

Test reliability may be concerned solely with the homogeneity of the items in a test (split-half; Kuder-Richardson) or may be concerned solely with stability of scores over time (test-retest) or may be concerned with both types of potential errors (parallel form; equivalent form). If you want to be confident that a given set of test questions are all measuring the same attribute, you want evidence of item homogeneity. If you want to be confident that a test score acquired today is about the same as it would have been if that test had been given yesterday or tomorrow, you want evidence of test score stability. If you want evidence that a test is both homogeneous and stable, you want evidence of parallel-form reliability. Finding evidence of satisfactory reliability of one type does *not* guarantee that the other type also is satisfactory.

In comparing the reliability of one test with another, you must always compare homogeneity estimates of one test against homogeneity estimates of another test, stability estimates of one against another, and so on. Estimates of test reliability are reported as a correlation coefficient (.92 or .87 or .73, etc.). Estimates of homogeneity generally are higher than estimates of combined homogeneity and stability. You must never make the error of assuming that a homogeneity estimate of .91 for Test F is better than a parallel form estimate of .82 for Test G. It may be, but it may not be. This is because parallel form estimates "allow" both errors of homogeneity *and* errors of stability to be included in the correlation estimates.

Most test users can judge reliability better by considering the standard error of measurement. A standard error of measurement, computed from each of the three types of reliabilities, enables a user to create a band score or a "confidence interval" (e.g., 10 to 18; 72 to 84, etc.) so that potential unreliability can be built directly into the interpretation of a test score. A test author or publisher who not only provides evidence of all three types of reliability but also provides the standard errors of measurement for each type clearly has done a better job of helping a test user make a wise decision than one who does not provide this information.

Norms

Judging whether or not a test author or publisher has attempted to develop test norms following accepted sampling and data-gathering procedures is a fairly simple task. Judging whether a set of test norms is truly accurate is an almost impossible task. You can and should check whether the standardization sample for a given instrument has satisfactory geographical balance, satisfactory balance on some reasonable socio-economic factor, satisfactory balance on ethnic, racial, and sex distributions, satisfactory representation across intended ages or grades, and so on.

It is reasonably easy to establish whether the author or publisher has tried to develop accurate norms. But the real hooker in data collection by sampling is the percentage response rate. If 90% of everyone or every school selected in a good statistical sample actually participate by taking the standardization edition of a test, you can rest easy. If 50% participate, you cannot help feeling very uneasy. Are those who refuse to participate really like the ones who do participate, or are they, perhaps, different in some systematic way? It is next to impossible to judge the real accuracy of a set of test norms when a substantial percentage of a sample refuse to participate. Norms may be highly accurate; they may not. You simply do not know. To compound this problem, it is possible for a set of test norms to be highly accurate, by happenstance, even when the rules of sample selection are knowingly violated. About the only thing that the typical user of a test instrument can do is to pick a test for which the author or publisher did follow accepted norming procedures, and then hope for the best. The test of time is a reasonably fair standard to apply in judging the accuracy of test norms. If many users have found the norms for a specific test to be realistic over a period of time, they probably are realistic.

Some published instruments in the career guidance/career assessment area have not been normed. Such instruments are not designed to provide information about counselees which allows for easy comparisons of counselee *vs.* counselee or of counselee *vs.* known groups. They often are designed primarily to be used as counseling tools and may be more useful for instruction and/or counseling than for evaluation.

Item Bias

A bias is not a bias is not a bias. There are many different perceptions of what constitutes test bias and many different perceptions about the importance of one type of bias versus another type of bias. This author believes that the most crucial type of test bias to guard against is test item bias: e.g., the six questions that many girls answer in a particular way because they look at the situations in these questions differently than boys; the seven questions that many bilingual Spanish-speaking students answer in a particular way because of cultural mores; the eight questions that many Blacks misinterpret because of dialectical considerations. A test item, then, is defined as being biased if it consistently elicits a different response from a particular group *because* of their sex or ethnic affiliation or race or some other characteristic.

Many attempts to reduce item bias have been made in the last decade. Wording that suggests stereotyping is avoided; words that may be interpreted differently by persons with different linguistic background are avoided; situations that suggest superiority or inferiority of different groups are avoided; and so on. Few tests developed before the early 1970s were screened for potential test item bias.

There are both judgmental and statistical approaches to the identification of potential item bias. Judgmental approaches concentrate on elimination of stereotyped situations, elimination of sex-specific wording or perhaps balancing items on sex specificity, elimination of words and phrases that may be offensive to some groups, elimination of references to things that are unfamiliar to some groups (e.g. rural/urban) or balancing such items. Statistical analyses concentrate on finding whether item difficulty varies from group to group and, even more important, whether distracter difficulties in multiple-choice questions vary from group to group.

While some reviewers attend to the potential of item bias, not all do. You may find it advantageous to scan the instruments you are evaluating in an effort to determine the degree of potential item bias. A part of the importance of this concern is the "appearance" of bias, independent of statistical evidence of its presence. It is to be hoped that, in a few years, test reviewers and test users will have less cause to be concerned about potential test bias, but until then potential item bias needs to be evaluated.

A USEFUL OUTLINE

In order to collect information on several instruments in such a way that it is most useful for selection decisions, practitioners will want to organize the information for meaningful comparison. One organizing scheme, offered by Westbrook (1987) is provided here.

Outline for Critical Analysis of a Standardized Test*

1. *Title*. Provide both the full title and the preferred acronym or short title.
2. *Author*. Give full name, title, and institution.

3. *Publisher*. Give name and mail address.
4. *Copyright date*. Give the date the instrument was first published and the date of each revision.
5. *Target Population*. State exactly the ages, grades, or special groups for which the test is intended.
6. *Purpose and recommended use*. Give these as intended by the author.
7. *Dimensions or areas that the test purports to measure*. List the sub-scales or give a description of the variables measured.
8. *Forms of the test*. What forms of the test are available? If the forms are not essentially the same, major difference should be mentioned. What evidence is presented on equivalence of forms?
9. *Similar tests by the same author*. Occasionally authors publish two or more tests that are similar but have different names. Sometimes long tests are shortened and given new titles. Give title, publisher, and date.
10. *Administration*. Describe briefly. The total time to complete the test should be indicated. If parts of the test are timed separately, mention how many "starting" points are necessary. Do the directions appear easy for the test administrator? For the test taker? Is the test largely self-administering? Are there objectionable features?
11. *Norm groups*. How many subjects were involved? Were they selected in such a way that they appear to be representative and appropriate for your setting? Are there norms for each group with whom you might wish to compare a person's score, i.e., norms for both sexes, age levels, curriculum majors, occupations, etc.?
12. *Interpretation of scores*. How are scores expressed (percentile ranks, standard scores, stanines, grade scores, etc.)? Is adequate assistance given for appropriate interpretation of the results?
13. *Scoring*. Describe procedures briefly, noting available options (hand/clerk/machine scoring).
14. *Source of items*. Where did the author get the items? What criteria were used for item selection? Are some items taken from other tests?
15. *Description of items*. Give a brief description of the major types of items used. Give attention to *item form* (multiple choice, analogy, forced choice, etc.) and *item content* (culture-free symbols, nonsense syllables, food preferences, occupational titles, etc.). Include typical examples of the major types of items used.
16. *Statistical item analysis*. Was an item analysis done to determine item discrimination and difficulty? What were the results?
17. *Method of validation*. For many tests this is related to items 14 and 15. What was done in planning and constructing the test to make it valid and useful? (This should not be a description of a study to demonstrate validity.) See 18.
18. *Validity as determined by the author*. Apart from what was presented in items 14–17, what has the author done to demonstrate the validity of the test? What correlations with other tests are presented? Has an external criterion been used to evaluate the usefulness of the scores? What specific "predictions" could you make about a person from his or her test score on the basis of the validity data presented?
19. *Validity as determined by others*. The recent literature should be consulted for studies. For what uses has the test been found to be valid?

20. *Reliability*. State how reliability was determined. Is it adequate for using the instrument with confidence?
21. *Expert opinion*. Give major questions, assumptions, strengths, and/or limitations noted by test experts in reviews of the instrument.
22. *Distinguishing characteristics*. Note what makes this test different from others in its construction and use.
23. *Cost*. Include one-time materials costs, recurring materials costs, and scoring costs.
24. *Desirable features*. In your opinion, what are the desirable features of the test?
25. *Undesirable features*. In your opinion, what are the problems you see in the test?
26. *References consulted*. Note your sources here briefly to facilitate relocation of the information if needed.

---

*Adapted from a handout developed for the presentation, "Selecting Appropriate Career Assessment Instruments," by Bert Westbrook at the Professional Development Institute, "Using Assessment in Career Development," at the AACD Convention, New Orleans, LA, April 21, 1987.

PERSONAL AND PROFESSIONAL JUDGMENTS

It is possible to rely solely on the opinions expressed in published reviews of an instrument to make a specific decision. It is possible to rely solely on personal examination of the test manual(s) and the test(s) itself to make a specific decision. More often than not, however, a review of the test reviews and of the instrument itself will leave you with two or three or more possibilities that "look good," and seem to be appropriate.

To make a final choice, it is highly advantageous to try out the several different tests that have passed the various criteria of suitability. Ideally, this is done in two stages. First and at a minimum, you should become familiar with the instruments by taking them yourself. In addition, most counselors can get the cooperation of a few students who would be willing to take one or more different test instruments with the full understanding that they will be helping the process of selecting a test that their peers may be taking in the future. Test developers have known for a long time that students can provide useful information about a test they have taken by answering questions such as:

1. Did you understand the questions?
2. Were the questions fair?
3. Were the directions clear and was the time reasonable?
4. Are your scores reasonable? Do they seem accurate?
5. Do the results relate to other things that you know or feel about yourself?
6. Are the results helpful in any way?
7. Would you recommend this instrument to your friends?

The counselor, in using a new test with a few students, will be able to develop an initial "feel" for its utility. Do the results confirm information already known about a student? Do they provide new insights? Would you be able to work better with students in the future if you had results from this instrument? The

34

wise buyer of a new automobile takes it for a road test; the wise buyer of a new career assessment instrument should put the instrument through a "testing" process. Additional references that may be useful to practitioners approaching the task of selecting an instrument include Grondlund (1981), Hills (1981) and Westbrook and Mastie (1983). See the references for more complete information on these resources.

IN CONCLUSION

The selection of a new instrument can be a learning experience for a counselor: it can be a challenge rather than a chore. It forces one to think about the types of information (both test and non-test) that may be helpful both to the counselor and to the counselees; it forces one to review the basic concepts of test development; and it forces one to apply common sense in a process of trying to improve the data base of your counselees. Ultimately, it contributes to making one a more thoughtful user of the results obtained from the tests or inventories that one elects to use.

REFERENCES

Grondlund, N. E. (1981). Test Selection, Administration, and Use. In *Measurement and Evaluation in Teaching*. New York: MacMillan, 275–302.

Hills, J. R. (1981). Finding, Choosing and Administering Standardized Tests. In *Measurement and Evaluation in the Classroom*. Columbus, Oh.: Merrill, 209–229.

Westbrook, B. W. and Mastie, M. M. (1983). Doing Your Homework: Suggestions for the Evaluation of Tests by Practioners. *Educational Measurement: Issues and Practice*, 2, 11–14, 26.

CHAPTER IV

Interpretation of Psychometric Instruments In Career Counseling

Interpretation of Psychometric Instruments in Career Counseling

Howard E. A. Tinsley
Professor of Psychology
Director, Counseling Psychology Program
Southern Illinois University at Carbondale
and
Richard W. Bradley
Professor of Educational Psychology
Southern Illinois University at Carbondale

Two principles constitute the foundation upon which skill is built in interpreting test inventories and other assessment instruments. First, interpretation must not be viewed as a discrete activity but conceptualized as a part of the ongoing counseling process. This means interpretation must be integrated into the flow of counseling. Counselors who take "time out" from being sensitive, warm, empathic, and caring individuals when conducting test interpretations engage in a practice detrimental to the overall counseling process. Remember, clients are people, not just a series of scores on psychometric instruments.

Second, it seems useful to think of assessment instruments as structured interviews which provide information about clients in an efficient manner. They should not be deified or thought of as magically providing answers. Tests provide counselors with a standard interview for clients, report descriptive information (scores) at an approximately known level of reliability, suggest inferences having an approximately known validity, accurately amass much experience (through the norm group) without being overly influenced by unusual cases, and save counselor time. In contrast, counselors generally conduct semistandard interviews, obtain descriptive information of unknown reliability, draw inferences that may be less valid than those of tests, take years to amass the experience the instrument provides at the beginning, and generally have a backlog of clients waiting to be seen.

Thus, assessment instruments are potentially valuable tools. Whether their value can be realized, however, continues to depend largely on skill in interpretation. The following discussion deals with four aspects of interpretation: counselor preparation, client preparation, delivery, and follow-up.

PREPARING FOR INTERPRETATION

Typically, measurement textbooks do a good job of explaining how to select appropriate instruments for use with their clients. Counselors who have not participated in the test selection process, however, must familiarize themselves with the instruments before attempting to interpret them. They can do this by self-administering and scoring the instruments and reviewing the results with colleagues (i.e., interpreting the instruments). This process usually motivates a counselor to find out more about the instrument.

As counselors gain experience in interpretation, they should consult the test manuals whenever necessary. Counselors should not be ashamed to admit that they cannot remember the meaning of some scores or that the implication of other scores is somewhat vague. Moreover, they should not fall into the trap of believing that they have become experts and do not need to consult reference sources after having used an instrument for some time. Many counselors seem to think that after they become reasonably proficient, they can dispense with preparation and simply interpret tests "off the cuff." This is not advisable. Assessment instruments should virtually never be interpreted in isolation but rather should be integrated with the other information available to present a unified picture. This takes thought beforehand. The process of preparing for interpretation can be conceptualized as involving two processes—gaining an understanding of the results and integrating this information with other knowledge about clients.

Understanding

The first thing to do in preparing for interpretation is to go over the results and ask, "What do these scores mean?" Although counselors cannot answer this question for clients, they can generate ideas or hypotheses to be investigated in the actual session. It is often helpful to go beyond the basic scores reported. Counselors should keep in mind that test scores are statistics that summarize client statements about themselves or about tasks they have performed. As such, counselors should not hesitate to review this information and raise questions with clients regarding the meaning of any of the statements counselors believe to be important. Sometimes various sources of information seem to be in contradiction. In such instances counselors must give careful thought to the meaning of these data. Often, subtle agreements among various portions of the data will, if noted, enhance the meaning of these results for clients. In still other instances, low or socially undesirable scores may be threatening to clients. Counselors must give careful thought to the presentation of this information to clients. All of these reasons suggest the importance of careful preparation.

During the preparation stage, counselors should take notes for use in the interview. Busy counselors will be seeing many clients each day and may be interpreting numerous tests and inventories. It is unwise to depend on remembering everything. Typically, they will remember highlights or major aspects, but the detail that enriches interpretations will be lost unless they have taken notes.

Integration

After counselors have a thorough grasp of the meaning of the test results, they must integrate this information with other available information. Frequently, school counselors will have other test scores, grades, teachers' anecdotal remarks, and information regarding the student's work history, family background, and, perhaps, scholastic major and career aspirations. Agency or mental health counselors may not have as complete a set of records to work from but will have interview data they gained before selecting instruments for clients. Interpretation involves integration of information, not just reporting statistical data or scores.

One of the first things to do in integrating information is to evaluate the consistency of the data. Are the test scores in agreement with or in conflict with the other data? If the scores are in conflict, counselors should attempt to determine why. They should check to see whether (a) the instrument was scored correctly, (b) the appropriate answer sheet was used, (c) the individual was compared with the proper norm group, and (d) the transformation from raw scores to standard scores was made properly. Each of these problems occurs at one time or another. One cardinal rule: Do not automatically believe the scores to be correct if they contradict other available evidence. Equally important, do not automatically disregard test results if they do not confirm expectations.

Order of Presentation

Any test interpretation must be determined in part by the emotional needs of clients. Clients do not always need information above all else. Counselors must be concerned with considerations such as whether the client has the ego strength to handle particularly threatening information. Thoughtful consideration of the best method of interpreting psychometric information may make a difference in its value to clients. The ability of counselors to do this depends on their perceptiveness and knowledge of their clients.

Counselors must consider the clients' frame of reference in planning the order of presentation. The plan adopted should be regarded as tentative and subject to modification as the interview unfolds. One strategy that has worked well for us is to briefly review with the client the instruments to be interpreted and then ask the client's preference regarding the order of interpretation.

Review

Counselors should reserve time to review their interpretation plans just before the interview. Good interpretation practice is more likely to result from having the information fresh in mind than from relying on cryptic shorthand notes that may have been made two weeks earlier.

PREPARING CLIENTS FOR TEST INTERPRETATION

Although the counselor and client may have decided jointly that a test or inventory is appropriate, it is ill advised to "hit" the client with an interpretation at the next session. Counselors should prepare clients for interpretation by reestablishing rapport. It may be helpful to summarize the previous interview or to find out what has happened since the previous session. It is important to give clients a chance to discuss anything that is really significant to them. Counselors should be perceptive enough to determine whether clients have needs more pressing than their need to learn about their test results. In short, counselors should begin test interpretation interviews much as they would any other interview.

Most clients come to the interview eager to learn about their results. Counselors can lead the interview into a discussion of the instruments when it is clear that their clients are ready for interpretation. It frequently helps to ask clients to begin by describing the test or inventory they took. Counselors may wish to ask clients, "Do you remember this test?" "What did you think about it?" or "What were your impressions of the test?" They should recall wtih clients the format and types of items used so clients can associate the results with the instrument they took. This, of course, is more important when clients have taken more than one instrument or when considerable time has elapsed between administration and interpretation.

In leading into the interpretation, it is also helpful for counselors to review with clients the types of information the instrument provides. For example, the fact that a person has interests similar to those of a musician does not mean that the person has musical ability. At this point it is also useful to review the norm group to which clients will be compared. In some instances counselors may wish to compare clients' performance with several norm groups. The nature of these norm groups and the differences between them should be made clear. Also, counselors should explain the inexact nature of test scores before beginning the interpretation and reiterate this from time to time during the test interpretation.

DELIVERY OF THE INTERPRETATION

Keeping Clients' Goals in Mind

During interpretation, counselors should relate results to the things clients want to know. The same performance on a test may be interpreted in several ways given different client goals. For example, a score of 110 on the General Learning Ability Scale of the General Aptitude Test Battery (GATB) could indicate for one client that his or her general intellectual ability is probably high enough to complete a BA in education. For another individual, the same score may indicate that successful completion of a doctoral program in philosophy will be quite difficult. Counselors can make the interpretation personal by keeping clients' goals in mind and interpreting results in terms of the kinds of decisions clients must make.

Keeping the Test Precision in Mind

Another important principle in interpreting results is to always keep in mind the precision of the test. Many clients come to counseling or testing situations thinking their results will have pinpoint accuracy. This tendency is easily observed with intelligence test scores. Everyone has no doubt heard people make statements such as, "My IQ is 135," indicating blissful ignorance of the fact that their true intellectual ability could be considerably higher or lower.

When interpreting test scores, counselors must be aware of the standard error of measurement. The outcome is not an exact score but a range. If the client has a T score of 45 on a test that has a standard error of measurement of 4 (based on a method of assessing reliability that is consistent with the use to which scores are being put), then the counselor could interpret the results by saying, ''The test results indicate that your ability probably falls somewhere in the range between 41 and 49.'' It is helpful to indicate the range on a profile to show clients visually the inexact nature of test scores—to simultaneously convey what counselors do know about the client's status and the limits to what they know.

Ranges may also be conveyed in other ways. As a school counselor, one of the authors tried to demonstrate this by using a set of nine stairsteps to report stanines. The testing company provided a series of single-digit scores (one for each section of an achievement test) printed on gummed labels to be attached to an informational flyer each student was given. The counselor and student would review each section of the test and place the score on the appropriate step. For example, if a student obtained a stanine of 4 in word usage, the counselor and student discussed the uncertainty as to whether the student was right on the edge, ready to fall down to step 3, or almost ready to jump up to step 5.

It is not always necessary to give clients exact scores or detailed technical information. The use of numbers in interpreting instruments is likewise not always necessary. The purpose of an interpretation is to transmit meaningful, useful information. Suppose a counselor was working with a young man who had a Wechsler Adult Intelligence Scale (WAIS) full-scale intelligence score of 101, a high school rank of 42/70 (the 40th percentile), a grade point average in high school of 2.50, and a scholastic aptitude score at the 30th percentile. One way of interpreting these results would be to give the client all the numbers and struggle to convey their meaning. What the client really needs to know, however, are the options available. For example, if someone with such a record asked, ''Can I get through college?'' the most appropriate response would be, ''I don't know. We do find, though, that people who have performed like you in high school and have similar scores on tests find college difficult. Some do make it but many do not. Based on your experiences in school, what do you think?'' Right to the point, this interpretation tells the client that neither the test nor the counselor are the ultimate answer, although both may provide some assistance. Furthermore, such interpretation of results leads counselor and client into a discussion of the information in a manner that should lead to a better understanding of the client's situation than either could obtain alone. This is one of the important contributions to counseling of good interpretation practice.

Minimizing Defensive Reactions

Interpretation of low or potentially unflattering scores is one of the more difficult tasks counselors are called on to do. Many counselors feel embarrassed interpreting such results to a client, which indicates a judgmental attitude on the counselor's part. Embarrassment in interpreting low or negative scores signifies a problem the counselor, not the client, needs to address. Counselors must not scold, disapprove, or feel sorry for clients who have low scores, and they must avoid the use of pejorative labels with any level of performance.

It is a simple fact that half the people who take well-standardized instruments will perform below the median. Counselors should not avoid low scores and by all means should not downgrade the importance or accuracy of these scores. Clients have come to counseling for help and need to know their weaknesses as well as their strengths. Counselors must leave open the possibility that the results inaccurately reflect the client's status but keep in mind that the important point is to get clients to talk about their level of performance and what it means to them. Point out the nature and implication of such scores but recognize that clients are the ultimate users of the information. Strive to give information that has meaningful implications for the decisions clients must make. At the same time, counselors must be sensitive to clients' feelings about their scores and deal with those feelings as appropriate.

Although it is important that counselors not avoid low or unflattering scores, they should not make such scores the center of interpretation. The client's goals should be the focus. If a client wants to improve social relations and obtains scores that are quite low on a characteristic such as "outgoing," this constitutes important information. A plan for developing more outgoing behavior is in order. The low score was simply a confirmation of the client's current status. As such, it provides additional focus to the counseling.

Low scores in academic areas can also be useful. Applicants to Ph.D. programs in counseling frequently have quantitative scores that are considerably lower than their verbal scores on the Graduate Record Examination. Talking about this low performance area and what it may mean when clients are faced with required statistics courses may assist clients in preparing for the realities to be faced in graduate school. For example, it may mean that they will have to take a lighter academic course load in the semesters they take statistics so as to give this weak area more attention.

Avoiding Jargon

Counselors should be aware that certain technical terms may interfere with clients' receptiveness to and understanding of the interpretation. Avoid terms such as intelligence (using instead scholastic aptitude or ability to learn things from books), neurotic, maladjusted, and perhaps, even masculinity and femininity. Such terms may arouse unfavorable connotations. Also, sensitive counselors should be perceptive enough to identify individually threatening terms.

A related consideration is that counselors should keep interpretations understandable. Counselors who rely on jargon or fancy phrases to convey outcomes probably do not have a clear understanding of the results. For example, the statement, "You have a moderate elevation on the psychasthenia scale of the MMPI," is meaningless to most clients. On the other hand, the statement, "Your scores on the test indicate that you are similar to persons who worry a lot, are nervous, and have a hard time making up their minds," conveys meaningful information to most clients. Try to phrase the interpretation in a language that will be easily understandable and inoffensive to clients.

Encouraging Feedback

Counselors should interpret instruments in a way that allows and encourages client participation. Counselors can elicit client feedback with statements such as, "What do you think about that?" "How does that compare with what you expected?" "How does that compare with what you think about yourself?" "Does that seem right to you?" "How do you feel about what we have discussed so far?" or "You seem disappointed with that score."

Eliciting client feedback is important for many reasons. Counselors need to know whether clients understand the information being presented, and they need to be aware of clients' attitudes or feelings toward the information. One technique that avoids the more obvious direct question is to ask clients periodically to summarize the interpretation. This gives counselors a chance to determine whether the client really understands the information and is helpful in keeping the talk ratio balanced. Counselors sometimes find it difficult to shift from the test interpretation, in which they have done most of the talking, back to a regular interview, in which clients are expected to do considerable talking, unless they have encouraged participation throughout the session. Furthermore, summarizing gives clients an opportunity to work at organizing and intergrating the information and to express any feelings they have about the information being presented.

Another technique that allows clients to work with and assimilate information is to ask them to speculate on the implications of the results. To do this, clients must organize and assimilate the test results with existing information. This technique goes further, however, and checks clients' understanding of the important implications of the results for decisions they must make.

One additional method of eliciting feedback should not be forgotten. Counselors should ask clients about any unusual responses they noted in reviewing clients' answer sheets. An oblique method of approaching the question is usually not necessary. For example, suppose the individual responded "true" to the MMPI statement, "Sometimes I feel as if I must injure either myself or someone else." The counselor could approach the subject by saying, "I noticed that on one of the items you replied that you have considered injuring yourself or someone else. Could you tell me more about that?" This general lead could then be followed by more specific questions as appropriate.

Using Profiles

The question sometimes arises, "Should the client be allowed to see the actual test profile?" In some vocational rehabilitation agencies, employment service offices, and public school settings, for example, counselors are discouraged from showing the results to clients. In contrast, Bradley (1978) suggested that the test booklet, answer sheet, and profile all be available for inspection. The so-called "truth in testing" movement has opened up accessibility to assessment materials.

Counselors should keep in mind that the purpose of discussing the results is to help clients learn something about themselves. Clients seem better able to understand what counselors are saying with visual aids that assist in organizing, clarifying, and simplifying the information presented. Moreover, clients seem to appreciate having something to take home that summarizes their performance. Counselors also may wish to encourage clients to take notes throughout the interpretation.

AFTER THE INTERPRETATION

After the actual interpretation, counselors should dictate their comments for incorporation into client case folders along with the test profile. This makes available for future reference a record of the results and what the client was told about the results. Most interpretations are not absolutely objective but depend on the counselor's perceptiveness of client needs, attitudes, and values. Thus, it is important to have some indication of the interpretation given the client.

It is important to recognize that the process of assimilating information from instruments is not confined to interpretation interviews. Counselors should continue to check client understanding of results and help them work with the information in later interviews. Learning is seldom achieved as a result of attempting something once. Clients can really learn about themselves only if they are given supervision and help in trying to understand the implications of their results. Likewise, counselors can learn to use tests, inventories and other assessment instruments in a skillful manner by trying to understand the implications of test results throughout counseling.

REFERENCE

Bradley, R.W. (1978). Person-referenced test interpretation: A learning process. *Measurement and Evaluation in Guidance*, *10*, 201–210.

NOTE: Significant portions of this chapter were abridged from the authors' original article in *Journal of Counseling and Development*, 1986, 64, 462–466, with permission of AACD.

CHAPTER V

Testing Competencies and Responsibilities: A Checklist for Counselors

Testing Competencies and Responsibilities: A Checklist for Counselors

Dale J. Prediger
Vocational Psychologist
American College Testing Program
and
Nancy J. Garfield
Director of Training
Psychology Service
Colmery-O'Neil Veterans Administration Medical Center
Topeka, Kansas

This checklist provides a practical means for counselors to assess their testing competencies and practices. It is intended to cover the basics and should not be viewed as a comprehensive statement of all responsibilities and competencies involved in testing. Since each item is considered to be important, there is no pass-fail score.

As used here, the term "test" subsumes the various types of instruments covered by this *Counselor's Guide*—single tests, test batteries, inventories, card sorts, and various self-report scales. The term "counselee" is meant to include anyone to whom tests are administered (e.g., a sixth grader, college senior, or adult in the labor force). Items in the Interpretation section of the checklist refer to the use of tests in individual counseling. Relevance of items to the use of tests with groups and in consultation with other professionals or parents should be evident. Although some checklist items address computer-based testing, the primary focus is on traditional uses of tests. Counselors interested in computer applications may wish to consult the *Guidelines for Computer-Based Tests and Interpretations* prepared by committees of the American Psychological Association (APA, 1986).

Much of the content of this revised checklist was adapted from resources cited at the end of this chapter. The American Association for Counseling and Development (AACD) policy statement, *Responsibilities of Users of Standardized*

Tests (APGA, 1980), was especially helpful. Another major resource was *Standards for Educational and Psychological Testing* (Committee to Develop Standards . . ., 1985). Several sections of the *Standards* focus on principles of test administration and use. Working papers of the Joint Committee on Testing Practices were also consulted in the fall of 1986. The Joint Committee, which consists of representatives from the American Educational Research Association, the American Psychological Association, and the National Council on Measurement in Education, plans to publish a code of fair testing practices and materials on test user qualifications in the latter part of 1987. (Contact the American Psychological Association Staff Liaison to the Joint Committee for specifics.) The American Association for Counseling and Development has contributed to Joint Committee work through liaison persons.

Counselors wishing to improve their testing skills in general will find Appendix A, "Sources of Information about Tests and Testing," to be helpful. Although a number of test selection and interpretation responsibilities are cited in this checklist, Chapter III ("Selecting an Instrument: Choice or Challenge?") and Chapter IV ("Interpretation of Psychometric Instruments in Career Counseling") provide more extensive suggestions.

BASIC CONCEPTS

Concepts important to the informed *use* of tests are listed below. Persons with final responsibility for *evaluating* and *selecting* tests will require knowledge beyond these basic concepts.

Use the following key in responding to the statements:
  3 = I am able to apply the concept and explain it to others.
  2 = I have some knowledge but little experience in applying the
       concept.
  1 = I have little or no knowledge of this concept.
Enter the appropriate number in the blank at the left of each statement.

---

1. STATISTICS USED IN TESTING AND TEST MANUALS

____ a. Mean, median, mode
____ b. Standard deviation
____ c. Frequency distribution
____ d. Normal distribution
____ e. Correlation coefficient

2. TYPES OF INSTRUMENTS

____ a. Measures of maximum performance
____ b. Measures of typical performance
____ c. Similarities and differences among self-reports, self-ratings, inventories, and tests
____ d. Similarities and differences among measures of intelligence, aptitude, ability, and achievement

3. SCORE REPORTING PROCEDURES

_____ a. Percentile ranks
_____ b. Standard scores (including stanines)
_____ c. Grade placement (equivalent) scores
_____ d. Score profiles and profile analysis
_____ e. Group similarity indices ("Your scores are similar to people who . . .")
_____ f. Expectancy (experience) tables
_____ g. Estimates of probability of success and/or level of success; standard error of estimate

4. STANDARDIZATION AND NORMS

_____ a. Standardized administration and scoring
_____ b. Limitations of raw scores
_____ c. Types of norms (e.g., local, national, gender, grade); their applications and limitations
_____ d. Norm-based vs. criterion-referenced interpretation

5. RELIABILITY

_____ a. Meaning of test reliability
_____ b. Sources of measurement error
_____ c. Types of test reliability (test-retest; parallel forms; internal consistency, including split-half)
_____ d. Standard error of measurement and error bands

6. VALIDITY

_____ a. Meaning of test validity
_____ b. Implications of test use for validation procedures
_____ c. Types of test validity (content, criterion-related, construct)
_____ d. Factors affecting test validity (e.g., the "criterion problem")
_____ c. Differential validity of test batteries for diverse criteria
_____ f. Potential sources of bias affecting validity

RESPONSIBILITIES/COMPETENCIES

Test user responsibilities and concomitant competencies are listed in the next three sections.

Use the following key in responding to the statements:

3 = I do this routinely—as a regular practice.
2 = I have done this on occasion.
1 = I do not do this—but should give it consideration.

NA = Not applicable to the tests I am using.
Enter the appropriate number in the blank at the left of each statement.

PREPARING FOR TEST USE

_____ 1. Avoid unnecessary testing by determining whether existing information can meet the needs of your counselees and institution.

_____ 2. Consider advertisements for tests, promotional brochures, catalog descriptions, etc., in the same manner as advertisements for any commercial product in a competitive marketplace.

_____ 3. Obtain and review up-to-date copies of the administration, interpretation, and technical manuals for any test you are seriously considering. If not qualified to evaluate the test, obtain help from a qualified supervisor or consultant.

_____ 4. Read professional reviews of the test—e.g., in the _Journal of Counseling and Development_, the Buros series of _Mental Measurements Yearbooks_, _Test Critiques_. (See Appendix A for availability.)

_____ 5. Determine whether the test's reading level is appropriate to your counselees.

_____ 6. Verify that the test items, norms, and score reporting procedures minimize bias due to gender, cultural background, disability, or age.

_____ 7. Know whether you possess the qualifications (e.g., specific training and/or experience) required for use of a given test. Apply the same criteria to anyone with delegated responsibility for test use.

_____ 8. Determine whether research shows that the test measures what you want it to measure; evaluate the basis for any cut-off scores or decision rules advocated for score interpretation.

_____ 9. Avoid a test that requires the comparison of a counselee's raw scores unless research shows that equal raw scores for each of the test's scales (e.g., interest types) indicate equal amounts of the characteristic being measured.

_____ 10. Determine that computer-administered tests meet the same standards as traditional paper-and-pencil tests. For ability tests and other timed measures, determine that norms are appropriate to computerized administration.

_____ 11. Examine the basis for occupational attribute descriptions (e.g., relevant abilities, work activities) used to link counselee characteristics (e.g., abilities, interests) to occupations. Determine whether the descriptions and links are justified.

_____ 12. Before final adoption of a test, evaluate usability by administering and interpreting it to a small number of counselees. (See subsequent checklist items.) If possible, arrange to take the test yourself.

ADMINISTRATION AND SCORING

_____ 1. Acquire the training necessary to administer the test. Study the directions for administration and know whether additional materials (e.g., timer, scratch paper) are needed.

_____ 2. Provide a training session for test administrators and proctors.

_____ 3. Ensure that reasons for testing are understood and accepted by counselees—why the test is being given; what the test can and cannot do; who will receive the test results; how they will be used.

____ 4. Maintain the security of test materials before, during, and after administration.

____ 5. Provide a testing room and psychological climate that allow each counselee to achieve optimal performance.

____ 6. Plan for special circumstances affecting the administration of the test (e.g., late arrivals, disabled persons, left handers).

____ 7. Ensure that test administration directions are followed explicitly and completely.

____ 8. Determine appropriate answers to questions about guessing, skipping questions, and using time efficiently.

____ 9. Note unusual behavior by any person(s) being tested. If the test results are not invalidated, consider whether a report of the unusual behavior should accompany the scores.

____ 10. Periodically rescore (perhaps with clerical help) a sample of machine-scored answer sheets to verify scoring accuracy.

____ 11. Periodically rescore a sample of "self-scored tests" to verify scoring accuracy. Routinely check the scores of counselees who, in your judgement, may have difficulty with self-scoring.

____ 12. Develop a system for dating, recording, maintaining the confidentiality of, and storing test results.

INTERPRETATION

____ 1. Provide test interpretations based on documented bridges between scores and their real-world implications. That is, be sure your test interpretations, including those provided on the score report and/or a computer terminal, are warranted by research conducted on the test.

____ 2. Initially, and periodically thereafter, discuss your test interpretations with a qualified colleague.

____ 3. Review, with the counselee, the purpose and nature of the test—why the test was given (e.g., its relevance to counselee goals); what the test can and cannot do; who will receive the test results.

____ 4. Obtain the consent of the counselee before using test results for purposes other than those described prior to testing.

____ 5. Consider whether a counselee's reading level, gender, cultural background, disability, or age may have influenced the test results. Take such information into account in any reports of results.

____ 6. Encourage counselees to discuss how they felt about the testing experience in general (e.g., did they see potential personal benefit?); their performance in particular; and any problems encountered (e.g., nervousness, fatigue, distractions).

____ 7. Provide a simple explanation of measurement error and its implications, especially for score differences on profiles.

____ 8. Help the counselee to think of test interpretations as hypotheses to be checked against past experience, compared with other information, tested via mutually planned activities, and periodically reviewed and modified.

____ 9. Apply good counseling techniques to test interpretation by—attending to the counselee first and test results second (e.g., by listening attentively and encouraging feedback); allowing sufficient time for the counselee to assimilate information and ask questions; checking the counselee's understanding from time to time and correcting any misconceptions.

_____ 10. Help the counselee begin (or continue) the career planning process by cooperatively identifying career options, steps for exploring the options, and criteria for evaluating the options.

_____ 11. Monitor and encourage career planning activities through informal contacts, scheduled progress reports, or follow-through counseling sessions.

_____ 12. In general, observe the Golden Rule of Testing: "Administer and interpret unto others as you would have them do unto you."

REFERENCES

American Personnel and Guidance Association. (1980). *Responsibilities of users of standardized tests* (APGA Policy Statement). Falls Church, VA: Author.

American Psychological Association Committee on Professional Standards and Committee on Psychological Tests and Assessment. (1986). *Guidelines for computer-based test and interpretations*. Washington, DC: Author.

Biles, L. W. (1977). Competency based preparation programs for counseling psychologists, counselor educators, and counselors. In American Psychological Association (APA) Division 17 Committee on Competency-Based Licensure in the Academic Psychology Setting, *A Report*. Washington, DC: APA.

California Personnel and Guidance Association (CPGA). (1976). *Assessment and evaluation in education* (CPGA Monograph 10). Fullerton, CA: CPGA.

Committee to Develop Standards for Educational and Psychological Testing; The American Educational Research Association, The American Psychological Association, and The National Council on Measurement in Education. (1985). *Standards for educational and psychological testing*. Washington, DC: American Psychological Association.

Dameron, J. D. (Ed.). (1980). *The professional counselor: Competencies, performance, guidelines and assessment*. Alexandria, VA: AACD (formerly APGA).

Monsebraaten, A. J. (1980). Certification in testing in Canada. *Journal of Employment Counseling, 17*, 211–216.

Westbrook, B.W., & Mastie, M.M. (1983). Doing your homework: Suggestions for the evaluation of tests by practitioners. *Educational Measurement: Issues and Practice, 2*(1), 11–14, 26.

NOTE: Significant portions of this chapter were taken from the authors' original chapter in *A Counselor's Guide to Vocational Guidance Instruments*, 1982, NVGA.

CHAPTER VI

Major Career
Assessment
Instruments

Descriptions and Reviews of 43 Instruments

Multiple Aptitude Batteries

Armed Services Vocational Aptitude Battery (ASVAB)

Department of Defense

Headquarters, U.S. Military Entrance Processing Command
2500 Green Bay Road, North Chicago, Illinois 60064-3094

Target Population: Grades 10–12 and post secondary students.

Statement of the Purpose of the Instrument: To provide counselors and students with information useful for educational and career guidance and counseling purposes; to provide military service recruiters with test score information on 11th grade, 12th grade, and post secondary students.

Titles of Subtests, Scales, Scores Provided: Seven composite scores: Academic Ability, Math, Verbal, Mechanical & Crafts, Business and Clerical, Electronics and Electrical, and Health, Social, & Technology. Ten subtests: General Science, Word Knowledge, Paragraph Comprehension, Numerical Operations, Arithmetic Reasoning, Math Knowledge, Auto & Shop Information, Mechanical Comprehension, Electronics Information, and Coding Speed.

Forms and Levels Available, with Dates of Publication/Revision of Each: ASVAB Form 14; 1984.

Date of Most Recent Edition of Test Manual, User's Guide, etc.: Counselor's Manual for ASVAB-14—1984; Technical Supplement to the Counselor's Manual—1985; ASVAB Test Manual—1984; "Exploring Careers" Student Workbook—1987.

Languages in Which Available: English only.

Time: Actual Test Time—144 minutes.
Total Administration Time—180 minutes.

Norm Group(s) on Which Scores Are Based: Nationally representative sample of American youth, ages 16–23, collected in 1980 by National Opinion Research.

Manner in Which Results Are Reported for Individuals
Types of Scores: Nationally representative percentile scores for each composite are provided to students and counselors, by grade level (10th, 11th, 12th and post-secondary), sex, and opposite sex. In addition, standard scores for each subtest are provided to counselors.

Report Format/Content
Basic Service: See Counselor's Manual.

Report Format/Content for Group Summaries
Basic Service: See Counselor's Manual.
Options: See Counselor's Manual.

Scoring

Machine Scoring Service

Cost of basic service per counselee: No cost.

Cost of options: Not available.

Time required for scoring and returning (maximum): 30 days.

Hand Scoring: Not available.

Local Machine Scoring: Not available.

Computer Software Options Available: Not available.

Cost of Materials

Specimen Set: No cost.

Counselee Materials: No cost: Your Career Starts Here—A Student's Guide to ASVAB-14; Military Career Guide: Employment and Training Opportunities in the Military (reusable); Exploring Careers (consumable workbook).

Additional Comments of Interest to Users: Workshops and self-instructional materials to assist counselors in the interpretation of ASVAB are available.

Published Reviews

Murphy, K. (1984). Armed Services Vocational Aptitude Battery. In D.J. Keyser & R.C. Sweetland (Eds.), *Test Critiques*, Kansas City, Mo: Test Corporation of America.

Jensen, A. (1985). Armed Services Vocational Aptitude Battery, Test Reviews, *Measurement and Evaluation in Counseling and Development*, 18, 32–37.

Reviewed By

Arthur R. Jensen
Professor of Educational Psychology
University of California, Berkeley

The new Armed Services Vocational Aptitude Battery (ASVAB) (Form 14, U.S. Department of Defense, 1984) is intended for all youth (ages 16–23) in grades 11 and 12 and in 2-year colleges. At present, 10th grade norms are in development. It requires approximately 3 hours to administer, of which 2 hours and 24 minutes are actual test-taking time, with the rest of the time for instructions. The ASVAB-14 comprises 10 subtests, each containing anywhere from 15 to 84 items (a total of 334 items) and taking anywhere from 3 to 36 minutes. The subtests are General Science (GS), Arithmetic Reasoning (AR), Word Knowledge (WK), Paragraph Comprehension (PC), Numerical Operations (NO), Coding Speed (CS), Auto and Shop Information (AS), Math Knowledge (MK), Mechanical Comprehension (MC), and Electronics Information (EI). All items are in a multiple-choice format, all with four choices. Separate electronically scorable answer sheets are provided.

Scores are not reported for the individual subtests, but instead are reported for seven overlapping composites of various subtests. The *academic composites* are Academic Ability (WK, PC, AR), Verbal (GS, WK, PC), and Math (AR, MK). The *occupational composites* are Mechanical and Crafts (AR, AS, MC, EI), Business and Clerical (WK, PC, MK, CS), Electronics and Electrical (GS, AR, MK, EI), and Health, Social, and Technology (WK, PC, AR, MC). Performance on each composite is reported in terms of a percentile score bsaed on four different reference populations: (a) grade/sex, (b) grade/opposite sex, (c) grade, and (d) youth population, ages 18–23.

ADMINISTRATION

Since 1966, when the ASVAB was introduced to the nation's high schools and colleges, it has increasingly figured in many schools' testing programs. Currently, more than 1.3 million students in some 14,000 schools take the ASVAB each year.

The ASVAB, originally devised by the U.S. Department of Defense (DOD) to select and classify individuals for military service, is now offered to schools free of cost by the DOD. The test materials and the administration, scoring, and reporting of results are all provided by the DOD; the school provides the pupils, a suitable room, and a block of time (about 3 hours). The ASVAB is not available under any other conditions than direct supervision by the DOD, which delivers the results to schools within 30 days. The security of the ASVAB and the standardization of its administration are probably greater than for any other comparable test available to schools.

STANDARDIZATION

One of the greatest advantages of the ASVAB-14 over previous forms is the quality of the standardization. In 1980, it was administered to a nationally representative sample of about 12,000 young men and women (ages 16–23). Blacks, Hispanics, and economically disadvantaged Whites were oversampled to permit sufficiently large samples of these minority subgroups for detailed statistical analyses to assess the ASVAB's psychometric properties, including cultural item bias. Statistics on the various subsamples then were weighted in accord with their actual proportional representation in the total youth population as the basis for the percentile equivalents of the raw scores in a nationally representative youth population, ages 18 to 23.

PSYCHOMETRIC CHARACTERISTICS

The ASVAB has undergone considerable development and psychometric sophistication since its inception. The ASVAB *Form 14* may be regarded as an exemplar of the state of the art for norm-referenced, group-administered, paper-and-pencil tests of mental abilities. This is not to say, however, that some of the suggested specific uses of the ASVAB can escape serious criticism. Its potential liabilities concern the manner of its uses, not its psychometric features. The quality of psychometric research on the ASVAB sets a high standard. Moreover, the total "package" offered by the DOD is attractive, impressive, and probably unmatched by any commercially available test. There are a number of different brochures and booklets describing the ASVAB for students, parents, counselors, and educators. The "Information Pamphlet" contains about 60 sample test items. The *Test Manual* and *Counselor's Manual* are exemplary in organization and readability.

Reliability

Reliabilities of the subtests and composites are entirely satisfactory and on a par with the best commercially published tests of general ability and scholastic aptitude. Internal consistency reliabilities range from .81 to .92 for various subtests.

Alternate-forms reliability coefficients for the seven ASVAB composites range between .90 and .95; internal consistency reliabilities are about the same.

Validity

The *Test Manual* contains 19 tables of validity coefficients for various composites of the ASVAB subtests for over 50 specialized military occupational training programs. The validity criteria are generally grades in training school. Validity coefficients on the whole are high, averaging .50 to .60, or near the upper range of validity coefficients for most selection tests used in the civilian sector.

The Academic Ability composite has been validated as a predictor of grades in high schools and 2-year colleges, with an average validity of about .40. In a sample of more than 1,000 high school students, the Academic Ability composite correlated .90 with the *California Achievement Test* and .85 with the *Differential Aptitude Tests*. These high correlations indicate that the ASVAB scores reflect mainly general cognitive ability, which is the predominant basis of the predictive validity of all aptitude batteries for virtually all occupations.

Factor Analysis

When the correlations among the 10 ASVAB-14 subtests in the total youth population sample are subjected to a principal factors analysis, only two significant factors emerge, a *very general* factor, or *g*, and a relatively small *speed* factor, with significant loadings only on NO and CS, the two most speeded subtests. Hence the various subtests and the composites composed of them can have exceedingly little *differential* validity for individual assessment or prediction. The subtests measure mostly *g*, with loadings ranging from .76 to .97, averaging about .90, or almost as high as reliability permits. The ASVAB measures mainly *g* and little else. But *g* is by far the chief agent in scholastic and occupational predictive validity; *profile* differences based on individual subtest scores or on composite scores based on groups of subtests add suprisingly little to predictive validity (see Hunter, 1984; Jensen, 1984, 1985).

Cultural Bias and Adverse Impact

Analyses designed to detect item biases and predictive bias by race (Blacks, Whites, Hispanics) and sex reveal no evidence of bias. The scores have comparable validity across race and sex. Blacks and Hispanics obtain lower scores comparable to their scores on other tests of general ability. Selection based on ASVAB scores, therefore, would not reduce *average impact*, i.e., the degree to which selection based on test scores results in a disproportionate rejection rate for members of any particular subpopulation whose mean score falls below the general average.

PRACTICAL USEFULNESS IN GUIDANCE

The ASVAB is useful in much the same way as an ordinary IQ test. Although the *Counselor's Manual* is full of cautions regarding the interpretation of the composite scores, the format of a *profile* of scores is apt to predispose many counselors to overinterpretation of the score profile for occupational choices. Occupational choice should be thought of more in terms of *general ability* plus *interests* than in terms of *differential* aptitudes, which really boil down to *g* + interests. Little stock should be put in the *profile* aspects of the ASVAB composites for individual counseling. The reliability of the *differences* between the various composite scores is much too low for individual prediction of *differential* occupational promise. Differences between profile points would have to be about 2 standard deviations to be worth noticing, and even then interpretation would be doubtful. Although the ASVAB is an excellent group test of general ability, it takes about 3 hours. There are much shorter tests that measure *g* with satisfactory reliability.

REFERENCES

Hunter, J. E. (1984). *The Validity of the ASVAB as a Predictor of Civilian Job Performance*. Rockville, MD: Research Applications.

Jensen, A. R. (1984). Test validity: G versus the specificity doctrine. *Journal of Social and Biological Structures*, 7, 93–118.

Jensen, A. R. (1985). Review of the Armed Services Vocational Aptitude Battery. *Measurement and Evaluation in Counseling and Development*, 18, 32–37.

U.S. Department of Defense (1984). *Armed Services Vocational Aptitude Battery (ASVAB): Test Manual*. North Chicago, IL: United States Military Entrance Processing Command.

NOTE: Significant portions of this review were abridged from the author's original review in *Measurement and Evaluation in Counseling and Development*, 1984, *17*, 93–118, with permission of AACD.

Differential Aptitude Tests (DAT)

G.K. Bennett, H.G. Seashore, A.G. Wesman

The Psychological Corporation
Harcourt Brace Jovanovich, Inc.
555 Academic Court,
San Antonio, TX 78204-0952

Target Population: Recommended for grades 8 through 12 and adults.

Statement of the Purpose of the Instrument: Provides an integrated battery of eight aptitude tests designed for educational and vocational guidance in grades 8 through 12 and adults.

Titles of Subtests, Scales Provided: Subtests: Verbal Reasoning, Numerical Ability, Abstract Reasoning, Clerical Speed and Accuracy, Mechanical Reasoning, Space Relations, Spelling, Language Usage; additional scale: VR + NA.

Forms and Levels Available, with Dates of Publication/Revision of Each: One level, 2 alternate and equivalent forms, V and W, published in 1981.

Date of Most Recent Edition of Test Manual, User's Guide, Etc.: 1981.

Languages in Which Available
   Czechoslovakian—Available from: Psychodiagnostiche a dedakticke test narodny, Podnik, 826 06 Bratislava, Namestic Ludovuch Miliccii 4 Czechoslovakia
   Hindi—Available from: Manasayan, 32, Netaji Subhash Marg, Darya, Ginj, New Delhi 110002 India
   Spanish (Mexico)—Available from: Liberia International, Av. Sonora 206, Mexico 11, D.F.

Time: Actual Test Time—Approximately 3 hours.
      Total Administration Time—Approximately 3 hours.
      (Computerized Adaptive Edition) Actual Test Time: The testing is self-paced, but usually lasts about 90 minutes.

Norm Group(s) on Which Scores Are Based: 64 school districts in 32 states, males and females, grades 8 through 12.

Manner in Which Results Are Reported for Individuals
   Types of Scores: Percentile Ranks and Stanines are reported for males and for females.
Report Format/Content
   Basic Service: List Report (Sold Separately), Record Label (Sold Separately), Individual Report (Sold Separately), Career Planning Report (When the DAT is administered together with the Career Planning Questionnaire) (Sold Separately).
   Options: Extra List Report, Extra Record Label, Extra Individual Report, Extra Career Planning Report, Local Norms, Computer Tape.

Report Format/Content for Group Summaries
Basic Service: N/A.

Options: Career Choice Report, Extra Career Choice Report, School and System Summaries (Includes Frequency Distribution), Career Planning Report Summaries, Extra Career Planning Report Summaries, Local Norms, Computer Tape.

Scoring
Machine Scoring Service: (Prices valid through December 31, 1987).

Cost of basic service per counselee: List Report: 1.40; Record Label: 1.35; Individual Report: 1.75; Career Planning Report 2.35.

Cost of Options: Extra List Report: first copy—.25, additional—.09; Extra Record Label: first copy—.27, additional—.17; Extra Individual Report: first copy—.37, additional—.24; Extra Career Planning Report: first copy—.60, additional—.37; Career Choice Report: .36; School and System Summaries: first copy—.27, additional—23.00, (per order); Career Planning Report Summaries: first copy—.27, additional—23.00, (per order); Local Norms: .19; Computer Tape: Basic charge of 35.00 per reel and .19 per pupil.

Time required for scoring and returning (maximum): 18–20 working days from date of receipt.
Hand-Scoring: Scored by counselor.

Time required for scoring: Not available.

Local Machine Scoring: Provisions/conditions/equipment required:

Equipment with the capability to score MRS or NCS Answer Documents and written permission from The Psychological Corporation required.

Computer Software Options Available
Computerized adaptive administration; standard administration on-line; scoring; interpretation; other: System Requirements: Apple IIe or IIc, or Apple II + with at least 64K RAM. Franklin Ace 1000 computers may also be used. Two disk drives are required. IBM version will be available late 1987.

Ways in which computer version differs: Computer administered and scored entirely by the computer which individually adapts the test to each student's ability and as he/she progresses through the test, automatically eliminating questions that are too easy or too hard. There are immediate test results and reduced testing time.

Cost of Materials: (Prices valid through December 31, 1987).
Specimen Set: DAT: 12.00; DAT Computerized Adaptive Version: 30.00.

Counselee Materials: *Test Booklets (package of 35): 85.00; MRC machine-scorable Answer Documents (DAT only package of 1000): 65.00; MRC machine-scorable Answer Documents (DAT with Career Planning Questionnaires—package of 100): 83.00; NCS machine-scorable Answer Documents (package of 100): 83.00; *Keys for hand scoring MRC Answer Documents (DAT only): 10.00; *Administrator's Handbook: 10.00; *Counselor's Manual: 10.00; One-Page Report Form with Profile (package of 100): 11.00; Six-Page Report Form "Your Aptitudes" (package of 100): 28.00; *Orientation Booklet (package of 35): 22.00; *Technical Supplement: 18.00; *Directions for Administering and Scoring: 3.25.

Computerized Adaptive Edition: Start-Up Package: Includes Diskette A, Diskette B/C, User's Manual, Diskette Jacket/Waiting List Form, 10 Orientation Booklets, 10 Score Report Folders; can be used to test 10 cases. Diskette B/C and the User's Manual are reusable: 95.00.

Replacement Package: Includes Diskette A, Diskette Jacket/Waiting List Form, 10 Orientation Booklets, 10 Score Report Folders; Can be used to test 10 cases, provided user already has Diskette B/C and the User's Manual: 49.00; Technical Report: 25.00.

*Indicates reusable materials

Published Reviews

Bouchard, T.J., Jr. (1978). In O.K. Buros (Ed.), *The Eighth Mental Measurements Yearbook.* Highland Park, N.J.: Gryphon Press.

Linn, R.L. (1978). In O.K. Buros (Ed.), *The Eighth Mental Measurements Yearbook.* Highland Park, N.J.: Gryphon Press.

Maria Pennock-Román
Research Scientist
Division of Measurement Research and Services
Educational Testing Service, Princeton, NJ

The Differential Aptitude Tests (DAT) are currently among the most widely used measures of multiple abilities. Unlike tests of general intelligence that give a single score, the DAT taps a greater variety of developed skills and knowledge in several key areas. This battery is primarily intended for use in educational and vocational counseling with students in Grades 8–12 or young adults.

Initially developed in 1947, it has been continually updated and restandardized on large, nationally representative samples. The most recent revision in 1982 included many changes in item content and illustrations. A special large-print edition for the visually impaired and a computerized-adaptive version are available. Several editions have been developed for use outside the United States, including translations into Spanish and at least five other languages.

DESCRIPTION

The battery is designed for ease in group administration in settings such as classrooms. There are two alternate forms of the test (V and W). The basic test specimen set for each form includes one booklet for all eight subtests, answer sheets, and three manuals, the *Administrator's Handbook*, *Directions for Administration and Scoring*, and *Technical Supplement*. The scoring can be done by hand, or one of several scoring services can be ordered using the forms provided in the specimen set. All materials are attractive and durable, with important directions within each test highlighted in colors.

Subtests

Three of the subtests tap primarily word or language skills: Verbal Reasoning (VR, 50 analogy items, 30 minutes), Spelling (Sp, 90 items, 20 minutes), and Language Usage (LU, 50 items, 20 minutes, measuring grammar, punctuation, and capitalization). The Numerical Ability scale (NA, 40 items, 30 minutes) tests arithmetic computation and simple algebra concepts.

The content of the other scales is less familiar. Clerical Speed and Accuracy (CSA, 2 parts, each with 100 items, 3 minutes per part) measures how quickly and accurately the examinee can select which letter or number combinations are identical. In Abstract Reasoning (AR, 45 items, 20 minutes), geometric designs are presented in a series, and the examinee must choose which one of several designs best completes the series. Space Relations (SR, 60 items, 25 minutes) has patterns representing three-dimensional figures that have been unfolded to lay flat. The figure that can be constructed from the given pattern must be identified. In Mechanical Reasoning (MR, 70 items, 30 minutes), pictures of mechanical devices or persons working with tools are shown. Examinees answer a question about each illustration based on their understanding of the laws of physics and mechanical principles.

Career Planning Questionnaire

The Career Planning program can be ordered in addition to the cognitive tests. It includes a career planning questionnaire which assesses the examinee's interest in activities and occupations. There is also a *Counselor's Manual* and an optional orientation booklet that contains test-taking hints, practice exercises for each test, and information on the program.

ADMINISTRATION

It is recommended that testing be carried out in two or more sessions because the total procedure takes approximately four hours (including distribution and collection of materials, giving directions, and answering questions). The directions are clear and complete. Special care must be taken with the CSA test, however, because its time limits are so short. It is important that the examinees realize that, unlike the other subtests, the answer sheet for CSA has the response options directly on it (not the letters corresponding to the answer options).

Testing in the fall is desirable because the spring norms are derived by interpolation and are not based on actual administrations.

NORMS AND SCORES

The battery of tests yields nine scores, one for each test with an additional $VR + NA$ score. The latter can be said to measure overall scholastic aptitude because it correlates highly with other group tests of ability yielding a single score. The interpretative materials for the DAT compare well with those of competing batteries.

Although some researchers have urged that the norms for males and females be combined, the publishers provide only separate-sex norms. For three tests— VR, NA, and AR—sex differences are small, and it does not matter which norms are used. In MR and SR, males tend to have higher scores; in LU, Sp, and CSA, females tend to have higher scores. It is recommended that students compare their scores against the norms for the gender group that dominates the career of interest (e.g., male norms for technical careers). In this way, students can evaluate their standing relative to probable competitors.

If the Career Planning Program service is selected for the group, students receive a computerized interpretive report based on their individual abilities, interests, and plans. The report evaluates the fit between the student's profile and the first three career options selected by him or her, and suggests alternatives if necessary. Besides the *Counselor's Manual*, individual case histories are given in *Counseling from Profiles: A Casebook for the Differential Aptitude Tests*.

RELIABILITY AND VALIDITY

The DAT is technically very sound. Most individual subtests for both forms have internal-consistency reliability coefficients in the low .90s for all grades and both sexes. Thus the DAT scales are likely to give much more stable profiles of skills than the shorter subscales of individually administered intelligence tests, such as *Block Design* in the Wechsler scales (Anastasi, 1982).

The data on correlations between corresponding tests on the V and W forms of the DAT indicate that the two forms are essentially equivalent and that the scores are quite stable over short intervals of time.

There are numerous studies showing that the DAT has substantial concurrent and predictive validity because it correlates well with other aptitude tests, standardized achievement batteries, course grades in specific subjects in Grades 8–12, college grades, and success in post-high school job training programs. However, the publishers report only one study of actual job performance, which involved only selected tests (Daniel, Wiessen, Trafton, & Bowker, 1982).

The best predictor of grades and job training is the *VR + NA* score; other tests do not contribute a differentially better prediction in the expected directions. For example, among the median correlations between tests and science grades for males, the highest were .53 and .48 for NA and *VR + NA* scores, respectively. Sp and LU correlated more highly with science grades than did the AR, MR, and SR tests. Similar results have been found with other batteries of this type (Anastasi, 1982; Cronbach, 1984).

SPECIAL CONCERNS

Counselors should bear in mind two overarching guidelines when using this test: (1) Rely on the *VR + NA* score as the primary basis for advising, and resist the temptation to overinterpret the other scores of lesser importance; and (2) suggest possible remediation and practice in skills to correct weaknesses in *any* specialized aptitudes (not just language usage).

The different measures do have much clinical appeal because they profile strengths for students with low general ability and reveal weak areas for the otherwise strong students. Nevertheless, the evidence from research studies overwhelmingly indicates that the overall *VR + NA* score is the best predictor of grades even in areas such as science and industrial arts. Some studies suggest that spatial and mechanical abilities may affect the pattern of occupational choice in the long run, but the evidence is scanty and weak at best for the specific tests of the DAT. Therefore, the sharp differentiations made by the publishers among the occupations listed as relevant to each skill should be taken lightly when advising students on the basis of the specialized subtests.

As cautioned in the *Handbook*, the tests should be considered measures of *developed* abilities; i.e., the distinction between aptitude and achievement tests is quite subtle at this age level. For example, educationally disadvantaged students who have not been exposed to mathematics concepts such as exponents and negative numbers may receive low scores on the NA test, even if they have the potential to master this material.

Although sex differences on the MR test are large, counselors should place little emphasis on these differences for vocational advising because the primary predictor for academic success in technical fields is the *VR + NA* score, which shows no gender differences. Advisors should be wary of discouraging females from entering male-dominated technical fields if they score poorly on MR but perform well on *VR + NA* and other relevant tests. Instead, such females could be encouraged to take courses in mechanical physics and industrial arts in order to strengthen their skills in these areas.

USABILITY

Less than two hours of training is required to familiarize examiners with group administration procedures, and answer sheets can be scored quickly by hand or machine. The battery can also be administered individually if instructions and time limits are strictly followed.

The DAT allows a fairer assessment of special populations such as the deaf or students with limited proficiency in English because it can measure reasoning and other aptitudes with less emphasis on verbal content.

In conclusion, I highly recommend this battery, provided that users abide by the aforementioned guidelines.

REFERENCES

Anastasi, A. (1982). *Psychological Testing* (5th ed.). New York: Macmillan Publishing Company.

Arnold, P., & Walter, C. (1979). Communication and reasoning skills of deaf and hearing signers. *Perceptual and Motor Skills*, *49*, 192–194.

Cronbach, L.J. (1984). *Essentials of Psychological Testing (4th ed.)*. New York: Harper & Row Publishers.

Daniel, M., Wiesen, J.P., Trafton, R.S., & Bowker, R. (1982, September). *The Relationship of Aptitudes to the Performance of Skilled Technical Jobs in Engine Manufacturing* (Tecnical Report 1982-5). Fort Worth, TX: Johnson O'Connor Research Foundation, Human Engineering Laboratory.

Deb, M. (1980). DAT as predictor of students' success in psychology. *Psychology Research Journal*, *4*(1), 23–28.

Sherman, J. (1980a). Mathematics, spatial visualization, and related factors: Changes in girls and boys, grades 8–11. *Journal of Educational Psychology*, *72*, 476–482.

NOTE: Significant portions of this review were abridged from the author's original review in Volume III of *Test Critiques* with permission of Test Corporation of America.

USES General Aptitude Test Battery (GATB)

United States Employment Service (USES)

United States Employment Service
Employment and Training Administration
200 Constitution Avenue, NW
Washington, DC 20210

Target Population: Grade 9–adult

Statement of the Purpose of the Instrument: The GATB measures the vocational aptitudes of individual in order to determine qualifications for the wide range of occupations for vocational guidance and selection.

Titles of Subtests, Scales, Scores Provided: The GATB consists of 12 tests measuring 9 occupational aptitudes.

Forms and Levels Available, with Dates of Publication/Revision of Each: There are four forms of the GATB, B-1002—Forms A, B, C, D. Form B is presently the only form available for use by approved organizations outside of the Employment Service system. Forms A and B, 1982—Forms C and D, 1983.

Date of Most Recent Edition of Test Manual, User's Guide, Etc.: 1982.

Languages in Which Available: English, Spanish.

Time: Total administration, 2½ hours.

Norm Group(s) on Which Scores Are Based: General working population and workers employed in particular occupations. (See Section III: Development, GATB, 1970 and Hunter, J.E. "Validity generalization for 12,000 jobs: An application of synthetic validity and validity generalization to the GATB." U.S. Dept. of Labor, Washington, DC, 1980.) Separate norms are also available for 9th and 10th graders.

Manner in Which Results Are Reported for Individuals
  Types of Scores: Standard scores are given as related to distributions of scores of people working in occupational groups. Standard scores on all nine aptitudes are calculated and can be related to Occupational Aptitude Patterns (OAPs). OAPs are combinations of GATB aptitudes with associated cutting scores. There are 59 OAPs.
  Report Format/Content: There is a nationwide scoring service available when NCS or Intran answer sheets are used. The service includes converting raw scores to aptitude scores, matching aptitude scores with OAPs, and printing Test Record Cards with results.

Report Format/Content for Group Summaries: Not available.

Scoring
  Machine Scoring Service
    Cost of basic service per counselee: $.70–$.75;
    Cost of options: none;
    Time required for scoring and returning (maximum): 3 days.
  Hand Scoring
    Scored by: counselor
    Time required for scoring: 20 minutes.
    Local Machine Scoring: Not available.

Computer Software Options Available: Not available.

Cost of Materials
  Specimen Set: (see below—no sample test available because of restrictions on test)
  Counselee Materials (see below)
  Test Book and Booklets: FORM B (only form available for use by outside approved organizations) Book I (Parts 1–4) $3.50 each; Book II (Parts 5–7) $2.25 each; Part 8 (not reusable) $6.50 per pad of 100; Pegboards & Pegs (Parts 9–10) plastic $26.50 each, wooden $19.50 each; Finger Dexterity Board (Parts 11–12) $15.50 each.
  Other Necessary Materials: Section I, Administration and Scoring, Forms A & B, 1982 $7.50; *GUIDE for Occupational Exploration*, 1979 $12.00; *Dictionary of Occupational Titles*, Fourth Edition, 1977 $23.00.

Additional Comments of Interest to Users: The GATB was developed by the United States Employment Service primarily for use by the State Employment Security agencies. Schools and other non-profit organizations which meet certain requirements may, at the option of the State Employment Security agency, be authorized to use the GATB for counseling or research. Inquiries must be directed to the appropriate State Employment Security agency.

Published Reviews
Keesling, J. W. (1985). In J. V. Mitchell (Ed.), *The Ninth Mental Measurements Yearbook*. Lincoln, Nebraska: The Buros Institute of Mental Measurements.
Borgen, F. H. (1982). In J. T. Kapes and M. M. Mastie (Eds.), *A counselor's guide to vocational guidance instruments*. The National Vocational Guidance Association.
Weiss, D. J. (1972). In O. K. Buros (Ed.), *The Seventh Mental Measurements Yearbook*. Highland Park, N.J. Gryphon Press.
Bechtoldt, H. P. (1965). In O. K. Buros (Ed.), *The Sixth Mental Measurements Yearbook*. Highland Park, N.J. Gryphon Press.
Carroll, J. B. (1965). In O. K. Buros (Ed.), *The Sixth Mental Measurements Yearbook*. Highland Park, N.J. Gryphon Press.

Reviewed by

J. Ward Keesling
Principal Systems Analyst
Advanced Technology Inc.

and

Charles C. Healy
Associate Professor
Graduate School of Education UCLA

The General Aptitude Test Battery (GATB) consists of 12 tests measuring nine occupational aptitudes: General Learning Ability, Verbal Aptitude, Numerical Aptitude, Spatial Aptitude, Form Perception, Clerical Perception, Motor Coordination, Finger Dexterity, and Manual Dexterity. The last two are measured with apparatus tests; the other seven aptitudes are measured by paper-and-pencil tests. Raw test scores are converted to standardized scores on each aptitude, with a mean of 100 and a standard deviation of 20. Test-retest reliabilities range from the mid-70s to .90.

THE GUIDE FOR OCCUPATIONAL EXPLORATION

The core of the occupational guidance system of which GATB is a part is the *Guide for Occupational Exploration* published by the U.S. Department of Labor (1979). The *Guide* partitions all of the occupations listed in the 1977 *Dictionary of Occupational Titles* into a hierarchical taxonomy consisting of 12 Interest Areas, within which are 66 Work Groups containing 348 Subgroups, within which are some 12,000 occupations.

The *Guide* is based on occupational titles that are nearly a decade old. It is noted, for example, that the occupation "word processor" is not in the *Guide*. Should one refer to the requirements of "typist" as a best guess?

USES relates scores on the GATB to this taxonomy via the Occupational Aptitude Pattern (OAP), which is a pattern of scores that identifies one or more Work Groups for which a candidate is "suited." The OAPs were derived from research on the specific Aptitude Test Batteries (SATBs).

THE CONCEPT OF SATBs

The SATBs are patterns of cutoff scores on the nine GATB aptitudes to be used in predicting whether or not a candidate is likely to be successful in specific occupations. Although there are nearly 470 SATBs given in the 1980 manual (Section IV), 92 of them are blank because they do not meet "current test development technology and research standards." This means that of the 12,000 occupations in the *Dictionary of Occupational Titles*, there are validated scales for less than 5%. Most of the validation studies are small scale, and there is

71

little evidence presented that these studies are very generalizable. Some attempt has been made to check for racial and sex bias in the scales, and some of the SATBs are marked as having potential problems in this regard.

Scores on the nine aptitudes measured by the GATB are highly correlated, making the choice of aptitudes and cutoff scores for an SATB unstable from study to study. The major problem with this instability in the constitution of the SATBs is that the final combination chosen for operational use is an arbitrary choice. It is not clear what additional factors guided these choices, or how these choices affected the analyses relating SATBs to the taxonomy of occupations.

THE USEFULNESS OF OAPs

To develop OAPs, USES made use of the SATB information in its files. For 31 of the Work Groups there were three or more SATBs for specific occupations in the group. (The SATBs now considered not to meet appropriate technical standards were apparently used in these analyses.) Within each Work Group these SATBs were examined to produce a "modal" OAP—a set of two or more of the "most commonly occurring aptitudes" and the median cutting score for those aptitudes. A candidate who meets or exceeds this pattern of scores is deemed qualified to explore occupations in the Work Group. Since different patterns of aptitudes and cutscores could serve as well as the operational SATBs, the choice of the "most commonly occurring aptitudes" is influenced by the arbitrariness of the choices of operational SATBs.

To summarize, the highly correlated nature of the aptitudes measured on the GATB results in instability of the pattern of aptitudes related to success in an occupation. In addition, the arbitrarily chosen SATBs result in uncertainty with regard to the aptitudes and cutscores to be included in an OAP and the prediction of OAPs for Work Groups having no SATB information results in further uncertainties.

VALIDITY IN COUNSELING HIGH SCHOOL STUDENTS

The validity evidence supporting the use of the GATB in counseling high school students is inconclusive. The results of the USES's own study (begun in 1958) are not fully reported, but the validity coefficients for this study apparently do not exceed .26. No evidence is presented regarding prediction of performance or satisfaction in specific occupations using the SATBs. (See Chapters 13 and 20 of Section III of the Manual for the GATB, 1970.)

It is worth noting that all of these studies predate the long slide in Scholastic Aptitude Test scores that may mark a profound change in the composition of the student population, or of the curricula to which they are exposed, either of which could alter the predictive validity of the GATB. (National Institute of Education, *Declining Test Scores*, Washington, D.C.: Author, 1976.)

Chapter 22 of Section III of the Manual for the GATB (1970) suggests using the OAP to locate Work Groups for which the counselee is suited, then narrow to specific occupations for which there are SATBs. The lack of evidence of predictive validity of the SATBs should discourage the latter practice. The evidence supporting the use of OAPs is weak, and an indication of being suited or not for a particular work group should be regarded as inconclusive by itself.

The Manual (Section III, pp 365–369) wisely suggests that counselors must integrate other information with the GATB test scores in guiding career choices. The Manual discusses assessment of: education and training, acquired skills, socio-economic factors, personal traits, physical capacities, leisure time activities, and interests. The USES has developed instruments particularly aimed at exploring interests (1981). In the spirit of using multiple perspectives to interpret GATB scores, this review concludes with advice for using the GATB in career counseling. Borgen (1982) offers additional advice and a plea for the USES to publish case examples to guide practicing counselors.

USING THE GATB IN COUNSELING

Despite their psychometric limitations, GATB scores may help clients in making reasoned estimates of their standing on the aptitudes relative to working adults. Several studies indicate that students and adults earn GATB scores which disagree with their estimates of the corresponding aptitudes. Rather than insisting that the GATB scores are the best estimates of the client's aptitudes, counselors can juxtapose the scores with the client's self-estimates to prime discussion of such issues as: How the client defines the domain of the aptitude, whether the client works carefully but slowly (the GATB tests are all speeded), the recency of the client's training and work experience relative to the aptitude, the client's comfort in demonstrating talents through tests, and whether the client is evaluating his/her talents against typical or atypical groups.

Although there is no direct empirical evidence that more reasoned self-estimates will benefit clients, the process of reviewing estimates and their bases is likely to increase the client's confidence in the estimates. Moreover, it is also likely to enable the client to more fully appreciate how to relate aptitudes to educational and work opportunities.

As long as the limitations of the SATBs and OAPs are understood, counselors can also use them in conjunction with expressed and inventoried interests in helping clients to explore career options. These occupational and work area profiles can be compared to the client's actual and reasoned self-estimated aptitude profile to identify occupations for exploration. They could also be used to open discussions of the feasibility of the client's seeking entry to occupations suggested by his/her interests. Sometimes clients find that their tested or estimated aptitudes are higher than the OAP or SATB cutoffs. That discrepancy can prompt reviewing whether the client will feel enough challenge in the occupation and whether the client aspires to advance.

When a client's scores and reasoned estimates are lower than the SATB cutoffs, client and counselor can discuss whether client experiences such as job success involving the aptitude do not contradict the low score. They can also consider whether strong interests or other abilities would compensate for the possible handicap of low aptitude. Sometimes, of course, a non-competitive profile can give clients permission to turn their aspirations toward occupational areas for which they are more likely to be competitive. In considering SATB and OAP comparisons along with data such as success in previous jobs and training, counselors should remember that aptitude scores have related more clearly to success in training and much less clearly to success or satisfaction in occupations (Ghiselli, 1966).

REFERENCES

Borgen, F. H. (1982). In J. T. Kapes and M. M. Mastie (Eds.), *A Counselor's Guide to Vocational Guidance Instruments*. Falls Church, VA: The National Vocational Guidance Association.

Ghiselli, E. E. (1966). *The Validity of Occupational Ability Tests*. New York: Wiley.

National Institute of Education (1976). *Declining Test Scores*. Washington, D.C.: U.S. Government Printing Office.

U.S. Department of Labor (1979). *Guide for Occupational Exploration*. Washington, D.C.: U.S. Government Printing Office.

U.S. Department of Labor (1970). *Manual for the General Aptitude Test Battery, Section III: Development*. Washington, D.C.: U.S. Government Printing Office.

U.S. Department of Labor (1979). *Manual for the General Aptitude Test Battery, Section II: Occupational Aptitude Pattern Structure*. Washington, D.C.: U.S. Government Printing Office.

U.S. Department of Labor (1980). *Manual of the General Aptitude Test Battery, Section IIA: Development of Occupational Aptitude Pattern Structure*. Washington, D.C.: U.S. Government Printing Office.

U.S. Department of Labor (1980). *Manual for the General Aptitude Test Battery, Section IV: Specific Aptitude Test Batteries*. Washington, D.C.: U.S. Government Printing Office.

U.S. Department of Labor (1981). *A New Counselee Assessment/Occupational Exploration System and its Interest and Aptitude Dimensions*. U.S. Employment Service Technical Report No. 35. Washington, D.C.: U.S. Government Printing Office.

NOTE: Significant portions of this review were abridged from the first author's original review in *The Ninth Mental Measurements Yearbook* with permission of the Buros Institute.

Interest Inventories

Career Assessment Inventory— The Enhanced Version (CAI)

Charles B. Johansson

NCS Professional Assessment Services
P.O. Box 1416, Minneapolis, MN 55440

Target Population: High schools, 2 & 4 year colleges, human resource departments and vocational rehabilitation programs.

Statement of the Purpose of the Instrument: The Enhanced Career Assessment Inventory is an interest inventory designed to measure one's occupational interests for use in career exploration and career decision making. The purpose of the enhanced version was to expand the scope of coverage to include more professionally oriented occupations.

Titles of Subtests, Scales, Scores Provided: Six general occupational theme scales, 25 basic interest scales and 111 occupational scales. Administrative indices and 4 non-occupational scales. (All scales constructed to be applicable to both genders.)

Forms and Levels Available, with Dates of Publication/Revision of Each: 1 form, 1986.

Date of Most Recent Edition of Test Manual, User's Guide, Etc.: Inventory and manual revised— 1986.

Languages in Which Available: English only. Original Career Assessment Inventory is available in Spanish and French.

Time: Actual Test Time—Approx. 30 minutes.
Total Administration Time—Approx. 40 minutes.

Norm Group(s) on Which Scores Are Based: General theme scales based on a normative sample of 900 adults; norms for occupational scales were developed by scoring occupational subgroup samples independently.

Manner in Which Results Are Reported for Individuals
Types of Scores: Standard scores and percent response.
Report Format/Content: Basic Service: Profile Report—graphically presents scores on each scale. Reverse side has preprinted interpretive information. Provided in duplicate.
Options: Narrative Report—provides scale descriptions, score interpretations and comparisons, and additional reference information; includes 3 page detachable counselor's summary.

Report Format/Content for Group Summaries
Options: Mean and standard deviation report; frequency distribution; item response report.

Scoring

Machine Scoring Service:

Cost of basic service per counselee: Profile: $2.90 when ordering quantities of 100 or more. Includes cost of answer sheet, scoring and report. Quantity discounts apply.

Cost of options: Narrative: $5.10 when ordering quantities of 100 or more. Includes cost of answer sheet, scoring and report. Quantity discounts apply.

Time required for scoring and returning (maximum): 24 hour turnaround.

Hand Scoring: Not available.

Local Machine Scoring

Provisions/conditions/equipment requires: MICROTEST® assessment software. Requirements: IBM* PC or PC/XT, parallel printer, NCS ScorBox® and MICROTEST software. Provides immediate on-site scoring and reports. Arion II® teleprocessing requirements: microcomputer, printer, modem and telephone. Provides inventory results in minutes using teleprocessing technology.

*IBM is a registered trademark of International Business Machines Corporation.

Computer Software Options Available: standard administration—on-line; scoring; interpretation.

Cost of Materials: Specimen Set: Includes manual and answer sheets for narrative and profile reports. Cost: $19.50. Counselee Materials: Combination test booklet and answer sheet. Profile: 1–4 $4.40; 5–29 $4.10; 30–49 $3.65; 50–99 $3.30; 100+ $2.90. Narrative: 1–4 $8.75; 5–29 $8.00; 30–49 $7.00; 50–99 $6.00; 100+ $5.10.

Additional Comments of Interest to Users: The 1986 enhanced version of the Career Assessment Inventory is more universally applicable than previous editions. The additional occupational scales, expansion of item coverage of the general theme scales and basic interest scales are reported in the revised manual.

Published Reviews

Bodden, J. (1978). In O. K. Buros (Ed.), *The Eighth Mental Measurements Yearbook*. Highland Park, N.J.: Gryphon Press.

Lohnes, P. R. (1978). In O. K. Buros (Ed.), *The Eighth Mental Measurements Yearbook*. Highland Park, N.J.: Gryphon Press.

Lohnes, P. R. (1982). In J. T. Kapes & M. M. Mastie (Eds.), *A Counselor's Guide to Vocational Guidance Instruments*. Falls Church, VA: National Vocational Guidance Association.

McCabe, S. D. (1985). In D. J. Keyser & R. C. Sweetland (Eds.), *Test Critiques, Vol. II*. Kansas City, MO: Test Corporation of America.

Sheridan P. McCabe
Associate Professor of Psychology
University of Notre Dame

The original Career Assessment Inventory (CAI) was patterned after the Strong-Campbell Interest Inventory but designed for a subject population that is not intending to pursue education at the college level. It was directed toward those moving toward immediate career entry after high school or who seek specific vocational preparation such as a business school or technical institute. It compares the interests of the test taker with those of workers in occupations requiring less than a four-year college education. The new enhanced version extends the basic instrument both by adding additional items and by developing scales which cover a larger spectrum of occupations, including those which demand collegiate or professional education. Thus, the enhanced CAI is an instrument intended to be applicable over a broad range of occupational levels including those spanned by both the Strong-Campbell and the preceding CAI. One particularly interesting feature which this test shares with the 1982 revision of the CAI is that careful steps have been taken to eliminate sex bias, including the utilization of combined male-female scales. The manual includes a point by point indication of how this test meets the National Institute of Education guidelines on the elimination of sex bias. The result is a good general-purpose vocational interest inventory which includes both content-oriented and empirically based scales and which is suitable for a general population, some of whom are college bound and others directed toward practical training or direct entry to the job market.

There are 370 items tapping preferences among three categories: activities, school subjects and occupations. Each is answered in the same five-choice format with options ranging from like very much to dislike very much. The items are presented in an attractive test booklet where the answers are recorded immediately adjacent to the items. The manual suggests that the reading level of the test is 8th grade. The test manual is a 214-page book which is clearly written and very complete. It is directed toward the test user, with the technical data on which the test is based included in appendices.

SCALES

Like the predecessor, the enhanced CAI uses the Holland Occupational Themes as its organizing principle. Scores are presented for each of the six General Themes. These are further divided into 25 component Basic Interest Scales, with both the General Themes and Basic Interest Scales based on the content of the items. There are 111 Occupational Scales that are also classified by the Themes which they represent. On these scales, the examinee's interests are matched to those of people who have been employed in an occupation for a number of years, have been given the appropriate training and have indicated job satisfaction.

Finally, there are a number of Administrative Indices that describe the response tendencies of the examinee as well as four non-occupational scales.

Scores on all of the scales are based on a standard score distribution with a mean of 50 and a standard deviation of 10. These standard scores were derived from the results of a reference group of 450 males and 450 females selected such that it is composed of 75 males and 75 females scoring highest on each of the six Themes. Thus scores between 43 and 57 on each of the General Themes and Basic Interests are regarded as average and neither high nor low. The scale is normed so that the mean of the criterion group is 50 with a standard deviation of 10. This is the same scale as is used on the earlier CAI and on the Strong-Campbell. The criterion groups are well described in the manual, including the relative proportion of men and women. The criterion groups range in size from 70 to 453. How they were selected, along with the date of the sampling, is presented in the manual.

VALIDITY

The manual presents a clear discussion of validity of the General Theme and Basic Interest Scales in terms of their content, construct and concurrent validity. Content validity was maximized by the use of an empirical-rational developmental strategy. The theoretical definition of the dimension to be measured by each scale was used to generate an item pool for that scale. Then items from that item pool were correlated with the total of the remaining items in order to select those items with the highest correlation. This resulted in a set of highly specific and cohesive scales that have a high relevance to the theoretical basis of the scale. Construct validity was investigated by correlations with similar scales on the Strong-Campbell. Finally concurrent validity is demonstrated by the distribution of occupational groups in a meaningful and logical order. For the occupational scales, the manual presents evidence of concurrent and construct validity. Concurrent validity is defined here as the ability of the scale to differentiate the criterion group from the reference group. The data in the manual suggest that the developmental strategy was successful in accomplishing this. Construct validity is demonstrated by presenting the correlations of the occupational scales with similar scales on the Strong-Campbell and the Kuder. The results with the Strong-Campbell show a median correlation of about .60.

RELIABILITY

Because this is a new test, test-retest reliability coefficients are not available for long intervals. The manual does report test-retest reliabilities for each scale for intervals of 1 week, 2 weeks, 30 days, and 2 or 3 months. These coefficients are quite appropriate and suggest that this instrument provides stable measures. For the shortest interval, they range from .80 to .96 with a median of .92. For the longest interval reported, the medial values are .82 for the Themes and Basic Interest Scales and .91 for the occupational scales. Based on research with the CAI over intervals as long as 7 years, the manual predicts that these values will be characteristic of the enhanced CAI for similar time intervals. This test appears to provide appropriately stable measures of interests.

SCORING

Like most interest inventories of this type and complexity, hand scoring is not feasible. However, the test publisher offers a scoring service that provides either profile or narrative reports. These are available either through a mail-in service, a teleprocessing service for those with computer telecommunication equipment, or software that runs on the user's own microcomputer. Both of these latter alternatives offer immediate availability of results.

USABILITY

The enhanced version of the CAI is an important addition to the repertoire of the counselor. It is a broad-spectrum vocational interest inventory that offers both content and empirical scores and extends to both professional and sub-professional level occupations. While the Strong-Campbell will continue to be the instrument of choice for individuals who are college bound, the enhanced CAI will be the interest inventory most useful for the larger group who are not. It provides very useful information in a clear and accurate fashion. Special features which commend it are the very complete and clear manual, the approach to minimize sex bias, the ease of administration, and the informative presentation of the results. On the last point, the report format is clear to an extent that could be deceptive. The quality of information that this test yields is great to the point that a good deal of training and theoretical sophistication is necessary for its adequate interpretation.

REFERENCES

Bodden, J. L. (1978). A review of the Career Assessment Inventory. In O. K. Buros (Ed.), *The Eighth Mental Measurements Yearbook*. Highland Park, NJ: Gryphon Press.
Johannson, C. B. (1986). *Manual for the Career Assessment Inventory*. Minneapolis: National Computer Systems.
Lohnes, P. R. (1978). A review of the Career Assessment Inventory. In O. K. Buros (Ed.), *The Eighth Mental Measurements Yearbook*. Highland Park, NJ: Gryphon Press.
McCabe, S. P. (1985). Career Assessment Inventory. In D. J. Keyser and R. C. Sweetland (Eds.) *Test Critiques, Volume II*. Kansas City, MO: Test Corporation of America.

NOTE: Some portions of this review were abridged from the author's original review in Volume II of *Test Critiques* with permission of Test Corporation of America. The present review is of a later version and substantial revision was made.

Career Occupational Preference System (COPS) Interest Inventory

R. R. Knapp, L. Knapp

EdITS
P.O. Box 7234, San Diego, CA 92107

Target Population: Seventh grade through high school, college and adult.

Statement of the Purpose of the Instrument: The COPS is used to measure job activity preference in 8 major career clusters for use in guiding both college and non-college bound examinees in job exploration and into educational & career decision making.

Titles of Subtests, Scales, Scores Provided: Science Professional, Science Skilled, Technology Professional, Technology Skilled, Consumer Economics, Outdoor, Business Professional, Business Skilled, Clerical, Communication, Arts Professional, Arts Skilled, Service Professional, Service Skilled.

Forms and Levels Available, with Dates of Publication/Revision of Each: Self-scoring 1982 Jr-Sr High and College; Machine scoring 1982 Jr-Sr High and College.

Date of Most Recent Edition of Test Manual, User's Guide, Etc.: COPSystem Technical Manual, 1984.

Languages in Which Available: English, Spanish, Braille, large print.

Time: Actual Test Time—20–30 minutes.
　　　Total Administration Time—30 minutes.

Norm Group(s) on Which Scores Are Based: Jr-Sr High and College.

Manner In Which Results Are Reported for Individuals
　Types of Scores: Percentile scores, verbal labels.
　Report Format/Content
　　Basic Service: Scores plotted on profile. Also receive descriptions of clusters, list of job titles, activity decision-making worksheets, for career and program planning.
　　Options: Self or machine scoring.

Report Format/Contents for Group Summaries
　Basic Service: Basic list report—Summarizes group scores, record labels, summary of interest categories by group, needs assessment summary.
　Options: May have summaries organized according to needs of school.

Scoring

Machine Scoring Service

Cost of basic coverage per counselee: $1.00.

Cost of Options: .15 for additional file copy. Basic list report $1.00, record labels .35, summary of interests .25, needs assessment summary .15/all per examiner.

Time required for scoring and returning (maximum): 10 days.

Hand Scoring: Scored by counselee; clerk; counselor. Time required for scoring: 15 to 20 minutes.

Local Machine Scoring: Provisions/conditions/equipment required: Optical scanner, microcomputer, and licensing agreement.

Computer Software Options Available: Standard administration: scoring; interpretation; group summaries.

Cost of Materials: Specimen Set $6.25; Counselee Materials: Self-scoring booklet & profile sheet per student: 25 $.69; 100 $.62; 500 $.59. Machine scoring booklet non reusable & scoring: 25 $1.36; 100 $1.32; 500 $1.30.

Additional Comments of Interest to Users: COPS keyed to outside sources and two job description kits available from EdITS. Also keyed to CAPS Ability Battery, COPES Values Survey.

Published Reviews

Bauernfeind, R. H. (1972). Review of the California Occupational Preference Survey. In O. K. Buros (Ed.), *Seventh Mental Measurements Yearbook*. Highland Park, NJ: Gryphon Press.

Bodden, J. S. (1972). Review of the California Occupational Preference Survey. In O. K. Buros (Ed.), *Seventh Mental Measurements Yearbook*. Highland Park, NJ: Gryphon Press.

French, J. W. (1972). Review of the California Occupational Preference Survey. In O. K. Buros (Ed.), *Seventh Mental Measurements Yearbook*. Highland Park, NJ: Gryphon Press.

Hansen, J. C. (1982). California Occupational Preference System. In J. T. Kapes & M. M. Mastie (Eds.), *A Counselor's Guide to Vocational Guidance Instruments*. Falls Church, VA: National Vocational Guidance Association.

Hansen, J. C. (1978). Review of California Occupational Preference System. In O. K. Buros (Ed.), *Eighth Mental Measurements Yearbook*. Highland Park, NJ: Gryphon Press.

Layton, W. L. (1978). Review of California Occupational Preference System. In O. K. Buros (Ed.), *Eighth Mental Measurements Yearbook*. Highland Park, NJ: Gryphon Press.

Reviewed By

Robert H. Bauernfeind
Professor of Educational Psychology
Northern Illinois University

The Career Occupational Preference System (COPS) (formerly the California Occupational Preference System) yields 14 job-activity interest scores. These scores represent occupational clusters that may be used as entries to most occupational information systems.

The authors write that:

. . . the career guidance process begins by assisting individuals in defining areas for occupational investigation which are specific and appropriate to their personal interests. Investigation of a great many related occupations within a given area broadens the scope of career exploration. Through this process individuals are more quickly and systematically introduced to those occupations in which they are likely to be occupied in years hence (Manual, 1984, p. 1).

The items present job activities (not job titles), written in straightforward English, each to be marked on a 4-point scale; L—Like very much; 1—like moderately; d—dislike moderately; D—Dislike very much.

Thus, sample items look like this:

	L	1	d	D
11. Sell housewares door to door	: : :	: : :	: : :	: : :
22. Take and compare fingerprints	: : :	: : :	: : :	: : :
(SCORING)	(3)	(2)	(1)	(0)

A few items in this 1982 instrument differ from earlier editions in three ways: (1) The authors have rewritten some items to reduce sex differences; (2) the authors have lowered the reading/vocabulary level of several items; and (3) the authors have changed a few items to bring them more in line with actual job activities in the American world of work. The factorial structure of the instrument, however, remains the same as before. Also, the COPS instrument still uses the graduated-response item format that allows clients to try to show their degree of feeling about each activity.

A very attractive feature of the COPS items is that the activities cited are rather mundane—non-glamorous. This means that high-scoring clients tend to "like" routine chores in the given occupational cluster.

THE 14 CLUSTER SCORES

The 14 cluster scores were developed and confirmed through an excellent series of multiple-factor analysis studies (Manual, 1984, pp. 2–4; pp. 30–32). Each cluster is based on 12 items and, since each item is scored 3, 2, 1, or zero, raw scores in each cluster can range from a high of 36 to a low of zero. The titles of the 14 clusters are provided in the publisher information, and detailed descriptions for each cluster are given in the Manual (1984, p. 3).

Each client receives a percentile-rank score for each of these 14 clusters. Because the COPS scores show high reliabilities, sizeable percentile-rank differences should be taken seriously.

NORMS

National norms data are presented in the Manual (1984, pp. 51–52) for junior high groups, senior high groups, and community college groups. While development of these norms seems offhand and unceremonious, three conclusions are suggested by the data shown: (1) Norms data for Grades 7–12 can be pooled into one set for boys and another set for girls; (2) community college groups

83

tend to show greater enthusiasm (higher raw scores) than the grades 7–12 groups; and (3) at both levels, norms for males are manifestly different from norms for females.

However, because the write-up about these national norms is so poor, COPS users are urged to consider development of local norms—local norms for males, and local norms for females.

RELIABILITY STUDIES

The 1984 COPS Manual shows a variety of reliability studies of the 14 scores. The data include Cronbach Alpha coefficients ranging from .86 to 91; parallel-forms coefficients ranging from .77 to .90; one-week test-retest coefficients ranging from .80 to .91; and one-year test-retest coefficients ranging from .62 to .80. These four sets of studies, based on students in junior and senior high schools, showed median reliability coefficients of .89, .86, .87, and .70, respectively (Manual, p. 36). These coefficients appear to be highly satisfactory for a short graduated-response instrument of this type.

SCALE INTERCORRELATIONS

The 1984 COPS Manual shows just one study of correlations among the COPS scores. This table, incomplete and hard to read, shows intercorrelations ranging from .66 to .12, with a median of .37 (1984, p. 33). This median intercorrelation of .37, which translates to 14 percent common variance among the COPS scales, is certainly satisfactorily low for scores in a graduated-response questionnaire.

RELATIONSHIPS TO OTHER MEASURES OF INTEREST

Authors of interest inventories (and personality inventories) seem to move out in different directions—with differing rationales, differing styles of item writing, and differing item-response formats. The COPS instrument is no exception.

Correlations between COPS scores and work-values (COPES) scores ranged from −.30 to a high of +.47; correlations between COPS scores and forced-choice (Kuder E) interest scores ranged from −.37 to a high of +.49; correlations between COPS scores and Holland Hexagon (VPI) scores ranged from −.15 to a high of +.54 (Manual, 1984, pp. 43–46).

Even more important, of course, are studies relating COPS scores to present or projected "real life" activities. The COPS Manual reports positive relations with declared college majors, areas of specialization in community colleges, and actual job/college situations one to three years later (1984, pp. 46–49). College-bound students tended to score higher than other students on the five "professional" scales; and in-college students tend to score higher than high school students on those same five professional scales (1984, pp. 50–52).

PREVIOUS CRITIQUES

The COPS instrument has received mixed reviews ever since it was first published in 1966:

L—Like very much (Bauernfeind, 1969)
l—like moderately (French, 1972)
d—dislike moderately (Bodden, 1972)
D—Dislike very much (Hansen, 1982)

As much as these four critics disagree with each other, there may be some agreements: (1) The instrument itself is well conceived and well written, with an attractive item format and answer sheet; and (2) The COPS manuals have through the years evidenced serious weaknesses in reporting national norms, intercorrelation studies, and especially studies of predictive validity.

SUMMARY

Every test package can be divided into two parts. One is the instrument, on which the client makes pencil-marks or whatever. The other is the manual in which the authors report validity studies, norms studies, and the like. On a scale of 1-to-10 the COPS Manual gets a 5 or 6. Some of the writing is confusing and, as noted above, there is a great need for more norms studies, more intercorrelation studies, and, of course, more predictive validity studies.

But the questionnaire itself gets a 10. The items are well-written and highly relevant to real life; the graduated-response format was developed with sensitivity; the pencil marks are easily scored; and most high school and college students enjoy marking the COPS questionnaire.

If one must make a career choice soon, of course the *Strong-Campbell* or the *Kuder KOIS* is to be preferred. But if one has time to explore—to try part-time jobs, to read, to talk to people—COPS stands out as an excellent instrument. This reviewer strongly endorses it as a propellent for career exploration.

REFERENCES

Bauernfeind, R. H. (1969). Review of the California Occupational Preference Survey. *Journal of Educational Measurement*, 6(1), 56–58.
Bodden, J. L. (1972). Review of the California Occupational Preference Survey. In O. K. Buros (Ed.), *The Seventh Mental Measurements Yearbook*. Highland Park, NJ: The Gryphon Press, 1403–1404.
French, J. W. (1972). Review of the California Occupational Preference Survey. In O. K. Buros (Ed.), *The Seventh Mental Measurements Yearbook*. Highland Park, NJ: The Gryphon Press, 1404–1405.
Hansen, J. C. (1982). California Occupational Preference System. In J. T. Kapes & M. M. Mastie (Eds.), *A Counselor's Guide to Vocational Guidance Instruments*. Falls Church, VA: National Vocational Guidance Association.
Manual for the COPSystem Interest Inventory (1984). San Diego, CA: Educational and Industrial Testing Service.

NOTE: Significant portions of this review were abridged from the author's original review in Volume V of *Test Critiques* with permission of Test Corporation of America.

Harrington O'Shea Career Decision-Making® System (CDM)

Thomas F. Harrington and Arthur J. O'Shea

American Guidance Service (AGS®)
Publishers' Building, Circle Pines
MN 55014-1796

Target Population: Grades 7–12 and adult.

Statement of the Purpose of the Instrument: The CDM is a systematized approach to Career Decision Making that integrates five major dimensions in choosing a career—abilities, job values, future plans, subject preferences, and interests. Based on a sound theoretical foundation the CDM provides individuals with a wealth of information to help in choosing a career and selecting a course of study or a job.

Titles of Subtests, Scales, Scores Provided: Responses to 120 interest items contribute to one of six interest scales: crafts, scientific, the arts, social, business, and clerical. Raw scores on the highest two or three interest scales are used to identify three or four career clusters for further exploration.

Forms and Levels Available, with Dates of Publication/Revision of Each: Self-scored (1982); Machine-scored (1982); Microcomputer version (TRS 80 models 3 and 4; Apple II and IIe and IIc) 1985.

Date of Most Recent Edition of Test Manual, User's Guide, Etc.: 1982—technical manual.

Languages in Which Available: English and Spanish.

Time: Actual Test Time—30–40 minutes.
      Total Administration Time—35–45 minutes.

Norm Groups(s) on Which Scores Are Based: Grades 7–12 randomly selected school districts.

Manner in Which Results Are Reported for Individuals
  Basic Service: Profile Report: Machine-scored, Interpretive folder: Hand scored

Report Format/Content for Group Summaries
  Options: Group summary report, narrative report.

Scoring
  Machine Scoring service
    Cost of basic service per counselee: $1.95;
    Cost of Options: Options available: contact publisher for prices;
    Time required for scoring and returning (maximum): 7 days via UPS.

Hand Scoring: Scored by counselee; Time required for scoring: 10–15 minutes.
Local Machine Scoring: Not available.

Computer Software Options Available: Computerized adaptive administration; standard administration; scoring; interpretation.

Cost of Materials: Specimen Set: $3.00; Counselee Materials: CDM self-scored (English and Spanish) package of 25 1–4 ea. @$34.00, 5–19 @$29.00, 20+ @$27.50; CDM Machine-scored Profile Report including scoring service (for 25 students) 1–4 @$66.00, 5–19 @$59.50, 20+ @$57.50—Micro CDM (50 administrators) $165.00 (can reorder diskettes. @$49.00 25 administrations).

Published Reviews

Droege, R.C. (1984). Review of the Harrington O'Shea Career Decision-Marking System. In D.J. Keyser & R.C. Sweetland (Eds.), *Test Critiques*: Volume I (pp. 322–327). Kansas City, MO: Test Corporation of America.

Westbrook, B.W., Rogers, B. & Covington, J.E. (1980). Harrington O'Shea Career Decision-Making System. *Measurement and Evaluation in Guidance, 13*, 185–188.

Willis, C. G. (1978). Review of Harrington O'Shea Career Decision-Making System. In O. K. Buros (Ed.), *Eighth Mental Measurements Yearbook*: Volume II (p. 1584). Highland Park, NJ: Gryphon Press.

Willis, C. G. (1982). Harrington O'Shea Career Decision-Making System. In J. T. Kapes & M. M. Mastie (Eds.), *A counselor's guide to vocational guidance instruments* (pp. 57–60). Falls Church. VA: National Vocational Guidance Association.

Reviewed By

Robert C. Droege
Retired, Formerly Research Psychologist
U.S. Department of Labor

The Harrington-O'Shea Career Decision-Making System (CDM) is an occupational interest-centered system designed to facilitate career decision making for youths and adults. The CDM is a good example of a new generation of comprehensive instruments involving systematic self assessment of vocationally relevant variables followed by focused career exploration. An earlier review (Willis, 1982) of the CDM appeared in the first edition of *A Counselor's Guide to Vocational Guidance Instruments*.

The CDM assumes that the individual should become actively involved in making his or her own career decisions. It provides for such involvement through a step by step process which includes: (1) self assessing occupational interests based on a 120-item interest inventory; (2) self reporting occupational preferences, school subjects liked, work values, and estimated abilities; (3) identifying promising occupational groups indicated by the above information; and (4) exploring specific occupations in these groups, using references usually available in school guidance offices and public libraries. For most individuals who have basic literacy skills, little or no outside help may be required throughout this process.

Clearly, the single most important self-assessment variable in the CDM is occupational interest, as measured by the Interest Survey. The survey consists of 120 job activity items, 20 for each of six Holland-type Career Interest Areas (Crafts, Scientific, Arts, Social, Business, and Clerical). This inventory is self scored and the combination of the two categories with the highest raw scores is identified as the individual's Career Code. The career code, in turn, is related to occupational groupings involving the interests represented by the code.

The system is designed primarily for use by teenagers and adults who are interested in making their own career decisions. In addition, counselors can use the information in counseling sessions, and school administrators may be able to use group summary reports for assessing course offerings and evaluating relevance of guidance programs in relation to student needs.

The authors of the CDM originally developed the system in 1976 and subsequently have prepared updated editions of the survey materials every two years until 1982. The current edition of the CDM Manual (Harrington & O'Shea, 1982) provides detailed descriptions of the materials and their rationale, information on administration, scoring, and interpretation, and the research basis for the system. One of the strengths of the CDM is its emphasis on career exploration, and incorporation of the *Guide for Occupational Exploration* (Harrington & O'Shea, 1984) in the exploration process was intended to enhance this strength. Use of this publication following identification of promising Career Clusters expands the potential for focused occupational exploration to virtually all occupations in the economy.

The CDM is available in a self-scored edition (in both English and Spanish), a machine-scored edition providing computerized scoring and reporting, and a microcomputer edition. The self-scored edition has important advantages over the machine-scored edition. These include: (1) maximizing involvement of the individual in all aspects of the process of career decision making, including interpretation and exploration, and (2) eliminating the need for a break in the assessment-exploration sequence to obtain computerized reporting of assessment results prior to career exploration. Not enough information about the microcomputer edition was available to evaluate its usefulness, although self-assessment instruments like the CDM should be easily adaptable to microcomputer applications.

PSYCHOMETRIC ASPECTS

In recognition of the importance assigned the Interest Survey, most of the research done on the CDM (as reported in the Manual) has been concentrated on this instrument.

Reliability coefficients are reported for the six Interest Survey scales. Internal consistency measures are uniformly high (.90s) for all scales and short-term test-retest coefficients range from .75 to .94. No data are reported on short-term stability of the self-reported variables (Stated Occupational Choice, School Subjects Preferred, etc.) in the CDM system. High self-scoring reliability (.98) is confirmation that self-administration is appropriate for the Interest Survey.

Some data on the construct validity of the CDM are reported, but they are limited to the Interest Survey portion. The most important evidence presented

88

indicates a degree of correspondence between summary occupational codes derived from the Interest Survey and those derived from other sources. However, the results are presented in terms of percentage agreement for code matches, and this information is difficult to interpret. The next edition of the Manual should also show correlation coefficients between Interest Survey scores and corresponding scores on other inventories (e.g., the Vocational Preference Inventory and the Strong Campbell Interest Inventory) for each of the six Holland themes.

Criterion-related data are presented in terms of concurrent and predictive validity against criteria of occupational or course status. The "validities" are shown as the extent to which Interest Survey codes agree with Holland occupational/educational codes for the samples tested. Although agreements are generally good, occupational/educational status is not a very relevant criterion. What the Interest Survey, and the CDM as a whole, is *really* about is facilitating career decision-making that will lead to entry into appropriate careers. Evidence of the CDM's usefulness for this purpose requires research on the extent to which CDM-takers who follow the occupational areas suggested by the results are more satisfied/successful than those who do not. Longitudinal validation research is required to study this question.

In addition to the research of the kind just described, developmental work to improve some specific aspects of the system is needed. Perhaps the most serious problem with the CDM approach is that it incorporates an unvalidated self-estimate of ability. Self-estimates of cognitive, perceptual, and manual aptitudes are promising areas for research, but such self-estimates have not yet been demonstrated to be sufficiently valid indicators of career potential to warrant their use in operating systems.

The Manual includes some standardization and normative data but these are of little interest since CDM authors do not recommend that clients' interest inventory results be based on norms.

CDM'S FUTURE

The 1984 review of the CDM by this author (Droege, 1984) concluded as follows:

"In summary, the CDM is an excellent example of a systems approach to career decision-making that is oriented to the needs of individuals who can do self evaluations of their occupational interests and of other important factors related to informed career choice. The authors have achieved a self administering, self scoring and self interpreting assessment and occupational exploration system with minimum requirements for counselor involvement. Improvements are possible, and assuming these will be made and appropriate validation research initiated, the CDM should have a bright future."

The above review was based on the 1982 edition of the CDM. As of late 1986 the CDM materials on sale have not been changed nor has a new Manual been published. (The Interpretive Folder has been revised to incorporate use of the *Guide for Occupational Exploration* in career exploration.) Over the four year period since 1982 it would seem that there would be some significant new research findings to report and that changes could be made in the Interest Survey or other aspects of CDM based on developmental or validation research findings. Also, users need reports of new research in progress. The future of the CDM will depend on whether confidence in its use can be supported by such research.

REFERENCES

Droege, R. C. (1984). Review of The Harrington-O'Shea Career Decision-Making System. In D. J. Keyser & R. C. Sweetland (Eds.), *Test Critiques*, Vol. I. Kansas City, MO: Test Corporation of America.

Harrington, T. F. & O'Shea, A. J. (Eds.) (1984). *Guide for Occupational Exploration* (2nd ed.). Circle Pines, MN: American Guidance Service.

Harrington, T. F. & O'Shea, A. J. (1982). *Manual for the Harrington-O'Shea Career Decision-Making System*. Circle Pines, MN: American Guidance Service.

Willis, C. G. (1982). Review of the Harrington-O'Shea Career Decision-Making System. In J. T. Kapes & M. M. Mastie (Eds.), *A Counselor's Guide to Vocational Guidance Instruments*. Falls Church, VA: National Vocational Guidance Association.

NOTE: Significant portions of this review were abridged from the author's original review in Volume I of *Test Critiques* with permission of Test Corporation of America.

Interest Determination, Exploration and Assessment System (IDEAS)

Charles B. Johansson

NCS Professional Assessment Services
P.O. Box 1416, Minneapolis, MN 55440

Target Population: Junior high, middle school and early high school.

Statement of the Purpose of the Instrument: IDEAS is a self-contained, self-contained, self-scorable interest inventory that serves as an introduction to career planning. It provides scores on 14 basic interest scales that help students identify and explore occupational areas of interest. The inventory booklet includes DOT/OOH references and suggested school courses.

Titles of Subtests, Scales, Scores Provided: Mechanical/Fixing, Electronics, Nature/Outdoors, Science, Numbers, Writing, Arts/Crafts, Social Serivce, Child Care, Medical Service, Business, Sales, Office Practices, Food Service.

Forms and Levels Available, with Dates of Publication/Revision of Each: 1 form, 1977.

Date of Most Recent Edition of Test Manual, User's Guide, Etc.: 1980.

Languages in Which Available: English only.

Time: Actual Test Time—20–25 minutes.
      Total Administration Time—20–25 minutes.

Norm Group(s) on Which Scores Are Based: Two norm groups: Students in grades 6–8 and in grades 9–12. Combined sex norms. Separate sex norms available in test manual.

Manner in Which Results Are Reported for Individuals
  Types of Scores: Raw and Standard Scores.
  Report Format/Content: Basic Service: Students plot profile report. Printed interpretive information is included in the IDEAS booklet.

Report Format/Content for Group Summaries: Not available.

Scoring
  Machine Scoring Service: Not available.
  Hand Scoring: a. Scored by: counselee; b. Time required for scoring: Actual test time and scoring take approximately 20–25 minutes.
  Local Machine Scoring: Not available.

Computer Software Options Available: Not available.

Cost of Materials: Specimen Set: Includes IDEAS booklet and manual. Cost: $5.75. Counselee Materials: Combination test booklet and answer sheet. For packages of 25: 1 package $24.00 ($.96 each); 2–9 packages $22.00 ($.88 each); 10–19 pkgs. $22.00 ($.80 each); 20+ pkgs. $18.00 ($.72 each).

Additional Comments of Interest to Users: IDEAS is updated every two years in conjunction with new editions of the OOH.

Published Review
Borman, C. (1982). In J. T. Kapes & M. M. Mastie (Eds.), *A counselor's guide to vocational guidance instruments*. Falls Church, VA: National Vocational Guidance Association.

Reviewed By

M. O'Neal Weeks
Professor, Department of Family Studies
University of Kentucky

The Interest Determination, Exploration and Assessment System (IDEAS) is a paper-and-pencil inventory developed by Charles B. Johansson in 1977, with revisions in 1978 and 1980. IDEAS was designed to aid students in secondary-level classes (grades 6–12) in the exploration of their vocational/career interests and introduce them to a variety of careers, most of which do not require a baccalaureate education for entry. This 112-item inventory consists of 14 scales which measure a student's interests in the following vocational areas: Mechanical/Fixing; Electronics; Nature/Outdoors; Science; Numbers; Writing; Arts/Crafts; Social Service; Business; Child Care; Medical Service; Sales; Office Practices; and Food Service.

Within each of the above categories the student's likes and dislikes for a number of subjects and activities are registered by use of a five-choice Likert scale, with responses ranging from "like very much," to "dislike very much." For students able to read at the sixth-grade level, the inventory can be self-administered, self-scored and self-interpreted. Upon completion of the inventory, students are given instructions for scoring their responses and for plotting the results on a profile sheet. This provides them with an overview of their career interests, followed by descriptions of careers with references to the *Dictionary of Occupational Titles* and the *Occupational Outlook Handbook* to encourage the student's further career exploration.

The test items in IDEAS were selected from a pool of items used in constructing the Career Assessment Inventory (CAI) which was also developed by Johansson. For those not familiar with the CAI, it has been referred to as a "blue collar" version of the Strong-Campbell Interest Inventory because it was designed primarily for use with non-college-bound student populations (Bodden, 1978). IDEAS is shorter and simpler than the CAI, using only those items from the CAI which are easily comprehended by students reading at a sixth-grade level.

SCORES AND NORMS

The inventory's 112 items are grouped into the 14 scales identified above. The responses to each item are summed, resulting in a composite score for each scale. These summary raw scores are then recorded on a profile sheet which provides students with an easy-to-interpret graphic representation of their career interests. Combined gender norms are also provided so that students may compare their scores with the scores of other students in their age group. Norms were established on the basis of scores for groups of males and females in grades 6 through 8 and males and females in grades 9 through 12. The data for standardization of IDEAS were based on the scores of students who had been tested with the CAI (Johansson, 1986). Unfortunately, the developer of IDEAS does not provide any information regarding the socioeconomic status, ethnic makeup, geographical location, or levels of academic performance of the populations on which the norms were established. Demographic information on the samples is limited to the gender and grade levels of the subjects (Weeks, 1985).

VALIDITY AND RELIABILITY

The manual which accompanies IDEAS includes impressive information regarding its content validity, construct validity, concurrent validity, and reliability. The correlations between the IDEAS scales and the scales on the CAI, on which the author seems to have conducted rather extensive research, are all quite high ($r = .91$ or above for all scales). IDEAS also correlated very well with the Strong-Campbell Interest Inventory and the Minnesota Vocational Interest Inventory ($r = .80$ or above for each correlation).

When using a measure of subjects' interests and preferences, the most important indicator of reliability is the stability of subjects' responses over time. IDEAS fares rather well on this criterion, as the author reports test-retest correlation coefficients ranging in the high .80s and .90s (Johansson, 1986). Given the validity and reliability of the inventories to which IDEAS was favorably compared, and given its own level of test-retest reliability, one can be reasonably confident that this is a valid and reliable instrument for measuring the vocational interests of students at the sixth grade level or above (Weeks, 1985).

RECOMMENDATIONS AND CAUTIONS TO USERS

IDEAS has several advantages warranting its recommendation for certain uses over some of the more complex vocational interest inventories, including the CAI which is longer and which requires machine scoring. IDEAS is (a) simple, quick and easy to administer; (b) can be scored and interpreted by the student; (c) gives the student immediate information about his or her career interests; and, (d) lends itself well to group administration. The latter point allows counselors to explore and discuss career interests and recommend pertinent classes and/or post-secondary courses of study to students in classes or other settings. "Such usage as a stimulus for class discussions and for further vocational exploration seems very appropriate, provided its users are cautioned not to allow their IDEAS profiles to weigh too heavily on vocational choices" (Weeks, 1985: p. 698).

In counseling individuals regarding career interests and choices, the IDEAS provides a good preliminary exploration of one's general career-related interests and can, therefore, serve as a good "springboard" for more in-depth counseling and guidance toward career choices. However, this reviewer believes that the inventory is too brief and cursory in its treatment of topics of interest to be used as a serious, conclusive assessment of one's career interests.

The prospective user of the IDEAS needs to be aware of several other minor concerns. First, in scoring the inventory, students are instructed to "copy each circled number onto the line to its right," but there are boxes rather than lines to the right of the circled numbers. While this is a very minor discrepancy in the instructions, some students may find it a bit confusing if attention is not called to it by the person administering the inventory. Second, some of the subjects used in the inventory seem a bit esoteric for the non-college-bound student exploring career options (e.g., astronomy and ecology). These, however, are exceptions and are not generally characteristic of the subjects covered in the inventory. Finally, although the inventory was developed for students in grades 6 through 12, it probably has limited usefulness with senior high students (grades 11 and 12). Its more appropriate and useful application is with middle school, junior high and early high school students.

To summarize,

"IDEAS is a well developed, well constructed, and validated inventory. It is easy to administer, score, and interpret. The major weaknesses are that IDEAS is appropriate for use [primarily] with populations interested in vocations that do not require a college education, and it has limited utility as a basis for in-depth vocational counseling and decision making. As a precursor of more extensive vocational testing, as a stimulus for discussion of vocational interest, . . . IDEAS has much to recommend it" (Weeks, 1985: p. 699).

REFERENCES

Bodden, J. L. (1978). Review of the Career Assessment Inventory, In O. K. Buros (Ed.), *The Eighth Mental Measurements Yearbook*. Highland Park, New Jersey: Gryphon Press.

Johansson, C. B. (1986). *Interest Determination, Exploration and Assessment System*. Minneapolis, Minnesota: National Computer Systems, Inc.

Weeks, M. O. (1985). Review of Interest Determination, Exploration and Assessment System, in J. V. Mitchell (Ed.), *The Ninth Mental Measurements Yearbook*. Lincoln, Nebraska: The University of Nebraska Press.

NOTE: Significant portions of this review were abridged from the author's original review in *The Ninth Mental Measurements Yearbook*, with permission of the Buros Institute.

Jackson Vocational Interest Survey (JVIS)

Douglas N. Jackson

Research Psychologists Press, Inc.
1110 Military Street, P. O. Box 984
Port Huron, MI 48061-0984

Target Population: High school age to adult.

Statement of the Purpose of the Instrument: To assist with educational and career planning by assessing vocational interests. Respondents are required to indicate a preference between two equally popular interests expressed as 289 paired statements.

Titles of Subtests, Scales, Scores Provided: 34 basic interest scales scores are presented in a sex-fair profile. Interest scales include work role dimensions and work style scales. Computer reports additionally provide scores for 10 general occupational themes, a profile of similarity to 17 educational major field clusters, a ranking of 32 occupational group clusters with narrative summary of the three highest ranked educational and occupational clusters, validity scales and other information.

Forms and Levels Available, with Dates of Publication/Revision of Each: Hand scored format published in 1977. Computer scored versions (Basic & Extended Report Versions) revised in 1985.

Date of Most Recent Edition of Test Manual, User's Guide, Etc.: Copyright date of current manual: 1977. Specimen Brochure (Free) containing additional suggestions on interpretation: Copyright 1978, 1985.

Languages in Which Available: English and French (Hebrew edition under development), Spanish (Booklet only).

Time: Actual Test Time—45 minutes.
Total Administration Time—1 hour.

Norm Group(s) on Which Scores Are Based: A subset of 500 males and 500 females drawn from the three normative sources: a representative sample of North American colleges and universities; a group of grade 12 students admitted to Pennsylvania State University; and a representative sample of high school students from grades 9 through 13 from the Province of Ontario.

Manner in Which Results Are Reported for Individuals
  Types of Scores: All three types of scores are used with various profiles. Handscored profile yields standard scores.
  Report Format/Content
    Basic Service: Some narrative text, preprinted, plus several profiles including Basic Interest Scales, General Occupational Themes, Educational & Occupational Clusters.
    Options: Extended Report includes additional narrative text and summary of the highest ranked educational and occupational clusters, with reading lists.

Report Format/Content for Group Summaries: Not available.

Scoring

Machine Scoring Service

Cost of basic service per counselee: Basic Report $3.25 for 24 or fewer with price quantity as low as $2.00 for 1,000 or more.

Cost of options: Extended Reports: $7.00 each for 24 or fewer quantity prices as low as $4.00 for orders of 1,000 or more.

Time required for scoring and returning: (maximum) 48 hrs. plus 1st class mail time.

Hand Scoring

Scored by: clerk; counselor.

Time required for scoring: approx. 5 minutes.

Local Machine Scoring: Interface with HEI 185 or NCS Sentry 3000 Scanners.

Computer Software Options Available: Standard admininstration on-line; scoring: Basic and Narrative Report Generation.

Cost of Materials: Specimen Set: Examination kit includes one manual, one handscored answer sheet and one handscored profile sheet, one machine scorable answer sheet that returns an extended report, and one reusable test booklet. $17.50.

Published Reviews

Covington, J. D. (1982). Jackson Vocational Interest Survey. In J. T. Kapes & M. M. Mastie (Eds.), *A counselor's guide to vocational guidance instruments*. Falls Church, VA: National Vocational Guidance Association.

Davidshofer, C. (1985). Review of Jackson Vocational Interest Survey. In J. V. Mitchell (Ed.), *Ninth Mental Measurements Yearbook: Volume I*. Lincoln, NE: University of Nebraska Press.

Reviewed By

Charles O. Davidshofer
Director, University Counseling Center
Associate Professor, Psychology
Colorado State University

The Jackson Vocational Interest Survey (JVIS) represents a relatively new attempt to assess academic and career interests. First published in 1977, the JVIS was developed using sophisticated factor-analytic procedures that produced scales which were generally homogeneous with respect to content, minimized response bias, and significantly decreased redundancy between scales.

RATIONALE

The JVIS assesses career interests from a different perspective from that used by other instruments such as the Strong-Campbell Interest Inventory or the Kuder Occupational Interest Survey. Rather than focusing on the item responses of various occupational criterion groups and the degree of similarity between the examinee's choices and those made by the reference groups, the JVIS was based on the premise that interest dimensions (scales) could be defined that would transcend individual occupational groups and permit the user to measure broader interest areas that would cut across a number of occupations. Jackson argues that this approach to interest measurement leads to better, more efficient and productive career exploration by focusing attention on important interest areas rather than restricting exploration to a few specific occupational groups.

FORMAT

The JVIS consists of 289 item pairs from which respondents select the interest activity they most prefer (e.g., choosing between "making decorative tiles" and "running a mimeograph machine in an office"). The items are grouped into 34 basic interest scales representing either specific types of work related activities (e.g., law, elementary education) or work environments requiring specific behaviors (e.g., planfulness, independence). Although the JVIS employs a forced-choice or ipsative item format, a complete pair-wise comparison among all 34 scales is not done. Instead, the 34 basic interest scales are divided into two subgroups of 17 each and paired between groups but not within subgroups. Exactly what effect this has on interpreting the relative strengths of all 34 scales remains unknown. The survey generally takes about 45 minutes to complete. The reading level of the items was designed to be at about the seventh grade level, but a review of some of the items suggests that it might be considerably higher. This could be a significant factor when using the JVIS with those from a more limited educational or impoverished background.

ADMINISTRATION AND SCORING

The JVIS permits both hand and machine scoring. There are separate answer sheets available for each option, however, and they are not interchangeable. The hand scoreable form of the survey is very easy and quick to score. The arrangement of the answer sheet permits scoring without the use of special scoring templates. The user only needs to count the items in both the rows and columns to obtain the 34 basic interest scores. In addition to the basic interest scales, the machine scoring form provides scores on 10 general occupational themes, administrative indices, information about the similarity of the respondent's interests to those of college students majoring in various academic programs, and data about how the examinee's interests compare to workers in 32 occupational groups. A computerized version of the JVIS is also available.

A separate profile sheet allows the conversion of the raw scores to standard scores and the comparison of the examinee's interests to those of both male and female general norm groups. Unfortunately, these general norm groups consist of a heterogeneous sample of adolescents in grades 9–12 and college students. The exact composition of these groups is not clearly stated in the manual, and therefore it is impossible to determine how representative they are of lower socioeconomic classes. A more serious objection to these norm groups concerns why it was constructed in such a heterogenous manner. No data are given showing whether the younger students demonstrated significantly different interest profiles from those in the college-age group. Previous research has shown, however, that certain interest dimensions are earlier developing (e.g., art, science) while others develop later in life (e.g., business, social service). It is not clear what effect combining such diverse age groups might have in masking such developmental aspects of interests.

RELIABILITY

Short term reliability estimates obtained on the JVIS indicate that it provides a rather stable measure of educational and career interests. Research has generally reported the reliability coefficients to be in the .80 to .90 range. Likewise, estimates of the internal consistency of the JVIS also appear to be in this same range. Because of the newness of the instrument, however, evidence for its long-term stability is not yet available.

VALIDITY

Evidence for the validity of the JVIS is still rather sparse. Early studies suggest that it can discriminate among college students in different majors along intuitively predictable lines. Similarly, a few of the occupational groups tested produce profiles with high interest scores in predictable areas. Yet some of the data reported raise questions about the discriminant validity of certain occupational scores (e.g., chemists scoring moderately high on the social worker scale). In general, most of the validity data reported are encouraging, but limited to demonstrations of concurrent and construct validity. Much more research needs to be done on occupational profiles before the predictive validity of the JVIS can be adequately assessed.

SUMMARY

The JVIS appears to be a valuable assessment tool for measuring general areas of interest. The manual states that it can be used with college and high school students, adults considering changing careers, advising students as part of college orientation and testing programs, employee classification and selection, and for research in vocational interests and student characteristics. It is probably especially useful in working with adolescents early in the career development process. One of its strengths is that it does not artificially limit the exploration process by focusing too narrowly on specific occupations, but rather directs attention on broader areas of interest. Another advantage is that it is relatively free of sex bias permitting open exploration of the full range of interests by both sexes because of its emphasis on work roles and styles. The possiblity of hand scoring is also an advantage for those wishing readily available information about interests.

The JVIS has three important shortcomings, however. First, its ipsative nature causes some difficulty. Juni and Koenig (1982) have shown that forced-choice items like those of the JVIS can lead to confusion on the part of respondents due to the multiplicity of statements contained in each item. Additionally, ipsative formats also contain inherent statistical limitations that can affect the psychometric properties of an instrument. Secondly, the administration time required to complete the test is somewhat lengthy compared to that of other interest measures on the market. Finally, there is not sufficient predictive validity data available yet to dictate its selection over more established interest measures.

REFERENCES

Covington, J. E. (1977). Test review: Jackson Vocational Interest Survey. *Measurement and Evaluation in Guidance, 12*, 49–52.

Jackson, D. N. (1977). *Jackson vocational interest survey manual*. Port Huron, Michigan: Research Psychologists Press.

Jackson, D. N., & Williams, D. R. (1975). Occupational classification in terms of interest patterns. *Journal of Vocational Behavior, 6*, 269–380.

Juni, S., & Koenig, E. (1982). Contingency validity as a requirement in forced-choice item construction: A critique of the Jackson Vocational Interest Survey. *Measurement and Evaluation in Guidance, 14*, 202–207.

Locklin, R. H. (1976). Predicting choice of an academic college from JVIS scores of college freshmen. University Park, Pennsylvania: The Pennsylvania State University Research Bulletin.

NOTE: Significant portions of this review were abridged from the author's original review in *The Ninth Mental Measurements Yearbook* with permission of the Buros Institute

Kuder General Interest Survey, Form E (KGIS)

G. Frederic Kuder

Science Research Associates, Inc.
155 North Wacker Drive, Chicago, IL 60606

Target Population: Students (from grade 6 through college) and adults (all ages).

Statement of the Purpose of the Instrument: Measurement of broad vocational interests, for use in counseling and initial vocational/occupational exploration for students in junior and senior high school and adults.

Titles of Subtests, Scales, Scores Provided: Outdoor, Mechanical, Computational, Scientific, Persuasive, Artistic, Literary, Musical, Social Service and Clerical.

Forms and Levels Available, with Dates of Publication/Revision of Each: Form E, Copyright 1963 with revisions in 1976.

Date of Most Recent Edition of Test Manual, User's Guide, Etc.: Manual, 1975—currently being revised.

Languages in Which Available: English only.

Time: Actual Test Time—approx. 40 minutes.
Total Administration Time—approx. 45–50 minutes.

Norm Group(s) on Which Scores Are Based: Male and female students in grades 6–8, 9–12, and male and female adults.

Manner in Which Results Are Reported for Individuals
Types of Scores: Percentile ranks.
Report Format/Content
Basic Service: Current—profile of percentile ranks for male and female norm groups with categorization into high, average and low interest; Revision—semi-narrative report with profile of results.
Report Format/Content for Group Summaries: Not available.

Scoring
Machine Scoring Service
Cost of basic service per counselee: $2.30 (sold in packages of 25 for $57.50 [1986 prices] price includes materials).
Time required for scoring and returning (maximum): Internal time—48 hours.
Hand Scoring
Scored by: counselee; clerk; counselor.
Time required for scoring: 30 minutes.

Local Machine Scoring: Available 4/87.
Provisions/conditions/equipment required: IBM PC plus NCS Sentry 3000 scanner—license required from SRA.

Computer Software Options Available: Available 4/87. Standard administration; scoring; interpretation; link to RIASEC classification system.

Cost of Materials: (1986 prices).
Specimen Set: $6.50 (M-S version contains complimentary survey including scoring).
Counselee Materials: Consumable hand-scored edition. $31.25 for 25 students;
Consumable machine-scored edition, $57.50 for 25 students (including scoring).

Additional Comments of Interest to Users: Revised manual and updated norms plus availability of local scoring version—available 4/87.

Published Reviews
Kirk, B. A. & Frank, A. C. (1982). Kuder General Interest Survey—Form E. In J. T. Kapes & M. M. Mastie (Eds.), *A Counselor's Guide to Vocational Guidance Instruments* (pp. 73–76). Falls Church, VA: National Vocational Guidance Association.
Lohnes, P. L. (1972). In O. K. Buros (Ed.), *Seventh Mental Measurements Yearbook:* Volume II. Highland Park, NJ: Gryphon Press.
McCall, J. N. (1972) In O. K. Buros (Ed.), *Seventh Mental Measurements Yearbook:* Volume II. Highland Park, NJ: Gryphon Press.
Stahmann, R. F. (1971). Kuder General Interest Survey—Form E. *Journal of Counseling Psychology, 18,* 191–192.
Williams J. A. & Williams, J. D. (1984). Review of the *Kuder General Interest Survey Form E.* In D. J. Keyser & R. C. Sweetland (Eds.), *Test Critiques:* Volume II (pp. 395–401). Kansas City, MO: Test Corporation of America.

Reviewed By

Jole A. Williams
Northwestern Mental Health Center
Crookston, Minnesota
and
John Delane Williams
Measurement and Statistics
University of North Dakota

The Kuder General Interest Survey—Form E (KGIS) is a 168-item interest inventory that catalogues measured interests—as opposed to claimed or expressed interests—of adolescents. It consists of eleven scales, ten of which reflect broad areas of interest to be measured: Outdoor, Mechanical, Computational, Scientific, Persuasive, Artistic, Literary, Musical, Social Service, and Clerical. The eleventh scale is the Verification Scale, designed to determine the sincerity of the responses. The survey has a forced-choice triad format and is partially ipsative in character. The limited sense in which it is ipsative is that some triads are scored for more than one scale.

The Kuder General Interest Survey has evolved from a series of Kuder vocational interest inventories published over a period of more than forty years. Its various forms, versions, and editions may be regarded as a family of related instruments that approach the measurement of interests from different perspectives and are designed for somewhat different purposes. Data from each part of the long series of experimental and published inventories became part of the foundation for later inventories. The earliest and the best known of these inventories is the Kuder Vocational Preference Record.

The KGIS, a revision and downward extension of the Kuder Vocational Preference Record, was developed in response to a need for an instrument to tap the measurable interests of young people, particularly at the junior high level. Designed for grades 6-12 it employs simpler language and an easier vocabulary than the earlier form, and requires comprehension of only a sixth-grade vocabulary.

ADMINISTRATION AND SCORING

The survey can be administered on a group or classroom basis. Although it is untimed, the manual (Kuder, 1975) indicates that students generally complete the Kuder in 45–60 minutes. A classroom teacher can administer the test, and no specialized skills are required, although familiarity with the manual would be helpful. Form E has both a hand-scorable and a machine-scorable version. The directions for the two versions differ slightly, principally because the hand-scorable version uses pins and corrugated paper. One possible area of difficulty with this version is the changing of answers, which is more cumbersome with pins than pencils and erasers. Students are told that if they want to change an answer, they must punch two more holes as close as possible to the undesired answer, then punch the new answer in the usual way. The novel use of the pin and difficulty of instructions might intimidate a sixth-grader (if not an adult), resulting in several unchanged, but inaccurate, answers.

Another problem area can be the hand-scoring process when scoring amounts to counting the number of circles with pin pricks through them, not including those with three pin pricks (changes). While this process is fairly routine, it may be too much of a challenge for younger examinees. Where it is financially feasible the machine-scoring version would seem to be preferable.

RELIABILITY AND VALIDITY

The studies reported in the manual are those done by the research staff. In all, they tested 9,819 students in grades 6-12, reporting information by socioeconomic level, region, and sex. Test-retest correlations are separately recorded for grades 6-8 and 9-12, together with means and standard deviations by sex. Although all (except one) test-retest reliabilities for the ten subscales are equal to or greater than .70, generally the older students achieved somewhat higher reliabilities. The Persuasive Scale may be somewhat problematical for younger students, showing test-retest reliabilities of .69 and .73 respectively for boys and girls in grades 6–8 on a six-week retesting. The Kuder Richardson 20 (KR 20) internal consistency reliabilities in grades 6–8 were between .72 and .89 for boys and .76 and .90 for girls. For grades 9–12, KR 20 reliabilities were between .86 and .92 for boys and between .80 and .90 for girls. Also reported are grade-by-grade reliabilities on each scale.

In general, the manual is very complete regarding reliability data. However, the very completeness might seem confusing to a person unaccustomed to evaluating reliabilities that are reported variously for four-week, six-week and four-year intervals. This poses no problem for sophisticated users, but may be confusing to beginning counselors. However, of more concern is that the manual does not have a separate section on validity. While the manual reports studies that clearly fall under this rubric, users looking for a specific section on validity will not find it. Problems concerning validity have also been addressed by earlier reviewers of other versions of the Kuder (Arnold, 1959; Layton, 1965). Additional validity concern of a middle class bias has been voiced by Husek (1965) and Kirk (1971). Because most students who take this survey are years away from an actual entry into a career, predictive validity is harder to assess; the other forms of the survey (Forms B and C) have shown some degree of acceptable validation, and by influence, Form E *should* also show validity. This does point to an area for longitudinal research regarding interests and occupational choices of adults in a comparison with their much earlier measured interests. Such research would best be explicatory if it were truly longitudinal and open ended; career choices would seem to be much more likely a continuous process in adulthood rather than a single event.

A BROADER CONCERN

If one conceptualizes future occupational success as a combination of interest, ability, and opportunity, it is clear that many measures of the first two constructs exist and that the Kuder is among the most respected among measures of interest. In addition, many different types of measures exist to measure many different aspects of ability. But careers cannot be made out of interest and ability alone if opportunities do not exist. Put another way, for those specifically looking for a measure of interest, the Kuder is definitely an acceptable measure. But interest is only one prong in the triumvirate of interest-ability-opportunity. Perhaps the most important prong, opportunity, has generated the least psychometric interest. That this would be so is not surprising. Opportunity is by far the hardest construct to define, but those who deal in career counseling should not ignore it, regardless of the difficulty of measurement and definition.

Even though the Kuder General Interest Survey most typically would be used by school counselors and classroom teachers working with students in grades 6–12, very little research has been done on the KGIS. Studies looking at its use with a variety of populations would seem to be most necessary. Some potential new applications might be (a) successful use with the developmentally disabled population—clients with mild to moderate levels of retardation—because of the simple language and easy vocabulary; and (b) use in rehabilitation counseling—usually with clients who have experienced change in physical and/or mental functioning—and are in need of thorough exploration of interests to reassess what is of interest to them in relation to their current capability.

REFERENCES

Arnold, D. L. (1959). Review of Kuder Preference Record—Personal. In O. K. Buros (Ed.), *The Fifth Mental Measurements Yearbook*. Highland Park, NJ: The Gryphon Press.

Harmon, L. W. (1978). Review of Kuder Preference Record—Vocational. In O. K. Buros (Ed.), *The Eighth Mental Measurements Yearbook*. Highland Park, NJ: The Gryphon Press.

Husek, T. R. (1965). Kuder General Interest Survey, Form E. *Journal of Educational Measurement*, 2, 231–233.

Kirk, B. A. (1971). A Review of the Kuder General Interest Survey. In O. K. Buros (Ed.), *Seventh Mental Measurements Yearbook* (p. 1024). Highland Park, NJ: Gryphon Press.

Kuder, G. F. (1975). *General Interest Survey (Form E)—Manual*. Chicago: Science Research Associates.

Layton, W. L. (1965). Kuder Preference Record—Personal. In O. K. Buros (Ed.), *The Sixth Mental Measurements Yearbook*. Highland Park, NJ: The Gryphon Press.

NOTE: Significant portions of this review were abridged from the author's original review in Volume II of *Test Critiques* with permission of Test Corporation of America.

Kuder Occupational Interest Survey, Form DD (KOIS)

G. Frederic Kuder

Science Research Associates, Inc.
155 N. Wacker Drive, Chicago, IL 60606

Target Population: Students (from grade 10 through college) and adults (all ages).

Statement of the Purpose of the Instrument: Measurement of occupational and college major interests, for use in counseling and occupational exploration.

Titles of Subtests, Scales, Scores Provided: 104 occupational scales, 39 college-major scales, 10 vocational interest estimates, and eight experimental scales. Scores on all scales reported, regardless of norm group, sex.

Forms and Levels Available, with Dates of Publication/Revision of Each: Form DD. Copyright 1956 with revision in 1964 and 1985.

Date of Most Recent Edition of Test Manual, User's Guide, Etc.: 1979 for General Manual, 1985 for Manual Supplement.

Language in Which Available: English only.

Time: Actual Test Time—approx 30 minutes.
Total Administration Time—approx 40 minutes.

Norm Group(s) on Which Scores Are Based: Men and women in specific occupational and college-major criterion groups.

Manner in Which Results are Reported for Individuals
  Types of Scores: Lambda correlations and percentile ranks, verification scale score.
  Report Format/Content
    Basic Service: Semi-narrative report form (2 copies) contains lists of occupations and college majors ranked by degree of similarity to criterion groups (ranking of vocational interests areas); interpretive information presented on reverse side of report form.
    Options: Audiocassette for interpretation.

Report Format/Content for Group Summaries: Not available.

Scoring
  Machine Scoring Service
    Cost of basic service per counselee: $3.50 (1986 price) (Package of 20 = $70.00; price includes materials).
    Cost of options: Audio cassette—$15.95 (1986 price).
    Time required for scoring and returning (maximum): 48 hours excluding mail time.
  Hand Scoring: Not available.
  Local Machine Scoring: Not available.

Computer Software Options Available: Not available.

Cost of Materials: (1986 prices).
Specimen Set: $6.50 (includes one complimentary survey and scoring/reporting).
Counselee Materials: $70 for 20 counselees (price includes scoring) Consumable machine-scored answer sheet.

Additional Comments of Interest to Users: Additional scales and revision of manual due by end of 1988. FastFax about occupations and college majors reported in KOIS due in 1988.

Published Reviews
Brown, F. G. (1982). Kuder Occupational Interest Survey, Form DD. In J. T. Kapes & M. M. Mastie (Eds.), *A Counselor's Guide to Vocational Guidance Instruments* (pp. 77–80). Falls Church, VA: National Vocational Guidance Association.
Brown, F. G. (1971). Kuder Occupational Interest Survey, Form DD. *Measurement and Evaluation in Guidance, 4,* 122–125.
Dolliver, R. H. (1972). In O. K. Buros (Ed.), *Seventh Mental Measurements Yearbook, Vol. II.* Highland Park, NJ: Gryphon Press.
Hunt, T. (1984). Review of the *Kuder Occupational Interest Survey, Form DD.* In D. J. Keyser & R. C. Sweetland (Eds.), *Test Critiques*: Volume I (pp. 406–410). Kansas City, MO: Test Corporation of America.
Jepsen, D. P. (1985). Kuder Occupational Interest Survey, Form DD. *Measurement and Evaluation in Counseling and Development, 17*(4),217–219.
Stahmann, R. F. (1971). Kuder Occupational Interest Survey, Form DD. *Journal of Counseling Psychology, 18,* 191–192.

Reviewed By

David A. Jepsen
Professor, Division of Counselor Education
The University of Iowa

The Kuder Occupational Interest Survey, (KOIS) Form DD, is designed for use with high school and college students for two purposes: (a) to help identify occupational options consistent with a student's interest patterns, and (b) to help this student choose occupations for exploration or commitment to entry. Students mark their most preferred and least preferred activity for each of 100 triads written in sixth grade reading vocabulary.

The *General Manual* (Kuder & Diamond, 1979) includes clear descriptions of the rationale for using an interest inventory, interest measurement innovations introduced in the KOIS, and score interpretation procedures. The book, *Activity Interests and Occupational Choice* (Kuder, 1977) and Kuder's earlier article stating his principles of interest measurement (Kuder, 1970) are helpful supplements because they delineate the rationale for KOIS construction and score interpretation. There are disappointingly few technical data included in the *General Manual* and *Manual Supplement* (Zytowski, 1985) considering the 30-year history of the item pool and the 20 years since Form DD was released.

NORMS AND SCORES

The 1985 revision of the KOIS Report Form is divided into four sections, each designed to explain, in plain language, one of the four different types of scales: Dependability, Vocational Interest Estimates (VIE), the College Major scales, and the Occupational scales.

Dependability of the scale scores is reported to the student in a narrative statement which is based on Verification scores, frequency of unreadable responses, and magnitude of the highest ranking College Major or Occupational scale score. Scores on ten VIE scales added to the 1985 KOIS Report Form are reported as percentile ranks compared with both male and female groups. Since KOIS items are derived from the early Kuder forms, it is theoretically possible to score KOIS items for the same scales, e.g., Persuasion, Outdoor, Mechanical. Scores on the College Major and Occupational scales are reported in rank order on male and female norms for 39 College Major scales and 104 Occupational scales. The numerical score is a Lambda coefficient representing the degree to which the student's responses are similar to the responses of each criterion group. Scores on all scales regardless of norm group gender are reported for all inventory takers. Thirty-nine occupational scales and 17 college major scales were developed on women subjects.

RELIABILITY AND VALIDITY

The reliability data are, appropriately, of the test-retest type covering the consistency of VIE, College Major, and Occupational profiles and consistency of differences between scale pairs for the latter two profiles. The VIE scales are quite short, and this may explain the modest test-retest reliabilities which range from .70 to .84. The data reported for the College Major and Occupational scale scores support claims for score consistency, but there are serious gaps. A few small samples were used and only four occupational scales were involved in studying the consistency of scale differences. Kuder's rationale for evaluating interests represents an important advancement. The comparison of a student's interest pattern to those of various college major and occupational groups (without using a general reference group) has improved the differentiation among occupational groups over previous inventories. The primary form of validity reported is that of concurrent validity. Groups of 100 persons each representing only 30 of the 143 College Major and Occupational scales were selected for study. The 30 were selected as most representative of "fields for which OIS scores are reported" (Kuder & Diamond, 1979 p. 29) rather than any reference to the general occupational structure. Consequently, the concurrent validity reported, substantial though it may be, must be considered selective.

The predictive validity data reported, most of which are supportive, use as criteria occupational *membership* rather than occupational *satisfaction*. Clearly the KOIS rests its case for validity largely on concurrent associations between scores and group memberships (Kuder & Diamond, 1979) and predictive associations with later occupational entry but *not* satisfaction (Zytowski, 1976). Despite its many advantages, the Kuder will have limited value in helping students choose occupations on the basis of satisfying outcomes until supporting predictive validity data are forthcoming.

USABILITY FOR PRACTITIONERS

An overall evaluation of the KOIS for use in counseling rests on the ability of the test to accomplish the purposes summarized in the first paragraph. The first purpose implies that the inventory provides an experience that stimulates the differentiations of particular occupations from a larger list, presumably a circumscribed population of occupations. What is apparent about the Kuder is that a very limited population of occupations is involved. No rationale for the selection of these particular occupations is provided in the manuals. At the least, a more restrained statement in both the *Manual* and interpretive materials would give the user a better feel for the instrument's limitations with regard to occupational differentiation.

The second purpose for the KOIS is made more explicit in Kuder's 1977 book: "The purpose of an occupational interest inventory is to help young people discover the occupations they will find most satisfying" (p. 7). Given this rationale a user would expect, as a minimum, information about the ability of the KOIS to predict occupational satisfaction. Only two studies are cited in the *Manual*; one is unpublished and both were conducted 30–35 years ago. The most recent study of predictive validity (Zytowski, 1976) supported the predictive validity of occupational *membership* criteria, but clearly failed to predict job *satisfaction*. Consequently, a major premise for the inventory has not been substantiated by empirical evidence.

SPECIAL CONCERNS

A few points about the KOIS item pool should be brought to the attention of the user. The *Manual* claims that the "items are activities that even sixth graders can understand" (Kuder & Diamond, 1979, p. 3). This claim is open to question since not *all* items are activities; for example, item number five requires the student to select from among three options "have good health, have good friends, have high social position." These options are clearly *not* activities but rather the *outcomes* of activities. At least three other items (numbers 50, 48, and 94) have similar content.

Kuder claims an advantage in using activity items rather than occupational title items because the former are more easily understood. There is a danger in equating recognition with understanding. Therefore, the general arguments Kuder uses against occupational title items can also be used against activity items: answers are susceptible to faking and young people may not be familiar with the activity especially when they have had no experience with it.

The interpretive materials imply that the *level* of satisfaction is indicated by KOIS scores. The KOIS provides information about the *direction* of activity interests (which activities are preferred) rather than the *intensity* of those interests (how strong the interest is). Ipsative scales create limits on the score interpretation that are not reflected in the *Manual* or interpretive materials.

In summary, the Kuder Occupational Interest Survey, Form DD, does well and perhaps better than any other interest inventory what it is designed to do, namely, assist students to differentiate among a limited group of occupations on the basis of similarity of interest patterns. Claims that go beyond this simple, but important, purpose are not substantiated by data or theory.

REFERENCES

Kuder, F. (1970). Some principles of interest measurement. *Educational and Psychological Measurement, 30*, 205–226.

Kuder, F. (1979). *Activity interests and occupational choice*. Chicago: Science Research Associates.

Kuder, F., & Diamond, E. E. (1979). *Kuder DD Occupational Interest Survey, general manual, second edition*. Chicago: Science Research Associates.

Zytowski, D. G. (1976). Predictive validity of the Kuder Occupational Interest Survey: A 12- to 19-year follow-up. *Journal of Counseling Psychology, 23*, 221–233.

Zytowski, D. G. (1985). *Kuder DD Occupational Interest Survey, manual supplement*. Chicago: Science Research Associates.

NOTE: Significant portions of this review were abridged from the author's original review in *Measurement and Evaluation in Counseling and Development* with permission of AACD.

Ohio Vocational Interest Survey: Second Edition (OVIS II)

David Winefordner

The Psychological Corporation
Harcourt Brace Jovanovich, Inc.
555 Academic Court
San Antonio, TX 78204-0952

Target Population: Recommended for students in grades 7 through college and adults.

Statement of the Purpose of the Instrument: OVIS II is an interest inventory and optional Career planning questionnaire and local survey designed to provide the student and counselor with background data for interpreting interest scores and to provide the school with summary data for planning guidance services and curriculum changes.

Titles of Subtests, Scales, Scores Provided: 253 job activities consolidated into the following groups: Manual Work; Basic Services; Machine Operation; Quality Control; Clerical; Health Services; Crafts and Precise Operations; Skilled Personal Services; Sports and Recreation; Customer Services; Regulations Enforcement; Communications; Numerical; Visual Arts; Agriculture and Life Sciences; Engineering and Physical Sciences; Music; Performing Arts; Marketing; Legal Services; Management; Education and Social Work; Medical Services.

Forms and Levels Available, with Dates of Publication/Revision of Each: One form, one level published in 1981.

Date of Most Recent Edition of Test Manual, User's Guide, Etc.: 1981.

Languages in Which Available: English only.

Time: Actual Test Time—30–45 minutes.
Total Administration Time—35–60 minutes.
Microcomputer Version: Actual Test Time: The examinee can complete OVIS II in one sitting (about 30 minutes) or over several sittings.

Norm Group(s) on Which Scores Are Based: 46,000 students enrolled in grades 8 through 12 in 10 geographical regions of the country.

Manner in Which Results Are Reported for Individuals
 Types of Scores: Percentile Ranks and Scale Clarity Indexes.
 Report Format/Content
  Basic Service: Student Report.
  Options: Extra Student Report; Career Planning Questionnaire Summary Report; Record Label; Local Norms; Magnetic Tape.

Report Format/Content for Group Summaries
Basic Service: Not available

Options: Group Guidance Report; Local Survey Summary Report; Local Norms; Magnetic Tape.

Scoring
Machine Scoring Service: (Prices valid through December 31, 1987).

Cost of basic service per counselee: Two copies of Student Report, $2.31.

Cost of options: Group Guidance Report Career Planning Questionnaire Report Summary, $.28; Local Survey Summary, $.31; Local Norms, $.19; Record Label, $.28; Extra Student Report, $.61; Magnetic Tape, Basic reel charge of $35.00 and $.19 per pupil.

Time required for scoring and returning (maximum): 18–20 working days from date of receipt.

Hand Scoring
Scored by: counselor.

Time required for scoring: N/A.

Local Machine Scoring
Provisions/conditions/equipment required: Equipment with the capability to score MRC or NCS answer documents and written permission from The Psychological Corporation required.

Computer Software Options Available: Standard administration on-line; scoring; interpretation; group summaries, System requirements: Apple II, Apple II+ or Apple IIe with 48 K memory, two disk drives and a printer.

Ways in which computer version differs: No basic service scoring charge as on publisher scoring, flexibility in administration, instant scoring.

Cost of Materials: (Prices valid through December 31, 1987).
Specimen Set: 7.50.

Counselee Materials: *Test Booklets (package of 35) (Includes Directions for Administering), $37.00; hand-scorable answer documents, (package of 35), $32.00; MRC machine-scorable Answer Documents, (package of 35), $20.00; NCS machine-scorable Answer Documents, (package of 35) $20.00; Norms and Scale Clarity Tables, (package of 10), $8.00; Career Planner, (package of 35) (Includes Directions), $20.00; *Handbook for Exploring Careers, $8.00; *Manual for Interpreting, $15.00; *Filmstrip Kit—"Your Interests", $45.00; *Filmstrip Kit—"Interpreting OVIS II", $45.00; *Combined Filmstrip Kits above, $85.00; *Directions for Administering, $2.50.

Microcomputer Version
Complete Package: Survey Master and Work Diskettes, Reporting Master and Work Diskettes, Utility Diskette, Analysis Diskette, 35 Student Information Booklets, Administrator's Manual. The original package permits local scoring of up to 35 records, plus one additional scoring for familiarization: $198.00.

Replacement Package: Analysis Diskette, 35 Student Information Booklets: $95.00

* Indicates reusable materials.

Published Reviews
Crites, J. O. (1985). In D. J. Keyser & R. C. Sweetland (Eds.), *Test Critiques, Vol. IV* (pp. 478–483). Kansas City, MO: Test Corporation of America.

John O. Crites
Northwestern University

Originally published as a paper-and-pencil inventory of vocational interests in 1970 and then revised extensively in 1983 as the OVIS II, but recently (1981; 1984) also available in a micro-computer version, the *Ohio Vocational Interest Survey* (OVIS) and *OVIS II/Micro* are published by the Psychological Corporation as measures of job-activity preferences for 23 job clusters cross-coded to cognate classifications by Data-People-Things in the *Dictionary of Occupational Titles* (DOT). Consisting of 253 (in the first edition, 280) job-activity statements, each of the current 23 interest scales is comprised of 11 items, which are answered along a Likert-type "liking" rating scale. Raw scores are transformed to percentile ranks and stanines for age, grade, and sex, local and/or national norm groups. A *scale clarity index* is also given which simply indicates whether ratings of items in a scale are consistently likes or dislikes. A variety of individual and group reports are available, as well as collateral materials such as the *Handbook for Exploring Careers* and the *Career Planner* (Ovis II).

A "Cubistic Model of Vocational Interests" (D'Costa, 1968; D'Costa and Winefordner, 1969) was formulated to serve as the schematic framework for the construction and development of the OVIS. The purpose of the Cubistic Model was essentially two-fold: first, to systematically define the domain to be measured; and, second, to link measures of the domain to the most widely used informational resource in the field of vocational counseling and guidance—the *Dictionary of Occupational Titles* (DOT). The "cube" is defined by the DOT tripartite classification of the components of work activity—Data, People, and Things. These three dimensions, in combination with three levels of "involvement" (High, Average, and Low) form a cube with 27 "cells." Most of the occupations in the DOT can be classified into the cubes, although 3 cubes were not used in the construction of the original OVIS and one has subsequently been eliminated.

Moreover, some cubes are measured by more than one OVIS interest scale, of which there are now 23, examples being Manual Work (002), and Medical (222).

NORMS

The OVIS was originally standardized on a well-selected national representative sample of over 20,000 male and female students in grades 8 through 12. Some gender differences were found on five scales. Separate scoring keys were then constructed and norms are reported on all scales separately by sex. Grade norms are also reported.

In the revision (OVIS II), only about one fourth of the original items were retained, and a new standardization on 16,000 students nationwide in grades 7 through 12 and 2800 college students (1st and 2nd year) was conducted. Some

112

clusters were dropped and others roughly equated, but the "cubistic" structure for the 23 OVIS interest scales was largely retained. Particular care was given to sex differences and a deliberate attempt was made to reduce gender bias as much as possible. Yet there are still differences on approximately 20 percent of the items. Therefore, the decision was made to report separate as well as combined sex norms—or none if requested.

RELIABILITY

Results on the reliability of the OVIS II are quite respectable. With a 4-week interval on samples of males and females in grades 8 and 10 (Ns = 564 and 318 respectively), the median stability coefficients for the 23 revised scales varied from .76 to .82, with a slight tendency to be higher for females. Findings are also reported on scale intercorrelations for OVIS II high school and college samples, based upon the national standardization, which are moderately positive, but with marked sex and educational level differences. Thus, the scales appear to be measuring different interests reliably, yet they are sufficiently interrelated to provide evidence for the cubistic model of interest organization.

For a 25 percent sample of the standardization group, Cronbach Alpha coefficients were calculated to estimate scale internal consistencies, all of which were greater than .83. Not only do the scales appear to be homogeneous by this criterion, but they more than adequately met other criteria for (1) own scale and (2) other scale correlations. In general, the OVIS interest scales are highly stable and internally consistent.

OTHER REVIEWS

The earlier edition (1970) of the OVIS was reviewed in the *Seventh Mental Measurements Yearbook* (1972), but much of these reviews, by Thomas T. Frantz and John W. M. Rothney, dealt with limitations of the inventory which were subsequently rectified in the 1983 edition. Some comments, however, are still relevant and echo the criticisms of this review. Frantz (1972, p. 1442) concludes, for example, that "No concurrent, or predictive or any kind of criterion-related validity information is offered." Rothney (1972, p. 1444) reiterates this criticism and adds his own:

"The authors do not discuss such matters as transparency of the items, deliberate or unintentional faking, arbitrary assignment of numbers to responses, elaboration of the obvious, superficiality of items, vocabulary difficulties, variability in moods and sets, forcing of choices when there is no genuine choice, and many other criticisms of the inventory approach that have appeared in the literature." These are criticisms which Rothney has made of most interest inventories. As long as there are no criterion-related validity data on the OVIS to show that "it works," these criticisms have to be taken into account.

VALIDITY

The careful conceptual development of the OVIS gives it considerable face validity. The process of item writing and editing provides content validity which, based upon the reviewer's expert opinion, is unusual for interest measures. There

113

are some nagging questions, however, that still need to be addressed. Foremost among these is: Why are some "cells" in the Cubistic Model *empty*? For the content and ultimately the construct validity of the OVIS to be coherent and compelling, an explanation for these lacuna is needed. Another, somewhat related, question concerns: What is the evidence for the assumption that ". . . the 11 job activities comprising each scale adequately represent all the jobs in the cluster of worker-trait groups defining the scale (Manual 1970, p. 4). Conspicuous by its absence, although evidently available for the standardization, are data on the factorial composition of the scales. Finally, there simply are *no* criterion-related validities reported in the Manuals. The only remotely relevant statement appears to be contradictory: ". . . use of the results (from the OVIS) in predicting future behavior is not considered to be as important as their immediate use in career orientation and vocational exploration. The validity and reliability of the instrument should be assessed in terms of how well it helps students, parents, and counselors to develop realistic plans for the *future*" (Manual 1970, p. 32; italics added). But the latter is exactly what criterion-related validity does.

USE IN CAREER COUNSELING

Two collateral booklets are available for use with the OVIS II—the *Career Planner* and the *Handbook for Exploring Careers*. The former is intended to take the student systemstically through a series of career exploration steps and interpretations of the *Student Report*, but, as well-designed as it is technically, it bogs down hopelessly in overly detailed and complex explanations of concepts and worksheets. It appears to have been written for self-administration but a student, particularly at the junior high school level, would need the guided assistance of a counselor or teacher. In contrast, the *Handbook for Exploring Careers*, which is a hybrid of the old D.O.T. Volume II and the new *Guide for Occupational Exploration*, comes off considerably better. It provides highly usable, condensed information about occupations in the 23 OVIS clusters with an attractive format and layout.

SUMMARY

There is no question that the OVIS has been carefully constructed and developed. The "Cubistic Model" provided an explicit conceptual schema for scale construction, as well as a "built-in" linkage with the world-of-work through the D.O.T. and G.O.E. occupational structure. The standardization and norm base are more than adequate for high school students and are also applicable to college students, to a somewhat lesser extent. The content and construct validity of the OVIS are articulate and compelling, although a much more extensive nomonological network of relationships with other variables for the latter is needed. If it were available, the criterion-related validity of the OVIS would be greatly augmented, since few, if any, data on it are reported in the Manual (1983).

If there are shortcomings of the OVIS, they are in its criterion-related (both concurrent and predictive) validity, as well as its appropriateness for use with adults. There are no adult norms reported to support its proposed use, in promotional materials, with ". . . adults with a mid-career change" or, for that matter, other decisional problems, although there is no reason why the OVIS could not be used with adults, given such norms.

In summary, the OVIS II is a well-constructed and conceptualized inventory of job activity preferences explicitly related to the occupational structure. It should be highly useful with high school and college students in their career planning and cognate educational choices.

REFERENCES

D'Costa, A. G. (1968). The differentiation of high school students in vocational education areas by the Ohio Vocational Interest Survey. Unpublished doctoral dissertation, Ohio University.

D'Costa, A. G., & Winefordner, D. W. (1969). A cubistic model of vocational interests. *Vocational Guidance Quarterly, 17*, 242–249.

NOTE: Significant portions of this review were abridged from the author's original review in Volume IV of *Test Critiques* with permission of Test Corporation of America.

Self-Directed Search (SDS)

John L. Holland

Psychological Assessment Resources, Inc.
P.O. Box 998
Odessa, FL 33556

Target Population: Junior and senior high school, college and university students, adults.

Statement of the Purpose of the Instrument: The SDS is a self-administered, self-scored, and self-interpreted vocational interest inventory and counseling tool used in career exploration and selection; based on Holland's theory of personality types and work environments.

Titles of Subtests, Scales, Scores Provided: Surveys Activities, Competencies, Occupations and Self-Estimates to produce Holland Occupational Codes (RIASEC) in 3-digits (Regular Form) or 2-digits (Form E).

Forms and Levels Available, with Dates of Publication/Revision of Each: Regular Form, 1970, 1977, 1985; Form E (Easy), 1970, 1973, 1979, 1985; Vietnamese Regular Form, 1970, 1977; Spanish Form E, 1970, 1979.

Date of Most Recent Edition of Test Manual, User's Guide, Etc.: Manual, Assessment Booklet, Occupations Finder, 1985; Alphabetized Occupations Finder, 1986; Manual Supplement, 1987. You and Your Career, 1985. College Major Finder, 1987.

Languages in Which Available: Spanish, Vietnamese, French, Chinese, Japanese, Arabic, Afrikaans, Danish, Dutch, and other languages and adaptations worldwide.

Time: Actual Test Time—35–50 minutes.
     Total Administration Time—35–50 minutes.

Norm Group(s) on Which Scores Are Based: High school students, college students, and adults ages 15–74.

Manner in Which Results Are Reported for Individuals
   Types of Scores: Raw Scores on homogeneous scales of equal length, percentiles, Holland Occupational Codes.
   Report Format/Content
     Basic Service: Assessment Booklet produces Holland Occupational Codes; Occupations Finder Booklet (1,156 occupations) keyed to Holland Occupational Code.

Report Format/Content for Group Summaries: Not available.

Scoring
   Machine Scoring Service
     Cost of basic service per counselee: $6.00 to $7.50.
   Hand Scoring
     Scored by: counselee; counselor.
     Time required for scoring: 5 minutes.

Local Machine Scoring: *Provisions/conditions/equipment required*: Administration, Scoring, and Interpretive software available for IBM-PC (and compatibles) and Apple II computer systems.

Computer Software Options Available: Standard administration on-line; scoring; interpretation. *Ways in which computer version differs*: Also administers My Vocational Situation, a vocational screening instrument.

Cost of Materials
  Specimen Set: $3.75; Manual, $12.00.
  Counselee Materials: Assessment Booklet = $.84; Occupations Finder (reusable) = $.78; Alphabetized Occupations Finder (reusable) = $.78; You and Your Career (reusable) = $.24; Spanish and Vietnamese Edition (Assessment Booklet and Occupation Finder) = $1.80.

Additonal Comments of Interest to Users: Forthcoming revisions, new 1985 Occupations Finder now contains 1,156 occupations; new Manual Supplement provides comprehensive and explicit interpretive information.

Published Reviews

Bodden, J. L. (1987). In D. J. Keyser & R. C. Sweetland (Eds.), *Test Critiques, Vol. V* (pp. 419–424). Kansas City, MO: Test Corporation of America.
Brown, F. (1972). *Measurement and Evaluation in Guidance*, 5, 315–319.
Campbell, N. J. (1985). In D. J. Keyser & R. C. Sweetland (Eds.), *Test Critiques, Volume II* (pp. 697–706). Kansas City, MO: Test Corporation of America.
Crites, J. (1978). In O. K. Buros (Ed.), *The Eighth Mental Measurements Yearbook*. Highland Park, New Jersey: Gryphon Press.
Cronbach, L. J. (1984). *Essentials of Psychological Testing*. 4th ed. New York: Harper & Row.
Cutts, C. C. (1977). *Measurement and Evaluation in Guidance*, 10(2) 117–120.
Dolliver, R. H., and Hansen, R. H. (1977). *Measurement and Evaluation in Guidance*, 10, 120–123.
Krieshok, T. S. (in press). *Journal of Counseling and Development*.
Seligman, R. (1974). *Measurement and Evaluation in Guidance*, 7, 138–140.

Reviewed by

N. Jo Campbell
Professor, Department of Applied Behavioral Studies
Oklahoma State University

The newly revised Self-Directed Search (SDS) is designed to be a self-administered, self-scored, and self-interpreted guide for high school students and adults desiring career planning assistance. Completion of the SDS results in a systematic study of the user's personal interests and abilities and is used to relate a self-assessment of competencies and preferred activities to 1,156 occupations listed in the Occupations Finder, a component of the SDS.

FORMAT

The SDS, based on Holland's theory of career choice, was developed using the hypothesis that the vocational choice process should involve a consideration of an individual's competencies, preferred activities, and self-ratings of abilities along with vocational interests. Six types of cognate personality orientations and environmental models—realistic (R), investigative (I), artistic (A), social (S), enterprising (E), and conventional (C)—identified by Holland's theory of vocational choice serve as the basis for relating one's self-assessments of abilities and interests to appropriate occupations. The basic premise underlying the SDS is that individuals are more likely to experience greater success, stability and satisfaction in their occupations if the work environment suits their personalities.

The SDS consists of two booklets, the self-assessment booklet and an occupational classification booklet, the Occupations Finder. The latter is available in alphabetized format or in a format using the R, I, A, S, E, C code letters. A booklet designed to assist in the interpretation of results of the self-assessment and a Professional Manual are also available.

The self-assessment booklet includes two self-ratings in six personal trait areas and six scales of 11 to 14 items per scale in each of three sections: Activities, Competencies, and Occupations. In an Occupational Daydreams sections, the users list careers they have considered. The six personality types and environmental models listed in Holland's theory are the bases of each category (R, I, A, S, E, C) assigned to each reponse made by the user.

SDS, Form E (Easy) was developed for use with adolescents and adults having limited reading abilities or educational levels below ninth grade (Holland, 1985). The scoring procedures for this shortened form have been simplified to yield two—rather than three—letter codes. The Form E occupation classification booklet, Jobs Finder, has been modified so the two-letter codes are used to identify appropriate occupations.

SCORES

The users score their own responses by summing the total occurrences of each letter (R, I, A, S, E, C) from the Activities, Competencies, Occupations, and Self-Estimates sections of the SDS. The Occupational Daydreams responses are not used in the scoring process, but are used as a type of check on the results. The three letters out of the possible six occurring most frequently form the user's summary code. The users then refer to the Occupations Finder to identify potential occupations having summary codes similar or identical to the user's summary codes. These potential occupations require patterns of interests and competencies that are most similar to the users' own patterns of self-estimates of skills and interests.

Scoring errors by users are a major problem, although revisions of the scoring procedures have simplified the process. Consequently, scores on the SDS should always be checked by a counselor or by a trained proctor.

The norm groups for the SDS scales and codes include more than 8,000 high school and college students and adults. The Professional Manual presents extensive sets of norms prepared using data collected using the 1971, 1977 and 1985 editions. Percentile ranks, raw score means and standard deviations, and score distributions are listed by sex and educational level.

118

RELIABILITY

The internal reliability (alpha) estimates of the summary scale range from .84 to .92 (Holland, 1985). Internal reliability (alpha) estimates range from .59 to .92 and tend to cluster in the .80s for the subscales of the SDS and are higher than estimates reported for earlier editions. Test-retest reliability estimates are provided for the earlier versions but not for the 1985 version. Holland (1985) reports internal reliability (K-8) estimates ranging from .56 to .92 for a sample of 236 seventh-graders who took Form E in a 1979 study.

VALIDITY

Evidence of concurrent validity of the 1985 edition of the SDS is reported for males and females, ages 14-74. Further evidence of validity is based in studies completed using the 1971 and 1977 editions. Gottfredson and Holland (1975) report that the high point SDS codes of male and female college freshmen were found to be consistent with the occupational choices of 43% of the males and 66% of the females three years after testing. Furthermore, McGowan (1982) reports that 73% of the vocationally undecided high school seniors in his study had received summary codes on the SDS that predicted their occupational choices four years later. The research of Rachman, Amernic and Aranya (1981) seems to support the hexagonal model of Holland's theory which serves as the basis for the SDS. However, Crites (1978) disagrees with the hexagonal model and calls into question the construct validity of the SDS when he states that Holland's model would be better represented by a 3-dimensional figure than by a hexagon.

Validity estimates for Form E are not reported. Holland states that the similarity between the items on the standard form and on Form E should result in similar estimates of validity for the two forms.

SUMMARY

The SDS, constructed using Holland's well-established career theory as the basis, can be used to supply helpful information regarding matches between work environments and the personal information users possess about their own personal interests and skills. A positive aspect of the SDS is the wide variety of alternative occupational choices included in the instrument. Counselors concerned with helping individuals make appropriate occupational plans in a fast changing world of work will find this aspect of the SDS very useful.

Several researchers have suggested SDS codes, scale scores, and responses to individual items are affected by the sex of the user. Cutts (1977) expressed such a concern when she reported females completing the SDS may receive higher conventional scores due to their work histories in clerical positions even though the vocational interests and plans of these females may be focused in other professions for which they are preparing while working in the clerical positions.

The value of the use of the SDS in unsupervised situations is limited in part by the scoring errors often made by unsupervised users. Therefore, the importance of providing trained clerical or counselor monitoring during test administration cannot be overly stressed. Of equal importance is the availability of counselors to discuss components of Holland's theory with users and to provide encouragement to the users regarding the exploration of potential careers indicated by the results of the SDS.

The SDS is most appropriately used in small group or individual counseling environments as a means for users to clarify their perceptions of careers and the process by which career choices are made. The contributions of the SDS as a valuable career counseling tool when used appropriately should be considered by both professional counselors and individuals desiring assistance in exploring viable career possibilities.

REFERENCES

Crites, J. (1978). Review of the Self-Directed Search. In O. K. Buros (Ed.), *The Eighth Mental Measurements Yearbook* (pp. 1608–1611). Highland Park, NJ: The Gryphon Press.

Cutts, C. C. (1977). Review of the Self-Directed Search. *Measurement and Evaluation in Guidance*, *10*, 117–120.

Gottfredson, G. D., & Holland, J. L. (1975). Some Normative Self-Report Data on Activities, Competencies, Occupational Preference, and Ability Ratings for High School and College Students and Employed Men and Women. *JSAS Catalog of Selected Documents in Psychology*, *5*, 192. (MS No. 859).

Holland, J. L. (1985). *The Self-Directed Search Professional Manual*. Odessa, FL: Psychological Assessment Resources, Inc.

McGowan, A. S. (1982). The Predictive Efficiency of Holland's SDS Summary Codes in Terms of Career Choice: A Four-Year Follow-up. *Journal of Vocational Behavior*, *20*, 294–303.

Rachman, D., Amernic, J., & Aranya, N. (1981). A Factor-analytic study of the construct validity of Holland's Self-Directed Search test. *Educational and Psychological Measurement*, *41*, 425–437.

NOTE: Significant portions of this review were abridged from the authors original review in Volume II of *Test Critiques* with permission of Test Corporation of America.

Strong-Campbell Interest Inventory (SCII)

E. K. Strong, Jr., Jo-Ida C. Hansen and David P. Campbell

Consulting Psychologists Press
(Agents for Stanford University Press)
577 College Avenue, Palo Alto, CA 94306

Target Population: Teens and adults, grades 8 and up.

Statement of the Purpose of the Instrument: The Strong measures occupational interests in a wide range of career areas. including professional, technical, nonprofessional, and vocational-technical. It has been used for making educational and occupational choices, exploring lifestyles (including avocations), choosing a college major, making employment decisions, mid-career evaluation and change, identifying and advising managerial candidates, helping to understand job satisfaction and dissatisfaction, guiding preretirement and retirement decisions, and conducting research studies on occupational interests.

Titles of Subtests, Scales, Scores Provided: Subtests include occupations, school subjects, activities, leisure activities, types of people, preference between two activities, and individual characteristics. On the profile sheet, scales are grouped into four categories: General Occupational Themes, Basic Interest Scales, Occupational Scales, and Administrative Indexes and Special Scales.

Forms and Levels Available with Dates of Publication/Revision of Each: Only form T325 is currently supported. Other forms are only translations of Form T325. Revised 1985.

Date of Most Recent Edition of Test Manual, User's Guide, Etc: Manual for the SVIB-SCII (1985). User's guide for the SVIB-SCII (1984).

Languages in Which Available: Spanish (Form T325S), French Canadian (Form T325FC), Hebrew (Form T325H), British (Form T325B), French, German, and Slovak are all available commercially. Research translations have been made in a variety of other languages.

Time: Actual Test Time—25 to 35 minutes.
Total Administration Time—Same.

Norm Group(s) on Which Scores Are Based: 1985 General Reference Sample (N = 600), half male and half female, constructed to represent the interests of People-in-General, composed of women and men from professional, vocational/technical, and nonprofessional occupations in all six of the General Occupational Theme types, from those without a high school diploma to those with doctorates.
Occupational Criterion Samples were normed by testing a sample of individuals from that occupation who were satisfied, successful, between the ages of 25 and 60, on the job for at least three years, and perform in the typical manner.

Manner in Which Results Are Reported for Individuals

Types of scores: Scores for the General Occupational Themes, Basic Interest Scales, Occupational Scales, and Special Scales are reported in standard scores (t-scores). Administrative Indexes are reported as percentages.

Report format/content

Basic service: Two page client profile with explanations of scores on the reverse includes all scales reported in an easily readable format. Includes two copies of profile—one for the client, and one for the counselor. No handscoring stencils available, only computer scoring.

Options: A three to six page interpretive report is available which elaborates on the individual scores as well as providing an overall interpretation of the profile.

Report Format/Content for Group Summaries

Options: Summary statistics (mean and standard deviations of scale scores) and data files on IBM PC floppy diskette are available.

Scoring

Machine scoring service: Cost of basic service per counselee: $2.20 to 3.65. Cost of options: $3.90 to 5.90.

Hand scoring: Not available.

Local Machine scoring service: IBM PC, PC/XT, PC/AT, or IBM-compatible microcomputer, serial port (asynchronous RS-232C adapter), DOS 2.0 or greater, and a multiple outlet power strip. Additionally, two specialized pieces of hardware are required, a controller and the appropriate CodeLock. The SCII Software Set includes three program diskettes and a user's guide.

Computer Software Options Available: Standard administration on-line; scoring; interpretation.

Cost of Material

Specimen set: $7.00.

Counselee materials: Test booklets (reusable) $8.75/25 booklets. Answer sheets $2.20 to $5.90.

Published Reviews

Campbell, D. P. (1978). Review of Strong-Campbell Interest Inventory. In O. K. Buros (Ed.), *The Eighth Mental Measurements Yearbook*, Volume II. Highland Park, NJ: Gryphon Press.

Crites, J. O. (1978). Review of Strong-Campbell Interest Inventory. In O. K. Buros (Ed.), *The Eighth Mental Measurements Yearbook*, Volume II. Highland Park, NJ: Gryphon Press.

Doliver, R. H. (1978). Review of Strong-Campbell Interest Inventory. In O. K. Buros (Ed.), *The Eighth Mental Measurements Yearbook*, Volume II. Highland Park, NJ: Gryphon Press.

Johnson, R. W. (1978). Review of Strong-Campbell Interest Inventory. In O. K. Buros (Ed.), *The Eighth Mental Measurements Yearbook*, Volume II. Highland Park, NJ: Gryphon Press.

Layton, W. L. (1985). Review of Strong Campbell Interest Inventory. In J. V. Mitchell, Jr. (Ed.), *The Ninth Mental Measurements Yearbook*, Volume II. Lincoln, NE: Buros Institute of Mental Measurements.

Lunneborg, P. W. (1978). Review of Strong-Campbell Interest Inventory. In O. K. Buros (Ed.), *The Eighth Mental Measurements Yearbook*, Volume II. Highland Park, NJ: Gryphon Press.

Steinhauer, J. C. (1978). Review of Strong-Campbell Interest Inventory. In O. K. Buros (Ed.), *The Eighth Mental Measurements Yearbook*, Volume II. Highland Park, NJ: Gryphon Press.

Tzeng, O. C. S. (1985). Strong-Campbell Interest Inventory. In D. J. Keyser & R. C. Sweetland (Eds.), *Test Critiques*, Volume II. Kansas City, MO: Test Corporation of America.

Westbrook, B. W. (1985). Review of Strong-Campbell Interest Inventory. In J. V. Mitchell, Jr. (Ed.), *The Ninth Mental Measurements Yearbook*, Volume II. Lincoln, NE: Buros Institute of Mental Measurements.

NOTE: Many other references to the SCII's predecessors, the SVIB-M and SVIB-F in previous Buros' MMY volumes.

Fred H. Borgen
Professor of Psychology
Iowa State University

The venerable Strong interest inventory now has a sixty-year history. Despite its deep roots and tradition, it has undergone remarkable expansion and revision in recent decades, while still retaining as its core E. K. Strong's (1927) innovation of empirically based occupational scales. Under David Campbell's leadership, the 1974 Strong-Campbell Interest Inventory (SCII) contained major conceptual and practical advances. These included merging the Women's and Men's forms of the inventory, adding Holland's typology as a central organizing feature, and adding homogeneous content-based scales. Now the 1985 SCII, led by Jo-Ida Hansen's massive research effort, contains capstone advances expanding the counseling utility of the revered "Strong." Most prominent of the latest revisions are 1) the completion of 15 years of research to produce sex-balanced scales with fair career options for women and men; 2) major extension of the coverage of the Strong with many more Occupational Scales for noncollege occupations (now representing 32 percent of the scales); and 3) a full-scale renorming to address concerns with possible societal changes in recent decades. All of this was accomplished with extensive national data collection from 142,610 people, so the current SCII is based on 48,238 satisfied workers in 207 occupational samples.

FORMAT, SCORING AND SCALES

Comprised of 325 items eliciting likes and dislikes for varied occupations and activities, the SCII has a sixth grade reading level and can typically be completed in about one-half hour. All scoring of the SCII is computer based, either through mail-in service, telephone linkage, or with software available for IBM-compatible microcomputers at the counselor's office. The profile provides three major kinds of scales, all organized within Holland's theoretical system of "personality" types. Representing Holland's RIASEC (Realistic, Investigative, Artistic, Social, Enterprising, and Conventional) types, the six General Occupational Theme (GOT) scales are the most general of the SCII scales. The second type of scale, the 23 Basic Interest Scales (BIS), tap somewhat more specific areas of interest. Thus, for example, four of the BIS—Science, Mathematics, Medical Science, and Medical Service—can be viewed as assessing more specific aspects of the Investigative GOT. The GOT and BIS are classed as *homogeneous* scales because they were developed to group items with high internal consistency and inter-pretability.

Continuing the approach pioneered by Strong, the 207 Occupational Scales are the third type of scales. These are called *empirical* scales to indicate that each is derived by surveying members of the particular occupation to identify the items they answer differently from people in a general reference (or norm) group. Thus, when a person receives a high score on, for example, the Photographer Occupational Scale, it is possible to tell that person, "you have interests similar to persons happily employed as photographers."

After very intensive scrutiny of sex differences in measured interests, the developers of the Strong have concluded that the most useful and valid results are achieved by creating separate occupational scales for females and males. Therefore, the current SCII continues Strong's initial practice of separate female and male occupational scales, but is augmented by Hansen's recent work to provide state-of-the-art scales for modern, sex-fair counseling. The 1985 SCII contains 101 pairs of parallel scales on the same occupation for women and men. Thus, there is a scale based on female geologists and one based on male geologists. (In addition, there are five scales based on only one gender; these are cases where it was not feasible to collect data on the other gender because so few people of that gender are currently employed in that occupation). Moreover, the carefully devised new reference groups—Women-in-General and Men-in-General—are based on recent data to reflect any recent changes in sex roles.

Finally, the profile includes special scales measuring Academic Comfort and Introversion-Extraversion, as well as administrative indices showing overall response tendencies.

RELIABILITY

The empirical construction of Occupational Scales typically results in heterogeneity of item content within scales. Thus, evaluating the internal consistency of these scales is not appropriate. Therefore, the developers of the Strong have emphasized the test-retest reliability of the scales, often over substantial time peiods. This kind of information about the stability of interests is essential for the predictive use of the inventory for career planning. Median retest reliabilities for the 1985 Occupational Scales were .92 for two weeks, .89 for thirty days, and .87 for three years. Over similar periods median reliabilities for the General Occupational Themes, Basic Interest Scales, and Special Scales ranged from .81 to .91. These results, and other studies of the Strong over decades-long intervals, indicate a high overall stability of interests that supports the use of the SCII for career planning. Of course, despite these average results, aware counselors know that single individuals may occasionally shift markedly in interests.

VALIDITY

Following the lead of Strong's extensive longitudinal research, predictive validity of the Occupational Scales has been a central feature for assessing the validity of the inventory. The typical strategy has been to give the inventory to young adults, and then, years later, determine their current occupation, and assess the agreement ("hit rate") between their original occupational scales and their current occupation. The newness of the revised SCII requires that such longitudinal studies be conducted in future years. However, it is reasonable to assume, because of similarity of methods of construction, that the hit rates for the current version will be comparable to those from longitudinal studies of earlier versions of the Strong. These results showed that the typical hit rate is

124

60–75 percent that college students will enter occupations predictable from their earlier scores.

Concurrent validity information is more readily obtainable for a revised Inventory. The *Manual* (Hansen & Campbell, 1985) provides extensive evidence on the capacity of occupational scales to differentiate people currently in the occupational groups surveyed for the revision. For example, the best SCII scale on this criterion is the female physicist scale, where the women physicists' scores overlapped only 13 percent with Women-in-General. The median overlap for all occupational scales is 36 percent, which can be considered a very adequate level of this kind of concurrent validity.

COUNSELING USE

Appropriately, counselors are urged not to overemphasize specific career predictions, but rather to use the SCII as a tool in a total counseling context aimed at helping clients develop general career planning strategies. The Holland organization of the results encourages a general understanding of the person and the world of work. The inventory is valuable both in developing possibilities for those undecided about career choice, and also in confirming choices for those who have already selected career directions.

Hansen's (1984) *User's Guide for the SVIB-SCII* is without peer in its value for counselors. Superbly written and organized, it is filled with specific advice on many issues related to the best use of the Strong. Besides providing an excellent introduction to the current inventory, it effectively covers such issues as atypical profiles, and use of the Strong with adult career changers, minorities, other cultures, and special populations. Further, it suggests specific sequential steps for career counseling interpretation of the Strong. Throughout the *User's Guide*, as well as the *Manual*, the emphasis is on using the inventory to assist clients with career exploration and self-understanding, yet also being attentive to other factors such as abilities and personal context that affect clients' lives.

SUMMARY

The latest revision of the SCII provides the counselor with even greater confidence and utility for the Strong, long respected for its psychometric excellence. The level of useful innovation and development that first Campbell, and now Hansen, have crafted in the Strong is nothing short of remarkable in the history of testing (cf. Borgen & Bernard, 1982; Walsh & Osipow, 1986). Together the *Manual* and the *User's Guide* are exemplars of how science and practice can be combined to use testing effectively in counseling. For continued reading about leading-edge issues in interest measurement, the volume edited by Walsh and Osipow (1986) is particularly recommended.

REFERENCES

Borgen, F. H., & Bernard, C. B. (1982). Review of Strong-Campbell Interest Inventory. *Measurement and Evaluation in Guidance, 14,* 208-212.

Hansen, J. C. (1984). *User's guide for the SVIB-SCII*. Stanford, CA: Stanford University Press.

Hansen, J. C., & Campbell, D. C. (1985). *Manual for the SVIB-SCII*, 4th Ed. Stanford, CA: Stanford University Press.

Strong, E. K., Jr. (1927). Vocational interest test. *Educational Record, 8,* 107-121.

Walsh, W. B., & Osipow, S. H. (Eds.). (1986). *Advances in vocational psychology: Volume 1. The assessment of interests.* Hillsdale, NJ: Erlbaum.

NOTE: Significant portions of this review were taken from the author's review in *Measurement and Evaluation in Guidance*, (1982) 14, 208–212 with permission of AACD.

USES Interest Inventory (USES-II)

United States Employment Service

United States Employment Service
Employment and Training Administration
200 Constitution Ave. NW, Washington, DC 20210

Target Population: Grade 9 to adult.

Statement of the Purpose of the Instrument: The Interest Inventory is used to relate occupational interests to the *Guide for Occupational Exploration's* Interest Areas (U.S. Department of Labor, 1979). Identification of the two or three highest interest areas for a counselee provides a basis for focusing occupational exploration. The Interest Inventory was also designed to be given with the General Aptitude Test Battery to provide the counselor information on both aptitude and interest.

Titles of Subtests, Scales, Scores Provided: A profile of scores on 12 scales is provided.

Forms and Levels Available, with Dates of Publication/Revision of Each: 1981 edition.

Date of Most Recent Edition of Test Manual, User's Guide, Etc.: 1982.

Languages in Which Available: English only.

Time: Actual Test Time—15–20 minutes.
      Total Administration Time—20 minutes.

Norm Group(s) on Which Scores Are Based: High school seniors, trade school or college students, out-of-school job applicants, employed workers, or adults in occupational training programs. Included minorities and equal numbers of males and females from both urban and rural areas.

Manner in Which Results Are Reported for Individuals
  Types of Scores: Standard scores, percentile ranks.
  Report Format/Content
    Basic Service: Score reports lists raw scores, standard scores and percentile ranking for each of the twelve interest areas.
    Options: If the Interest Inventory is administered in conjunction with the GATB, score reports give the individual aptitude profile, the interest profile, and Occupational Aptitude Patterns (OAPs) that correspond to each of the 12 interest areas (see GATB review).

Report Format/Content for Group Summaries: Not available.

Scoring
  Machine Scoring Service
    Cost of basic service per counselee: $.75 (three day)—$.95 (one day).
    Cost of options: Interest Inventory and GATB: Counselor Report (just results) $1.40–$2.00; Interpretative Report $1.80–$2.60.
    Time required for scoring and returning (maximum): 3 days.

Hand Scoring
Scored by: counselor.
Time required for scoring: 10 minutes.
Local Machine Scoring: Not available.

Computer Software Options Available: Not available.

Cost of Materials
Counselee Materials: USES Interest Inventory $11.00 per 100; Manual for USES Interest Inventory $4.50 per copy (reusable); Guide for Occupational Exploration, 1979 $12.00 per copy (reusable); Combined B, C, D GATB answer sheet and II (Machine scoring) $19.00 per 100.

Additional Comments of Interest to Users: The USES Interest Inventory is on restricted sale, available only to State Employment Security agencies, and organizations which have obtained approval from State Employment Security agencies. The State Testing Supervisor can be contacted for further information.

Published Reviews

Bolton, B. (1984). Review of *United States Employment Service Interest Inventory*. In D. J. Keyser & R. C. Sweetland (Eds), *Test Critiques*: Volume III (pp 673–681). Kansas City, MO: Test Corporation of America.

Reviewed By

Brian Bolton
Professor, Arkansas Research and Training Center in Vocational Rehabilitation, University of Arkansas

The United States Employment Service Interest Inventory (USES-II) is a self-report instrument that measures the respondent's relative strength of interests in 12 broad categories of occupational activity. The USES-II is a central component of the U.S. Department of Labor's Counselee Assessment/Occupational Exploration System. The 12 occupational interest areas constitute the primary theme of the *Guide for Occupational Exploration* (GOE) (U.S. Department of Labor, 1979a).

All 12,000 occupations in the U.S. labor force were allocated to the 12 interest areas by occupational analysts using a standardized procedure. Because the occupations within each of the 12 interest areas are extremely heterogeneous with respect to educational and aptitude levels required, it was necessary to cluster occupations within the interest categories. This task was accomplished by identifying 66 work groups, each with corresponding Occupational Aptitude Patterns (OAPs) that are measured by the General Aptitude Test Battery (GATB). Thus, each of the 66 work groups is characterized by a unique combination of interest preference *and* minimal aptitude requirement (for details see Droege, 1987).

DESCRIPTION

The USES-II consists of 162 items of three types: (1) job activity statements (e.g., guard airport security, sell life insurance, and conduct studies on economics), (2) occupational titles (e.g., biologist, dairy farmer, bookkeeper), and (3) life experiences (e.g., play a musical instrument, tour a tree nursery, teach surfboard riding). The examinee responds to each item using a 3-choice format: Like (L), Dislike (D), or Not Sure (?). Only the "Like" responses are counted as preferences in calculating interest area scores. The USES-II measures the relative strengths of the respondent's occupational interests in each of the following 12 areas: artistic, scientific, plants and animals, protective, mechanical, industrial, business detail, selling, accommodating, humanitarian, leading-influencing, and physical performing.

The USES-II should not be confused with another occupational interest instrument developed by the U.S. Department of Labor, the Interest Check List (ICL) (U. S. Department of Labor, 1979b). The ICL contains 210 work activity statements keyed directly to the 66 *GOE* work groups. Although the ICL uses the same response format as the USES-II, there is no provision for calculating interest scores. Rather, the ICL was conceived as a counseling aid that would permit joint counselor-counselee exploration of specific expressions of occupational interests.

PRACTICAL APPLICATIONS

The USES-II was designed for use by counselors and guidance personnel working in institutional settings concerned with occupational exploration and career·development of youth and adults. These settings include employment agencies, vocational rehabilitation facilities, high schools, and vocational-technical institutes. It is apparent from the brief description of the Counselee Assessment/Occupational Exploration System above that by itself the USES-II would not be particularly helpful in facilitating vocational decision making. In almost all situations the GATB would have to be administered concurrently with the USES-II to make realistic use of the latter. For counselors who simply wish to encourage a counselee to use the *GOE*, with proper precautions, the ICL would be a helpful starting point.

The USES-II can be appropriately used with the general adult population aged 16 years and above. The reading level required by the 162 items appears to be about third grade, but it would be easy to prepare an audio-tape version for administration to poor readers. Administration of the USES-II to individuals or groups of examinees is a straightforward task that can be accomplished by a psychometric aide or trained secretary; completion time is estimated to be 15–20 minutes. Directions for administering the USES-II are detailed in the USES-II manual (Intran Corp., 1982).

Two versions of the USES-II are available: First, a four page form published by the Government Printing Office that can only be hand-scored. Second, a four page folder published by the Intran Corporation which can be either hand-scored or machine-scored by the Intran Scoring Service. A booklet that combines the USES-II with the standard Intran GATB answer sheet entitled Occupational AIM (Aptitude-Interest Measurement) is also available from Intran. It can be either hand-scored or machine-scored by Intran Scoring Service. Hand scoring of the

USES-II is easy and rapid and does not even require the use of scoring stencils. For high-volume testing programs, however, the machine scoring service would greatly reduce turn-around time for agency counselors, especially if a computer-generated report is desired.

Raw scores are translated into standard T-scores using a large, geographically and racially representative normative sample. Because there are substantial gender differences on several scales (*e.g.*, males score higher on Mechanical and Physical Performing and females score higher on Business Detail and Humanitarian), percentile scores are calculated for male and female examinees using the corresponding segment of the normative sample. Thus, two sets of derived scores are generated for each counselee providing comparisons with the general population and with the same-sex population.

TECHNICAL CHARACTERISTICS

The USES-II is the product of a careful program of developmental research (Intran Corp., 1982). Factor analysis of 307 occupational activity items that covered all worker-trait groups in the third edition of the *Dictionary of Occupational Titles* identified eleven interest factors. The factors were highly similar for males and females. To evaluate the comprehensiveness and usefulness of the eleven interest categories, occupational analysts allocated samples of occupations to the eleven areas defined by the factors by matching major job activities to the activities comprising the interest factors. Results of this judgmental process demonstrated that the factors could provide the foundation for a functional occupational classification system. However, a small group of occupations in entertainment, recreation, and sports could not be allocated to any of the eleven categories, necessitating the addition of a twelfth area, Physical Performing, to complete the USES occupational interest system.

The USES-II was administered to 6,530 persons, half of whom were high school seniors, trade school, or college students. The remaining half were out-of-school job applicants, employed workers, or adults in occupational training programs. This sample, which includes Black, Hispanic, Native American, and Oriental respondents and approximately equal numbers of males and females, constitutes the normative sample for the calculation of USES-II derived scores as described above. The USES-II was designed to meet the National Institute of Education's (Diamond, 1975) guidelines for sex fairness in interest inventories.

Hoyt reliability coefficients, which are lower-bound estimates for the corresponding test-retest reliabilities, range from .84 to .92 for the twelve scales. Scale intercorrelations are typically in the .30s and .40s, indicating that the USES-II scales are relatively independent of one another. Due to the recent completion of the USES-II and associated counseling tools, no studies of predictive validity or counseling utility have been reported in the measurement or vocational guidance literature. However, a statistical investigation of the vocational interests of adult handicapped persons by Brookings and Bolton (1986) replicated most of the USES-II interest categories. A confirmatory factor analysis by Brookings and Bolton (1987) provided strong support for all 12 USES-II interest scales. It can be assumed that the U.S. Department of Labor will publish validity and utility studies of the USES-II in conjunction with their ongoing programmatic research on test development and occupational exploration.

SUMMARY

The USES-II is the only interest inventory designed to be used with the most thoroughly occupationally validated multiaptitude test available (the GATB) and is directly linked with an occupational exploration system that encompasses all jobs in the U.S. economy. Four specific strengths of the USES-II deserve special mention: (1) the psychometric foundation of the instrument is outstanding; (2) the excellent normative sample is representative of the entire U.S. labor force; (3) the interest structure is consistent and interchangeable with Holland's vocational typology; and (4) machine scoring and computer-generated reports are available through the Intran Corporation.

REFERENCES

Brookings, J., & Bolton, B. (1987, August). *Confirmatory parcel analysis of the USES Interest Inventory*. Paper presented at the meeting of the American Psychological Association, New York City.

Diamond, E. E. (Ed.) (1975). *Issues of sex-bias and sex-fairness in career interest measurement*. Washington, DC: National Institute of Education.

Droege, R. C. (1987). The USES testing program. In B. Bolton (Ed.), *Handbook of measurement and evaluation in rehabilitation* (2nd ed.) (pp. 169–182). Baltimore, MD: Paul Brookes.

Intran Corporation (1982). *Manual for the USES Interest Inventory*. Minneapolis, MN: Author.

U.S. Department of Labor (1979a). *Guide for occupational exploration*. Washington, DC: U.S. Government Printing Office.

U.S. Department of Labor (1979b). *Interest Check List*. Washington, DC: Government Printing Office.

NOTE: This review was abridged from the author's original review in *Test Critiques: Vol. III* with permission of the Test Corporation of America.

Vocational Interest, Experience and Skill Assessment (VIESA)

ACT Staff Members

American College Testing Program (ACT)
Career Services Area
P. O. Box 168, Iowa City, Iowa 52243

Target Population: Grade 8 through adult.

Statement of the Purpose of the Instrument: VIESA helps counselees expand self-awareness, learn how the world of work is structured, and begin to explore personally relevant career options. Through the "World-of-Work Map," counselees relate information about themselves to 500 occupations employing over 95% of the labor force.

Titles of subtests, scales, scores provided: Unisex Edition of the ACT Interest Inventory (UNIACT), Work-related Experience Inventory, and Self-ratings of Skills. Each provides results for data, ideas, people, and things work tasks. Job values are also assessed.

Forms and Levels Available, with Dates of Publication/Revision of Each: Level 1: Grades 8–10 (1983/1986); Level 2: Grades 11–adult (1983/1986).

Date of Most Recent Edition of Test Manual, User's Guide, Etc.: *VIESA User's Handbook (Revised 2nd Edition)*, 1984.

Languages in Which Available: English only.

Time: Actual Test Time—untimed.
Total Administration Time—45 minutes (plus optional follow-through).

Norm Group(s) on Which Scores Are Based: Nationally representative samples (1983) consisting of approximately 15,000 8th, 10th, and 12th graders in 115 schools.

Manner in Which Results Are Reported for Individuals
Types of Scores: World-of-Work Map "region" scores; quartiles.
Report Format/Content
Basic Service: A counselee's trial job choices and interest, experience, and skill results are reported as World-of-Work Map regions.

Report Format Content for Group Summaries: Not available.

Scoring
Machine Scoring Service: Not available.
Hand Scoring: *Scored by*: counselee; clerk (optional); counselor (optional).
Time required for scoring: Included in 45 minute total administration time.
Local Machine Scoring: Not available.

Computer Software Options Available: Not available.

Cost of Materials
Specimen Set: $5.00 per level. Includes *VIESA User's Handbook*.
Counselee Materials: $23.75 per level for package of 25 Career Guidebooks and Job Family Charts.

Additional Comments of Interest to Users: VIESA is a self-scored "short form" of ACT's Career Planning Program (CPP). The machine-scored CPP also includes an ability test battery and a narrative report of results.

Published Reviews
Association for Measurement and Evaluation in Guidance Committee to Screen Career Guidance Instruments. (1981). *AMEG Newsnotes, 16*(3), 6.
Collins, M. A. (1986). *Guidance & Counseling, 1*(5), 73–75.
Krauskopf, C. J. (1978). In O. K. Buros (Ed.), *The Eighth Mental Measurements Yearbook*. Highland Park, N.J.: Gryphon Press.
Mehrens, W. A. (1977). *Measurement and Evaluation in Guidance, 10*, 185–189.
Read, R. W. (1982). In J. T. Kapes & M. M. Mastie (Eds.), *A counselor's guide to vocational guidance instruments* (pp. 97–100). Falls Church, VA: National Vocational Guidance Association.

Reviewed by

William A. Mehrens
Professor of Measurement
Michigan State University

Vocational Interest, Experience and Skill Assessment (VIESA) "is a self-scored inventory of career-related interests, experiences, and skills supplemented by an informal ranking of job values" (ACT *User's Handbook*, 1984, p.1). It is a short form of the Career Planning Program. VIESA is designed to stimulate and facilitate self/career exploration for those persons in the early states of educational or vocational planning. The primary goals of VIESA are to help individuals (a) expand self-awareness; (b) develop career awareness; (c) identify personally relevant career options; and (d) begin exploring and evaluating their career options.

GENERAL DESCRIPTION

VIESA is composed of eight basic units. The first unit is a short, one page introduction to the key notions of people, data, things and ideas. Unit two is composed of 60 of the 90 interest items used in the Unisex edition of the ACT

Interest Inventory (UNIACT). Thirty are scored on a Data/Ideas Scale and 30 are scored on a Things/People Scale. An option is provided for the counselees to complete the other 30 UNIACT items if scores are desired on Holland's six interest types. In unit three the counselees are asked to identify one of three skills at which they think they are best within each of the four broad skill areas: people, data, things, and ideas. Then they designate the skill at which they are best from among the four they have identified and mark the appropriate regions on a World-of-Work Region Chart. In unit four counselees name their first "trial job choice" and find its job family in the list provided. In unit five counselees are requested to list at least three job possibilities based on ones identified from the two most appropriate World-of-Work map regions and the Job Family Charts. Unit six provides one page of tips for exploring jobs and unit seven asks counselees to review seven job values and identify the three that are most important to them. In unit eight counselees mark work-related experiences and find regions in the World-of-Work Map that correspond to these.

The *User's Handbook* suggest that units one through five can be completed in about 40 minutes and that units six through eight be completed as homework or during a follow-through session. The reading level of the various components of VIESA is 6.6 to 6.7. There are two levels (Level I for grades eight through ten and Level 2 for 11th graders through adults) of the inventory.

NORMS AND SCORES

Some normative data exist for the VIESA on the UNIACT and the Work-Related Experience Inventory. The norms were obtained in the spring of 1983 using nationally representative samples of students in grades 8, 10, and 12. The schools were stratified by public or private school and by estimated enrollment in the grade. Further, there was an attempt to obtain geographic region and socio-economic status representativeness. We are told in the *User's Handbook* that more schools were contacted than were needed because of anticipated non-responses. However, we are not told what proportion of the schools contacted actually participated in the norming. We are referred to an unavailable *Psychometric Handbook* for further information regarding the norming.

Raw scores on both the UNIACT and the Work-Related Experience Inventory are referenced to combined-sex norms. Because the items for the UNIACT were chosen based (in part) on their lack of differentiation between the sexes, combined-sex norms give approximately the same information as would separate sex norms. Of course, one could question the wisdom of intentionally not choosing items that show different answer patterns for the two sexes. The basic reason given for such an inventory construction process is that "sex differences in the responses to many interest items may reflect the differential effects of sex-role socialization on males and females without necessarily reflecting differences in basic interests" (Prediger and Hanson, 1978, p. 89). The rationale for the combined sex norms for the Work-Related Experience Inventory is that the work-related experiences of males and females differ markedly and that, "given the purpose of the experience inventory. . . . these differences should be reflected in the scores" (ACT *User's Handbook*, 1984, p. 11). Both rationales are subject to debate.

Because only two scales are reported from the UNIACT, the norms themselves are not presented in the *User's Handbook* or the guidebook for the students.

Rather, the two scores are plotted on a grid. The Data/Ideas Scale and Things/People Scale are placed on the vertical and horizontal margins and lines are drawn across and down the grid. The intersection lies in one of 12 regions. This placement gets translated to the comparable region on the World-of-Work Region Chart. The *User's Handbook* informs us that if we wish to translate UNIACT raw scores into standard scores and percentile ranks we can refer to the (nonexistent) *Psychometric Handbook*.

The Work-Related Experience Inventory scores are reported by three broad categories—upper quarter, middle half, and lower quarter. It is suggested, and I agree, that this broad categorization is adequate for the exploratory functions served by the Work-Related Experience Inventory

RELIABILITY AND VALIDITY

An *Interim Psychometric Handbook* reports internal consistency estimates of the reliability of the six UNIACT Holland scales that range from 0.80 to 0.93. No internal consistency data are available on the Data/Items Scale or the Things/People Scale. Three-week stability coefficients are available for high school seniors. For the six separate scales these range from 0.77 to 0.89. For the Data/Ideas scale the stability coefficient is 0.87 and for the Things/People Scale it is 0.82.

A draft revision of the *Interim Psychometric Handbook* reports internal consistency estimates of reliability of the four Work-Related Experience Scales ranging from 0.68 (grade 10, Ideas) to 0.87 (grade 12, Things). An *ACT Informal Report* (dated 10/86) states that over a three week period 85% of the ninth graders and 60% of the 11th graders selected the same skill area at initial testing and at retest.

For job values, three-week stability indices show test-retest correspondence rates ranging from 0.47 to 0.90 (median = 0.85) for grade 9, and from 0.64 to 0.92 (median = 0.85) for grade 11. Work-related experiences stability estimates ranged from 0.81 to 0.92 for grade 9 students and from 0.86 to 0.93 for grade 11 students. While I am reasonably satisfied with the reliability data presented, it is certainly a shame that the data were not obtained before October of 1986.

The *Technical Report* for the UNIACT (1981) provides a fair amount of evidence on the validity of the UNIACT. However, because only 60 of the 90 items and two of the eight scales are typically used in the VIESA, those data are of limited relevance. There are basically no validity data reported for VIESA. VIESA itself is described as a teaching module as well as a measurement tool. It supposedly promotes self-knowledge, teaches key concepts about the world of work, and encourages further career exploration. I suspect it does that, but it would be nice to have some evidence.

USABILITY

The *User's Handbook* provides fairly extensive information regarding how to administer, interpret and use the VIESA. As stated in the handbook, anyone preparing to use VIESA should be familiar with the *User's Handbook*.

SUMMARY

For the most part, VIESA is a well designed teaching module. It incorporates the use of the UNIACT for which there are reasonable reliability and validity data. It is unfortunate that some of the reliability data on the other component parts of the VIESA were not available earlier. It is also unfortunate that there are basically no validity data available for any component except the UNIACT. In spite of the lack of appropriate data, I believe the VIESA is likely a useful instrument. Students do need catalysts for career and self exploration. The VIESA is likely a good catalyst.

REFERENCES

ACT. (1986, Oct). *VIESA Test-retest data for work-related skills, job values, and work-related experience*. ACT Informal Report. Iowa City, Iowa: The American College Testing Program.

ACT. (1985). *Interim Psychometric Handbook for the 3rd edition ACT Career Planning Program*. Iowa City, Iowa: The American College Testing Program.

ACT (1984). *User's Handbook: Revised Second Edition*. Iowa City, Iowa: The American College Testing Program.

ACT. (1981). *Technical Report for the Unisex Edition of the ACT Interest Inventory (UNIACT)*. Iowa City, Iowa: The American College Testing Program.

Prediger, D. J. & Hanson, G. R. (1978). Must interest inventories provide males and females with divergent vocational guidance? *Measurement and Evaluation in Guidance*, 11, 88–98.

Vocational Interest Inventory (VII)

Patricia W. Lunneborg

Western Psychological Services
12031 Wilshire Blvd., Los Angeles, CA 90025

Target Population: High school students and college freshmen.

Statement of the Purpose of the Instrument: Measures student's relative interest in 8 occupational areas—to help student isolate his or her strongest interests and relate them to specific education programs and occupations. Based on Anne Roe's *Psychology of Occupations*.

Titles of Subtests, Scales, Scores Provided: Service, Outdoor, Business Contact, Science; Organization, General Culture; Technical, Arts and Entertainment.

Forms and Levels Available, with Dates of Publication/Revision of Each: One form with 112 forced-choice items, 1981.

Date of Most Recent Edition of Test Manual, User's Guide, Etc.: 1981.

Languages in Which Available: English only.

Time: Actual Test Time—20 minutes.
   Total Administration Time—20 minutes.

Norm Group(s) on Which Scores Are Based: VII scores are based on longitudinal research tracking thousands of high school students through college. VII scores are compared to those of former students, who took the VII as high school juniors or seniors, then went on to successfully complete specific college degrees.

Manner in Which Results Are Reported for Individuals
   Types of Scores: Raw scores and percentile equivalents.
   Report Format/Content
      Basic Service: Complete interpretive analysis, including both a Profile of Scores and a College Major Profile. Also, 8-page Guide to Interpretation.

Report Format Content for Group Summaries: Not available.

Scoring
   Machine Scoring Service
      Cost of basic service per counselee: As little as $3.80 per student.
      Time required for scoring and returning (maximum): 8-hour turnaround.
   Hand Scoring: Not available.
   Local Machine Scoring
      Provisions/conditions/equipment required: VII microcomputer diskette for IBM PC, XT, or AT and compatibles.

Computer Software Options Available: on-line; scoring; interpretation.

Cost of Materials
  Specimen Set: Manual functions as specimen set. 1 Manual, $24.50; 2 or more $21.75 each.
  Counselee Materials: Computer scored Answer Sheet

Published Reviews
Hanson, J. (1985). Review of the Vocational Interest Inventory. In James V. Mitchell, Jr. (Ed.), *Ninth Mental Measurements Yearbook, Volume II* (pp. 1677–78). Lincoln, Nebraska: The Buros Institute of Mental Measurements.
Johnson, R. W. (1985). Review of the Vocational Interest Inventory. In James V. Mitchell, Jr. (Ed.), *Ninth Mental Measurements Yearbook, Volume II* (pp 1678–79). Lincoln, Nebraska: The Buros Institute of Mental Measurements.

Reviewed By

John D. Krumboltz
Professor of Education and Psychology
Stanford University

The following is a transcript of a fictitious interview between a curious high school junior (S) and a well trained career counselor (C), who has spent hours studying the *Manual for the Vocational Interest Inventory* (Lunneborg, 1981).

A COUNSELING SCENARIO

S: Hello. I took the *Vocational Interest Inventory (VII)* a few weeks ago, and I am wondering if you would explain the results to me.

C: Certainly. I have the results of your VII right here. What is it that you would like to know?

S: The names of some occupations where the people working in them have interests similar to mine.

C: I'm sorry, there is no validity data of that type here in the VII manual.

S: Oh, that's strange. I thought that something entitled *Vocational Interest Inventory* would give me some information about vocational interests. What is it good for?

C: I could make a stab at trying to predict what you're going to major in when you go to college.

S: I'm not even sure I'm going to college, but okay, tell me what you think I'm going to major in.

C: Before I do that, I will need to have your factor scores on each of three dimensions.

S: No factor scores are reported here in my printout.

C: Yes, I know, but there are some difference scores that correlate quite well with the factor scores.

S: Okay then, use the difference scores.

C: I really can't use the difference scores because I don't have any formula available to combine them.

S: Then you really can't make a prediction because you have neither my factor scores nor a formula for combining them.

C: That's true, but if I did, I could make a prediction about which of 11 possible groups of college majors you would eventually choose.

S: You mean these 11 majors listed here in Table 18?

C: Yes, that's right.

S: But I don't see any of the common majors that I might be interested in, like English, mathematics, chemistry, physics . . .

C: That's because a number of majors were combined to form categories like "Humanities" and "Health Professions."

S: Then if you did have the necessary information you could at least tell me with high accuracy which of these groups I would be likely to major in.

C: I think it's only fair to tell you that even if I had all the necessary information, my predictions would be wrong 77% of the time.

S: What? You would be wrong 77% of the time? What's the good of making predictions then?

C: I can do better in some majors. The very best I can do is for people who enter nursing, and then I am wrong only 53% of the time.

S: You're still wrong more than half the time with your very best predictions. What about your worst predictions?

C: I must confess that for people majoring in the humanities, I am wrong 98% of the time, and for those in biological science, I am wrong 97% of the time.

S: If that's the best you can do, what's the use of even taking this VII?

C: Well, on the average, I can predict somewhat better than random chance.

S: Predict my future major better than random chance? I could do that by myself. Why didn't you just give me a list of these eleven groups of college majors and ask me which one I'm going to major in? Why did I need to fill out a questionnaire with 112 questions?

C: Now, wait a minute. There is more validity information here in the manual. In Table 25 are some correlations between the unobtainable factor scores on your VII and the SCII Occupational Scales.

S: If I wanted to know what scores I would get on the *Strong-Campbell Interest Inventory*, why wouldn't I just take the *Strong-Campbell Interest Inventory*? I was hoping that this VII would be more reliable.

C: There is a section in the VII manual beginning on page 27 about reliability.

S: Oh, yes. Look at Table 7. There are some very high correlations, .85, .86, oh, and look, there's a .91 and another .91. Don't high correlation coefficients mean that the test is very good?

C: I'm afraid these are correlations of half the test with the total test.

S: Is that what is known as a split-half correlation coefficient?

C: Unfortunately not. These are part-whole correlation coefficients. A score from half the test is correlated with the score from the whole test.

S: But the score on part of the test makes up some of the score on the total test, so wouldn't that produce an artificially high correlation coefficient?

C: Yes, it would.

S: Isn't it misleading, then, to include those correlation coefficients under the heading of reliability?

C: It might be to a casual reader of the manual, but if you study the footnotes carefully and figure out what the abbreviations must mean, you can eventually deduce that the table consists of part-whole correlations, not conventional reliability coefficients.

S: At least there is some other evidence about reliability reported here for the 1975 version of the VII. Is that the form I took?

C: We can't be sure, but later on in the VII manual, there is an indication that you took another version that was prepared after 1978 and has benefited from several item analyses.

S: Then the reliability and validity of this new version must be better than the figures reported for the 1975 version here in the manual.

C: Not necessarily. The revisions were not undertaken for the purpose of increasing reliability or validity.

S: Why were they undertaken?

C: To reduce sex bias.

S: What's sex bias?

C: Sex bias here means that males and females on the average did not answer each item in the same way.

S: Well, males are interested in different things than females.

C: That's true on the average, but strenuous efforts have been made here to eliminate any item that was answered differently by males than by females.

S: Wouldn't it be important to include items that are related to future vocations, even if some of them are favored more by one sex than the other?

C: Only if we were interested in maximizing the validity of the test for predicting vocational choice. However, there is an important social problem that needs our attention; namely, that males and females do not choose to go into the same occupations in the same proportions.

S: Shouldn't we be allowed to go into any occupation we want?

C: Sure, but there are not enough males who want to go into the arts, service, and cultural domains and not enough females who want to go into business, technical, and outdoor domains. There are some important people who think that the same percentage of each sex should go into each domain.

S: So a scientific measuring instrument is altered? Would they alter a thermometer if they didn't like the temperature? Isn't the notion of equal opportunity becoming confused with equal percentages?

C: I think the whole purpose of the VII is to promote equal opportunity by minimizing differences between the sexes.

S: Then the VII yields scores that do not discriminate between males and females?

C: Well, no. Despite the strenuous efforts, six out of eight subscales still do discriminate between the sexes.

S: Are there separate norms for males and females then?

C: No, mixed-sex norms are used. The author is hoping that future revisions will "bring the proportions of the sexes even closer together" (p. 50).

S: Do males show a greater interest in technical things than females?

C: Yes, on the Technical scale, males score about 1 standard deviation higher.

S: Then a female interested in technical things would earn a lower percentile in Technical with these mixed-sex norms than she would if she could compare her scores with females only?

C: Yes.

S: Wouldn't she tend to be discouraged from entering technical-type occupations because of these mixed-sex norms?

C: She might be.

S: I thought this VII was supposed to encourage more females to enter technical fields. Doesn't the use of mixed-sex norms actually defeat the goal of encouraging people to consider nontraditional occupations?

C: Students receive individual statements urging males to look into service, culture, and arts and females into business, technical and outdoor if they have scores at or above the 50th percentile.

S: So the VII does treat males and females differently?

C: Yes, for the present, "the VII *must* call attention to sex in its interpretative materials" (p. 50).

S: I find this computerized printout that compares my scores to the scores of people in different college majors to be quite confusing.

C: What seems to be the trouble?

S: I have scores on four dimensions, and each one seems to recommend a different major. Which one should I pay attention to?

C: I found that confusing, too. Your scores on each dimension are derived by subtracting one interest score from another.

S: On the Organization-Outdoor dimension, I appear very high on the organization end, higher even than political science and economics majors.

C: Don't you have a strong interest in organization?

S: No, look, I'm only at the 34th percentile, but since I'm lower still on the outdoor end (12th percentile), the difference between them is large.

C: There is a discussion of this problem in the VII manual, but I'm afraid there is nothing in the guide to interpretation nor on your computer printout to clarify the confusion. We are advised by the manual to call your attention to the dimensions on which you have high interests.

S: Hey, look at Table 10. Am I reading this right? Only 15/100 of 1% of students whose highest score was in business actually intend to choose business as their vocation.

C: Oops. I think there is a mistake here and in several other tables, too. Those numbers must be proportions, not percentages as the title indicates.

S: Even so, only 15% of the students whose highest score was business intend to go into a business career. It doesn't sound to me as if the scores people get on the test correspond very well with what they say they want to do.

C: It is true that in seven out of eight of the interest areas, the majority of people intend to go into some vocation unrelated to their highest score.

S: I'd like your frank evaluation of this VII. Is it a good inventory?

C: Good for what purpose?

CONCLUDING REMARKS

As a method for stimulating thoughtful discussion of career alternatives, the VII's list of questions might be as good as any other. However, it is not empirically keyed to various occupations. The primary criterion for predictive validity has been college majors, and the VII does a poor job of predicting this somewhat irrelevant criterion. Data are presented showing the concurrent correlation coefficients of the unobtainable factor scores with the Occupational Scales of the *Strong-Campbell Interest Inventory*. But since the *Strong-Campbell Interest Inventory* is identified only by its acronym, an uninformed reader of the manual might be led to think that the VII has been validated against membership in actual occupations. The first table under the heading of reliability contains artifactually inflated part-whole correlations. The Profile of Scores, where each

141

student's percentile scores on eight scales are summarized, seems straightforward and easy to interpret. However, when the scales are reorganized into "dimensions" and each person's scores are plotted in relation to the average scores of students in some college major categories, strange distortions occur. The results could be extremely misleading, even to sophisticated test interpreters.

There is no method for combining scores to identify a most likely college major, let alone potential occupations. Virtually all the research has been in the state of Washington, so students attempting to generalize about college majors in other states would be taking an unknown risk. The same norms are used for both males and females, even though the evidence indicates significant differences between the sexes on six of the eight scales. However, if it were important for political purposes to choose an interest inventory that gave the outward appearance of having no "sex bias," the VII might be an attractive candidate. Frankly, I would prefer to use some other interest inventory.

NOTE: Significant portions of this review were abridged from the author's original review in *Measurement and Evaluation in Counseling and Development*, 1985, *18* (1), 38–41 with permission of AACD.

Measures of Work Values

Minnesota Importance Questionnaire (MIQ)

David J. Weiss, René V. Dawis and Lloyd H. Lofquist

Vocational Psychology Research
University of Minnesota, N620 Elliot Hall
75 East River Road, Minneapolis, MN 55455

Target Population: Adults and high school students, ages 16 and above, of both sexes. Reading level is approximately grade 5.

Statement of the Purpose of the Instrument: The MIQ is designed to measure twenty (or 21) psychological needs (and their six underlying values) found relevant to work satisfaction. The MIQ permits comparison of individual needs with measured reinforcers or benchmark occupations representative of the major fields and levels of the work world. Need-reinforcer correspondence allows the prediction of job satisfaction.

Titles of Subjects, Scales, Scores Provided: Needs: Ability Utilization, Achievement, Activity, Advancement, Authority, Company Policies and Practices, Compensation, Co-workers, Creativity, Independence, Moral Values, Recognition, Responsibility, Security, Social Service, Social Status, Supervision-Human Relations, Supervision-Technical, Variety, Working Conditions. Values: Achievement, Altruism, Autonomy, Comfort, Safety, Status Validity: Logically Consistent Triads.

Forms and Levels Available, with Dates of Publication/Revision of Each: Paired form—1975; Spanish edition also available; Ranked form (1975).

Date of Most Recent Edition of Test Manual, User's Guide, Etc.: User's manual was published in 1981; Counseling use of the MIQ (1975); Manual for the Minnesota Importance Questionnaire (1971).

Languages in Which Available: Paired form available in Spanish and English; Ranked form available only in English.

Time: Actual Test Time—Paired: 30–40 minutes; Ranked: 15–25 minutes.
   Total Administration Time—same.

Norm Group(s) on Which Scores Are Based: Occupational correspondence scores are based on occupational reinforcer ratings from employees and supervisors in 185 occupations representative of the world of work.

Manner in Which Results Are Reported for Individuals
   Types of Scores: Need and value scores are intra-individual adjusted z-scores.
   Report Format/Content
      Basic Service: Two-page computer profile. Page 1 represents need and value score graph. Page

144

2 reports individual's need correspondence with reinforcer patterns of 90 benchmark occupations.

Options: MIQ Extended Report is same format as standard report but provides report of individual's need correspondence with reinforcer patterns for 185 occupations.

Report Format/Content For Group Summaries: Not available.

Scoring

Machine Scoring Service

Cost of basic service per counselee: $3.00. All costs subject to change without notice.

Cost of options: Report plus duplicate copy: $3.15; Extended report: $3.25; Extended report plus duplicate copy: $3.45.

Time required for scoring and returning: (maximum) In-house turnaround is one work day.

Hand Scoring: Not available.

Local Machine Scoring: Not available.

Computer Software Options Available: Not available. On-line administration and interpretation planned for 1987.

Cost of Materials

Specimen Set: $11.00.

Counselee Materials: Test booklets (reusable) $.70 each 10 to 99 copies; $.67 each 100 to 249; $.64 each 250 or more. Answer sheets (not reusable) $.12 each; MIQ manual: $8.50; *Occupational Reinforcer Patterns* $20.00 each.

Additional Comments of Interest to Users: The 1981 MIQ profile features the addition of 6 value scales, and the revised correspondence report includes additional occupations and an improved correspondence index.

Published Reviews

Albright, L. E. (1982). Minnesota Importance Questionnaire. In J. T. Kapes & M. M. Mastie (Eds.), *A Counselor's Guide to Vocational Guidance Instruments* (pp. 77–80). Falls Church, VA: National Vocational Guidance Association.

Albright, L. E. (1978). Review of the Minnesota Importance Questionnaire. In O. K. Buros (Ed.), *Eighth Mental Measurements Yearbook*: Volume II (p. 1671). Highland Park, NJ: Gryphon Press.

Benson, P. (1984). Review of the Minnesota Importance Questionnaire. In D. J. Keyser & R. C. Sweetland (Eds.), *Test Critiques*: Volume II (pp. 481–490). Kansas City, MO: Test Corporation of America.

Zedek, S. (1978). Review of the Minnesota Importance Questionnaire. In O. K. Buros (Ed.), *Eighth Mental Measurements Yearbook*: Volume II (p. 1671). Highland Park, NJ: Gryphon Press.

Reviewed By

Philip G. Benson
Assistant Professor of Management
College of Business Administration & Economics
New Mexico State University

The Minnesota Importance Questionnaire (MIQ) was developed to measure an individual's vocational needs and values. Essentially, the authors of the MIQ suggest that adjustment to work involves satisfactoriness (i.e., the ability of the worker to perform the job adequately) and satisfaction (i.e., the worker's feeling of reward resulting from job performance). Within this framework, the MIQ measures those aspects of work that are especially salient reinforcers for an individual. A matching of such needs with the reinforcers found in an occupation results in a better match of worker and job.

The MIQ can be used in either of two forms utilizing a paired comparison format or a ranked form. The paired form requires the examinee to indicate which of two job characteristics is more important to him or her in an idealized job. Because the MIQ measures twenty characteristics of jobs, the paired form requires that 190 such pairs be evaluated. The ranked form consists of 21 groups of five work value statements; each group ("item") requires the test taker to rank order the importance of the five values included. In either format, the MIQ measures 20 different aspects of work. Through factor analyses, these have been grouped into six underlying dimensions or values.

The MIQ report, which can be provided by Vocational Psychology Research, avoids the difficulty of hand scoring the MIQ. In addition, various potentially useful types of information are provided. The 20 scales are grouped into their corresponding values, and scores (range of -1.0 to $+3.0$) are given for each. While technically it is possible for scores to range from -4.0 to $+4.0$, the range used will include the vast majority of scores in practice. Scores outside the report range are noted.

In addition, the report has a visual profile of the relative scores for each examinee. This profile is also used to match each person to a number of benchmark occupations, based on profile similarity of the examinee and the reinforcers generally available in the occupation. Finally, the satisfaction of the examinee for each of the benchmark occupations is predicted as "Satisfied," "Likely Satisfied," or "Not Satisfied." It is likely that counselors will find these comparisons to benchmark occupations extremely useful in career counseling.

The MIQ is untimed and self-administered, which requires a minimum of input from the examiner. Typically, the paired form requires 30–40 minutes to complete in contrast to approximately 20 minutes for the ranked form. For either form of the MIQ, test booklets are reusable. Machine scoring, available from the publisher, is not mandatory but is recommended as hand scoring is extremely time consuming. Machine scoring also results in the formal report described earlier, which most users will find very helpful.

POTENTIAL USES

According to the manual (Rounds, Henly, Dawis, Lofquist, & Weiss, 1981), the MIQ can be used to advantage in three areas; these areas include vocational counseling, career planning, and job placement. As a counseling tool, the MIQ can help an individual identify his or her particularly salient psychological needs as manifested in work settings. By matching work environments with such needs greater satisfaction should result for the counselee.

In career planning, the MIQ can identify the types of occupations that have reinforcer systems especially congruent with the examinee's needs. This is done largely by comparing the individual's need profile with the reinforcers typically found in selected occupations. These Occupational Reinforcer Patterns (ORPs) have been described for 148 benchmark occupations (Borgen, Weiss, Tinsley,

Dawis, & Lofquist, 1972; Rosen, Hendel, Weiss, Dawis, & Lofquist, 1972), and additional ORPs are reportedly being developed.

As a job placement test, the MIQ is recommended as a means of maintaining employees' job satisfaction. It is suggested (Rounds et al., 1981, p. 3) that this should maximize productivity and minimize turnover, absenteeism, tardiness, accidents, and injuries.

It is likely that the clearest applications of the MIQ are to be found in vocational psychology and rehabilitation, especially in counseling individuals regarding their future work plans. The test could be used with individuals who are entering the workplace for the first time (i.e., new high school graduates) or with individuals who are, of necessity or choice, changing careers/occupations later in life (e.g., the vocationally disabled). Other applications and research uses are likely found in such diverse fields as industrial/organizational psychology, industrial sociology, industrial relations, and business management.

RELIABILITY AND VALIDITY

The clearest single review of MIQ reliability and validity studies can be found in the technical manual (Gay, Weiss, Hendel, Dawis, & Lofquist, 1971). Reliability data are presented in terms of the internal consistency of scales, the temporal stability of scales, and the temporal stability of profiles. In all three areas, the reported reliabilities seem to be acceptably high, although information is lacking on the level for each specific scale. Across 20 scales in nine samples (sample sizes ranged from 27 to 283, with a median size of 73), median internal consistency reliabilities are approximately .80 (range of median reliabilities was .77 to .81). However, these median reliabilities fail to address the internal consistency of each individual scale.

Median test-retest reliabilities are reported as ranging from .48 to .89 with the higher values corresponding to immediate retests. The longest two time frames considered, nine months and ten months, had a median reliability of .49 and .53, respectively. Again, these data do not clearly establish the reliability of each individual scale score.

Median values for profile stability are reported as ranging from .70 to .95. Such profile stabilities indicate that the general pattern (profile) of scores tends to be more reliable than individual scale scores, and are important for the use of the MIQ in counseling. Essentially, this suggests that profiles may be more useful in interpretation of MIQ results than are individual scale scores. Overall, reliability seems adequate based on any of the reported approaches to its assessment. However, greater attention to the reliability of each scale score would be helpful.

One advantage to the use of a paired comparison format is that it allows reliability to be assessed in terms of triadic inconsistency. In theory, if a respondent makes statements across pairs, and those responses are logically inconsistent, the reliability of the test can be questioned. For example, if I prefer one work value statement (A) over another (B), prefer the second (B) over a third (C), but prefer the third (C) over the first (A), my responses can be questioned. The paired form of the MIQ uses a count of such triadic inconsistency to invalidate tests which are suspect. In addition, data suggest that such a procedure is warranted.

The technical manual (Gay et al., 1971) summarizes the validity data for the MIQ in three ways. First, structural validity (i.e, content and discriminant validity) is reported through use of factor-analytic data. These data suggest that the MIQ subscales are sufficiently distinct to be treated as separate dimensions.

In addition, a number of validity studies are reported for the MIQ. While these emphasize concurrent validation designs, in general validity of the MIQ is again supported. All 20 scales of the MIQ have been shown to statistically discriminate among nine occupational groups (group sizes ranged from 71 to 1897, median of 285). Thus, there are differences in MIQ profiles among different occupational groups, and these tend to be consistent with theory.

Finally, an early form of the MIQ has shown group differentiation among various occupational groupings, between disabled and non-disabled workers, and between white collar workers and pre-employment college students. In each case observed differences are consistent with theoretical predictions. While these data do not reflect directly on the present form of the MIQ, it does suggest that the items and constructs are likely related to meaningful groupings of workers.

Considering all of the results summarized by Gay et al. (1971), it is reasonable to conclude that the MIQ is at least reasonably valid in appropriate applications. Other, more recent studies also support the validity of the MIQ (Elizur & Tziner, 1977; Stulman & Dawis, 1976). After several decades of systematic research, the MIQ has been shown to have reasonable empirical support.

CAUTIONS IN USE

While the MIQ is generally a commendable effort, a few cautions should be raised for potential users. First, it is not clear that ORPs are as strongly related to occupational groupings as the MIQ manuals would have one believe. Most ORPs are based on a minimum of 20 responses by supervisors and/or job incumbents, and a large proportion use fewer than 50 raters. As an index of an entire occupational grouping, it is not clear that such small samples are adequate. In addition, for some scales it is likely that organizational variations can lead to wide divergence within an occupation. Published ORPs should be used with some care.

It is also likely that ORPs will change over time. For example, the published ORP for a Certified Public Accountant is based on an all-male sample of raters, but many women have entered this profession in recent years. Caution in interpretation is again recommended.

While either form of the MIQ can be used, many counselors will find that 190 pairs require excessive time in administration. Unless the paired form is specifically needed, most users may well want to use the shorter, ranked form.

A major shortcoming of the MIQ is the relatively old technical manual. The MIQ has been heavily researched, and the theory which it supports has undergone revision since the manual was published in 1971. It would be helpful if the technical manual could be appropriately updated.

In spite of such potential criticisms, the MIQ is overall a very good measure of work needs and values. Given appropriate professional attention, its use is recommended.

REFERENCES

Borgen, F. H., Weiss, D. J., Tinsley, H. E. A., Dawis, R. V., & Lofquist, L. H. (1972). *Occupational Reinforcer Patterns*: I. Minneapolis, MN: Vocational Psychology Research, University of Minnesota.

Dawis, R. V., & Lofquist, L. H. (1984). *A psychological theory of work adjustment: An individual-differences model and its applications*. Minneapolis, MN: University of Minnesota Press.

Elizur, D., & Tziner, A. (1977). Vocational needs, job rewards, and satisfaction: A canonical analysis. *Journal of Vocational Behavior*, *10*, 205–211.

Gay, E. G., Weiss, D. J., Hendel, D. D., Dawis, R. V., & Lofquist, L. H. (1971). *Manual for the Minnesota Importance Questionnaire*. Minneapolis, MN: Minnesota Studies in Vocational Rehabilitation.

Rosen, S. D., Hendel, D. D., Weiss, D. J., Dawis, R. V., & Lofquist, L. H. (1972). *Occupational Reinforcer Patterns:* II. Minneapolis, MN: Vocational Psychology Research, University of Minnesota.

Rounds, J. B., Jr., Henly, G. A., Dawis, R. V., Lofquist, L. H., & Weiss, D. J. (1981). *Manual for the Minnesota Importance Questionnaire: A measure of vocational needs and values*. Minneapolis, MN: Vocational Psychology Research, University of Minnesota.

Stulman, D. A., & Dawis, R. V. (1976). Experimental validation of two MIQ scales. *Journal of Vocational Behavior*, *9*, 161–167.

NOTE: Significant portions of this review were abridged from the author's original review in Volume II of *Test Critiques* with permission of Test Corporation of America.

Salience Inventory (SI)

Dorothy D. Nevill and Donald E. Super

Consulting Psychologists Press
577 College Avenue, Palo Alto, CA 94306

Target Population: Teen and adult, grades 9 and up.

Statement of the Purpose of the Instrument: The SI is designed to fill a gap in the array of tools of career development researchers and practitioners. It was designed to assess the relative importance of five major life roles in individuals and cultures. In order to understand a person's readiness to make career decisions, one needs to know the relative importance that he or she attaches to study, work, homemaking, leisure, and community service. In order to interpret scores on a vocational interest inventory, one must know how important work is to the student or adult, as well as the nature and degree of exposure to work and occupations. Similarly, in educational, leisure, and marital counseling the relative importance of the role in question is an essential bit of information. The SI quickly and objectively provides this information.

Titles of Subtests, Scales, Scores Provided: Scales include scores for study, work, community, home, and leisure for each of three areas: participation, commitment and value expectations.

Forms and Levels Available, with Dates of Publication/Revision of Each: There is only one form of the U.S. version of the Salience Inventory, published in 1985.

Date of Most Recent Edition of Test Manual, User's Guide, Etc.: Manual for the Salience Inventory (1986).

Languages in Which Available: Different forms of the SI have been translated from the English language version by researchers participating in the international Work Importance Study. These translations include: Polish, Portuguese, Italian, and Hebrew. Other countries which have translated the SI include: Yugoslavia, Czechoslovakia, and India. Canadian and Australian versions are available as well.

Time: Actual Test Time—30 to 45 minutes.
      Total Administration Time—Same

Norm Group(s) on Which Scores Are Based: In its development the SI was administered to 2000 youth and adults in the United States. Current normative samples for the United States include high school (N = 574), college (N = 776), and adult (N = 379). It should be noted that currently a full scale national sample is being tested. Data on this national sampling will be available in the near future.

Manner in Which Results Are Reported for Individuals
  Types of Scores: Scores are reported as raw scores on the current profile; however, normative data are published in the manual. Computerized scoring yields a percentile score for both males and females.

150

Report Format/Content

Basic service: The SI is easily handscored when the number of profiles is small. Otherwise, automated scoring services are available from the publisher. A one-page profile which reports the scores for each of the 15 scales is the outcome for either method.

Report Format/Content for Group Summaries
Basic service: NA
Options: Summary statistics (mean and standard deviations of scale scores) and data files on IBM PC floppy diskette are available. Cost: $25.00.

Scoring
 Machine scoring service
   Cost of basic servie per counselee: $3.00 to $4.50.
   Time required for scoring and returning (maximum): 24–48 hours.
 Hand scoring: Keys not necessary, and easily handscored for small number of profiles.

 Local machine scoring service: Not available.

Computer Software Options Available: Not available.

Cost of Material
 Specimen set: $11.00. **Counselee Materials:** Test booklets (reusable): $16.50/25 booklets; Answer sheets: $14.50/50 sheets; Profiles: $10.50/50 sheets.

Additional Comments of Interest to Users: Inventory was developed out of the Work Importance Study, an international consortium of vocational psychologists led by Dr. Donald E. Super. Especially useful in cross-cultural setting.

Published Reviews
 None, new instrument.

Reviewed By

Donald G. Zytowski
Counseling Psychologist, Student Counseling Service
Professor, Department of Psychology
Iowa State University

Practicing career counselors know what many career theorists do not: that people vary widely in their attraction to the idea of working. Only Donald Super (1980) has taken cognizance of this possibility in his concept of the life-career rainbow. This concept specifies that there are a number of life roles in addition to that of worker, and that they occupy different degrees of importance as people progress through their lives.

Super and his colleague, Dorothy Nevill, have made the life career rainbow manifest in their new Salience Inventory (SI). In brief, the SI purports to measure participation, commitment, and value expectations for five roles: Studying, Working, Community Service, Home and Family, and Leisure, all of which are assumed to be important in understanding a person's readiness to make career decisions and plans.

The instrument is a product of Super's Work Importance Study, and is the first psychological assessment, to my knowledge, to be developed in a multinational framework. The concepts and their verbal representations were reviewed by panels representing the different perspectives of agnostic, Catholic and Protestant nations, of Capitalist, Socialist, and Communist economies, and of developed and developing nations of North America, Europe, and Asia. It is said to be available in seven languages, although publication of the present edition is exclusively in English.

HOW DOES THE SI WORK?

Early in the inventory booklet, the five life roles are carefully described. It is crucial that the inventory taker understand them, for they are referred to throughout. Despite the multinational origin of the instrument, some of the descriptions seem steeped in U.S. and Western European concepts: Community Service names Scouts and Red Cross, political parties and trade unions, few or none of which exist in Communist countries.

The importance of each life role is assessed from three different perspectives, one behavioral and two affective. The behavioral component, Participation, is assessed by asking the inventory-taker to respond to ten items, such as accomplishing something in, talking to people about, or reading about each of the five life roles. One of the affective components, Commitment, contains ten items. This calls on the inventory-taker to respond to such items as the personal importance of, what they would be proud to do well in, or the admiration for people who are good at each of the life roles. The second affective approach is Value Expectations, which asks the inventory-taker to report the opportunity for each role to fulfill a list of 14 values, quite similar to those of Super's (1970) earlier instrument, The Work Values Inventory. A sampling of the value descriptions includes, "using all your skills and knowledge," "knowing that your efforts will show," "making life more beautiful" and the like. A short form of the SI omits the Commitment assessment.

The response format is a four-point Likert scale, varying from "never" or "rarely" for the behavioral component, and "little" or "none" for the affective components, through "almost always or always" and "a great deal."

The answer sheet is standard optical scan, with additional items to assess educational level, marital and employment status, field of employment, occupational level of father, mother, and spouse, and satisfaction with four of the five life roles. The manual does not remark on how the information from these additional items is to be used.

PSYCHOMETRICS

The manual is clearly marked "Research Edition," which signals that no norms are available. The implications of this lack, which the authors intend to remedy, are discussed below.

Means and standard deviations for each of the 15 scales (five roles by three perspectives) are reported for groups of American, Canadian, and Yugoslavian high school and college students, and adults, and Portuguese high school students, separately by sex. One can observe many interesting national, age, and gender-related differences supporting the use of the SI in crosscultural research. The scales show good internal consistency coefficients, all in the .80s or .90s, and an intercorrelation matrix appears as it should, except that the Participation and Commitment measures are not as independent as the authors expected they would be.

The SI has some problems with stability. Ten of the 15 test-retest correlations are less than .70 (interval not given). Value expectations are the least stable, with a median r of .58 in a range from .37 to .67. Despite mounting a study to uncover the reason for this, the authors are at a loss to explain it.

USES

Several applications of the SI are suggested in the manual. These include; tracking developmental changes in the status of life roles, uncovering occupational and cultural differences, studying role conflict, and surveying the impact of education on the valuation of differing roles.

Irrespective of the labeling of the SI as a research edition, a substantial discussion of the counseling use of the instrument is given, using raw scores. Such use requires ipsative interpretation, or intra-individual comparisons, on the order of "You seem to give more value to the work role than you do to the home and family role." The authors correctly state that such interpretations require the number of items in each scale and the scoring weights to be equal, which is the case for the SI. I would add that it also requires the mean item response popularities to be the same for each scale, or that they be equated by means of standard scores based on norms. Consider a high school male who has scored 25 on leisure participation and 20 on the study participation scale. One might assume that for this person leisure is more important than study, until it is realized, from the preliminary data reported in the manual, that the mean score for high school males on leisure is about 31, while the mean score for study is 20. Thus, this student is well below the mean on leisure, but at about average on study, quite a different state of affairs than the raw scores would seem to indicate.

Super (personal communication, November 10, 1986) argues that the implications for use are different: "Just as one interprets profiles taking the standard error of measurement into account for each variable, one should allow for overlap in the case of raw scores based on the same number of items." He expanded on this idea in his chapter in Zytowski (1973).

The manual describes how hand-scoring is done, and says that the publisher is prepared to do large-quantity machine scoring, but provides no information on how to obtain this service, nor describes the form in which machine scored results are reported.

SUMMARY

The SI is an attractive idea. At this time, though, I must say it is incompletely realized. It is quite correctly identified as a research edition, awaiting norms, and perhaps tapping one construct which is not inherently stable. I look forward to the SI when it is more fully flowered.

REFERENCES

Super, D. E., (1970). *Work Values Inventory*. Boston: Houghton-Mifflin.

Super, D. E., (1980). A life-span, life-space approach to career development. *Journal of Vocational Behavior*, *16*, 282–298.

Zytowski, D. G. (Ed.). (1973). *Contemporary approaches to interest measurement.* Minneapolis, MN: University of Minnesota Press.

Values Scale (VS)

Donald E. Super and Dorothy D. Nevill

Consulting Psychologists Press
577 College Avenue, Palo Alto, CA 94306

Target Population: Teen and adult, grades 8 and up.

Statement of the Purpose of the Instrument: Values are objectives that one seeks to attain in order to satisfy a need. The VS is designed to measure both intrinsic and extrinsic values, the former being inherent in the activities, the latter outcomes of the activity. The VS is an asset in individual counseling, group assessment, career-development workshops, needs surveys, and research with other variables such as interests, career maturity, sex, and socio-economic status.

Titles of Subtests, Scales, Scores Provided: Scales include Ability Utilization, Achievement, Advancement, Aesthetics, Altruism, Authority, Autonomy, Creativity, Economic Rewards, Life Style, Personal Development, Physical Activity, Prestige, Risk, Social Interaction, Social Relations, Variety, Working Conditions, Cultural Identity, Physical Prowess, and Economic Security.

Forms and Levels Available, with Dates of Publication/Revision of Each: There is only one form of the Values Scale, published in 1985.

Date of the Most Recent Edition of Test Manual, User's Guide, Etc.: Manual for the Values Scale (1986).

Languages in Which Available: Different forms of the VS have been translated from the English language version by researchers participating in the international Work Importance Study. These translations include: Polish, Portuguese, Italian, and Hebrew. Other countries which have translated the VS include: Yugoslavia, Czechoslovakia, and India. Canadian and Australian versions are available as well.

Time: Actual Test Time—30 to 45 minutes.
      Total Administration Time—Same.

Norm Group(s) on Which Scores Are Based: In its development the VS was administered to 3000 youths and adults in the United States. Current normative samples include high school (N = 199), college (N = 548) and adult (N = 396). It should be noted that currently a full scale national sample is being tested. Data on this national sampling will be available in the near future.

Manner in Which Results Are Reported for Individuals
    Types of Scores: Scores are reported as raw scores on the current profile; however, normative data are published in the manual. Computerized scoring yields a percentile score for both males and females.
    Report Format/Content
      Basic Service: The VS is easily handscored when the number of profiles is small. Otherwise,

155

automated scoring services are available from the publisher. A one-page profile which reports the scores for each of the 21 scales is the outcome for either method.

Report Format/Content for Group Summaries
  Options: Summary statistics (means and standard deviations of scale scores) and data files on IBM PC floppy diskette are available. Cost: $25.00.

Scoring
  Machine scoring service: Cost of basic service per counselee: $3.00 to $4.50.
    Cost of options: Not available.
    Time required for scoring and returning (maximum): 24–48 hours.
  Hand scoring: Keys not necessary, and easily handscored for small number of profiles.
  Local machine scoring service: Not available.

Computer Software Options Available: Not available.

Cost of Material
  Specimen set: $11.00.
  Counselee materials: Test booklets (reusable): $13.50/25 booklets; Answer sheets: $14.50/50 sheets; Profiles: $10.50/50 sheets.

Additional Comments of Interest to Users: Inventory was developed out of the Work Importance Study, an international consortium of vocational psychologists led by Dr. Donald E. Super. Especially useful in cross-cultural setting.

Published Reviews
  None, new instrument.

Reviewed By

Lenore W. Harmon
Professor of Educational Psychology
University of Illinois

The Values Scale (VS) is an instrument which was devised for use in the Work Importance Study (WIS), an international project spanning eight years and a dozen nations at the time of publication of this inventory. The purpose of the WIS was to gain crosscultural understanding of the relative importance of various life roles and the values that individuals attempt to fulfill through work and other life roles. The VS reviewed here is the United States version, which has some commonalities and some differences with the values measures used in other countries, but its crosscultural origin gives it some unique characteristics.

The WIS attempted to assess the full range of values, both work values and more general values, which influence people's behavior in different types of cultures. Values were defined by research teams from several countries. Sample items were written and preliminary analyses at the national level resulted in a reduction in the number of items as well as the number of scales. Each participating research team agreed to use five items to define each of the common

156

values with three of these being used in all cultures and selected by consensus after a review of the preliminary data. The additional two items were those that correlated most highly with the international items in the national data, providing that at least two items must tap work values and two must tap general values.

In addition to its crosscultural pedigree, the VS is firmly rooted in a developmental model of assessment for career counseling. This includes in addition to values, the assessment of work salience and career maturity. One of the major contributions of this model is that it points out that values can be realized in several life roles, not just in work roles. The model is beautifully spelled out in the second chapter of the manual. The fourth chapter contains an excellent case study which utilizes the model very faithfully and completely, illustrating the use of various assessment devices—not just the VS. These materials notwithstanding, the VS is published as a research instrument, and the authors place most emphasis on its use in research. They suggest that its use as a counseling aid may be "explored" but provide careful cautions about its shortcomings for individual assessment.

SCORES

Each of the twenty-one scales has five items scored on a four point scale. The score for a scale is the total points for the five items. The items are arranged on a machine scorable answer sheet in a way which makes it very easy to hand score the inventory. The manual contains instructions for hand scoring, although the publisher will score the inventory.

It is not totally clear from the manual how the scores should be treated. In the case study presented the total scores for each scale seem to have been divided by five to produce scale scores ranging from one to four. In the tables of means and standard deviations presented for high school students (N = 199), college students (N = 548) and adults (N = 396), the mean scores seem to be based on the total scores (undivided) with a range of 5–20. The authors point out that the scores are ipsative and that the proper comparison to make is among the scores for a given individual. Although means and standard deviations are given for the groups mentioned above as well as for several cross national groups, complete norms are not given. Data from more representative groups are currently being collected and norms will be forthcoming. In any case, there is enough information available now to compute a standard error of measurement for each scale, which would provide some guidance in interpreting score differences. My very rough estimate of the standard error for college students based on a median test-retest reliability of .72 and a median standard deviation of 2.9 is about 1.5. Thus, one would be able to interpret scores differing by 3 points on a scale ranging from four to 20 with some degree of confidence. Of course, many of the scales have higher reliabilities so the standard error would be smaller. The point to be made here is that this kind of information would be most helpful in interpreting intra-individual score differences.

Although the authors found no significant differences in the mean scores for males and females on any scale, they do insist that a knowledge of the sex of the respondent is necessary to scoring the inventory, for some unexplained reason.

RELIABILITY

Alpha coefficients, which measure scale homogeneity, range from .67 to .83 with a median of .78 for the high school group, from .65 to .87 with a median of .79 for the college group, and from .67 to .87 with a median of .77 for the adult group. Test-retest correlations are given for two college groups (N = 83 and 140). The respective ranges and medians are .52 to .82, median = .74, and .59 to .80, median = .72. Unfortunately, the retest interval is not specified. The manual cautions against interpreting the least reliable of these scales with too much assurance. Factor scales are being developed in an attempt to improve reliability.

VALIDITY

The care with which the items for the VS were developed and refined supports the content validity of the inventory. In suggesting research uses for the VS in chapter four, the authors present data on occupational differences, cultural differences, socialization, and life stage which support the construct validity of the VS. Additional support comes from the similarity of factor analyses conducted across age groups in the United States. No predictive validity data are available yet but follow-up studies are planned using some of the standardization samples.

CAUTIONS AND CONCLUSIONS

The authors indicate that the VS is ready only for "exploratory" use in counseling. The reviewer agrees, and suggests its use only by counselors who are willing to 1) consult the manual carefully to determine which scales are reliable enough for use with the groups with which they work, 2) calculate the standard errors of measurement for the scales, and 3) use the measure, as it was intended, as a part of a careful and complete plan for assessment of career development. One additional caution is that several of the scales seem to have a rather low "ceiling" for certain populations. Five or six of the 21 scales for each group (high school, college, adult) are negatively skewed. Thus, intra-individual comparisons might be even more difficult to accomplish among the high scores on an individual's profile.

The VS is a well developed and promising inventory up to this point. Much more work should be done before it can be used in any routine way in counseling. Currently it is suggested only for use by the most psychometrically sophisticated counselors. Those who are interested in career development will find it a very useful tool for research.

REFERENCES

Nevill, D. D. & Super, D. E., (1986). *The Values Scale: Theory, application, and research manual* (Research Edition). Palo Alto, California: Consulting Psychologists Press.

Super, D. E. & Nevill, D. D. (1986). *The Values Scale*. Palo Alto, California: Consulting Psychologists Press.

Career Development/
Maturity Instruments

Adult Career Concerns Inventory (ACCI)

Donald E. Super, Albert S. Thompson, Richard H. Lindeman, Roger A. Myers and Jean P. Jordaan

Consulting Psychologists Press
577 College Avenue, Palo Alto, CA 94306

Target Population: Adults (out of school or college, 18 or older), all occupational levels, literate (8th grade reading).

Statement of the Purpose of the Instrument: To help identify the vocational developmental tasks with which adults (young and old) are concerned, and to classify these by developmental stages (exploratory, establishment, maintenance and disengagement) or types or processes.

Titles of Subtests, Scales, Scores Provided: Stages: Exploration, Establishment, Maintenance, Disengagement. Substages: Crystallization, Specification, Implementation, Stabilizing, Consolidating, Advancing, Holding, Updating, Innovating, Decelerating, Retirement Planning, Retirement Living.

Forms and Levels Available, with Dates of Publication/Revision of Each: Adult form, 1985.

Date of Most Recent Edition of Test Manual, User's Guide, Etc.: 1987.

Languages in Which Available: English only.

Time: Actual Test Time—15 to 30 minutes.
  Total Administration Time—20 to 40 minutes.

Norm Group(s) on Which Scores Are Based: Various literate occupational groups, semi-skilled to professional/managerial; various cities and regions; samples of convenience (described). Norming now being completed (1987).

Manner in Which Results Are Reported for Individuals
  Types of Scores: Temporarily: ratings on a 5 pt. scale (Likert scores); manual provides percentiles.
  Report Format/Content
    Basic Service: (1) career stage and substage profile, (2) rosters of Likert scores and percentiles, (3) group reports.

Report Format/Content for Group Summaries
  Basic Service: Rosters of Likert scores and percentiles.

Scoring

Machine Scoring Service
   Cost of basic service per counselee: $3.50 each, or $2.75 each for 25 or more.
   Time required for scoring and returning (maximum): Typically 24 hours.
Hand Scoring
   Scored by: counselee; clerk; counselor
   Time required for scoring: 10 minutes or less.
Local Machine Scoring: Not available.

Computer Software Options Available: Not available.

Cost of Materials
Specimen Set: To be announced.
Counselee Materials: Manual—To be announced, Guide to ACCI—To be announced; Booklets
(with scoring profiles): Pkg. of 25 (reusable if not hand scored) $5.00 ($4.50 if 10 or more);
Answer sheets (not prepaid): Pkg. of 50—$13.50 ($12.50 if 10 or more).

Additional Comments of Interest to Users: Manual, Guide available Fall, 1987. Has been in
research and development use since 1973, in the Career Pattern Study, Work Importance Study,
etc., with several revisions. Used also in research in developmental assessment.

Published Reviews
None, new instrument.

Reviewed By

Edwin L. Herr
Professor of Education
Head of the Division of Counseling
and Educational Psychology and Career Studies
The Pennsylvania State University
and
Spencer G. Niles
Assistant Professor of Counselor Education
University of Virginia

During the last twenty years or so, the needs of adults for career guidance
and career counseling have become more visible, and the settings in which such
services are provided have expanded. However, the availability of measures of
career development in adults has lagged behind the expansion of other services
to them. Most current measures of career maturity either yield global scores or
have focused solely on the measurement of career maturity among adolescents.
In contrast, the Adult Career Concerns Inventory (ACCI) is a new instrument
designed to assess planfulness, one aspect of career adaptability in young and
in mature adults.

RATIONALE

Although career adaptability, the term Super believes is more appropriate than career maturity when applied to adults, is a multi-dimensional quality, several studies have found planfulness to be the most important group factor related to career maturity (Gribbons & Lohnes, 1968; Myers et al., 1971). Factor analysis of the ACCI shows that it assesses adult planning attitudes and planfulness. In assessing planfulness, the ACCI measures the degree of concern expressed in the major developmental tasks of an adult occupational career. These concerns are organized by type and by the substage at which they are most commonly encountered even though the available fact sheet about the inventory recognizes that many of the tasks are faced at more than one life stage as people cycle and recycle through their careers. As pointed out in the preliminary manual, the ACCI does not seek to assess factors such as information and use of resources due to the fact that these tend to vary across occupations, organizations, and communities (Super, Zelkowitz & Thompson, 1975).

DESCRIPTION

The ACCI was first developed in order to collect data in the final follow-up of the Career Pattern Study (Zelkowitz, 1974). The ACCI has since undergone several revisions. The current form consists of 61 items, five in each of the three substages of each of four career stages. An additional item is included in order to assess the individual's current career change status. The reading difficulty of the items is estimated to be at the eighth grade level.

Examinees are informed that the inventory consists of statements related to career concerns (e.g., "deciding what I want to do for a living," "advancing to a more responsible position," "having a good life in retirement"). Individuals are instructed to consider how strong each of these concerns is to them at this point in their career. The five response items range from No Concern to Great Concern. Most examinees can complete the ACCI in less than 30 minutes.

Scores are available both for stages and for substages. In addition to a total score for the Exploratory Stage, substage or task scores are possible for Crystallizing, Specifying, and Implementing a Vocational Preference. The Establishment Stage yields a total score, and scores for concern with Stabilizing, Consolidating, and Advancing. The Maintenance Stage score is broken into subscores, but they are considered to be methods of coping rather than successive substages: Holding One's Own, Updating and Innovating. The Disengagement Stage has both a total score and substage scores for Planning for Retirement, Retiring and Living in Retirement.

The ACCI is advertised as being a self-scored instrument. The scoring procedure yields scores which are recorded on a Career Concerns Chart and a Career Stage Profile. The Career Concerns Chart provides weighted sums and average scores for each substage. Total weighted sums and average scores are also provided for each life stage. Each of the four stage averages (i.e., Total Exploration, Total Establishment, Total Maintenance, and Total Disengagement) are then plotted on the Career Stage Profile in order to present a graphic summary of the career development tasks that are currently of most concern to the examinee. Scoring can be completed in 15 to 30 minutes.

While the instructions for scoring are relatively straightforward, additional information concerning profile analysis could be provided. Since self-scoring does not necessarily allow for accurate self-interpretation, the recommendation that examinees should discuss their results with a counselor could be more explicitly made.

RELIABILITY AND VALIDITY

The reliability of the research form of the ACCI was computed by two methods. Using the odd-even method of the split-half test of reliability, the reliability was found to be .93 after the application of the Spearman-Brown prophecy formula. Using the coefficient alpha measure of reliability a coefficient of .86 was obtained for the research form of the ACCI. More recent data provided in the dissertation of Mahoney (1986) revealed alpha coefficients at .90 for the ACCI. Super et al. (technical manual in process) have reported reliability coefficients in the .80s for substage scores of the inventory.

Validity data provide an indication of the degree to which an instrument measures what it purports to measure. At this point in time, one must proceed with a degree of caution in attempting to assess the validity of the current form of the ACCI. This caution is due to the fact that validity data in the preliminary manual of the ACCI are drawn from earlier forms of this instrument. (The updated manual is in process). The preliminary manual discusses the content validity, construct validity, and criterion-related validity of the ACCI.

Information in the manual indicates that the validation process of the preliminary forms of the ACCI involved numerous revisions and factor analyses resulting in items which clearly clustered under their appropriate stages and substages, thereby offering support for the content validity of the earlier forms of the ACCI.

The authors point out the difficulty in establishing the construct validity of the ACCI due to the fact that there was no established measure of career maturity for adults at the time that the ACCI was developed. Using subjects from the Career Pattern Study, the authors found that men who were administered the ACCI at the mid-career stage were more concerned with the tasks of the Establishment and Maintenance stages than with those of the Exploration and Decline stages. Additional studies which offer support for the construct validity of the ACCI are reported in the preliminary manual.

A recent study by Cron and Slocum (1986) lends support to the criterion-related validity of the ACCI. These researchers found that the ACCI was a useful measure in distinguishing between the job attitudes and the career stages of a sample of salespeople (e.g., salespeople in the Exploration stage were less involved in their jobs, did not feel that their job was challenging, and did not feel as successful as salespeople in other career stages). A study by Morrison (1977) found that managers between the ages of 37 and 55 and rated as non-adaptive appeared to be fixated at the Exploration stage or to be recycling through the Exploration stage according to their scores on the ACCI. Conversely, managers in the study who were rated as being adaptive had completed all of the tasks of the Exploration stage and many of the Establishment stage tasks according to their responses on the ACCI.

In summary, the evidence from the numerous studies referenced in the preliminary manual provides more than adequate support for the validity of the preliminary forms of the ACCI. It is expected that the updated manual will provide evidence which is just as convincing with regard to the validity of the current version of this instrument.

SUMMARY

The ACCI appears to be useful as a diagnostic and counseling instrument. The Career Stage Profile provides a clear graphic portrayal of the examinee's current career concerns. This information can be useful as counselors attempt to plan interventions aimed at increasing their client's planfulness as well as their readiness to make various career decisions. Since career development often does not proceed in a smooth linear progression through the developmental career stages, the ACCI can also be used to identify individuals who may be in the process of recycling through career stages and, therefore, in need of additional counseling assistance. As norms for various adult occupational groups become available, comparisons can be made among groups in order to more fully understand the various kinds of career problems and issues confronting specific groups of individuals.

By assessing the career adaptability or planfulness of adults, the ACCI fills a need that is not being met by other measures of career maturity. One concern is the lack of technical data for the current version of the ACCI. While this concern is lessened by the fact that the technical data from the preliminary manual are supportive of the reliability and validity of the earlier forms of this inventory, the technical manual soon to be published will be essential for researchers and counselors using the instrument.

REFERENCES

Cron, W. L., & Slocum, J. W., Jr., (1986). The influence of career stages on salespeople's job attitudes, work perceptions and performance. *Journal of Marketing Research, 23*, 119–129.

Gribbons, W. D., & Lohnes, P. R., (1968). *Emerging Careers.* New York: Teachers College Press.

Mahoney, D. (1986). An exploration of the construct validity of a measure of adult vocational maturity. Unpublished doctoral dissertation, Teachers College, Columbia University.

Morrison, R. F. (1977). Career adaptivity: The effective adaptation of managers to changing role demands. *Journal of Applied Psychology, 62*, 549–558.

Myers, R. A., Lindeman, R. H., Forrest, D. & Super, D. E. (1971). Preliminary report: Assessment of the first year of the use of the ECES in secondary schools of Genessee County, Michigan. New York: Teachers College, Columbia University.

Super, D. E., Thompson, A. S., Lindeman, R. H., Myers, R. A. & Jordan, J. P. (in process) Career Concerns Inventory: Technical manual.

Super, D. E., Zelkowitz, R. S., & Thompson, A. S. (1975). Career Development Inventory, Adult Form I: Preliminary manual for research and field trial. New York: Teacher's College, Columbia University.

Zelkowitz, R. S. (1974). The Construction and Validation of a Measure of Vocational Maturity for Adult Males. (Doctoral dissertation, Teachers College, Columbia University) Ann Arbor Michigan, University Microfilms, No. 75-18.

Assessment of Career Decision Making (ACDM)

V. A. Harren (Test); and
J. N. Buck & M. H. Daniels (Manual)

Western Psychological Services
12031 Wilshire Blvd., Los Angeles, CA 90025

Target Population: High school and college students.

Statement of the Purpose of the Instrument: To evaluate student's decision-making style and progress on three decision-making tasks (adjustment to school, selection of an occupation and of a major).

Titles of Subtests, Scales, Scores Provided: Decision-making Styles scales (Rational, Intuitive, Dependent); Decision-making Tasks (DMT): School Adjustment (Satisfaction with School, Involvement with Peers, Interaction with Instructors) DMT: Occupation Scale; DMT: Major Scale.

Forms and Levels Available, with Dates of Publication/Revision of Each: One form available; used with both high school and college students, although option not to administer DMT: Major Scale to HS students unless they intend to obtain postsecondary training.

Date of the Most Recent Edition of Test Manual, User's Guide, Etc.: 1985.

Languages in Which Available: English only.

Time: Actual Test Time—20 minutes.
Total Administration Time—same.

Norm Group(s) on Which Scores Are Based: High school and college students (includes community college sample). Separate norms by sex and grade at college level and where indicated in high school sample (see Manual, p.48).

Manner in Which Results Are Reported for Individuals
Types of Scores: Raw scores, T-scores, percentiles. Also evaluate significant differences between scores and pattern of Decision-making Styles scores.
Report Format/Content
  Basic Service: Fully interpretive computer report provided. Includes group summary and an individual report for the counselor and an individual report for the student.

Report Format/Content for Group Summaries
  Basic Service: Provides ID, age, sex, raw scores, and indicates whether any special validity considerations were identified. Identifies students who may be in need of either group or individual counseling.

Reviewed By

Dale J. Prediger
Vocational Research Psychologist
American College Testing Program

The Assessment of Career Decision Making (ACDM) is a 94-item self-report inventory intended for individual or group use with high school and college students. As a supplement to the preceding publisher's description, I wish to emphasize some unique assets of the ACDM. First, the ACDM follows Harren's model of career decision making (Harren, 1979), a model grounded in the work of Tiedeman and O'Hara (1963). Second, the ACDM combines measures of progress with career (educational and vocational) decision-making tasks with measures of decision-making styles. I know of no other serious efforts to assess career decision-making styles. Third, the ACDM assesses progress with school/college adjustment—a here-and-now, career-related task. Fourth, the ACDM explains the implications of scores in plain English via narrative reports for counselors and counselees. Furthermore, the companion 15-unit Career Planning Program provides an efficient group intervention for addressing needs revealed by the ACDM.

SCORES AND NORMS

The ACDM provides percentile ranks and standard scores for nine scales. Three scales (30 items) assess career decision-making styles (Rational, Intuitive, and Dependent); four scales (24 items) assess school/college adjustment (Satisfaction with School, Involvement with Peers, Interaction with Instructors, and School Adjustment—overall); and two scales (40 items) assess progress with career planning tasks. The first scale, Decision-Making Tasks: Occupation, measures "the degree of commitment and certainty the student feels towards his or her choice of a future occupation" (Buck & Daniels, 1985, p. 2). The second scale, Decision-Making Tasks: Major, has a similar purpose. It can be omitted for counselees not attending or considering college.

High school and college norms (550 and 2,495 students, respectively) are based on convenience samples, an approach to norming that is common among competing instruments (e.g., see Crites, 1973, 1978; Osipow, 1980; Thompson, Lindeman, Super, Jordaan, & Myers, 1981). Procedures for reporting normative standing were chosen to minimize gender differeneces. Differences across ethnic groups were reported as "generally small." Local norms can be developed from the "ACDM Group Summary," part of the standard scoring service.

INTERPRETIVE REPORTS

ACDM results for individuals are discussed in a multi-page "Counselor's Report" that is largely narrative in style. (Tables in the *ACDM Manual* list the score ranges that trigger interpretive phrases.) After a description of a counselee's standing on a particular scale, the narrative "goes into further detail regarding the particular pattern of responses that resulted in that score" (Buck & Daniels, 1985, p. 9). This unique feature, which is based on subsets of items within a given scale, enriches the description of ACDM results. However, the item subsets are not identified, and criteria for referencing one subset rather than another are not described. ACDM users could benefit from a discussion of the basis for the response pattern interpretations.

Another unique feature of the Counselor's Report is a section addressing score differences. Within the decision-making styles area, school/college adjustment area, and occupation/major area, the scores for pairs of scales are compared. Scores are cited as being different "only if the probability of the observed difference occurring by chance is less than 5%" (Buck & Daniels, 1975, p. 22). Also, the probability of obtaining a given score combination is reported via verbal categories. These procedures are certainly an improvement over reporting scores as if they were precise or "true." However, the *ACDM Manual* could be more explicit regarding how the probabilities are determined—e.g., how measurement error and scale intercorrelations are taken into account.

A third unique feature of the Counselor's Report is a two-page section titled "Analysis of Predominant Decision-Style Pattern." Research regarding decision-making styles supports four style patterns for the three ACDM Style Scales: high rational, high intuitive, high dependent, and high intuitive-dependent. A counselee's similarity to students with each of these four style patterns is reported in the form of a probability. Thus, statistics are used to enhance clinical profile interpretations.

The ACDM "Student's Report," intended for use in a "face-to-face meeting," is also largely narrative in style. A nine-scale percentile rank profile (similar to the profile in the Counselor's Report) is presented, and interpretations are provided for the style, adjustment, and occupation/major areas. As noted above, ACDM scores are based on counselee self-report. Hence, one may question the benefit in telling a counselee, "You are moderately satisfied with school." "You have not made an occupational choice." "You may feel a need to decide on a major" (e.g., see the sample Student Report in the *ACDM Manual*.) Counselors, of course, can benefit from such information in preparing for an interview or in screening a student for counseling. However, the chief value of the ACDM report for counselees appears to lie in the decision-making styles section. From this section, counselees learn about basic types of decision-making styles. In addition, self-reports of decision-making behaviors are organized and described in a way that may be both new and useful to many counselees.

RELIABILITY

Internal consistency reliability coefficients were obtained in two studies at the high school level and two studies at the college level. Across the nine scales, the coefficients ranged from .49 to .92, with a median of .72. Although coefficients in the low end of the range are discomforting, they are not unusual for instruments in this relatively new area of assessment (e.g., see Crites, 1978; Thompson et al., 1981). Standard errors of measurement are listed by grade and gender.

VALIDITY

It is ironic that the *ACDM Manual* appears to suffer from a plethora of validity-related studies. Although study results are organized by the usual topics (i.e., content validity, criterion-related validity, and construct validity), the variety of scales, samples, designs, and analyses makes the results difficult to assimilate. The manual authors, themselves, appear to get lost in the data at times. For example, in a study of the four School Adjustment Scales, corrections with eight "psychosocial adjustment measures" were obtained. The 32 correlations were cited as supporting the convergent and divergent validity of the scales (Buck & Deniels, 1985, p. 57). The correlations ranged from − .30 to .28, with a median of − .02. Although 10 of the 32 correlations were statistically significant, such results appear to indicate divergence, but not much convergence.

Harren's (1979) career decision-making model provides an alternative approach for gaining perspective on ACDM validity. The model suggests a number of hypotheses regarding relationships among ACDM scales, relationships with other scales, group differences, and intervention effects. ACDM validity data could be structured around key hypotheses. Marginally relevant and weak studies could be excluded or cited in an appendix. To the extent that the hypotheses are supported, both Harren's model and the ACDM would be supported.

Without such a structure, the overall impression provided by the mass of data presented in the *ACDM Manual* is one of relatively weak trends supporting ACDM validity. However, there are contradictions in the data. (There always are—hence, the need for structure to guide their interpretation.) There are also notable gaps—e.g., are the School Adjustment Scales related to drop-out and persistence, as purported?

168

CONCLUDING STATEMENT

Some very sophisticated thinking and research have gone into the ACDM. Most of its scales are unique among those currently available to practitioners. The ACDM narrative reports are innovative and appear to be useful for needs assessment and career counseling in high school and college settings. (The *ACDM Manual* cautions against use in other settings). Special concerns have already been noted.

Clearly, the ACDM has generated a large amount of research. The results of the research (as reported in the *ACDM Manual*) do not provide a solid case for the validity of the ACDM, considered as a whole. Among the diverse scales on the ACDM, the Occupational and Major Scales appear to have the best support.

REFERENCES

Buck, J. N., & Daniels, M. H. (1985). *Assessment of Career Decision Making (ACDM) manual*. Los Angeles: Western Psychological Services.

Crites, J. O. (1973). *Career Maturity Inventory theory and research handbook*. Monterey, CA: McGraw-Hill.

Crites, J. O. (1978). *Career Maturity Inventory theory and research handbook* (2nd ed.). Monterey, CA: McGraw-Hill.

Harren, V. A. (1979). A model of career decision making for college students. *Journal of Vocational Behavior, 14*, 119–133.

Osipow, S. H. (1980). *Manual for the Career Decision Scale* (2nd ed., rev. 1980). Columbus, OH: Marathon Consulting and Press.

Thompson, A. S., Lindeman, R. H., Super, D. E., Jordaan, J. P., & Myers, R. A. (1981). *Career Development Inventory--Volume 1: User's manual*. Palo Alto, CA: Consulting Psychologists Press.

Tiedeman, D. V. & O'Hara, R. P. (1963). *Career Development: Choice and Adjustment*. New York: College Entrance Examination Board.

Career Decision Scale (CDS)

Samuel H. Osipow

Psychological Assessment Resources, Inc.
PO Box 998, Odessa, FL 33556

Target Population: High school & college.

Statement of Purpose of the Instrument: Clarify the antecedents of indecision and provide a total indecision score.

Titles of Subtests, Scales, Scores Provided: Certainty scale and Indecision scale.

Forms and Levels Available, with Dates of Publication/Revision of Each: Not available.

Date of Most Recent Edition of Test Manual, User's Guide, Etc.: Feb 1987.

Languages in Which Available: English only.

Time: Actual Test Time—10 minutes.
        Total Administration Time—15 minutes.

Norm Group(s) on Which Scores Are Based: High school; college, continuing educ. students, returning women students.

Manner in Which Results Are Reported for Individuals
  Types of Scores: Percentile ranks.
  Report Format/Content:
    Basic Service: See above.

Report Format/Content for Group Summaries: Not available.

Scoring
  Machine Scoring Service: not available.
  Hand Scoring:
    Scored by: clerk; counselor.
    Time required for scoring: Two minutes.
  Local Machine Scoring: Not available.

Computer Software Options Available: Not available.

Cost of Materials
  Counselee Materials: Kit (Manual and 50 Test Booklets): $26.95; Manual: $8.00; Pkg. 50 Test Booklets: $19.50.

Additional Comments of Interest to Users: New manual for 1987 edition.

Published Reviews
Allis, M. (1984). Review of the Career Decision Scale. *Measurement and Evaluation in Counseling and Development, 17*, 98–100.

Harmon, L. W. (1985). Review of the Career Decision Scale. In J. V. Mitchell, Jr., (Ed.), *Ninth Mental Measurements Yearbook*: Volume II (p. 270). Lincoln, NE: University of Nebraska Press.
Herman, O. D. (1985). Review of the Career Decision Scale. In J. V. Mitchell, Jr. (Ed.), *Ninth Mental Measurements Yearbook*: Volume II (p. 270). Lincoln, NE: University of Nebraska Press.
Slaney, R. B. Review of the Career Decision Scale. In D. J. Keyser & R. C. Sweetland (Eds.), *Test Critiques*: Volume III (pp. 138–143). Kansas City, MO: Test Corporation of America.

Reviewed By:

Robert B. Slaney

Associate Professor of Counseling Psychology
The Pennsylvania State University

The Career Decision Scale (CDS) by Osipow, Carney, Winer, Yanico, and Koschier (1976, 3rd rev.) represents the earliest published attempt to develop an instrument that measures the components or antecedents of career indecision. The scale consists of nineteen items that measure the degree to which respondents report that the individual career-related items describe them and their particular circumstances. There are sixteen items (3–18) that describe the components of vocational and/or educational indecision. Two initial items measure the respondents' reported decidedness, comfort with, and knowledge about implementing a career choice and a college major respectively. The final item has a free response format so respondents can insert descriptions of their unique circumstances relative to career indecision.

The entire scale is contained on a small 4-page booklet that has detailed, clear instructions on the front page for responding to the simple format. A sample question and answer are followed by the nineteen items. Opposite each item are the numbers 4, 3, 2 and 1 (4 = "exactly like me"; 3 = "very much like me"; 2 = "only slightly like me"; 1 = "not at all like me"). Respondents are asked to circle the number which most accurately describes their situation in response to each of the items.

PRACTICAL APPLICATIONS/USES

This scale is potentially useful to career counselors, researchers and teachers of a variety of courses and programs on educational and vocational exploration and/or career decision-making. It provides an estimate of career indecision and its antecedents as well as an outcome measure for determining the effects of a variety of interventions relevant to career choice or career development. Although the scale was developed to relate specific interventions to particular antecedents of career indecision, this approach has not received much attention. However, for counselors it makes sense to examine the responses of clients to the individual items to identify particular issues that need to be explored.

The Career Decision Scale can be administered to large groups as well as individually. It was designed for use with high school and college students. Although no reading level is noted in the manual, the language is clear and simple and seems appropriate for the intended audience. There is no specified time limit but 10 to 15 minutes is usually enough time to complete the scale. Scoring involves summing the numerical values that were circled for items 3–18. This yields an objective score for career indecision with higher numerical values representing higher degrees of career indecision. Items 1 and 2, which indicate decidedness about the choice of a career or college major, are not included in the career indecision score and are scored in the opposite direction. Item 19 is not scored and may offer clues to issues that are of concern to respondents. Thus far, however, the published studies on the scale have simply ignored Item 19.

TECHNICAL ASPECTS

An article by Osipow, Carney, and Barak, (1976) was the first published paper on the current version of the Career Decision Scale. The article contains an impressive amount of data on the scale. Seven undergraduate samples (N = 737) were involved in an elaborate plan to gather data on relevant groups. The hypothesis that students requesting help in career decision making would score higher on the scale than students not requesting such help was supported. Students requesting career counseling had significantly higher scores on the Career Decision Scale than students who did not request counseling. The results were mixed for students in courses on educational-vocational exploration. It was found, as expected, that the career indecision scores for two groups of students in courses on educational-vocational exploration declined while the scores for introductory students and two groups of students in a course on personal effectiveness did not change. Items 3–18, as expected, were almost all negatively correlated with Items 1 and 2. The above results provide clear support for the construct and concurrent validity of the scale and its individual items.

Test-retest reliabilities calculated over two-week intervals on the summary scores yielded values of .90 for 56 introductory students and .82 for 59 students in a course on personal effectiveness. Osipow et al. (1976) also conducted a factor analysis on the 16 indecision items and found that four factors accounted for over 81% of the variance. Osipow et al. (1976) said the first factor seemed to have two basic elements that involved a lack of structure and confidence in approaching decision making and choice anxiety. The second factor was seen as suggesting a perceived or actual external barrier to a preferred choice and questions about alternative possibilities. Factor three was interpreted as an approach-approach conflict. The fourth factor seemed to indicate a personal conflict over making the decision. One of the implications of the factor analysis was that perhaps interventions could be devised to respond to the factors that were found.

More recent studies have added to the initial support for the validity of the Career Decision Scale. Slaney, Palko-Nonemaker, and Alexander (1981), using a large sample (N = 857), divided subjects into career decided and undecided groups. There were statistically significant differences in the expected direction for the summary scores, the factor scores, and all of the individual items. A factor analysis replicated Osipow et al's first factor but otherwise the factor structure was unclear. Rogers and Westbrook (1983) found clear support for the construct and concurrent validity of the scale. They factor analyzed the responses of 175 students to the Career Decision Scale and found two factors which coincided with the second and third factors found by Osipow et al. (1976). They concluded that the match of these two factors indicated "some degree of convergent validity for the CDS" (p. 84). Overall the rapidly expanding research on the construct and concurrent validity of the Career Decision Scale seems quite promising although the factor structure of the scale needs additional clarification (Harmon, 1985; Slaney, in press).

CRITIQUE

The current edition of the manual provides succinct, articulate and accurate summaries of the published and unpublished research that has been conducted on the scale. It is nicely produced and includes, in addition to the research summary, a table of contents, 39 references, a copy of the Career Decision Scale and 53 pages of tables. It is a rich source of data for potential users and researchers. Because of the rapidly developing research on the scale the manual is in need of revision and, in fact, a revised manual is currently being prepared (Osipow, personal communication).

For the Career Decision Scale, a number of issues, mostly minor, remain unclear or in need of additional investigation. For example, the amount of information available on the initial stages of the development of the scale is minimal. How was it determined that there were 16 antecedents of career indecision? Why not more or less? What revisions took place at what points and for what reasons? A more important issue concerns the lack of clarity of the factor structure. In turn, this lack of clarity may be related to the lack of clarity that exists in some of the items. For example, item 11 requires subjects to give one response to the following statements: "Having to make a career decision bothers me. I'd like to make a decision quickly and get it over with. I wish I could take a test that would tell me what kind of a career I should pursue." These three statements seem at least potentially independent of each other. The need for clarifying the factor structure does seem important, especially if the future development of the scale is to involve career interventions that are based on this structure.

On the other hand, if the research done thus far is predictive, there may be less need to be concerned about clarifying the individual items or the factor structure. Almost all of the studies have used the scale as a unidimensional measure of career indecision. Used in this way, the scale has received an impressive amount of empirical support for its test-retest reliability and its construct and concurrent validity. It can be concluded that the Career Decision Scale is a brief, easily administered, valid and reliable measure of career indecision.

REFERENCES

Harmon, L. W. (1985). Review of Career Decision Scale. In J. V. Mitchell, Jr. (Ed.), *Ninth Mental Measurements Yearbook Vol. 11*, (p. 270). Lincoln NE: The University of Nebraska Press.

Osipow, S. H. (1980). *Manual for the Career Decision Scale*. Columbus, OH: Marathon Consulting and Press.

Osipow, S. H., Carney, C. G., & Barak, A. (1976). A scale of educational-vocational undecidedness: A typological approach. *Journal of Vocational Behavior, 9*, 233–243.

Rogers, W. B., & Westbrook, B. W. (1983). Measuring career indecision among college students: Toward a valid approach for counseling practitioners and researchers. *Measurement and Evaluation in Guidance, 16*, 78–85.

Slaney, R. B. (in press). The assessment of career decision making. In W. B. Walsh and S. H. Osipow (Eds.). *Advances in Vocational Psychology, Vol. II., Career Decision Making, Development and Maturity.* Hillsdale, NJ: Erlbaum.

Slaney, R. B. (in press). The assessment of career decision making. In W. B. Walsh and S. H. Osipow (Eds.), *Advances in Vocational Psychology, Vol. II., Career Decision Making, Development and Maturity.* Hillsdale, NJ: Erlbaum.

NOTE: Significant portions of this review were abridged from the author's original review in Volume II of *Test Critiques* with permission of Test Corporation of America.

Career Development Inventory (CDI)

Donald E. Super, Albert S. Thompson, Richard H. Lindeman, Jean P. Jordaan and Roger A. Myers

Consulting Psychologists Press, Inc.
577 College Ave., Palo Alto, CA 94306

Target Population: School Form—grades 8–12; College & University Form for that population.

Statement of the Purpose of the Instrument: Assessing career development and vocational or career maturity; helping students make educational & career plans; assessing readiness to make career decisions.

Titles of Subtests, Scales, Scores Provided: Eight scales: Career Planning; Career Exploration; Decision-Making; World of Work Information; Knowledge of Preferred Occupational Group; Career Development—Attitudes; Career Development—Knowledge and Skills; Career Orientation Total.

Forms and Levels Available, with Dates of Publication/Revision of Each: School Form: 1979; College and University Form: 1981.

Date of Most Recent Edition of Test Manual, User's Guide, Etc.: Technical Manual: 1984; User's Manual—1981; Supplement to User's Manual—1982.

Languages in Which Available: English only.

Time: Actual Test Time—untimed—typically takes 60 minutes.
Total Administration Time—Not available.

Norm Group(s) on Which Scores Are Based: School Form: 5,039 students grades 9–12. College & University Form: 1,826 students from 13 different colleges & universities.

Manner in Which Results Are Reported for Individuals
Type of Scores: Standard scores, percentiles, response analysis (percents).
Report Format/Content
Basic Service: above scores plus descriptions of scales and group roster (names, scores, grade, sex) plus group means and standard deviations.

Report Format/Content for Group Summaries
Basic Service: If 100 or more answer sheets are sent at one time, percentiles for individuals based on the local group and the national norms will be provided; separate rosters for each subgroup if submitted by subgroup.

Scoring
  Machine Scoring Service
    Cost of basic service per counselee: Machine scoring is included in the cost of the pre-paid
    answer sheets.
    Time required for scoring and returning (maximum): 24 hr. turnaround.
  Hand Scoring: Not recommended.
  Local Machine Scoring
    Provisions/conditions/equipment required: with computer version; codelock key, controller,
    IBM PC. Optical scanner is also available for scoring of multiple paper & pencil administrations.

Computer Software Options Available: Standard administration on-line; scoring; interpretation;
group summaries.
Ways in which computer version differs: Allows local storing of data; with purchase of an optical
scanner, large numbers of paper & pencil administrations can be scored immediately.

Cost of Materials
  Specimen Set: $16.00.
  Counselee Materials: (quantity discounts available) Manual (2 volumes) = $20.00; Reusable
  test booklets = $17.00/25; Prepaid answer sheets = $33.00/10 (quantity discounts available).

Additional Comments of Interest to Users: New student profile available; PC computer version
can be purchased as part of a set of tests.

Published Reviews
Hansen, J. C. (1985). Career Development Inventory. *Measurement and Evaluation in Counseling
  and Development, 17*(4), 220–224.
Pinkney, J. W. (1985). Review of Career Development Inventory. In J. V. Mitchell (Ed.), *Ninth
  Mental Measurements Yearbook*: Volume I (p. 271). Lincoln, NE: University of Nebraska Press.

Reviewed by

Don C. Locke
Professor and Head, Department of Counselor Education
North Carolina State University

The publication of the Career Development Inventory (CDI) in 1979 and 1981 was a major psychometric event. The CDI, rationally derived and based on Super's theoretical model of career development, was constructed to give an indication of an individual's readiness to make wise vocational choices (Super, Crites, Hummel, Moser, Overstreet, and Warnath, 1957). The fact that the authors spent a considerable amount of time refining the instrument is reflected in the fact that it has the most thorough research base of any career development instrument (Johnson, 1985).

The CDI is available in a School Form (grades 8–12) and a College and University Form. Both forms consist of 120 gender-fair items which are divided into two parts. Part one includes four subtests which measure Career Planning (prior planning and amount of planning), Career Exploration (career information

176

sources and the usefulness of the sources), Decision-Making (knowledge and insight into career decisions), and World-of-Work Information (knowledge of career development tasks). Part two is "Knowledge of Preferred Occupational Group" and measures the results of an individual's explorations that should precede selection of a training program or occupation.

The CDI yields eight scale scores, one for each of the previously mentioned subtests, and three additional scale scores based on combinations of several of the subtests. The three additional scales are Career Development Attitudes (Career Planning and Career Exploration combined), Career Development Knowledge and Skills (Decision Making and World-of-Work Information combined), and Career Orientation Total (Career Planning, Career Exploration, Decision Making, and World-of-Work Information combined). This Career Orientation Total scale score approaches a measure of career or vocational maturity but is not titled as such since it only includes four of the five dimensions of vocational maturity.

The administration of the inventory should present few problems to counselors or students. The directions are clear and the inventory can be completed in about 60 minutes. The reading level appears to be easy for most students but there are long sentences and the inventory requires a great deal of reading. Hansen (1985) concluded that a major portion of the inventory is appropriate for only 11th and 12th grade reading levels. The CDI answer sheets are designed for machine scoring. The authors recommend against hand scoring since a different key is needed for each of 20 occupational groups. For those with access to a personal computer and an optical scanner, a PC scoring version can be purchased. Individual scores are reported as standard scores with a mean of 100 and standard deviation of 20.

APPLICATIONS/USES OF THE CDI

The CDI results have three primary applications in schools or colleges:

1. To provide diagnostic data and predictors for use in individual counseling.
2. As a survey instrument in planning career development programs.
3. As outcome measures in evaluating programs and research.

The CDI was designed to assess students' readiness to make sound educational and vocational choices. Since students differ widely in their readiness to make these decisions (Super & Overstreet, 1960), counselors must determine a level of vocational development before planning some intervention. Intervention can be developmental, preventive, or remedial, and differential strategies are required for each type of intervention. Scores from the CDI can be useful in pinpointing the specific area(s) in need of some intervention. Scores can also help in determining whether individual counseling, structured learning, or exploratory techniques are needed. The CDI data, when combined with aptitude test data, interest inventory data, and school records should be sufficient background to plan some career development experiences for students.

A CDI group profile is provided if 100 or more answer sheets are sent for scoring at one time. This group profile provides the counselor with a clear picture of the career planning needs of the group. Such a picture is useful in formulating appropriate objectives and components of a career development program. The diagnostic use of the CDI is crucial to developing a career development program based on individual needs.

Since the CDI was designed to measure vocational development, scores can be used to measure outcomes or change for program evaluation. Similar uses can be made of the CDI for research purposes. The goals of career education programs often include positive changes in things like awareness, exploration, and decision-making, factors which are measured by the CDI.

TECHNICAL CHARACTERISTICS

The publication of the Technical Manual in 1984 was a positive addition to needed information on the psychometric characteristics of the CDI. The Technical Manual provides background information on the theoretical model of vocational maturity, background research on development of the inventory, validity and reliability data on both forms, data concerning profile types and occupational group preferences, and uses of the CDI in surveys, program planning/evaluation, and assessment/counseling.

The procedures used in developing the items, factor analyzing them, and checking for the validity and reliability of the final form of the inventory appear to be generally sound. Procedures for weighing items are not described in the manuals. Normative data have been derived from a sample of over 5,000 high school students and over 1800 college students. In both instances the samples were based on convenience and were not representative samples. Users are encouraged to develop local norms for specific populations.

One of the admirable features of the CDI is the quality of the sections in the Technical Manual on reliability and validity. Test-retest correlations are reported for both forms for two- and three-week intervals. On the eight scales of the School Form these correlations range from .36 to .90 for 668 high school students. The correlations for the three combined scales are somewhat higher, ranging from .74 to .84.

It is difficult to justify the lower reliability coefficients on Knowledge of Preferred Occupational Group (.36), World-of-Work Information (.49), and Decision-Making (.51). One might have expected greater care in construction and selection of items for these subtests to yield sufficiently high reliability coefficients.

Considerable attention has been given to the validation of the CDI, and the treatment of validity in both the User's Manual and the Technical Manual is good. Content validity is based on the career development model consisting of five dimensions. The items for each dimension in the CDI were drawn from two studies (Super & Overstreet, 1960; Jordaan & Heyde, 1979). The intercorrelations between the dimensions were high enough to justify the construct of career maturity and even though only two factors emerged from discriminant analysis of the sample, five dimensions were derived. Evidence of construct validity is based on sex, grade and curriculum program differences. Correlations between the CDI and other career development measures revealed that the CDI does measure variables resembling those measured by other instruments. Correlations indicating significant relationships are also reported between the CDI and measures of scholastic ability.

178

SUMMARY

A theory of career development, followed by an instrument to assess dimensions of that theory, has been successfully implemented with the development of the CDI. The inventory itself leaves little to be desired in the way of layout, typography, administration, or scoring. The materials accompanying the inventory are clear and straightforward in presenting the CDI and the work that has been done so far.

The authors indicate that no cross-cultural comparisons have been attempted. Such an admission assumes that all students share the same culture and that cross-cultural studies would only involve those between residents of different countries. The user must be cognizant of the fact that the inventory is subject to students' prior experiences and that for some culturally different populations the CDI might yield some falsely immature ratings.

If one assumes that the costs associated with the CDI are reasonable, then a decision must be made as to whether students, particularly in junior and senior high school, can benefit from such an expenditure. This reviewer believes that they can. It seems clear that the inventory should yield data decidedly useful to high school and college students who desire diagnostic or survey information relating to future educational plans.

REFERENCES

Hansen, J. C. (1985). Career Development Inventory. *Measurement and Evaluation in Counseling and Development*, 17, 220–224.

Johnson, S. D., Jr. (1985). Career Development Inventory. In D. J. Keyser & R. C. Sweetland (Eds.), *Test critiques: Volume IV*. Kansas City, MO: Test Corporation of America, 132–143.

Jordaan, J. P., & Heyde, M. B. (1979). *Vocational maturity in the high school years.* New York: Teachers College Press.

Super D. E., Crites, J. O., Hummel, R. C., Moser, H. P., Overstreet, P. L., & Warnath, C. F. (1957). *Vocational development: A framework for research*. New York: Teachers College Press.

Super, D. E., & Overstreet, P. L. (1960). *Vocational maturity of ninth grade boys.* New York: Teachers College Press.

Career Maturity Inventory (CMI)

John O. Crites

CTB/McGraw-Hill
2500 Garden Road, Monterey, CA 93940

Target Population: Norms are for grades 6–12; also used above grade 12.

Statement of the Purpose of the Instrument: To measure the development of the client's career maturity in terms of attitudes toward career choice and competency to make decisions.

Titles of Subtests, Scales, Scores Provided, Etc.: Attitudes Toward Career Decision-Making: Decisiveness, Involvement, Independence, Orientation, Compromise; Competence in Career Decision-Making: Self-Appraisal, Occupational Information, Goal Selection, Planning, Problem Solving.

Forms and Levels: Attitude, Form A-2; 50 items, 1 scale (1978). Attitude, Form B-1; 75 items, 1 50-item scale (as above) and 5 subscales (1978). Competence Test, no total scale; 5 subtests (1978).

Date of Most Recent Edition of Test Manual, User's Guide, Etc.: 1978.

Languages in Which Available: English only.

Time: Actual Test Time—untimed.
    Total Administration Time—approximately two hours.

Norm Group(s) on Which Scores Are Based: School children at each grades, 6–12.

Manner in Which Results Are Reported for Individuals
   Types of Scores: Standard scores, national percentiles, stanines.
   Report Format/Content
     Basic Service: Individual Career Maturity Profiles, 2 copies plus home report.

Report Format/Content for Group Summaries
   Basic Service: none—users select separately priced options.
   Options: class record sheet, administrative summary, right response summary, frequency distribution, label, class roster reorganized, pre- and post-class record sheet.

Scoring
   Machine Scoring Service
     Cost per counselee of basic service: $1.18 per student, profile only.
     Cost of options: priced separately, approximately 12¢ to 45¢ per student for each option.
     Time required for scoring and returning (maximum): 21 working days.
   Hand Scoring
     Scored by: clerk; counselor.
     Time required for scoring: 20 minutes, including norms look-up.

Local Machine Scoring: Not available.
Computer Software Options Available: Not available.

Cost of Materials
Specimen Set: $10.80.
Counselee Materials: Reusable Attitude and Competency Test booklets—$2.25 each, answer sheets—17¢ to 29¢ each (consumable).

Published Reviews
Katz, M. R. (1982). In J. T. Kapes and M. M. Mastie (Eds.), *A counselor's guide to vocational guidance instruments*. Falls Church, VA: National Vocational Guidance Association.

Reviewed By

Robert B. Frary
Professor, Learning Resources Center
Virginia Polytechnic Institute and State University

The Career Maturity Inventory (CMI) consists of an attitude scale and a knowledge test. These instruments may be used completely independently of each other and hence will be discussed separately. Both arose from research beginning in the 1960s and remain unchanged since publication in 1978. Norms for both instruments are derived from the scores of about 74,000 students tested during the years 1973 through 1976. The comments which follow are based largely on information in the second editions of the CMI's *Administration and Use Manual* (Crites, 1978a) and its *Theory and Research Handbook* (Crites, 1978b).

ATTITUDE SCALE

Description and Use

The attitude items are career or work-related statements to which the examinee responds true or false, for example, "There is only one occupation for each person," and "The most important part of work is the pleasure which comes from doing it." Although characterized as measuring attitudes, the true-false responses are scored as correct or incorrect, with total scores based on the number of correct responses.

Two versions of the Attitude Scale are available. Form A-2, is designated as the screening scale. It has 50 items and provides a single score. The manual recommends that these scores be used for counseling or for evaluating career education. Presumably, a counselor might view very high or very low scores as possibly representing generally good or deficient attitudes about matters such as planning a career or seeking employment. Also, mean screening scores for a group, perhaps pre- and posttest, might be used to determine the effectiveness of some educational effort designed to improve attitudes in the areas just mentioned.

The second version of the Attitude Scale, Form B-1, has 75 items, including the 50 from the screening scale. It is designated as the counseling form, and provides five subscores, namely, Decisiveness in, Involvement in, Independence in, Orientation to, and Compromise in Career Decision Making. These scores might be used to provide a more definitive basis for counseling than that from the screening scale alone. In addition, they might be used for a more detailed analysis of the effects of educational or interventive efforts with respect to attitudes toward work.

Norms are by grade level (6 through 12) and provide percentile ranks and standard scores (mean = 50, s.d. = 10). They are provided for each of the five subscales of the Counseling Form B-1 as well as for the Screening Form A-2. Commendably, the top scores on all five of the rather short screening scales correspond to higher than the 90th percentile.

Technical Considerations

The items of the screening scale, Form A-2, were selected on the basis of congruence with theory underlying career development and empirical performance, mainly with respect to differentiation across grade levels. The resulting internal consistency reliability estimates for total scores ranged from .73 to .75, not very high for a scale of this length. Test-retest reliability estimates were similar. Empirical evidence of validity is available in two forms, weak but statistically significant correlations with other relevant measures, and mean score changes for groups undergoing interventive procedures designed to change attitudes toward work.

Determination of items constituting the subscales of the counseling scale, Form B-1, was based largely on the extent to which responses to items with content in common were empirically interrelated. The process used assigned only 47 of the 75 items to subscales. Of the remaining 28 items, 22 appear on the screening scale, and six are not used in any scale. Internal consistency reliability estimates for scores from the five subscales range from .5 to .72, generally satisfactory for scales of this length. Their intercorrelations range from .18 to .55, acceptably low for scales purportedly measuring different constructs.

The low intercorrelations among the subscales of the counseling scale explain why the internal consistency reliability estimates for the screening scale are relatively low. This scale contains items from all five counseling subscales. Items from three counseling scales, Decisiveness in, Involvement in, and Orientation to Career Decision Making, constitute 23 of the 50 items of the screening scale. Hence, scores from this scale must be viewed as a conglomerate mainly involving these constructs.

Critique

A technical problem arises from the fact that the Attitude Scales are essentially tests. The administration instructions provide no admonition against omitting items; hence a diffident examinee may get a low score, while an examinee who marks all items at random could get many more right. If comparison with the norms (already over 10 years old) is not a goal of testing, the test user might well consider strongly urging examinees not to omit items on the attitude scales. At the least, counselors should be sure that low scores are not simply the result of omissions.

Another possible problem with the Attitude Scales is the large proportion of negatively worded items. For example, only seven of the 50 items on the screening scale are considered "true." This may engender some kind of response bias, especially among brighter students who are used to seeing a balance between true and false statements on tests.

At a broader level, one must wonder whether the Attitude Scales measure attitudes as generally conceived or knowledge about what are conventionally accepted as proper approaches to career planning. The fact that these concepts can apparently be taught through fairly brief educational exposure suggests the latter. Also, the increase in scores with grade level may suggest better ability to deduce what answers are more plausible or desirable as children grow older rather than actual changes in attitude. On the other hand, empirical research has reported acceptably low correlations between CMI attitude scores and variables such as intelligence (Alvi & Kahn, 1982, and Chodzinski & Randhawa, 1983). Regardless, cautious interpretation of CMI attitude scores is recommended.

COMPETENCE TEST

Description and Use

Five subtests comprise the Competence Test, Form A-1, namely Self Appraisal, Occupational Information, Goal Setting, Planning, and Problem Solving. Each subtest has 20 multiple-choice items with four active choices and a "don't know" choice. As expounded in the *Theory and Research Handbook*, the items were written to be consistent with theory underlying the dimensions of knowledge required for effective career planning. As in the case of the attitude items, the final selection of knowledge items was based on their tendency to be easier at higher grade levels and their ability to distinguish high and low scorers within a grade level.

Competence Test score use is recommended in the manual for studying career development, assessing curricular and guidance needs, evaluating career education, and testing in career counseling. The manual gives appropriate caveats and suggestions in these areas.

Competence Test norms like those for the Attitude Scale are by grade level (6 through 12) and provide percentile ranks and standard scores. Each subtest has its own norms. (There is no composite score.)

Technical Considerations

Internal consistency reliability estimates for scores from the subtests range from .58 to .90. These estimates cover grades 6 through 12 and are generally in an acceptable range for tests of this length. Development of the competence subtests did not involve selection of items on the basis of their lack of relationship to scores from other subtests as was the case for the attitude subtests. Therefore, it is not surprising that scores from competence subtests are somewhat intercorrelated, with observed intercorrelations ranging from .45 to .71.

Empirical evidence of validity of the competence scores of the CMI is largely negative in nature. For example, they should not correlate meaningfully with variables representing personality constructs, and this has largely been found to be the case. One would expect, on the other hand, moderate but not strong relationships with variables such as grade level, grade-point-average, and intelligence. These relationships too have largely been found to be satisfactory. Several studies have investigated the extent to which the various competence scales and the attitude scales measure different constructs consistent with the theory underlying scale construction. The evidence has been mixed. For example, Westbrook, Cutts, Madison & Arcia (1980) found relationships among the attitude and competence measures which were not consistent with their supposed distinct natures. Chodzinski & Randhawa (1983) found better support for the theory underlying these scales but also noted weakness in distinguishing attitudes from competencies.

Critique

The use of the "don't know" response for the competence items represents a serious error in judgement in the opinion of this reviewer. The only valid reason for using this response is to control error variance associated with completely random guessing among all the choices of an item. Indeed, the instructions to examinees state, "If you have no idea, indicate 'don't know.' " Thus, even a hint of knowledge or the ability to identify an incorrect choice should be enough to yield a response of other than "don't know." Complete ignorance for a number of items should be rather unusual if the test is being used in an appropriate setting. What happens in reality is that timid or diffident examinees choose "don't know" much more often than aggressive examineees with the same knowledge level. Since each response other than "don't know" has a chance of being right, the scores of the aggressive examinees tend to be higher than those of their equally able but timid coexaminees. If comparison of results to the norms is not planned, it would be desirable to alter the instructions to examinees, telling them to answer all items regardless of knowledge. This would be the only way to insure elimination of personality factors from the scores.

A minor but vexing characteristic of the competence tests is the way the answer choices are designated. To prevent use of answer sheets not purchased from the publisher, choices are designated A through E and F through K (omitting I) on alternating items.

Perhaps the weakest aspect of the competence tests is the rather high intercorrelations among their scores. Part of the variance in common with all of the competence subtests is obviously due to intelligence and maturity. However, the subtest score relationships with variables representing these constructs in various studies have been modest. Therefore, there may well be a pool of common knowledge about careers and work that is not adequately distinguished by the theory underlying the CMI. More research is needed in this area.

RECOMMENDATIONS

While flawed, the CMI has, for the most part, reasonable and well-documented psychometric charcteristics. While possibly slightly dated in terms of its norms and item content, its scores can be related to results in over 200 published references. These factors speak in favor of its use, given the need to measure attitudes and knowledge about careers and working. On the other hand, there are competing inventories that measure many of the same constructs and have better psychometric characteristics. However, none of these is based on exactly the same theoretical base as the CMI, and hence at least some of their scores measure different constructs or emphasize different aspects of broader constructs.

If after reviewing several inventories, the researcher or counselor concludes that the CMI seems to cover most closely what needs to be measured, then it should be used.

REFERENCES

Alvi, S. A., & Khan, S. B. (1982). A study of the criterion-referenced validity of Crites' Career Maturity Inventory. *Educational and Psychological Measurement*, 42, 1285–1288.

Chodzinski, R. T., & Randhawa, B. S. (1983). Validity of Career Maturity Inventory. *Educational and Psychological Measurement, 43*, 1163–1173.

Crites, J. O. (1978a). *Administration and use manual* (2nd ed.). Monterey, CA: CTB/McGraw-Hill.

Crites, J. O. (1978b). *Theory and research handbook* (2nd. ed.). Monterey, CA: CTB/McGraw-Hill.

Westbrook, B. W., Cutts, D. D., Madison, S. S., & Arcia, M. A. (1980). The validity of the Crites' model of career maturity. *Journal of Vocational Behavior, 16*, 249–281.

My Vocational Situation (MVS)

John L. Holland, Denise C. Daiger and Paul G. Power

Consulting Psychologists Press
577 College Avenue, Palo Alto, CA 94306

Target Population: Teens and adults, grades 9 and up.

Statement of the Purpose of the Instrument: The MVS is a brief two-page questionnaire that seeks to determine which of three possible difficulties—lack of vocational identity, lack of information or training, and environmental or personal barriers—may be troubling a client seeking help with career decisions. The sheet may be filled out by someone waiting for an interview and tabulated at a glance by the counselor; it may suggest useful clues for the interview itself and treatments relevant to each client's needs.

Titles of Subtests, Scales, Scores Provided: Scales include Vocational Identity, Occupational Information, and Barriers.

Forms and Levels Available, with Dates of Publication/Revision of Each: Only one form of the MVS is available—1980.

Date of Most Recent Edition of Test Manual, User's Guide, Etc.: Manual—1980.

Languages in Which Available: English only.

Time: Actual Test Time—5 to 10 minutes.
       Total Administration Time—same.

Norm Group(s) on Which Scores Are Based: The MVS was administered to persons in high schools, colleges, and businesses (N=824). Sample was designed for a great range in age (16–69), level of training (high school freshmen to doctorates in engineering and social sciences), and kind of work (factory workers, office workers, scientists, personnel workers, and others).

Manner in Which Results Are Reported for Individuals
    Types of Scores: Scores for the three scales are first collected as raw scores with normative data (sample means and standard deviations) available in the manual. All of this is done by the person administering the test. No profile sheet is available.
Report Format/Content for Group Summaries: Not available.

Scoring
    Machine Scoring Service: Not available.
    Hand Scoring: The MVS is easily handscored.
    Local Machine Scoring Service: Not available.

Computer Software Options Available: Not available.

Cost of Material
    Specimen Set: $1.50.
    Counselee Materials: Test booklet $5.00/25 booklets.

Published Review
Tinsley, H.E.A. (1985). My Vocational Situation. In D. J. Keyser and R. C. Sweetland (Eds.), *Test Critiques*, Volume II. Kansas City, MO: Test Corporation of America.

Reviewed By

Bert W. Westbrook
Professor of Psychology
North Carolina State University

My Vocational Situation (MVS), published in 1980 by Consulting Psychologists Press, is authored by John Holland, Denise C. Daiger and Paul G. Power. The manual does not indicate the level or group for which it is intended, but the data are based on its administration to high school students, college students, and workers.

According to the manual, My Vocational Situation "appears to be useful for assessing a client's need for vocational assistance and for assigning clients to two or three kinds of treatments: (1) those for clients with a poor sense of identity who need experience, career seminars, personal counseling, (2) those for clients with a clear sense of identity who need only information and reassurance, and (3) those for clients who exhibit a combination of these needs" (p. 7, manual).

The instrument provides measures of Vocational Identity, Occupational Information, and Barriers. Vocational Identity (VI) is defined as "the possesion of a clear and stable picture of one's goals, interests, personality, and talents" (p. 1, manual). According to the manual this is a trait which "leads to relatively untroubled decision making and confidence in one's ability to make good decisions in the face of inevitable environmental ambiguities" (p. 1, manual). The Occupational Information (OI) scale is a measure of "need for vocational information, most of which is available in printed form; the counselor can quickly direct the client to the appropriate materials" (p. 1, manual). The Barriers (B) score provides an indication of "perceived external obstacles to a chosen occupational goal" (p. 1, manual). The manual asserts that "a *yes* response to one or more of the items or the listing of an idiosyncratic obstacle may enable the counselor to focus promptly on a significant problem area" (p. 1, manual).

MVS is self-administered, individually or in a group, and can be completed "by most people in ten minutes or less" (p. 2, manual). Responses are marked on the single-sheet booklet and can be hand-scored in "about ten seconds without templates" (p. 2, manual).

SOURCE AND DESCRIPTION OF ITEMS

The manual does not indicate the precise source of the items, but it does indicate that the instrument has its origins in the indecision literature, the older counseling diagnostic schemes, and experimental studies of the effects of interest inventories, workshops, and career education programs on clients.

The MVS contains three types of items. The 18 VI items are true/false items such as "No single occupation appeals strongly to me." The OI items are yes-no items such as "I need information about how to find a job in my chosen career." The four B items are also yes-no items such as: "I have the following difficulty: I am uncertain about my ability to finish the necessary education or training."

NORM GROUPS

The manual does not present percentile norms for any group. However, it does present the means and standard deviations for sample of high school students (185 males, 311 females); college students (132 males, 134 females); full-time workers (138 males, 143 females); and graduate students and faculty (15 males, 14 females).

INTERPRETATION OF SCORES

Scores are expressed in raw scores. The VI score is the total number of *false* responses to the 18 items in the scale. Mean scores range from 9.19 for female high school students to 13.93 for male graduate students and faculty.

The OI score is the number of *No* responses to the four statements in item 19. Mean scores range from 1.77 for female college students to 3.67 for female high school students.

The B score is the number of *No* responses to the four statements in item 20. The scores range from 1.82 for female high school students to 3.57 for female graduate students and faculty.

VALIDITY

To support the construct validity of the MVS, the manual presents a table of intercorrelations based upon a combined sample of 824 persons in high schools, colleges, and businesses, ranging in age from 16 to 69, in occupations from factory workers to scientists, and in education from high school freshman to Ph.D.

The intercorrelation variables include: age, number of occupations being considered, number of different types of occupations named (using Holland's six categories), VI score, OI score, B score, and five-point ratings on five attributes: (a) This person appears well-organized, (b) This person appears at loose ends, (c) This person seems self-confident, (d) This person seems tense and uncomfortable, and (e) This person seems competent to handle his/her life well. Intercorrelations are presented separately by sex.

The manual states that "we hypothesized that the VI and OI scales should be positively correlated with age. They are" (p. 4, manual). Age is correlated .29 with VI and .32 with OI for males; the correlations for females are .06 and .15 respectively. The authors do not explain their rationale for expecting age to be correlated only with these two particular variables.

The authors also hypothesized that "The three scales were expected to be negatively correlated with the variety and number of vocational aspirations a

188

person lists in the MVS'' (p. 6, manual). All of the correlations are negative, as hypothesized, with a median of $-.16$. However, contrary to expectation, VI scores were not the most negatively correlated with vocational aspirations.

The external ratings correlate as hypothesized with VI with one exception: There is no relation between VI and "appears tense and uncomfortable."

The manual also offers the "normative data" to support the validity of the MVS. Because the mean scores on VI increase systematically and monotonically from high school students to college students to full-time workers to graduate students and faculty, the authors conclude that the VI scale "clearly increases with age, training, and degree of specialization" (p. 6, manual). However, the scores on the OI and B scales do *not* increase systematically and monotonically across the four groups, and the authors conclude that the "haphazard sampling makes any conclusion premature" (p. 6, manual).

There is a possibility that haphazard sampling is a source of invalidity for all three scales. Perhaps a more reasonable explanation for the OI and B scales' inconsistent performance has to do with their low reliabilities.

RELIABILITY

The KR20 reliability estimates are in the upper .80s for the VI scale. Reliabilities for OI are lower among college students and workers (.79, .77) and much lower among high school students (.39, .44). Reliabilities for the B scale are low among college students and workers (.45, .65), and seriously low among high school students (.23, .23). Only four items comprise each of the latter two scales.

Apparently, the data are based upon the original 20-item VI scale rather than the current form; if so, the reliability of the current form would be lower than reported.

QUESTIONS, CONCERNS AND ISSUES

Although the MVS is offered as "an experimental diagnostic scheme" rather than a test, there are several reasons why psychometric standards should be applied to it. First, the parts of the MVS are referred to as scales and users will likely treat them as measuring instruments. Second, the test booklet does not indicate that it is intended for research use only. Third, the manual indicates that the MVS is intended for operational use, that it can be used to make practical decisions about individuals and groups.

The manual does not present data to support such claims as: (a) "for assigning clients to two or three kinds of treatments," (b) "to identify real external barriers to a particular career choice," (c) "to locate those people in high schools, colleges, and adult programs of career development who are in greatest need of orientation programs."

The "haphazard sampling" cited (p. 6, manual) make it difficult, if not impossible, to interpret the scores. Students in different grades are grouped together as high school students; the type of college student is not described; full-time workers are not described; and 15 graduate students and faculty are grouped together to constitute a normative group.

Validity data are based, for the most part, upon how well the scales correlate with other variables according to theoretical expectation. However, the manual does not explain the theoretical framework for the hypotheses. Reliability estimates of the OI and B scales cannot be considered adequate for making decisions about persons.

The OI scale should perhaps have been named needs assessment or information needs. The term occupational information has been used most frequently to indicate the amount of knowledge one has about occupations.

The items on the V scale resemble items found on measures of indecision. Since several measures of indecision are available, one wonders why the VI scale was not correlated with one of them.

The table of intercorrelations of the eleven variables used in the construct validation study does not report the means and standard deviations which would be very helpful in interpreting the correlations. For example, how many occupations, on the average, are people considering?

The manual does not report any reliability estimates for the ratings. Also, it is not clear how well the raters knew the persons they were rating.

This reviewer has serious concerns about the intercorrelations data used to support construct validity. Some of the correlations are based upon 229 to 300 persons, while other correlations are based on 70 to 115 persons tested. Which persons were left out? The high school students? The college students? Some other subgroup of the sample? The small n may not be as serious as the fact that we do not know to which population the correlations can be generalized. Perhaps a more serious problem is that persons from different age and grade levels have been pooled.

SUMMARY

In summary, this reviewer does not feel that the MVS is ready for generalized use. The instrument can be improved by refining and articulating the theoretical framework, by increasing the length of the scales, by increasing the reliability of the scales, by administering the MVS to well defined samples, and by collecting more data to support its construct validity. It is an interesting and potentially useful instrument, but much more research is needed before it can be used to make decisions about persons.

NOTE: Significant portions of this review appeared in J. V. Mitchell, Jr. (Ed.), *Ninth Mental Measurements Yearbook Vol. II*. Lincoln, NE: The University of Nebraska Press.

Combined Assessment
Programs

ACT Career Planning Program (CPP)

ACT Staff Members

American College Testing Program (ACT)
Career Services Area
P.O. Box 168, Iowa City, Iowa 52243

Target Population: Grade 8 through adult.

Statement of the Purpose of the Instrument: The CPP helps counselees expand self-awareness, learn how the world of work is structured, and begin to explore personally relevant career options. Through six job clusters, the World-of-Work Map, and a narrative report, the CPP relates information about counselees to 500 occupations employing over 95% of the labor force.

Titles of Subtests, Scales, Scores Provided: Ability Test Battery (6 scores); Self-rated Abilities (9 scores); Unisex Edition of the ACT Interest Inventory (6 scores); Work-related Experience Inventory (6 scores). Each provides results for data, ideas, people, and things work tasks. Job values are also assessed.

Forms and Levels Available, with Dates of Publication/Revision of Each: Level 1: Grades 8–10 (1983/1986); Level 2: Grade 11–adult (1983/1986).

Date of Most Recent Edition of Test Manual, User's Guide, Etc.: ACT Career Planning Program Counselor's Manual (3rd Edition), 1983.

Languages in Which Available: English only.

Time: Actual Test Time—111 minutes.
     Total Administration Time—168 minutes.

Norm Group(s) on Which Scores Are Based: Nationally representative samples (1983) consisting of approximately 15,000 8th, 10th, and 12th graders in 115 schools.

Manner in Which Results Are Reported for Individuals
    Types of Scores: Stanines, percentile ranks, World-of-Work Map "region" scores, and verbal labels based on stanines.
    Report Format/Content
        Basic Service: Two-page report provided. Page 1 organizes abilities, interests, experiences, and trial job choices into appropriate job clusters. Page 2 provides narrative interpretation and stanine score profiles.
        Options: Responses for up to 14 local option items can be printed on the score report or list report.

Report Format/Content for Group Summaries
Options: Counselee list report; counselee results on magnetic tape; 19-page Group Summary Report with 36-page *Interpretive Guide*.

Scoring
Machine Scoring Service
Cost of basic service per counselee: Included in cost of answer folders and interpretative materials.
Cost of Options: Group Summary Report and list report ($40.00 each, for all persons tested); magnetic tape ($50.00 for all persons tested).
Time required for scoring and returning (maximum): 5 to 9 days (2 scorings per week).
Hand Scoring
Scored by: counselee; clerk; counselor.
Time required for scoring: about 5 minutes (ability tests only).
Local Machine Scoring: Not available.

Computer Software Options Available: Standard administration on-line; scoring; interpretation; Ability Test Battery administered and scored off-line.
Ways in which computer version differs: Scoring and interpretation are components of DISCOVER, ACT's computer-based career planning system.

Cost of Materials
Specimen Set: $6.50 per level. Includes *Counselor's Manual* and *Interim Psychometric Handbook*.
Counselee Materials: $.50 per level for Assessment Booklet with test items (reusable); $4.00 per level for answer folder, scoring, score report, and 24-page Career Guidebook; $.50 per level for self-scored answer booklet for Ability Test Battery.

Additional Comments of Interest to Users: A self-scored "short form" of the CPP is provided by the Vocational Interest, Experience, and Skill Assessment (VIESA). VIESA substitutes self-ratings of skills for the CPP Ability Test Battery.

Published Reviews
Barnette, W. L, Jr. (1973). *Journal of Counseling Psychology, 20,* 389–394.

Healy, C. C. (1973). *Measurement and Evaluation in Guidance, 5,* 509–512.

Johnson, R. W. (1978). In O. K. Buros (Ed.), *The Eighth Mental Measurements Yearbook.* Highland Park, NJ: Gryphon Press.

Mehrens, W. A. (1982). In J. T. Kapes & M. M. Mastie (Eds.), *A counselor's guide to vocational guidance instruments* (pp. 132–135). Falls Church, VA: National Vocational Guidance Association.

Reviewed By

Alan G. Robertson

Research Associate, Institute for Research and Development in Occupational Education, Center for Advanced Study City University of New York

The Career Planning Program (CPP) is a set of assessment measures for use in high schools or two-year colleges where occupational interest and related ability testing can be integrated with a multi-dimensional occupational exploration program. The measurement approach is grounded in the job classification and clustering theories advanced by Roe, Super and Holland. Student background and work experiences data are included in the profile reports.

The publisher advises that the CPP should be used EARLY in career guidance programs ONLY to stimulate career self exploration and give wideband signposts for exploration. Counselors should order the Interim Psychometric Handbook (IPH) from the publisher for detailed information on test theory, construction, and statistics, the latter derived from earlier test editions, to supplement the Counselor's Manual.

DESCRIPTION OF MATERIALS

The CPP instruments consist of timed and untimed test-type measures of interests and abilities, and student self-reporting and self-assessment machine-scored questionnaires. Sample scripts and outlines for conducting student, parent and faculty orientation and interpretation meetings and press releases for local publications are provided. An optional section permits the addition of locally determined items. Score reports can be referenced to accompanying career exploration activity materials, including World of Work maps.

In the initial Career Family List execise, students review 179 job titles ranging from semi-skilled to highly skilled professional occupations and enter first and second choices on the machine-scored answer form, indicating degree of interest in each. Five questions ask if the student needs school help with basic, study, or writing skills, choosing school electives or exploring a future occupation.

The Work-Related Experience Scales require counselees to indicate how frequently they have participated in 90 activities; many of these are passive or avocational but nevertheless related to the same six Job Cluster areas.

The Self-Ratings of Abilities questionnaire asks students to rate themselves, as compared to other students their age, in nine areas titled: Scientific, Creative/Artistic, Literary, Helping Others, Meeting People, Sales, Management, Organization and Manual Dexterity.

The Unisex edition of the ACT Interest Inventory (UNIACT) is incorporated into the CPP. Students report their preferences as "like-indifferent-or dislike" for 90 work-task activities in the six areas of Holland's theory of careers (1973).

The Abilities Measures consist of six norm-referenced timed subtests in several aspects of reading comprehension, numerical skills, language usage, mechanical reasoning, space relations and clerical skills.

ADMINISTRATION

Levels 1 & 2 can be administered simultaneously to mixed grade groups; directions and timing of subtests are identical. Three optional testing time schedules given in the manual permit administration of the entire battery in one, two or three sessions; the administration manual gives very explicit start-stop directions for each testing time option. Total administration time including preliminaries is approximately 166 minutes. One staff proctor is recommended for each 30 examinees.

CAREER DATA ORGANIZATION

The ACT-OCS job classification system of the 13,800 occupations identified as "unique" is the primary analysis method used in the CPP. The IPH presents extensive references in support for the basic work task activity and work preference *bipolar* approach.

NORMS

The 1983 edition is normed on a national sample of 15,400 public and private school students in grades eight (6,342), ten (5,322), and twelve (3,768). A description of the sampling plan, the rationale for adjustments to school data in final norm generation, and a comparison of the test norming population with national census data to determine whether demographic imbalances were significant are described in the IPH. Data include breakouts of student sex, U.S. geographic region of residence, and percent below proverty level for grades eight and ten, plus racial and ethnic data for students in the norming sample. National norms tables in Appendix B include means and standard deviations for measured abilities in stanines, and both self-rated abilities and first and second occupational choices in percentages.

VALIDITY

Validity data in the IPH from research on earlier postsecondary editions illustrate convergent and diverent validity by subtest intercorrelations, the Ability Measures' predictive validity of students' school and college performance, and CPP effectiveness in differentiating among students by their course program. Supplementary data are presented from a followup study conducted six years later that related test scores to occupational pursuits, interest scores to job satisfaction, and interest and experience scores to the incumbent's occupation. Extensive statistical tables are explained in detail by accompanying narratives.

RELIABILITY

Both the IPH and Counselor's Manual caution that CPP reliability data should be regarded in the context of the "wideband approach" as defined by Cronbach and Glaser. "No problem" if the test is used for self/career exploration purposes within a career development program *as the CPP should be used*. Reliability estimates determined by the Kuder-Richardson formula are given for five of the six ability measures for grades eight, ten, and twelve. Mean scores, standard deviations, and standard errors of estimate are presented by subtest within these grades (IPH only).

READING DIFFICULTY OF MATERIALS

The Dale-Chall Readability Index indicates that on Level 1, the difficulty ranges from grade 5.5 for test booklet directions to 8.5 for the work-related self-reporting experiences section. Level 2 ranges from 5.5 for test booklet directions to 9.5 for the Background and Plans unit. The Reading Ability exercise is constructed with a low to middle difficulty "floor" but with a high "ceiling." Despite only 40 test items, student chance level scores are reported as "below what would be expected."

SCORING AND REPORTING

Student *self-assessment* on the nine abilities and self reporting of background variables are cross-related to the ability and interest test *scores* through the ACT scoring service processes. Although a consumable self-scoring answer sheet option is available for the ability measures only, users of the reusable booklet MUST use the ACT machine scorable answer sheet and scoring service to obtain the new two-page score report. The cost of the answer sheet includes scoring. The individual reports include a narrative interpretation designed to start career exploration in "high" areas, expanded descriptions of the six job clusters and summarized biographical information. Test results are given in stanines and profile plots. A student interpretative guide is available.

SEX BIAS

The first page of the CPP Counselor's Manual cites the close attention paid to the *Guidelines for Assessment of Sex Bias and Sex Fairness in Career Interest Inventories*, developed in 1975 under the auspices of the National Institute of Education. The IPH presents a detailed rationale supported by research that if sex-balanced items can be developed at the test item level, sex-balanced scales can be produced reflecting them. Combined-sex norms are used.

OTHER CONSIDERATIONS

Group data from the CPP could be used in a variety of applications for curriculum and instructional planning. Ability test scores could be analyzed at the local level to predict success rates on required state minimum competency examinations and target potential students in need of basic skills remediation.

In the reviewer's judgment, there is insufficient explanation in the Counselor's Manual of how the score reports can be used for educational counseling and programming. The IPH table headings predicting H.S. GPAs and course grades from ability measures lack specificity.

Several of the data and format criticisms in a review of an earlier post-secondary edition in *Measurement and Evaluation in Guidance* (Healy, 1973) appear to have been addressed in the 3rd edition. The *Psychometric Handbook* listed in the CPP Manual as available in 1984 and replacing the IPH will not be available until late 1987–88. It should contain results of post-1983 studies, and add to the already extensive bibliography in the IPH.

REFERENCE

Healy, C. C. (1973). Review of the ACT Career Planning Program. *Measurement and Evaluation in Guidance*, 5, 509–512.

Apticom

Jeffery A. Harris, Howard Dansky and Bonnie Zimmerman

Vocational Research Institute
Philadelphia Jewish Employment and Vocational Service
2100 Arch Street, Philadelphia, PA 19103

Target Population: English or Spanish speaking disadvantaged job applicants, high school or special education students and vocational rehabilitation clients.

Statement of Purpose of the Instrument: To provide a quick vocational assessment in three major areas: aptitudes, interests and educational levels. Apticom's purpose is to combine aptitude, interest and academic skills into meaningful job recommendations in the form of work groups and job titles.

Titles of Subtests, Scales, Scores Provided: Measures ten U.S. Department of Labor aptitudes (i.e., G, V, N, S, P, Q, K, F, M, and E), 12 *Guide for Occupational Exploration* interests, and language and mathematics skills.

Forms and Levels with dates of Publication/Revision of Each: One form, manuals copyrighted 1985.

Date of Most Recent Edition of Test Manual, User's Guide, etc: 1985.

Languages in Which Available: English and Spanish.

Time: Actual Test Time—Aptitude test times total to 28 minutes and 15 seconds; interest inventory—
20 minutes; language and math skills—25 minutes.
Total Administration Time—1½ to 2 hours.

Norm Group(s) on Which Scores are Based: Aptitudes—standardized on adults in U.S. and Canada 9th and 10th grade score adjustment options. Interest inventory—secondary students and employed adults. Reading and mathematics—criterion referenced to US. Department of Labor's General Educational Development (GED) levels.

Manner in Which Results Are Reported for Individuals
Types of Scores: Aptitudes reported in standard scores and percentiles; interests reported in standard scores; educational skills reported in criterion achieved.
Report Format/Content: A separate profile sheet for each of the three test types can be used for hand scoring. Results can be printed directly from Apticom computer or downloaded to a PC.

Report Format/Content for Group Summaries: Not available.

Scoring

Machine Scoring Service: Not available.

Hand Scoring: Hand scoring by clerk or counselor. Test scores converted to aptitude scores and these are compared to OAP's; interest scale scores converted to standard scores; math and language scores compared to criteria.

Local Machine Scoring: If the user has a printer that is compatible with the dedicated Apticom computer, the test results can be scored and the results printed for each student/client.

Computer Software Options Available: Not applicable.

Cost of Materials: Single Apticom unit, $5,350.00; Single Apticom unit with printer, $6,000.00; Midi System (2 Apticom units, master control, 2 printers), $12,400.00; Maxi System (4 Apticom units, master control, 4 printers), $22,300.00; Spanish/Bilingual Kit (overlays/manual), $495.00.

Published Reviews

Botterbusch, K. F. (1987). *Vocational Assessment and Evaluation Systems: A Comparison*. Menomonie, WI: Materials Development Center.

Reviewed By

Karl F. Botterbusch

Materials Development Center
Stout Vocational Rehabilitation Institute
University of Wisconsin-Stout

The Apticom is a computerized assessment or testing system developed by the Vocational Research Institute (VRI) division of the Philadelphia Jewish Employment and Vocational Services (JEVS). Designed for English or Spanish speaking disadvantaged job applicants, high school or special education students, and rehabilitation clients, the purpose of the system is to provide a quick vocational assessment of three major areas: aptitudes, interests and educational levels. Apticom then combines aptitude, interest and academic skills into meaningful job recommendations.

The aptitude part of the system is based on the U.S. Department of Labor definitions of 10 of the 11 aptitudes (except Color Discrimination), with much of the design and test item formats closely resembling those of the General Aptitude Test Battery (GATB). The Occupational Interest Inventory is based on the twelve interest areas (e.g., Artistic, Selling) defined in the *Guide for Occupational Exploration* (GOE). This interest measure was developed from the United States Employment Service (USES) Interest Inventory. The Educational Skills Development Battery was derived from the General Educational Development (GED) Language and Mathematics scales; there are six levels of these two GED scales.

DESCRIPTION

The system contains administrative and technical manuals. The administration manual begins with very detailed directions and diagrams for setting up the administration and scoring equipment. There follows a separate section for each test within each battery. All instructions to be read verbatim are contained in "shadow boxes"; the accompanying demonstrations are also printed. The administration manual also contains detailed procedures for both hand and machine scoring, and various conversion charts and tables. The format promotes easy use and the content of the manual is complete. The technical manual consists of development and interpretation sections for each of the three parts of the battery. These sections contain explanations that are easy to follow and understand for all development steps.

The self-contained Apticom consists of a dedicated computer and several testing devices. The major device is a plastic board approximately 18 by 24 inches, containing an array of holes that correspond to test answers. Except for the apparatus tests, all test items are contained on plastic overlays that are placed on this board. The client uses a wand to select between alternatives. The system also includes various computer controlled devices for measuring the dexterity aptitudes. The heart of the system is a dedicated computer that is necessary for all administration and scoring. An optional printer can be connected directly to the control console. The results can also be downloaded to an IBM PC or IBM compatible computer for storing results.

All administration instructions are read directly from the manual and most are accompanied by some demonstration. Only the power tests specifically designed to assess verbal aptitude and language skills contain items beyond the fourth grade reading level. Except the interest inventory, the computer contains preset times for each test. The system beeps and turns the control lights off when the predetermined time is up for each test.

SCORING AND REPORTING

There are two basic ways to score the Apticom results. In the manual procedure, the raw test scores are read from a display following each test. There are three Apticom profile sheets used in hand scoring.

1. The Individual Aptitude Profile consists of data and client identification information, followed by a chart that plots the 11 tests measuring the ten aptitudes. It is possible to chart a grade adjustment for ninth and tenth grade students. As with the GATB, the standard error of measurement (SEm) can be added to each aptitude score. A percentile equivalent can also be calculated.
2. The Occupational Interest Inventory Profile Sheet consists of two charts for plotting the 12 GOE interest areas. Interest inventory scoring is based on the frequency of "like" responses.
3. The Educational Skills Development Profile Sheet contains client identification information and scores on each of the first four GED scales.

If a printer is available, the dedicated computer performs all scoring and prints the final report complete with explanations of all test variables. The contents of the standard report are: (1) The Aptitude Test Battery section contains the raw and standard test scores for each of the 11 tests. Aptitudes are given in standard scores and percentiles as well as graphically. (2) The Occupational Interest Inventory gives the number of "like", "?" and "dislike" scores for each of the 12 interest areas and the percentile for each score, compared to the entire norm group and to male and female subgroups. Standard scores and a graphic display are presented for each interest scale. A statistical idiographic analysis is also conducted to establish the client's high interest area(s). (3) The Educational Skills Development Battery section contains the number of correct responses for each of the four GED levels and a content analysis of the items missed.

The heart of the final report is the Vocational Recommendations section. This section lists all four-digit GOE codes (i.e. Work Groups) considered viable based upon the client's high interest areas and aptitude scores (when the latter are compared against GATB Occupational Aptitude Patterns). The report also includes examples of specific jobs, with *Dictionary of Occupational Titles* (DOT) codes, and General Educational Development (GED) and Specific Vocational Preparation (SVP) requirements. The recommendation section, then, provides cross-classification of interest, aptitude and educational levels.

NORMS, RELIABILITY AND VALIDITY

The aptitude battery was developed on selected samples of young adults in the U.S. and was standardized on adults in the U.S. and Canada. The interest inventory contains two separate norms: (1) secondary students and (2) employed adults. Because the educational battery was developed using a criterion referenced approach, norming was not necessary. In general all samples are fully described and most are of adequate size. The development of norms was straightforward and technically sound.

Internal consistency, standard error of measurement (SEM) and test-retest reliability coefficients are given for all tests. Aptitude test-retest reliabilities range between .65 and .89, with most being higher than .80. Although these are adequate, the SEm's are rather large when compared to aptitude score distributions. Alpha coefficients and test-retest reliabilities were provided for the 12 interest areas. These results are compared to the USES Interest Inventory. The shorter Apticom interest scales have in almost all cases just as high or higher reliability coefficients than the USES II. No reliability data were reported for the educational skills tests.

The aptitude tests and interest inventory were validated against their U.S. Labor Department counterparts. Correlations between Apticom and GATB aptitudes were in the .80s for the three cognitive aptitudes, in the .60s for the perceptual aptitudes, and the .50s for dexterity skills. The manual also compares factor analyses of the GATB and Apticom aptitudes. The GATB factor structure resulted in two factors, interpreted as cognitive/perceptual and motor. The Apticom has three factors: cognitive, perceptual and motor. The Apticom developers rightly interpreted this as a strong indication of the soundness of the Apticom aptitude tests. The interest inventory was validated against its USES counterpart. Correlations reported for three samples ranged from .67 to .90. When the length of the Apticom interest inventory is taken in account, these are quite high. The Educational Skills Development Battery was developed using a content validity approach in which all test items were rated by experts for their GED level. Thus,

201

at present all reported validity is based on correlations with widely used USES tests. Although the reported results are very impressive, the Apticom definitely needs empirical validation studies.

SUMMARY

The Apticom is designed either to provide a quick assessment of a person's vocational capabilities or to be used as an initial screening device before a longer vocational evaluation. The central part of the system is its ability to combine the three factors commonly used in vocational testing, i.e. aptitudes, interests and academic performance levels. Of these the relationship between aptitudes and interests is the most critical.

The initial development of the Apticom has resulted in a technically sound test battery. The remarkable thing about this development is that the highly speeded Apticom tests have reliability coefficients that meet or exceed those of the much longer USES tests. Although the reported construct validity is an excellent beginning, the instrument definitely needs concurrent and predictive validation research.

The manuals are easy to understand and follow. The standard printed report is complete with all necessary information provided, and the physical apparatus is easy to operate and control. These features, plus the short administration time and the reported technical aspects, make the Apticom an impressive instrument.

REFERENCES

Evans, L. (1985, June). A survey regarding placement and performance of students receiving vocational evaluation in the Region V Vocational Evaluation Center. Lake Charles, LA: Vocational Evaluation Center, 2323 Sixth Street, 70601.

Evans, L. (1986, May). A survey regarding placement and performance of students receiving vocational assessments. (Technical Report). Lake Charles, LA: Region V Vocational Assessment Center, 2423 Sixth Street, 70601.

Greene County School Systems Apticom Assessment. (1986). Greenville City, TN: Author.

NOTE: Significant portions of this review were abridged from the author's original review in Botterbusch, K. F. (1987) *Vocational Assessment and Evaluation Systems: A Comparison*. With permission.

(

Career Survey

Ohio Department of Education and
John W. Wick, Northwestern University
Jeffery K. Smith, Rutgers University
Donald L. Beggs, Southern Illinois University
John T. Mouw, Southern Illinois University

American Testronics
P.O. Box 2270, Iowa City, Iowa 52244

Target Population: Grades 7–12 adult.

Statement of the Purpose of the Instrument: This instrument provides students, clients and their counselor with information that will stimulate the counseling process, encourage the exploration of career areas that may not have been previously considered, and provide a means for relating long-range career plans to short-range educational decisions.

Titles of Subtests, Scales, Scores Provided: INTEREST SCALES include: Accommodating/Entertaining; Humanitarian/Caretaking; Plant/ANimal Caretaking; Business Detail; Sales; Numerical; Communication/Promotion; Science/Technology; Artistic Expression; Educational/Social; Mechanical; and Medical. Ability Scales include: Verbal and Nonverbal.

Forms and Levels Available, with Dates of Publication/Revision of Each: Only one form/level is available; copyright 1984.

Date of Most Recent Edition of Test Manual, User's Guide, Etc.: Copyright, 1988.

Languages in Which Available: English only.

Time: Actual Test Time—Interest, not applicable; Ability, 24 minutes.
  Total Administration Time– Approximately 74 minutes

Norm Group(s) on Which Scores Are Based: Interest: Both same sex and combined sex norms are available for grades 7–8, 9–10, and 11–12. Ability: Grade level norms are available for grades 7, 8, 9, 10, 11 and 12.

Manner in Which Results Are Reported for Individuals
  Types of Scores: Interest: Same Sex and Combined Sex Percentile Ranks by grade level group (7–8; 9–10; 11–12) Ability: Grade level percentile rank, plus estimated ACT Composite, SAT Composite, and GATB-G score.

Report Format/Content

Basic Service: Career Profile (2 copies for each student) including percentile ranks for 12 interest scales and the 2 ability scales; estimated ACT and SAT Composites, plus GATB-G; (includes narrative reporting).

Options: Student Label and Educational Planning Report highlighting for each client areas of study that may relate to current interests.

Report Format/Content for Group Summaries:

Basic Service: Counselor's List Report provides a summary of scores for each student/client including same sex and combined sex percentile ranks, average item response (interest only) and consistency with which client answered interest items.

Options: Group Guidance Report—groups students of like interest for possible small group career exploration activities.

Scoring

Machine Scoring Service

Cost of basic service per counselee: $1.17.

Cost of options: (per student/client) Student Label—$.21; Group Guidance Report—$.32; Educational Planning Report—$.53; (extra) Career Profile—$.42; Magnetic Tape—$42.40 plus $.16.

Time required for scoring and returning (maximum): guaranteed 15-day turnaround.

Hand Scoring

Scored by: counselor.

Time required for scoring: 10–15 min. per client.

Local Machine Scoring: Yes.

Computer Software Options Available: Yes.

Cost of Materials

Specimen Set: $15.00

Counselee Materials: Career Survey Booklets (reusable) with Directions for Administration and Orientation Booklets (reusable) 35 for $26.25; Ohio Career Interest Survey Booklets (no ability) with Directions for Administration and Orientation Booklets (all reusable) 35 for $23.85; same for clinic or college counseling centers (no Orientation Booklets) 35 for $21.75. Machine scorable answer sheet (consumable) including Career Planning Booklets 35 for $21.20; same answer sheet without planning booklets 35 for $16.95. Other career resource materials are available from the publisher.

Published Reviews

None to date

Reviewed By

Christopher Borman
Professor, Department of Educational Psychology
Texas A&M University

The Career Survey consists of two parts: an interest survey called the Ohio Career Interest Survey and an ability test called the Career Ability Survey. The interest test has 12 scales with 11 items per scale. The 132 items in the interest test are scored on a five-point scale ranging from "dislike very much" to "like very much." The interest survey also has seven additional items that measure expressed interests relating to best-liked job tasks, best-liked school subjects, and future educational goals. The Career Ability Survey has two parts: (1) verbal reasoning is measured by 22 verbal analogy items; (2) nonverbal reasoning is measured by 18 items divided equally between two item types—number series and figural relationships.

The Ohio Career Interest Survey was developed by staff members from the Ohio Department of Education who worked with Ohio schools in using the Ohio Vocational Interest Survey (OVIS) and used their experience to develop this instrument. A two-dimensional model of people-things and data-ideas was used to develop the Ohio Career Interest Survey. Twelve interest scales originally containing 600 items were reduced to 11 items per scale. The Counselor's Guide (provided with the test and similar to a test manual) explains how the items were assigned to scales and how the final items were selected, but no data are given to support this selection process. The items of the interest inventory are stated as job tasks. Results of the Ohio Career Interest Survey are linked to the Worker Trait Group arrangement of jobs developed by the Department of Labor and to the Military Occupation Specialties used by the Department of Defense.

Approximately 500 ability test items were written and field tested with 8,000 students per grade (7–12) to develop the Career Ability Survey. From this pool three types of items were selected for inclusion in the test: verbal analogy, number series and figural relationships. Item selection criteria are described in the Counselor's Guide, but no data are given to support the selection of the 40 items that comprise the ability test.

NORMS AND SCORES

The Career Survey was designed for students in grades 7 through 12 and for use with adults. The survey was normed nationally in 1983 and 1984, and a list of participating schools is included in the Counselor's Guide. The norm sample seems to be a representative sample of secondary school students from across the country, but this observation is based only on visual examination of a table listing school districts and number of participants per grade level included in the norm sample. National norm group percentile ranks are provided for both the interest and ability scales. For the 12 interest scales, separate norm tables are provided for males, females, and combined sex groups of the following grade combinations: 7/8, 9/10, and 11/12. The test materials state that 11–12 grade norms are to be used for college-age individuals and young adults. For the two ability subtests (verbal and nonverbal), norm tables are provided separately for each grade (7 through 12). On the ability test, separate tables are not provided for males and females because sex differences on the ability subtests were negligible.

RELIABILITY

The internal consistency of the Ohio Career Interest Survey was tested using Cronbach's coefficient alpha with Ohio studies of 6,000 to 7,000 students per grade level. The coefficients for the 12 scales ranged from .86 to .93 indicating very respectable internal consistency. With 10-day intervals, test-retest reliability coefficients were calculated for samples of students in grades eight, nine and ten. Test-retest reliabilities for the interest survey ranged from .79 to .92 with the median reliability being .86. These data indicate that the 12 scales included in the Ohio Career Interest Survey are stable over time.

Reliability of the Career Ability Survey was assessed using the Kuder-Richardson Formula 20 and split-half method with a sample of approximately 1,500 students in grades 7–12. Reliabilities reported by grade level for the verbal and nonverbal sections of the test ranged from .62 to .84. Coefficients for all grades combined were .80 (KR-20) and .81 (split-half) for the verbal test, and .73 (KR-20) and .78 (split-half) for the nonverbal test. These data indicate satisfactory internal consistency for the ability test, but no data are reported on its test-retest reliability.

VALIDITY

Construct validity for the interest survey was established by a two-step process: (1) theoretical relationships were predicted from the two-dimensional model used to develop the instrument, and (2) the "fit" between observed and theoretical relationships was examined. Data presented in the Counselor's Guide tend to support predictions from the test model. Criterion validity for the 12 interest scales was investigated by relating measured interests to satisfaction with job training experiences in selected vocational training programs. Graduates (N = 996) from nine vocational training programs at 16 vocational schools completed the interest survey and a questionnaire measuring overall satisfaction with job tasks that they were trained to perform. The data reported generally supported the hypotheses that a satisfied group of students in a particular training program would show significantly higher interest on certain specified items and scales than a dissatisfied group and that the satisfied group means would be significantly higher than the standardization means for the same scales. Additional validation studies with students in other training programs or with actual workers in different occupations would add considerable support to the validity of the instrument.

The Career Ability Survey was written by the four authors who wrote the Developing Cognitive Abilities Test (DCAT), and one of the validity studies compares Career Ability measures with DCAT results. Data indicate that the verbal subtest is moderately to highly correlated with the DCAT verbal subtest while the nonverbal subtest is moderately correlated with the DCAT quantitative and spatial subtests. The Career Ability Survey was also correlated with the General Aptitude Test Battery (GATB), the American College Test (ACT), and the Scholastic Aptitude Test (SAT). Data indicate a substantial relationship between the verbal scale of the Career Ability Survey and the verbal scale of the GATB. There is a moderate relationship between the nonverbal scale of the Career Ability Survey and the numerical and spatial scales of the GATB. Finally, the Career Ability Survey subtests have substantial correlations with subtests of the ACT and SAT.

USABILITY

Although the Career Survey consists of two separate tests, both of these tests are included in one test booklet to allow them to be administered together. The interest survey is also included by itself in a separate booklet if the desire is to administer only the interest test. Directions for administration of the Career Survey are clear and easy to follow. The instrument can be hand scored, and scoring directions are given in the Counselor's Guide. Machine scoring is recommended and provided by the test publishers. A career profile is provided where the scores are presented in a visual fashion. Also, the profile reports results in words as a part of a personalized narrative for each student.

The Career Survey is new among career guidance instruments, but it offers the potential for being very useful, especially since it includes both an interest inventory and an ability test. Reliability data for the interest inventory indicate respectable internal consistency and stability. Reliability data for the ability survey indicate satisfactory internal consistency, but no information is reported on test-retest reliability. Evidence is presented supporting the construct and criterion validity of the interest survey, but further studies with more diverse populations are needed. Considerable evidence is provided in the Counselor's Guide supporting the criterion validity of the ability survey. The Career Survey is well developed in terms of providing detailed directions and support materials (career profile, career planning booklet, and career guidance activities) that test administrators and students/clients can use in interpreting results.

NOTE: This review was abridged from the author's original review which will appear in *The Tenth Mental Measurements Yearbook* with permission of the Buros Institute.

Occupational Aptitude Survey and Interest Schedule (OASIS)

Randall M. Parker

PRO-ED
5341 Industrial Oaks Blvd, Austin, TX 78735

Target Population: 8th–12th grade students.

Statement of the Purpose of the Instrument: To assist junior high and high school students in vocational exploration.

Titles of Subtests, Scales, Scores Provided: Aptitude Subtests: Vocabulary, Computation, Spatial Relations, Word Comparison, & Making Marks. Scores: Verbal Aptitude, Numerical Aptitude, Spatial Aptitude, Perceptual Aptitude, & General Ability. Interest Scales: Artistic, Scientific, Nature, Protective, Mechanical, Industrial, Business Detail, Selling, Accomodating, Humanitarian, Leading—Influencing, Physical Performing.

Forms and Levels Available with Dates of Publication/Revision of Each: One form 1983.

Date of Most Recent Edition of Test Manual, User's Guide, Etc.: 1983.

Language in Which Available: English only.

Time: Actual Test Time (Aptitude) 35 minutes, (Interest)—untimed
Total Administration Time (Aptitude) 45 minutes, (Interest)—Approx. 30 minutes.

Norm Group(s) on Which Scores Are Based: 1,398 8–12th grade students from 11 states.

Manner in Which Results are Reported for Individuals
 Types of Scores: Raw scores, percentiles, and stanines.

Report Format/Content for Group Summaries: Not available.

Scoring
 Machine Scoring Service: Not available.
 Hand Scoring
  Scored by: clerk; counselor.
  Time required for scoring: 5 minutes or less.
Local Machine Scoring: Not available

Computer Software Options Available: Not available.

Cost of Materials
  Specimen Set: $19.00
  Counselee Materials: Complete Aptitude Kit = $49.00; Test Booklets (10) = $15.00 (reusable); Answer Sheets (50) = $19.00; Aptitude Manual = $19.00. Complete Interest Kit = $59.00, Test Booklets (25) = $12.00 (reusable); Answer Sheets (50) = $15.00; Profile Sheets (50) = $15.00; Interest Manual = $21.00; Software = $59.00 (Unlimited Administration)

Published Reviews
Remer, R. (1986). Review of the Occupational Aptitude and Survey Interest Schedule (OASIS). *Journal of Counseling and Development*, 64(7), 467–468.

Reviewed by

Rory Remer

Associate Professor, Educational and Counseling Psychology University of Kentucky

The *Occupational Aptitude Survey & Interest Schedule* (OASIS) (Parker, 1983) is designed to provide aptitude and interest information for secondary students' career exploration. The battery consists of two instruments, the Aptitude Survey (AS) and the Interest Schedule (IS).

APTITUDE SURVEY

Parker's goal was to develop a short and usable instrument similar to the GATB and the DAT. The three power and two speeded subtests of the AS require a total working time of only 35 minutes; the goal of brevity was clearly attained.

Number right scoring is used for all five subtests. Although number right scoring is convenient (and hence popular), it provides little immunity from contamination by response set and/or test wiseness in certain test situations. This characteristics in the AS subtests raises questions as to what they measure—the intended attribute or response sets.

Scores

Number right scoring is easily accomplished for all subtests, and normative tables are easy to understand and use. Raw scores, five-point scores, percentile ranks, and stanines are produced and displayed in a student profile on the back of the answer booklet. Stanines are also plotted on a grid to assist presentation. Discussion is provided concerning the limitations of various types of scores. It would be helpful to include a score range or band, using the standard error of measurement in plotting scores to help make clear to clients the unimportance of minor differences (Mehrens & Lehmann, 1985). Such safeguards against overinterpreting minor differences are especially important with measures of moderate reliability.

Parker contended that five-point scores indicating the suitability of examinees for various occupations should be useful in matching clients' aptitutes to particular occupations, and this may be true. The derivation of these scores seems to be based on the comparability of the AS to the GATB. Without validation of AS scores against more direct criteria, such as occupational work samples, the use of the five-point scores seems questionable.

Norms

Comparison of the sample to 1980 census figures indicates that the sample deviated in a statistical sense with respect to the variables considered—sex, ethnicity, region or residence (urban or rural). How seriously these discrepancies affect the usefulness of the scores is hard to say, particularly in a sample of junior high school students. Still, providing a basis for comparing the norming sample goes far beyond the efforts of most developers. The manual's suggestion that users produce local norms is a good one, depending on how the information is to be used. Although local norms are often useful for achievement tests, they make little sense for aptitude tests where comparisons are to a broader spectrum of people.

Validity and Reliability

Although the development of the AS is carefully described, data supporting the claims for validity and reliability are relatively meager. The main case made for AS validity is its comparability to the GATB, a claim which is only partially supported by the evidence presented.

Reliability estimates range from .70 to .94 (median range .78 to .90), depending on subtests and grade. No discussion is offered concerning the reliability of profiles, a topic elucidated by Anatasi (1985). Although the profile should not be used to judge differences among subtests, the plotting of profiles will almost certainly lead to such comparisons.

INTEREST SCHEDULE

The IS was designed to provide a low cost instrument that would not require the use of computers for scoring. In an era of reduced funding for education in general and guidance functions in particular, attaining this aim would certainly be worthwhile.

The instrument consists of 20 stimulus items for each of the 12 IS scales. Item response options are "like," "dislike," and "neutral." The first 120 items are job titles, while the last 120 are job activities that are widely associated with various occupations (e.g., "use firearms safely to enforce the law"). One wonders whether presenting all the job titles first could create a particular mind set that might influence examinees' subsequent reactions to job title-related activities.

The source of item content for the job activities (The *Guide for Occupational Exploration*) seems somewhat undesirable. Assessing reactions only to activities "judged recognizable and understandable" does little to expand a person's perspective or to enrich the information base provided by an interest inventory. Also, it would seem useful to include some job activities that are contrary to popular conceptions of the occupations involved.

Scores

Scoring procedures are as simple as those of a 12-scale, 240-item instrument can be. The instructions are clear, and the formating facilitates the procedures.

The report form is easily understood and has the advantage of presenting female, male and total group percentile norms for each scale on a single document. It should facilitate interpretation. The section of the form that presents profile scores would be improved by use of confidence bands (Mehrens & Lehmann, 1985).

The instructions, suggestions and admonitions for interpreting the IS include some excellent points. For example, the warning that no occupation is exclusively male or female in orientation is effectively given. Some of the sample cases, however, do not seem well chosen or constructed.

An additional caution should have been included in the section of the manual concerned with interpretation. Because there is evidence that interests do not crystalize until about age 18, care in the use of any interest information with younger students, particularily junior high school students, should be emphasized.

Validity and Reliability

The technical data presented to support the use of the IS have somewhat more difficulties attendant than those offered for the AS. Content validity is based on comparability with U.S. Employment Services (USES) publications. Construct validity of the 12 subscales is supported by factor analytic evidence, but should be improved through multi-trait/multi-method and criterion related approaches. The problem with the normative sample is the same as for the AS. There is an excellent handling of sex bias issues through balancing and norming procedures.

The Administrative Scale focuses on the validity of administration. Data that come from examinees' responses (e.g., percentage of "like" responses) may prove valuable to counseling. Such information may provide hints concerning examinees' level of career development and maturity, or even involvement in the whole exploration process. For example, someone who likes everything may not have a well-developed value system; someone who dislikes all activities may have personal adjustment problems or may object to the measurement process. The scale is not as yet validated, however. The concept itself is intriguing and promising, but if it is not ready, then the appropriateness of presenting it seems questionable, at least as part of the validity data proper. When the work on it has been completed it should provide uniquely useful data to counselors and students.

Test-retest scale reliabilities obtained over a five-week period ranged from .66 to .91, (median range .86 to .92) with a moderate median of .82. Alpha reliability coefficients by sex and grade are also reported for each scale, ranging from .78 to .94.

SUMMARY

Both components of the OASIS present limited validity evidence at the present time, problematic normative data, moderate reliability, and insufficient cautions concerning the interpretation of differences between scores. The IS also has insufficient cautions concerning the instability of interests in younger examinees and from content that fails to transcend commonly perceived job activities. Some of the worthwhile aims of the developer are attained, at least in a limited sense. The manner in which the test manuals present the technical information does a disservice to the claims made. As the battery now stands I can at best recommend its use with a great deal of caution and would personally prefer more development and validation be done before suggesting any more positive action.

REFERENCES

Anastasi, A. (1985). Interpreting results from multiscore batteries. *Journal of Counseling and Development, 64*, 86–89.

Mehrens, W.A., & Lehmann, I.J. (1985). Interpreting test scores to clients: What score should one use? *Journal of Counseling and Development, 63*, 317–320.

Parker, R.M. (1983). *OASIS (Occupational Aptitude Survey and Interest Schedule.)* Austin, TX: PRO:ED.

Note: Significant portions of this review were abridged from the author's original review in *The Journal of Counseling and Development* with permission of AACD.

Planning Career Goals (PCG)

American Institutes for Research

CTB/McGraw-Hill
2500 Garden Road
Monterey, California 93940

Target Population: Grades 8 through 12.

Statement of the Purpose of the Instrument: To provide career guidance information regarding the client's values, interests, abilities, career information, and career and educational plans.

Titles of Subtests, Scales, Scores Provided: Interest and Information in each of 12 Career Groups. Ability scores for 10 Abilities as well as weighted Ability scores for each of the 12 Career Groups. A narrative report that combines and compares all three scores in the 12 Groups. A graphic profile of scores in Interest areas and Ability measures.

Forms and Levels Available, with Dates of Publication/Revision of Each: There is only one form and one level of each of the tests. The copyright dates are 1975 and 1976.

Date of Most Recent Edition of Test Manual, User's Guide, Etc.: 1976.

Languages in Which Available: English only.

Time: Actual Test Time—278 minutes for all parts.
　　　Total Administration Time—add 20 minutes for handling materials.

Norm Group(s) on Which Scores Are Based: Students in each of the grades who participated in the equating study, plus the Project TALENT population on whom the original research was based.

Manner in Which Results Are Reported for Individuals
　Types of Scores: Raw scores, percentile ranks, weighted interpretation of scores, narrative reports.
　Report Format/Content
　　Basic Service: A two page report with graphic and narrative presentation of all scores and their interpretation relative to each other. For example for the Career Group for which a client expressed most interest, all scores are compared.
　　Options: A translucent report showing the profiles in the same proportion as those that are presented in the Career Data Book allows the client to superimpose the profile over those showing similar scores for each of over 100 careers. Thus one could see, for example, that engineers did better in math in high school than the client.

Report Format/Content for Group Summaries: Not available.

Scoring
　Machine Scoring Service
　　Cost of basic service per counselee: $1.77.

213

Cost of options: $.70 for translucent profile.
Time required for scoring and returning (maximum): 3 weeks.
Hand Scoring: *Scored by*: clerk; counselor.
Time required for scoring: 30 minutes.
Local Machine Scoring: Not available.

Computer Software Options Available: Not available.

Cost of Materials
Specimen Set: $10.00.
Counselee Materials: Complete Battery, reusable: $88.50 for materials for 25; Answer sheet, consumable: $50.50 for materials for 50.

Published Reviews
Super, D.E. (1982). In J.T. Kapes & M.M. Mastie, (Eds.), *A counselor's guide to vocational guidance instruments*. Falls Church, VA: National Vocational Guidance Association.

Reviewed By

Dean Nafziger

Laboratory Director, Far West Laboratory for Educational Research and Development San Francisco, California

Planning Career Goals (PCG) consists of career guidance materials centered about a set of tests and interest inventories developed as a part of the Project TALENT research conducted by the American Institutes for Research. The stated purpose of the PCG is to "assist guidance and counseling personnel in helping students in Grades 8–12 make realistic and long-lasting educational and career plans."

The authors of PCG have attempted to produce a guidance device which includes assessment instruments, reporting mechanisms for students and counselors, and guidance materials. The intended use of the tests and materials is for students to take a battery of instruments comprising measures of values, interest in various careers, information about career-related areas, and abilities which can be compared with the high school profiles of persons in various occupations or occupational groups.

It is important for the user to understand that the research information underlying the PCG pertains to the characteristics of the assessment instruments and to their interpretation. However, the effectiveness of the battery in meeting its purpose of promoting long-lasting plans has not been evaluated.

Also, the user should be aware that no modifications or new revisions have been made since its initial publication in 1976. This lack of attention to updating the instrument should concern potential users.

TEST BATTERY CONTENT

Four types of data are gathered from students by the test battery—values; interests, information and abilities. Data regarding a student's values are gathered through 15 questions printed directly on the battery answer booklet. The student is asked to indicate the degree of importance of various needs and activities related to quality of life, e.g., material well-being, having and raising children, or expressing self.

Interest data are gathered through a separate Interest Inventory booklet comprising three parts. In the first part, students indicate the extent to which they think they would like each of 104 listed occupations. In the second part, students indicate how much they think they would enjoy each of 99 occupational activities. In the third part, students are asked to indicate how much they would enjoy each of 97 different activities which they are likely to find somewhat familiar.

Data about student information are gathered using a separate Information Measures booklet consisting of 240 items. The Information Measures items "sample knowledge that individuals would have acquired if they had studied about an occupation or participated in activities related to an occupation." Items were chosen to provide an indication of knowledge that individuals have gained in each of the 12 occupational categories.

Data about student abilities are gathered for ten areas: reading comprehension (40 items), mathematics (24 items), abstract reasoning (22 items), creativity (24 items), mechanical reasoning (25 items), English (48 items), quantitative reasoning (22 items), vocabulary (60 items), visualization (25 items), and computation (76 items). Items for all areas except computation are included in the Ability Measures booklet. The computation scale, a speeded test, is in a separate booklet designed to facilitate finding and marking answers.

Taken together, the test battery provides a comprehensive assessment as a basis for career planning, and this is one of the prominent features of the instrument. At the same time, the comprehensiveness leads to a weakness in the test. Namely, it is difficult for a counselor to learn and understand the different parts of the test and its related materials. This difficulty is compounded by the failure of any one of the accompanying descriptive documents to fully illuminate the counselor, and by some modest inconsistencies in these documents. The three descriptive documents that accompany the test battery are an Examiner's Manual, a Counselor's Handbook, and Technical Bulletin No. 1.

SCORING AND REPORTING

Procedures for using and scoring the tests are well delineated, although this information is scattered among the three descriptive documents. Scoring may be done by hand scoring stencils or through a scoring service. Hand scoring the entire battery takes about one and a half hours per student and, for some sections of the battery, it would be quite complex. It seems that there are few circumstances in which hand scoring would be advantageous.

215

The primary report for students is the career planning report, available only when scoring service is purchased. Three types of information are included in the report. First, students' responses on the interests, information and abilities tests are summarized for each of the 12 occupational groups. Percentile ranks are given (for both male and female norm groups) for each of the ten scores within the abilities test. Second, comparisons are shown between students' scores on values, interests, information and abilities and the scores of individuals employed within each of the 12 occupational categories. Third, a computerized narrative report about certain of the responses is given.

The report provides considerable information to the students. Except through portions of the narrative report, however, no synthesis of the information across the various types of data obtained on each student is provided. No overall career profile is developed, and it is not clear how a student should interpret results if different profiles occur in different portions of the test battery. This plethora of information without a synthesis seems, to this reviewer, to put too much of a burden on the student. Counselors should be prepared to provide considerable assistance to students in interpreting information.

A second report is the career planning profile that can be purchased as an option from the scoring service or produced through handscoring. This report allows students to compare their interest and ability profiles with those of individuals in specific occupations as well as in occupational groups. In addition to the two individual student reports, group reports are available.

TECHNICAL DATA

Means, standard deviations, and intercorrelation coefficients for the values items, Interest Inventory, Information Measures, and Ability Measures, and split-half reliability coefficients and standard errors of measurement on the latter three measures are reported for each of grades 8 through 11. There are no data for Grade 12. Reported reliability coefficients for the Interest Inventory range from .84 to 1.00 (sic), from .63 to .89 for Information Measures,, and from .68 to .94 for Ability Measures (with corrections made to prevent exaggerations that could occur because of the speededness of the computation section).

Because the PCG is based upon longitudinal data from a large national sample of students, validity data should be extensive. The test authors assert that predictive validity exists because the predictive weights for the occupational profiles are based upon data from people in various career groups obtained when they were in high school. However, some important questions about the validity data have not been addressed. Do those within career groups have similar profiles that are distinctive from those in other career groups? Are the predictive weights developed using only those who are satisfied with their career choices? Are the predictive weights based upon those who have been in a career category for an adequate period of time? Are the predictive weights based upon an adequate number of individuals for every career category? Despite the extensive research behind the PCG, its validity has not been thoroughly demonstrated.

SUMMARY

Planning Career Goals is a comprehensive career guidance system, developed through a large-scale research effort, that gathers several types of data on students

216

and provides guidance materials related to the assessment instruments. Despite its research base, users should be cautioned about some apparent shortcomings in the test battery. In particular, information from the test battery seems difficult to use because no synthesis of the results is provided, and the methods used for developing the predictive weights for the career profiles leave the validity of the profiles in question. The test developers should improve the descriptive documents so that each has a clear purpose and communicates to its intended audience. Users of the materials should be given guidelines on how to combine the information from all parts of the test battery, especially when discrepancies occur. Data demonstrating the appropriateness of the criterion group for the development of the predictive weights should be provided. Finally, an evaluation of the PCG is needed to determine its effectiveness in meeting the goal of its authors to promote long-lasting and realistic career plans.

Note: Significant portions of this review were abridged from the author's original review in *The Eighth Mental Measurements Yearbook* with permission of the Buros Institute.

System for Assessment and Group Evaluation (SAGE)/ Compute-A-Match

Evaluation Component:
Schabacher and Associates, Greenwich, NJ
Raymond G. Wasdyke, Educational Testing Service
and Charles Loch, Creative Development Associates
Computer Component:
Neal Grosson, Orion Software

Train-Ease Corporation
47 Marble Avenue, Pleasantville, NY 10570

Target Population: EMR, TMR, LD, disadvantaged, displaced workers, persons with various disabilities with some test modification. Suggested use with persons 15 years and older. Vocabulary does not exceed 4th grade level unless a higher level of language ability is being tested.

Statement of the Purpose of the Instrument: Compute-A-Match was developed to match the aptitudes, educational levels, attitudes, and temperaments of people to jobs and training.

Titles of Subtests, Scales, Scores Provided: Vocational Interest Inventory (VII): relates to and utilizes the 12 interest areas of the Guide for Occupational Exploration.
Cognitive and Conceptual Abilities Test (C-CAT): relates to the Dictionary of Occupational Titles reasoning, math, and language levels and yields raw scores which are then converted to GED levels of 1–5.
Vocational Aptitude Battery (VAB): relates to the 11 DOT aptitude requirements and yields raw scores which are then converted to aptitude levels of 1–5 used by the Department of Labor.
Assessment of Work Attitudes (AWA): yields raw scores, converted to an attitudinal index developed and normed by authors of test.
Temperament Factor Assessment (TFA): elicits a client's preferred temperaments which relate to the Department of Labor's ten temperament factors.

Forms and Levels Available, with Dates of Publication/Revision of Each: One form, one level available. SAGE (Vocational Battery) published in 1980; JOBS (Computer Match) published in 1982; Autoscore published in 1983; Compute-A-Match combined version of three components) published in 1985.

Date of Most Recent Edition of Test Manual, User's Guide, Etc.: 1985 with some 1986 revisions.

Languages in Which Available: English only.

Time: Actual Test Time—69 minutes.
Total Administration Time—2½ hours.

Norm Group(s) on Which Scores Are Based: School Composite (Jr. and Sr. H.S. students—ages 15–21); Competitive Employment (UAW, GM, Ford); Vocational Technical (students participating in vocational training programs); Low Functioning (IQs 40–112).

Manner in Which Results are Reported for Individuals
   Types of Scores: GED and vocational aptitude levels utilized by DOL.

Report Format/Content
   Basic Service: Computer printout containing vocational profile, training sites, possible jobs, job descriptions.
   Options: The SAGE results, used without the JOBS, can be reported on the SAGE Profile Form, which includes the Raw Score Conversion Profile, Occupational Match Form, and the Observation Record.

Report Format/Content
   Basic Service: Client Bank

Scoring
   Machine Scoring Service: Not available.
   Hand Scoring
   Scored by: clerk; counselor.
   Time required for scoring: 30 minutes.
   Local Machine Scoring
   Provision/conditions/equipment required: Optical card reader, computer with JOBS software.

Computer Software Options Available: Does not apply. SAGE does not require computer for administration or scoring. Autoscore automates the scoring process, and JOBS is a computer program. Compute-A-Match is the combined package of the three components.

Additional Comments of Interest to Users: INFOSTAT (software which will generate statistical analysis of client data including standard deviation, correlations, and graphs.

Published Reviews

Botterbusch, K. F. (1983). *A Comparison of Computerized Job Matching Systems* Menonomie, WI: Materials Development Center.
Botterbusch, K. F. (1986). *A Comparison of Computerized Job Matching Systems* Menonomie, WI: 2nd ed., Materials Development Center.
Botterbusch, K. F. (1980). *A Comparison of Commercial Vocational Evaluation Systems* Menonomie, WI: Materials Development Center.
Botterbusch, K. F. (1982). *A Comparison of Commercial Vocational Evaluation Systems* Menonomie, WI: 2nd ed., Materials Development Center.

Field, T. (1984). (Ed.). *A Directory of Micro-Computer Software for Disabled Persons*, Athens, GA.

Fry, R. (1983). *Job Opportunity Based Search (J.O.B.S.)* Vocational Evaluation and Work Adjustment Bulletin, Vol 16, 145–146.

Reviewed By

Regis J. Jacobs
Assistant Director, Special Education Division
Oakland Schools, Pontiac, Michigan
and
Bernard A. Gucwa
Consultant, Measurements and Guidance
Macomb Intermediate School District
Mt. Clemens, Michigan

The System for Assessment and Group Evaluation (SAGE)/Compute-A-Match is composed of five separate components which, when combined, form a total vocational assessment package. The components are: 1) a vocational aptitude battery (consisting of 11 subtests), 2) a vocational interest inventory, 3) a measurement of General Educational Development, 4) an assessment of attitudes toward others in working environment and 5) an assessment of temperament. Taken together, the testing units address all of characteristics described by the *Dictionary of Occupational Titles* (DOT).

Central to this system is the Vocational Aptitude Battery (VAB). Eleven aptitudes are evaluated in this battery through the following timed subtests:

1. *Verbal*—An evaluee is to indicate which of four possible words are "the same as" or "opposite of" a given word.
2. *Numerical*—The evaluee is to indicate the correct answer to twenty-five story problems using a multiple choice format.
3. *General*—Three separate sub-sections of this component use paper and pencil tasks which relate to a) verbal reasoning, b) arithmetic reasoning, c) form perception.
4. *Spatial*—A hands-on task which requires the evaluee to assemble a system of interlocking wheels using a picture of a total assembly as a model.
5. *Form Perception*—Evaluee is required to select a matching form, such as washers or nuts, from photographic samples.

6. *Clerical Perception*—Four distinct subtests which call for evaluee to a) match names, b) match telephone numbers, c) file alphabetically, d) sort by zip code.
7. *Motor Coordination*—Evaluee is to depress buttons as a light appears above them on an electronic panel.
8. *Finger Dexterity*—Evaluee is required to assemble a small pressure coupling consisting of five small parts.
9. *Manual Dexterity*—Evaluee is required to assemble a series of electronic connectors.
10. *Eye-Hand-Foot Coordination*—Using a joy stick and foot bar, evaluee is required to line up lights on an electronic console.
11. *Color Discrimination*— Evaluee is required to match colors from photographs using a multiple choice format.

NORMS AND SCORES

The normative population for the aptitude section of SAGE offers the evaluator four comparative groups. The school composite group consists of 1220 15 to 21 year olds. The competitive employment group is 400 auto workers. The vocational training group consists of 650 vocational students. The low functioning group consists of school age persons with I.Q.'s from 40 to 112. Users are encouraged to develop local norms. National norms have not been developed. Raw scores are converted to the GED aptitude levels of 1 to 5 used by the Department of Labor.

RELIABILITY

The issue of stability of test scores is addressed in SAGE by the application of standard error of measurement values in converting raw scores to a five-level standard score report format. In so doing, the developers increase the reliability of the reported scores by approaching the evaluation as a wide band, low fidelity procedure.

Test-retest coefficients reported for the manipulative tests and color discrimination range from .63 for clerical sort to .91 for motor coordination. All correlations are significant to at least the .01 level. KR-20 reliability coefficients are reasonably high.

VALIDITY

Concurrent validity is suggested through a comparison of SAGE scores to GATB and Valpar scores using a table for conversion to DOT levels. The authors offer this table as a means of predicting the aptitude levels into which VAB scores will fall. Seven of the ten correlation coefficients reported in this analysis have r > .60. The Eye-Hand-Foot aptitude correlates to Valpar at r = .39.

A variety of item analysis data and validity data are presented for each section. Validity data include correlations with ratings and other tests; the majority of these are at acceptable levels.

USABILITY

Ease and speed of testing are major selling points for SAGE. As many as six to eight evaluees can be tested as a group in as little as 2½–3 hours by an evaluator. However, school users may find that the management of more than four or five students at a time is difficult and will likely require the provision of an assistant. The evaluator should be trained prior to using the system.

A hand-written report is easily developed from conversion tables, and interpretation to students is done using a bar g raph depicting their performance on a five point scale on which point three is average.

A computer job matching system (Compute-A-Match) is available at added cost for the creation of a detailed report on feasible jobs and training opportunities. Please note that the Compute-A-Match Program can be used with SAGE, but that the use of SAGE is not dependent upon it.

As is the case with all of the job matching systems, higher functioning evaluees will receive exhaustive lists which will need to be limited by interest and temperament, and less able evaluees will primarily see tending and service occupations on their reports. This is not intended as a criticism. More qualified persons will yield more job titles. Since the GED is a critical factor in the resulting reports, the counselor will want to be particularly attentive to these scores.

The user will also want to consider the portability feature of SAGE. Although most of the testing material can be packed into three easily handled double width suitcase type boxes, the evaluator will need a station wagon size cargo area to transport. In transit, the Eye-Hand-Foot Coordination test is particularly susceptible to damage, and the manual cautions against overextending the movement of the joy stick and rudder bar.

In summary, SAGE offers an integrated package of test instruments which can provide a general vocational profile (worker trait profile). The VAB emphasizes a "hands-on" manipulative testing approach that brings a work sample approach to aptitude testing and can be complemented with quick tests for GED, interests, attitude and temperament. This instrument is best used as a broad screening, general tendency indicator and should not be relied upon for discrete occupational/vocational placement.

REFERENCES

Botterbusch, K.F. (1987). *Vocational Assessment and Evaluation Systems: A Comparison*, Menominee, WI: Materials Development Center, University of Wisconsin-Stout.

Botterbusch, K.F. (1982). *Sage-System of assessment and group evaluation, Vocational Evaluation and Work Adjustment Bulletin*, 15 (1) 32–34.

Cronbach, L.J. (1970). *Essential of Psychological Testing*. Third Edition. New York: Harper and Row.

Irvin, L.K. & Gersten, R.M. (1984). Validating Vocational Assessment of Severely Mentally Retarded Persons: Issues and Application. *American Journal of Mental Deficiency*, 88, 411–417.

World of Work Inventory (WOWI)

World of Work, Inc.

World of Work, Inc.
2923 N. 67th Place
Scottsdale, AZ 85251

Target Population: Ages 15–65, high schools, colleges, rehabilitation facilities, displaced home-makers, prisons, business and industry.

Statement of the Purpose of the Instrument: To aid in the selection of occupations and careers appropriate and consistent with the job related temperaments, aptitudes and interests of the individual.

Titles of Subtests, Scales, Scores Provided: Job satisfaction indicators, aptitude for learning, school achievement, and career interests.

Forms and Levels Available, with Dates of Publication/Revision of Each: World of Work Inventory—1971, revised 1973 and 1980. Modified Version (5th grade level), revised 1985.

Date of Most Recent Edition of Test Manual, User's Guide, Etc.: 1987—4th edition.

Languages in Which Available: English and Spanish.

Time: Actual Test Time: Not timed; a power test.
      Total Administration Time: 2–2½ hours.

Norm Group(s) on Which Scores Are Based: Ages 13–65, grades 8–16 +; high schools (public and private); community/junior colleges; universities; prisoners; technical colleges; vocational rehabilitators; vocational counselors; businesses.

Manner in Which Results Are Reported for Individuals
  Types of Scores: Raw scores plus bar graph (interests, aptitudes, and temperaments).

Report Format/Content
  Basic Service: Bargraphs and dictionary plus Dictionary of Occupational Titles codes.
  Options: Six to eight page interpretation, one page summary with job recommendations.

Report Format/Content for Group Summaries
  Basic Service: Statistical summary.

Scoring
  Machine Scoring Service
    Cost of basic service per counselee: Approximately $2.50 per person for non-profit entities; $6.50 per person for profit making entities.
    Cost of options: Statistical summary—$10.00. Narrative summary—$10.00, for profit-making entities; $5.00 for non profit.
    Time required for scoring and returning (maximum): 12 hour turnaround time.
  Hand Scoring: Not available.

Cost of Materials
  Specimen Set: For profit making entities—$37.95: for non-profit entities—$27.95 POSTPAID.
  Counselee Materials
    Reusable: Testbook, Interpretation Manual, Mini-Manual.
    Non/Reusable: Occupational Exploration Worksheets. Prices vary with quantity, please write
    for price sheet.

Additional Comments of Interest to Users: All test materials are discounted to non-profit organizations; interpretive summary available.

Published Reviews
Botterbusch, K.F. (1987). *Vocational Assessment and Evaluation Systems: A Comparison.* Materials
  Development Center, Stout Vocational Rehabilitation Institute.

Reviewed By

Wilbur L. Layton
Professor and Chair
Department of Psychology
Iowa State University

The World of Work Inventory (WOWI) was developed about 20 years ago by Robert Ripley. It was reviewed by the present author in the *Eighth Mental Measurements Yearbook* (Layton, 1978) and by Locke (1977) in *Measurement and Evaluation in Guidance*. Both reviewers criticized the WOWI because the evidence for reliability and validity was meager, and norms were inadequate. Layton concluded, "Unfortunately, the psychometric properties of the inventory are not developed to the point that this reviewer can recommend the use of the inventory in work with individuals." . . . "Considerably more research covering reliability, validity, and norms must be carried out before the worth of the inventory can be ascertained." Locke (1977, 1982) stated, "Although these are important advantages, they are not significant enough to warrant recommendation of the WOWI over either the Strong Campbell Interest Inventory or the Kuder Occupational Interest Survey (Form DD). Both these measures have more reported validity and reliability data, more research, and more occupational normative data than the World of Work Inventory." The present manual of interpretation for the WOWI refers to the work of Robert Ripley as having established the reliability and validity of the inventory but does not present details of the Ripley research and does not present a bibliographic reference to that work. A separate manuscript describes a small test-retest study. The interpretative materials currently available in the Specimen Set for the WOWI have not sufficiently addressed the need for adequate psychometric evidence to demonstrate that the inventory is measuring something in a reliable way, and that that something is of value in the counseling and education of adolescents and adults.

According to the manual of interpretation provided by the WOWI publisher, "The three basic parts of the W.O.W. Inventory are designed to measure the whole person in relation to his or her total individual differences. The Career Interest Activities section explores the individual's preference for tasks and activities relevant to the jobs in which most people are engaged. The Job Satisfaction Indicators section includes 12 temperament factors related to worker placement and adjustment. The Vocational Training Potentials section measures the individual's possession of entry level skills or the possible potentials for benefitting from further training." . . . "The World of Work Inventory has been developed as a multiple purpose instrument in which the results may be used for better career exploration, career decisions, job placement, education and training programs selections, and local research." The WOWI was intended for use with clients from early adolescence to adulthood.

The inventory consists of four sections: Identifying Information, Career Interest Activities, Vocational Training Potentials, and Job Satisfaction Indicators. The identifying information section allows the subject to record vital statistics, stated occupational choices, and best-liked school subjects. The career interest activities section contains job related activity items to which the subject responds "like," "neutral," or "dislike." The vocational training potential section purportedly measures six aptitude-achievement areas: verbal, numerical, abstractions, spatial form, clerical, and mechanical-electrical. The abstractions and spatial form items are considered to be aptitude oriented, and the clerical and mechanical-electrical items are meant to be achievement oriented. The verbal and numerical items measure "the more traditional ability to do public school work of aptitude-achievement." The job satisfaction indicators section covers 12 job temperament areas; the subject is asked to respond "like," "dislike," or "neutral" to a job temperament indicator such as "going to movies alone."

The career interest activities scales are keyed to the job classifications scheme in the Dictionary of Occupational Titles (DOT), and the job satisfaction indicators are keyed to the job temperaments listed by the U.S. Department of Labor. This attempt to coordinate the inventory with DOT is about the only laudatory aspect of the WOWI.

Seventeen basic occupational area worksheets containing 117 career family areas are coordinated with the inventory profile results. These worksheets were designed to allow for personal involvement in occupational exploration by the test taker.

VALIDITY

Little evidence of validity is given in the manual of interpretation. It does give means and standard deviations for selected groups. The basis of selection is not given. Also presented in the manual are correlations with miscellaneous interest, mechanical ability, and personality tests. The number of cases is small and of unlisted origin. From an examination of the data one can only conclude that evidence for validity is meager and weak.

NORMS

No norms, in the generally accepted sense of being based on representative groups, are given in the manual of interpretation. For the Vocational Training

Potentials, several norm tables in loose leaf form are available but one cannot determine the source of the norms from the information given. The authors assume a normal distribution of raw scores for the Vocational Training Potentials and without supporting evidence being presented in the manual they use standard scores based on the normal curve to report the Vocational Training Potentials, The Career Interest Activities and Job Satisfaction Indicators scales are interpreted according to the relative placement of scores to each other on a given profile.

INTERPRETIVE MATERIALS

The authors have made a considerable effort to provide interpretive materials. In addition to the large manual there are a mini-manual and an audio cassette to help users learn the system. A new narrative report form can be provided. It is too bad that the WOWI's psychometric characteristics as reported cannot support such efforts.

SUMMARY

The authors are to be commended for their attempts to relate the WOWI on an individualized basis to the Dictionary of Occupational Titles (DOT) and the world of work. As has already been indicated the inventory needs further research to establish its reliability and validity, and adequate norms need to be provided. This reviewer suggests that the WOWI publisher rely on the *Standards for Educational and Psychological Testing* (American Psychological Association, 1985) and use the technical standards for test construction as a guide to providing information that will enable prospective users to properly evaluate and use the inventory. The publisher has provided a laudable amount of interpretation aides. The Guide to Career Families can be very useful as an interviewing aid even without the WOWI. One should keep in mind, however, that the Strong-Campbell and Kuder are much better established than the WOWI in assessing vocational interests, and the Self Directed Search with its materials related to the DOT surpasses the WOWI in that approach. As a final comparison, the DAT and GATB are better established as measures of vocationally related aptitudes.

The basic approach of assessing interests, aptitudes, and personality in a single measuring instrument is an idea worthy of development. The WOWI needs further developmental work before this reviewer would feel comfortable about recommending its use.

REFERENCES

American Psychological Association. (1985). *Standards for educational and psychological testing*. Washington, DC: Author.

Layton, W. L. (1975). Review of World of Work Inventory. In O.K. Buros, (Ed.), *The Eighth Mental Measurement Yearbook*. Highland Park, NJ: The Gryphon Press.

Locke, D. C. (1977). Review of the World of Work Inventory. *Measurement and Evaluation in Guidance*, 10, 62–64.

Locke, D. C. (1982). Review of the World of Work Inventory. In J. T. Kapes & M. M. Mastie (Eds.), *A counselor's guide to vocational guidance instruments*. Falls Church, VA. National Vocational Guidance Association.

NOTE: Significant portions of this review were abridged from the author's original review in *The Eighth Mental Measurements Yearbook* with permission of the Buros Institute.

Personality
Measures

Myers-Briggs Type Indicator (MBTI)

Isabel Briggs Myers and Katharine C. Briggs

Consulting Psychologists Press, Inc.
577 College Ave., Palo Alto, CA 94306

Target Population: High school through older adults (can be used down to 4th grade; requires 8th grade reading).

Statement of the Purpose of the Instrument: To make the theory of psychological types described by C. G. Jung understandable and useful in people's lives. To provide a measure of Jung's theory of types.

Titles of Subtests, Scales, Scores Provided: Four bipolar scales: Extraversion—Introversion, Sensing—Intuition, Thinking—Feeling, Judgment——Perception. Preference scores reported for each scale.

Forms and Levels Available, with Dates of Publication/Revision of Each: Form G, 126 items is the standard form, revised 1977; Form F (166 items): Form AV (abbreviated, self-scoring version, 50 items) form J (290 items, research: 1985); Form G, Self Scorable (94 items).

Date of Most Recent Edition of Test Manual: 1985.

Languages in Which Available: English and an official version in Spanish but translation available in Japanese, Italian, and French.

Time: Actual Test Time: No time limit but typically takes 20–30 minutes.

Norm Group(s) on Which Scores Are Based: Form G Restandardization performed on 2,225 students grades 4–12 and 3,362 college freshmen. Norms available on over 55,971 people.

Manner in Which Results Are Reported for Individuals

Types of Scores: Raw score for each of eight preferences; Four preference scores indicating relative strength of preference; Four type letters indicating direction preference (type). Computer scoring also generates for each bi-polar scale: one continuous score, one standard score for preferences, one standard score for word pairs, and one standard score for phrases.

Report Format/Content
Basic Service: Definition of preferences, type, preference scores, description of all 16 types.
Options: Group type tables.

Report Format/Content For Group Summaries
Basic Service: Type table showing number and percent of each type in the group.

Scoring
Machine Scoring Service
Cost of basic service per counselee: Depends on number scored: ranges from $4.50 to $3.00/person if more than 50 are scored together.
Time required for scoring and returning (maximum): 24 hour. turnaround.
Hand Scoring
Scored by: clerk; counselor.
Time required for scoring: 3–4 minutes.

Local Machine Scoring
Provisions/conditions/equipment required: Requires a personal computer (IBM compatible) and two pieces of hardware (a code lock with scoring algorithms and a controller). With additional optical scanner, local group scoring available immediately.

Computer Software Options Available: standard administration on-line; scoring: interpretation:
Ways in Which Computer Version Differs: Stores responses in a file for research.

Cost of Material
Specimen Set: $3.00
Counselee Materials: Report form—$5.50/50; Form G, (reusable) question booklets—$9.50/25; answer sheets—$6.50/50; Introduction to Type—$1.25.

Additional Comments of Interest to Users: Instrument supported by a non-profit ed/res group: Center for Applications of Psychological Type; an international users group: Assoc. of Psychological Type; Journal of Psych. Type; over a dozen books; new research form available.

Published Reviews
Carlvn, M. (1977). An assessment of the Myers-Briggs Type Indicator. *Journal of Personality Assessment*, 41 (5), 461–473.

Comrev, A. L. (1983). An evaluation of the Myers-Briggs Type Indicator. *Academic Psychology Bulletin, 5*, 115–129.

Devito, A. J. (1985). Review of the Myers-Briggs Type Indicator. In J.V. Mitchell (Ed.), *The Ninth Mental Measurements Yearbook, Volume II* (pp 1030–1032). Lincoln, NE: The Buros Institute of Mental Measurements.

McCaulley, M. H. (1981). Jung's theory of psychological types and the Myers-Briggs Type Indicator. In P. McReynolds (Ed.), *Advances in Psychological Assessment, Volume V*, (pp. 294–352). San Francisco: Jossey Bass., Inc.

Carl G. Willis
Counseling Psychologist
University of Missouri-Columbia
and
Tom L. Ham
Research Associate
University of Missouri-Columbia

The Myers-Briggs Type Indicator (MBTI) is a forced-choice, self-report inventory which reflects over six decades of thinking and research efforts in the adaptation of Carl Jung's theory of conscious psychological type. The theory assumes a developmental and dynamic model which incorporates the apparently random array of human behavior into an orderly and consistent form. Jung's theory is viewed as a "powerful way for illuminating everyday observations about individual styles of information gathering and decision making" (Myers & McCaulley, 1985, p. iii).

Although a modified Form G, a 94 item self-scorable instrument, and a Form J, a 290 item research edition with 27 subscales, have recently been released, this review concerns only Forms F and G.

The MBTI classifies individuals along four relatively independent bi-polar dimensions. An individual is assigned one of the two preferences from each dimension. The first dimension describes a general attitude toward the world. Preferences are described as being either extraverted (E), where the orientation is outward to other persons and objects, or introverted (I), where one's main focus is upon internal representations of events and reactions. The second dimension describes preferences in perception. One tendency is sensing (S), which refers to reliance on actual sensory realities and established facts. The converse perceptual style is intuition (N), which is more globally based, focusing on the use of insight and construal of possibilities from the sense data. The third dimension could be described as a judging of information function. Information is seen as processed by preference for either thinking (T), relying on reason and logic, or feeling (F), relying more on personal values, especially concern for effects on others. The final dimension generally reflects attitudes toward closure on decision making. The judging (J) preference reflects a tendency toward quick, firm decisions, while the perceiving (P) attitude prefers to delay decisions, usually in an effort to gain more information. In addition, the J-P dimension is used to determine which of the four functions (i.e., sensing, intuition, thinking, or feeling) is dominant and which is the auxiliary.

TECHNICAL CHARACTERISTICS

Several representative type career tables are presented in the manual with brief discussions of the percent of individuals in each of the 16 possible type combinations. The career tables are presented with sex neutral comparisons for all types. A useful comparison concerns the SCII and the Kuder DD occupational scales. The MBTI with over 180 different occupations actually contains more scales for occupations than the SCII with 106 (Hansen & Campbell, 1985) and the Kuder DD with 75 (Zytowski, 1985).

Correlations on split-half continuous scores with the Spearman-Brown prophecy formula correction provide estimates of reliability on many samples ranging from .43 to .88 for E-I, .34 to .91 for S-N, .00 to .88 for T-F, and .28 to .92 for J-P. The correlations reported below the .60's are for younger, under achieving, or educationally disadvantaged individuals. Stability in types category scores using test-retest intervals from five weeks to five years provide a proportion of reclassification into the same preference from 72% to 89% for E-I, 64% to 92% for S-N, 68% to 88% for T-F, and 66% to 90% for J-P.

In terms of validity information, the MBTI manual reports scores are correlated with at least 28 other psychometric instruments—suggesting a good map to assist a counselor. The theory based Jungian constructs are supported with much data and extensive criterion validation.

Mean preference scores by age groups from 15–17 to 60 plus for each one-letter type are presented for Forms F and G. Although there seems to be amazing consistency of mean continuous scores throughout the lifespan (not the same people tested over time), the sensing and judgment types do increase with age. If the sampling of Form F (N = 52,848) and Form G (N = 30,308) are representative of an adult population, the major type code for both forms is ESTP. For a more thorough discussion of reliability and validity information, the reader is referred to an earlier review and discussion (Willis & Ham, 1984).

VOCATIONAL SUMMARY

Though not specifically designed as a vocational assessment instrument, the MBTI has been widely and diversely applied in the career development realm. A major use of the MBTI is for career exploration. It can provide both self-assessment data as well as vocational information via type distribution information among occupational titles. Broadening of different career options is facilitated by the MBTI. The MBTI theory can also provide a cognitive framework for organizing career information. Widespread use of the MBTI in employment settings suggests its value as a tool in work adjustment.

Because of the MBTI's utility for vocational applications, some cautionary notes are appropriate. The MBTI assesses personal styles, but is not a comprehensive personality test, vocational or otherwise. Abilities are not directly assessed, though easily inferred by the overzealous counselor. Similarly, values need to be interpreted within the limits of the test, being careful to use the type descriptions as suggestive rather than confirmatory data. For example, assuming that all introverts, because of their more internal focus, do not value working with people would be a naive mistake. Assumptions regarding vocational maturity are potential problems as well. A common example would be to automatically ascribe the label of vocational immaturity to a person whose type doesn't match an aspired-to occupation (e.g., an INFP type person seeking a career in an area dominated by ESTJ types). Finally, the MBTI should not be used as a substitute for vocational interest assessment, though this may be the most tempting of all. In fact, the Manual indicates the utility of having a diversity of types in a work setting, even though the tendency for preferences to cluster in certain occupations is unmistakable.

SPECIAL CONSIDERATIONS

Administration time for the MBTI is relatively brief, and it can be quickly scored with scoring programs. However, no specific scoring programs are available summarizing occupational information. In clinical use, a common complaint regards forced-choice format of self-descriptive items. This often occurs when clients perceive their personal characteristics as varying across situations. The item content itself, however, tends to evoke very little negative reaction.

Use of the MBTI for career choice assumes predictive validity. Given the difficulties associated with collecting such data, there is expectedly much less research support for the MBTI's predictive validity. Furthermore, a clinical suggestion in the 1985 Manual is that individuals sometimes respond to the MBTI with different role sets, such as "work self," "ideal self," "school self," as opposed to the desired "shoes-off self." In essence, giving repeated administrations can yield different type indications based on the mental set at testing time. This essentially seems to be an admission that the dimensions being tapped by the MBTI can be significantly affected by situational factors. In other words, persons in an "NF job" may tend to score more NF as a result of the job's influence. This is counter to the assumptive belief that because of their NF personality they selected themselves into a "NF" job.

In general, the MBTI is a good instrument based on its substantive theoretical and empirical bases. The extensive manual provides the user with a plethora of useful information. However, a typical point of confusion in the interpretation of the MBTI involves the determination of the dominant/auxiliary processes. The manual does provide an excellent, understandable elaboration of this process.

Another concern is the possibility that the mood or test-taking attitude of an examinee could well distort the type which is calculated for that individual. How a client intends to use the information gleaned from a type classification could introduce errors without any indices to correct them.

An extremely positive aspect of the MBTI is the test manual. Having perused many different test manuals, these authors definitely believe that the MBTI Manual is among the top two or three currently available for use. The theory and data bases, the extensiveness of the reported information, and its readability, are supportive of the MBTI for use in career counseling. Yet, counselors using the MBTI need much more than a cursory perusal of the manual and the literature. They need understanding of the theory.

REFERENCES

Hansen, J. C. & Campbell, D. P. (1985). *Manual for the SVIB-SCII* (4th ed.). Stanford, CA: Stanford University Press.

Myers, I. B. & McCaulley, M. H. (1985). Manual: *A Guide To The Development And Use of The Myers-Briggs Type Indicator*. Palo Alto, CA: Consulting Psychologists Press.

Willis, C. G. & Ham, T. L. (1984). Myers-Briggs Type Indicator. In D.J. Keyser & R.C. Sweetland (Eds.), *Test Critiques*, Volume I. (pp 482–490). Kansas City, MO.: Test Corporation of America.

Zytowski, D. G. (1985). Kuder DD manual supplement. Chicago: Science Research Associates.

NOTE: Significant portions of the review were abridged from the authors' original review in Volume I of *Test Critiques* with permission of Test Corporation of America.

PERSONAL SKILLS MAPS (PSM)

Darwin B. Nelson and Gary R. Low

Life Skills Center, P.C.
P.O. Box 8848, Corpus Christi, TX 78412

Target Population: Separate instruments for elementary students, secondary students, and adults.

Statement of the Purpose of the Instrument: To provide a research-based positive assessment of intrapersonal, interpersonal, and life management skills directly related to achievement, performance, adjustment and healthly living.

Titles of Subtests, Scales, Scores Provided: Skills of self-esteem, assertion, interpersonal comfort, empathy, drive strength, decision making, interpersonal aggression, deference, change orientation, time management, sales orientation, commitment ethic, stress management, and physical wellness.

Date of Most Recent Edition of Test Manual, User's Guide, Etc.: Personal Skills Map Manual, 1981.

Languages in Which Available: English, Spanish, French, and Finnish.

Time: Actual Test Time—30–50 minutes.
Total Administration Time—50–75 minutes.

Norm Group(s) on Which Scores Are Based: General adult, adolescent, business and industry.

Manner In Which Results Are Reported For Individuals
  Types of Scores: Graphic profile of standard score.
  Report Format/Content:
    Basic Service: Report includes graphic profile on one sheet with a definition of skills and illustration of the meaning of high and low scores on the back.

Report Format/Content for Group Summaries
  Basic Service: None.
  Options: Descriptive statistics for groups available upon request.

Scoring
  Machine Scoring Service: Not available.
  Hand Scoring: *Scored by*: counselee: clerk.
    Time Required for Scoring: 20 minutes.
  Local Machine Scoring: Not available.

Computer Software Options Available: Not available

Cost of Materials
  Specimen Set: Education/schools $7–$5 each. Business/industry $10–$7 each.

Published Review
Carlson, R.D. (1987) In D.J. Keyser & R.C. Sweetland (Eds.), *Test Critiques*, *Volume V* (pp 318–325). Kansas City, MO: Test Corporation of America.

234

Roger D. Carlson

Willamette University

The major purpose of the development of the Personal Skills Map: A Positive Assessment and Personalized Learning Model (PSM) was to "construct a positive assessment instrument that would result in a self description for the person which identified personal strengths and areas of needed change for personal growth and creative living" (Nelson and Low, 1981, p.5). The authors developed the PSM from an ostensibly humanistic and holistic perspective. The skills which the PSM purports to measure are: intrapersonal skills (self esteem, growth motivation), interpersonal skills (assertion, interpersonal awareness, empathy), career/life skills (drive strength, decision making, time management, sales orientation, commitment ethic, stress management), personal communication style (interpersonal assertion, interpersonal agression, interpersonal deference), and personal change orientation.

USABILITY

The PSM has been used in clinical, counseling, educational, industrial/organizational, criminal justice, and medical settings. The following areas for its use are suggested by the authors which might be appropriate for the career counselor: life transition/adjustment counseling, career/life planning and management, positive adult development, life transition, personalizing skill building groups and professional development classes, stress management, personal wellness groups, communication skills building, and relationship skills development. No training specific to its administration or interpretation is required for its purchase or use.

FORMAT

The PSM is designed to be a self-administering paper and pencil test. The PSM is printed on six pages of a test booklet, and answers are marked on a separate machine scorable answer sheets. One quite practical problem in using the PSM is that turnaround time for scoring is lengthy. (In the writer's experience, it can take two weeks to receive profiles—a problem which seems to defeat the purpose of computerized scoring). There is no remedy in hand scoring because keys are not released to professionals. The only remedy is a more expensive self-scoring form.

The 300 items are grouped in two parts: the first 63 items describe possible reactions to situations. The remaining items are self descriptions outside of situational contexts. The respondent is asked to rate each item in terms of being most descriptive of him/herself, sometimes descriptive, and least descriptive. The scale is untimed and completion time ranges from 45 to 75 minutes.

Besides the main form which is contained in a reusable booklet and used with separate answer sheets, there also is a 244 item self-scoring non-reusable form and a form which was developed for use with adolescents aged 13 through 18 years (PSM-A). The PSM has also been translated into the Finnish language. The present review pertains to the adult English language version in the non-self-scorable format.

PROFILE

Scoring is accomplished by sending the answer sheets to the Life Skills Center, P.C. in Corpus Christi, Texas, and Castro Valley, California. Normally, computerized scoring services are prepaid with the cost of the answer sheets when ordered. The profile of the PSM, a computer generated, full color standard form called a "person map," lists all of the dimensions of the PSM. Along each dimension an individual's standard score is graphically indicated. Standard scores below 40 (one standard deviation below the norm) are labeled as areas in need of change, those over 60 (one standard deviation above the norm) are labeled as skill strengths, and those between 40 and 60 (one standard deviation below to one standard deviation above the norm) are considered "average or expected level of personal skills development when compared to a general adult population" (Nelson and Low, 1981, p. 10). On the reverse of the profile form is interpretive material for the user. The forms are designed to be given directly to the client.

TECHNICAL ASPECTS

The PSM (adult version) consists of 300 items which were developed from an original pool of 1300 items. Each item was determined to have content validity by virtue of the judgments of professionals as to what scale was most appropriate for its placement. The PSM was normed on a random sample of 1400 normal adults. Demographic characteristics of the sample are not explicited in the manual except to say that the sample was chosen in order to represent a cross section of "the education, counseling, and business populations" (Nelson and Low, 1981, p. 45). The adolescent version of the scale was normed on 1157 adolescents aged 13 to 19 years enrolled in a wide variety and size range of public and private secondary schools. Five per cent were identified as juvenile offenders. Fifteen per cent of the sample included black students, and 12 per cent of the sample included Mexican-American students.

Construct validity was obtained by administering the scale to three groups and obtaining means and t-ratios comparing them. Statistically significant differences were found between (1) mental health professionals (n = 100), (2) normal adults (n = 99), and (3) persons voluntarily seeking counseling and psychotherapy services at outpatient treatment facilities during their first week of therapy (n = 122).

Concurrent validity was studied by scale to scale correlations with other scales such as the Personal Orientation Inventory, the Edwards Personal Preference Schedule, the 16 PF, and the MMPI. Because the first three instruments generally correlated positively with the PSM, and the MMPI does not, the authors surmise that they have been successful in their attempt to build an instrument which measures normal "healthy" personality.

Test-retest reliability coefficients derived from two test administrations of the PSM to 24 undergraduate college students separated by a one week interval range from .64 to .94 on the various scales. Since the test is meant to detect change in personal skills that can be brought about by a number of sources, unlike other personality scales the PSM is not meant to reveal constant stable aspects of personality. Therefore, according to the authors, the PSM profiles should not be expected to remain stable over time. The authors warn that the test should not be used for unobtrusive assessment purposes. The authors present research on the PMS which shows that responses on the PSM can be deliberately faked to a significant degree. With those considerations, reliability estimates probably ought not to be taken as serious indicators of test stability. No internal consistency reliability studies are reported in the manual. Score reports are in terms of exact scores; standard errors are not included in score reports.

Although factor analysis was not conducted on the PSM, the authors surmise that because intercorrelations reveal that 11 skill scales are positively correlated, those skills contribute to a common factor. Negative correlations exist between interpersonal agression, interpersonal deference, and change orientation with all other skills.

SPECIAL CONCERNS

The important concern for the purposes of the career counselor, is the possible independence and irrelevance of personality strengths and "deficits" to *occupational* strengths and deficits to which the PSM seems insensitive and not designed to detect. Besides having the numerous theoretical and technical problems, the relevance and appropriateness of the valid use of the PSM in the career counselor's practice must be seriously questioned.

REFERENCES

Nelson, D. B. & Low, G. R. (1979). *Personal Skills Map: A Positive Assessment and Personalized Learning Model.* Corpus Christi, Texas: Institute for the Development of Human Resources.

Nelson, D. B. & Low, G. R. (1981). *Personal Skills Map: A Positive Assessment of Career/Life Effectiveness Skills: Manual.* Corpus Christi, Texas: Institute for the Development of Human Resources.

NOTE: Significant portions of this review were abridged from the author's review in Volume V of *Test Critiques* with permission of Test Corporation of America.

Sixteen PF Personal Career Development Profile (PCDP)

Verne Walter

Institute for Personality and Ability Testing
1801 Woodfield Drive, Savoy, Illinois 61874
(P.O. Box 188, Champaign, IL 61820)

Target Population: 16 and up, younger age in high school settings.

Statement of the Purpose of the Instrument: An interpretive report based on the 16 PF, the PCDP interprets personality influences on occupations and careers. The report paragraphs deal with how the person solves problems, copes with stress, interacts with others, and matches up with different occupational settings.

Titles of Subtests, Scales, Scores Provided: Basic personality factor scores plus personality-based version of occupational themes like Holland's.

Forms and Levels Available, with Dates of Publication/Revision of Each: One version of the PCDP, can only be generated from 16 PF, Forms A, A + B, C, or C + D. Form A or A + B are the preferred combinations. Form A/B last revised in 1968 (rdg level = 7.5); Form C/D in 1969 (rdg level = 6.5).

Date of Most Recent Edition of Test Manual, User's Guide Etc.: Administrator's Manual—1986, 16PF Handbook 1980, PCDP Manual, 1985.

Languages in Which Available: PCDP available in English only; 16PF testing materials available from IPAT in Spanish; German and French versions available from foreign distributors.

Time: Actual Test Time: approx. 45–60 minutes.
  Total Administration Time: 50–60 minutes.

Norm Group(s) on Which Scores Are Based: High school, college, general population adult.

Manner in Which Results Are Reported for Individuals
  Types of Scores: All scores are found on the last two pages of the report, following the narrative interpretation. Scores are sten scores (range 1–10. ave. = 5.5 st. dev. = 2.0.)

Report Format/Content
  Basic Service: on six pages of highly integrative narrative plus two score pages.
  Options: PCDP + additional self-administered exercises based on PCDP.
Report Format/Content For Group Summaries
  Basic Service: Group summary format.
  Options: At additional cost, can provide group data on the scores of the 16PF factors; and, can run PCDP based upon model profile of the group.

Scoring

Machine Scoring Service
Cost of Basic Service per counselee: $16 per report-less, if pre-purchased in quantities of 5 or more.
Cost of options: PCDP + exercises based on PCDP + $2.00 additional.
Time required for scoring and returning (maximum) 24 hour turnaround time at IPAT (1 day + shipping).
Hand Scoring: Not available.
Local Machine Scoring: Not available.

Computer Software Options Available: Interpretation (software not available, but if user has computer + modem + printer, can link directly with our computer for immediate turnaround).

Cost of Materials
Specimen Set: PCDP (Personal Career Development Profile)—$22.85 (computer report).
Counselee Materials: Nothing is reusable for counselee.

Additional Comments of Interest to Users: Manual available for helping user understand contents of report and score pages.

Published Reviews

Bloxom, B. M. (1978). Review of the Sixteen personality factor questionnaire. In O. K. Buros (Ed.), *Eighth Mental Measurements Yearbook.* Highland Park, N.J.: Gryphon Press. Vol. I, (pp. 10077–1078).

Bolton, B. F. (1978). Review of the Sixteen personality factor questionnaire. In O. K. Buros (Ed.), *Eighth Mental Measurements Yearbook.* Highland Park, N.J.: Gryphon Press. Vol. I, (pp. 1078–1080).

Butcher, J. N. (1985). Review of the Sixteen personality factor questionnaire. In J. V. Mitchell (Ed.), *Ninth Mental Measurements Yearbook. Vol. I.* Lincoln, NE: University of Nebraska-Lincoln, Buros Institute of Mental Measurements. (BRS Document Reproduction Service No. AN 0910-679)

Fleenor, J. (1986). Review of the Personal career development profile: Using the 16 PF for vocational exploration. *Measurement and Evaluation in Counseling and Development,* 18, (185–189).

Mossholder, K. M. (1985). Review of the Personal career development profile. In J. V. Mitchell (Ed.), *Ninth Mental Measurements Yearbook Vol. I.* Lincoln, NE: University of Nebraska-Lincoln, Buros Institute of Mental Measurements. (BRS Document Reproduction Service No. AN 915-2082)

Walsh, J. A. (1978). Review of the Sixteen personality factor questionnaire. In O. K. Buros (Ed.), *Eighth Mental Measurements Yearbook.* Highland Park, N.J.: Gryphon Press. Vol. I, (pp. 1081–1083).

Wholeben, B. E. (1985). Review of the Sixteen personality factor questionnaire. *Test Critiques* Vol. IV, (pp. 595–605). Kansas City, MO: Test Corporation of America.

Zuckerman, M. (1985). Review of the Sixteen personality factor questionnaire. In J. V. Mitchell (Ed.), *Ninth Mental Measurements Yearbook Vol. I.* Lincoln, NE: University of Nebraska-Lincoln, Buros Institute of Mental Measurements. (BRS Document Reproduction Service No. AN 0910-679)

Brent Edward Wholeben

Senior Graduate Faculty
Department of Educational Leadership and Counseling
The University of Texas at El Paso

The Personal Career Development Profile (PCDP) (Walter, 1977; latest revision, 1985), is a computer-generated interpretation in narrative form of the Sixteen Personality Factor Questionnaire (16PF) developed by Cattell (1949; latest revision, 1969). The seven or eight pages of narrative discuss the respondent's personality profile based upon the 16PF according to nine (9) interpretable patterns important to occupational exploration: testing orientation, problem solving, coping with stressful conditions, interpersonal interactions, organizational role and work setting, career activity interests, personal career life-style considerations, and occupational comparisons.

The 16PF, which provides the basis for PCDP interpretations, is an objective test of 16 multidimensional personality attributes arranged in omnibus form. Conceptualized as a broad, multi-purpose measurement of the "source traits" of individual personality, the 16PF provides a global representation of an individual's coping style, the person's reactive stance to an ever fluid and transactional environment, and that individual's ability to perceive accurately certain specific environmental requisites for personal behavior.

The PCDP, in addition to interpreting the career-oriented personality of the respondent, classifies the degree to which the respondent possesses leadership qualities. Based upon this classification, a comparison with the personality assessments of professionals from 34–35 careers is provided.

NORMS AND SCORES

The PCDP is based upon a respondent's answers to a series of situational questions supplied by the 16PF; the total number of questions is dependent upon the form of the 16PF (Form A or B, 187 items; Form C or D, 105 items). The resulting personality profile is interpreted for the occupational setting using sten scores derived from significantly high/low attribute patterns based upon each of the 16PF norms: gender, high school versus adult, and incidence of college training.

Combinations of individual personality attributes are used to suggest the respondent's probable reaction to a variety of occupational situations common to most careers (e.g., coping with stress). Several of the predictor equations utilized are based upon previous research by other investigators in the area of career preference. In particular, the PCDP relies heavily upon the occupational choice theory of Holland (1973). Holland's six career personality orientations (enterprising, social, artistic, investigative, conventional, and realistic) are paralleled by the PCDP's respective occupational themes (venturous, nurturing, creative, analytic, procedural, and mechanical).

The relationship of the respondent's personality to those professionals considered successful in various careers is reported in sten score format; high sten scores imply high personality relationships between respondent and professionals in specific occupations, while low scores imply low relationships. The choice of direct career comparisons is based upon the respondent's preponderance towards leadership qualities.

RELIABILITY

Dependability coefficients (short interval, test-retest) for the 16PF, the measurement basis of the PCDP, demonstrate relatively acceptable coefficients of .70 magnitude and higher. Equivalence coefficients (primary factor intercorrelations from different testing forms) for the 16PF are generally low, suggesting that two or more test administrations using different forms may provide useful complementary, rather than redundant, personality information.

VALIDITY

Multiple correlation "loadings" for each of the six PCDP occupational themes range from a high of .61 (venturous) to a low of .37 (each of procedural and nurturing). Cross-validation correlations between each of the PDCP themes and Holland's orientations range from a high of .60 (venturous/enterprising) to a low of .16 (each of analytic/investigative and mechanical/realistic). Factor comparisons among PCDP theme-pairs range from a high of .56 (mechanical to analytical) to a low of − .03 (creative to venturous).

PRACTITIONER USABILITY

Used with care, the PCDP is an excellent tool for career awareness in the high school curriculum and occupational exploration for adults. In either case, the results should be viewed as a "basis for further discussion" rather than a criterion-based assessment of specific career potential in the respondent.

SPECIAL CONCERNS

It must be remembered that the transient situational emotional state of the respondent at the time of administration will distort the way the individual interprets each question. For career interests which might necessitate a closer scrutiny of personality patterns than required for alternative occupations (e.g., in the case of careers which allow access to sensitive information), two administrations utilizing different forms might be advisable.

While the narrative is easily read, many of the "labels" of personality denote operational definitions which are distinctly different from more common "street" usage; e.g., disciplined-compulsive. Without the assistance of trained professionals, a respondent could easily misinterpret the narrative comments.

REFERENCES

Cattell, R. B., Eber, H. W., & Tatsuoka, M. M. (1970). *Handbook for the sixteen personality factor questionnaire (16PF)*. Champaign, IL: Institute for Personality and Ability Testing, Inc.

Holland, J. L. (1973). *Making vocational choices: A theory of careers*. Englewood Cliffs, NJ: Prentice-Hall.

Karson, S., & O'Dell, J. W. (1976). *Guide to the Clinical Use of the 16PF*. Champaign, IL: Institute for Personality and Ability Testing, Inc.

Krug, S. E. (1981). *Interpreting 16PF profile patterns*. Champaign, IL: Institute for Personality and Ability Testing, Inc.

Walter, V. (1985). *Personal career development profile* (3rd Ed.). Champaign, IL: Institute for Personality and Ability Testing, Inc.

Wholeben, B. E. (1985). Review of the Sixteen personality factor questionnaire. In *Test Critiques, Vol. IV*, (pp. 595–605). Kansas City, MO: Test Corporation of America.

NOTE: Significant portions of this review are abridged from the author's review in Volume IV, *Test Critiques* with permission of Test Corporation of America.

Temperament and Values Inventory (TVI)

Charles B. Johansson
and
Patricia L. Weber

NCS Professional Assessment Services
P.O. Box 1416, Minneapolis, MN

Target Population: Grade 9 to adult.

Statement of the Purpose of the Instrument: Assess work-related temperament and reward values. The temperament scales assess how an individual reacts to various activities and situations, while the reward scales measure what aspects of a job an individual finds most rewarding.

Titles of Subtests, Scales, Scores Provided: Temperament scales include: Routine-Flexible; Quiet-Active; Attentive-Distractable; Serious-Cheerful; Consistent-Changeable; Reserved-Sociable; Reticent-Persuasive. Reward Values scales include: Social Recognition, Managerial/Sales Benefits, Leadership, Social Service, Task Specificity, Philosophical Curiosity, and Work Independence.

Forms and Levels Available, with Dates of Publication/Revision of Each: one form, 1976.

Date of Most Recent Edition of Test Manual, User's Guide, Etc.: Manual, 1977.

Languages in Which Available: English only.

Time: Actual Test Time—approx. 30 minutes.

Norm Group(s) on Which Scores Are Based: Six age/sex groups: adolescents (male & female); young adults (male & female); and older adults (male & female).

Manner in Which Results Are Reported for Individuals
  Types of Scores: Standard scores and percent responses.
  Report Format/Content
    Basic Service: Profile Report: presents standard scores and a graphic display of all the Inventory's scales and indexes. Reverse side had preprinted interpretive information.
    Options: Interpretive Report: provides individualized information for evaluating job possibilities and long-range career choices; includes 2-page detachable summary.

Report Format/Content for Group Summaries: Not Available.

Scoring
  Machine Scoring Service
    Cost of basic service per counselee: Profile: $2.80 when ordering quantities of 100 or more. Includes cost of answer sheet, scoring and report. Quantity discounts apply.

Cost of options: Interpretive: $4.75 when ordering quantities of 100 or more. Includes cost of answer sheet, scoring and report. Quantity discounts apply.
Time required for scoring and returning: (maximum) 24 hour turnaround.

Hand Scoring: Not available.
Local Machine Scoring
Provisions/conditions/equipment required: Arion II℗ teleprocessing. Requirements: microcomputer, printer, modem and telephone. Provides inventory results in minutes using teleprocessing technology.

Computer Software Options Available: Not available.

Cost of Materials
Specimen Set: Includes profile and interpretive report answer sheet and manual. Cost: $15.50.
Counselee Materials: Combination test booklet and answer sheet. Profile: 1–4 $4.25; 5–29 $4.00; 30–49 $3.65; 50–99 $3.30; 100+ $2.80; Narrative: 1–4 $8.50; 5–29 $7.75; 30–49 $6.75; 50–99 $5.75; 100+ $4.75.

Additional Comments of Interest to Users: While fully functional by itself, the TVI is part of a comprehensive career guidance system which includes the Career Assessment Inventory—the Enhanced Version, the Self-Description Inventory and the Word and Number Assessment Inventory (WNAI).

Published Reviews
Schrank, F. A. (1984). In D. J. Keyser & R. C. Sweetland (Eds.), *Test Critiques, Vol. I*, Test Corporation of America. Westport Publishers, Inc.
Wheeler, W. G. (1985). In J. V. Mitchell (Ed.), *The Ninth Mental Measurements Yearbook*, University of Nebraska-Lincoln, Lincoln, Nebraska: University of Nebraska Press.
Zucherman, M. (1985). In J. V. Mitchell (Ed.), *The Ninth Mental Measurements Yearbook*, University of Nebraska-Lincoln, Lincoln, Nebraska: University of Nebraska Press.

Kenneth G. Wheeler
Associate Professor of Human Resource Management
University of Texas at Arlington

The Temperament and Values Inventory (TVI) consists of two sets of scales designed to be used primarily in guidance counseling at the high school level and career counseling at the young adult level. The temperament section of the inventory consists of seven Temperament Scales measured by 133 true-false items. These temperament scales measure personal characteristics related to career choice and include: Routine-Flexible, Quiet-Active, Attentive-Distractible, Serious-Cheerful, Consistent-Changeable, Reserved-Sociable, and Reticent-Persuasive. The second section of the inventory relates to individual preferences for reinforcers in the work situation using 97 Likert-style items on a five point scale ranging from very important to very unimportant. These reward values scales include: Social Recognition, the degree to which individuals want to be liked and respected by others; Managerial/Sales Benefits, the value placed on rewards related to managerial and sales positions such as fringe benefits and bonuses; Leadership, the extent to which individuals desire to be in positions where they make decisions affecting other people; Social Service, the emphasis placed on caring for others; Task Specificity, the degree to which individuals want to know what is expected of them or prefer freedom and flexibility; Philosophical Curiosity, the desire to know and understand the laws of nature and question beliefs of society; and Work Independence, the importance placed on determining the best way to do a job with little supervision.

NORM GROUPS AND SCORES

The scales are normed on six separate groups (three age groups by sex): 272 females and 179 males from 15 to 19 years old, 320 females and 214 males from 20 to 25, and 559 females and 488 males from 26 to 55. The manual for the TVI provides means and standard deviations for each of these groups and includes a brief discussion of the differences for all of the TVI scales for these norm groups. There is a limited comparison of minority and nonminority males and females that shows potential differences on several of the scales from the TVI. The sample sizes are very small, and the category of minority group is not differentiated into any subgroups.

The raw scores on each of the scales are converted to standard scores with a composite mean of 50 and a standard deviation of 10. The scores are reported on a graph format with vertical lines marking the 25th and 75th percentiles. The average of scores for males and females are also indicated on each scale, allowing the interpretation of scores in relation to the individual's sex.

RELIABILITY

In counseling students and young adults on current and future career choices, it is important to have measures of temperaments and values that are relatively stable over time. The reliabilities of the TVI scales were determined by administering the scales to a group of mostly employed adults with an approximately equal split of males and females. The test-retest reliabilities were calculated for one- and two-week intervals with samples of 41 and 27, respectively. These reliabilities are quite acceptable, ranging from .79 to .93 with a median of about .88. Since these reliabilities are influenced by actual changes in the temperaments and values of individuals, it is expected that measured reliabilities for younger age groups and over longer time periods would be lower.

VALIDITY

A primary concern in establishing the usefulness of the TVI in vocational and career counseling is the validity of the TVI scales. The manual provides good support for concurrent validity in terms of differentiating between individuals who were currently employed in 68 different occupations. However, this analysis is limited by very small sample sizes, with several occupations including only five respondents. No predictive validation evidence is provided.

A construct validation approach is also used to establish the relation between the scales on the TVI and similar scales on other established inventories. Relatively small sample sizes limit detailed discussion in the manual to three other well-established inventories: the Strong Campbell Interest Inventory based on a sample of 123, the Career Assessment Inventory based on a sample of 197, and the Self-Description Inventory based on a sample of 320. The results support high convergent validity for scales measuring similar constructs and good divergent validity for scales measuring dissimilar constructs.

The manual also indicates content validity for the scales on the basis of careful scale construction to assure that the composition of each scale reflects the relevant dimensions of that category. Evidence of a high internal consistency of items comprising each scale is also provided in the manual as support for the content validity of the TVI.

ADMINISTERING THE TVI

Although the TVI could be utilized by itself, it might be most useful as a supplement to other instruments as part of a more comprehensive career counseling program. One possibility in addition to the Strong-Campbell Interest Inventory (SCII) is to provide input concerning the individual's personal characteristics and desired reinforcements in the work situation not included in the SCII (Schrank, 1984).

The instructions for completing the TVI are included on the same four-page form as the answer sheet and test items, making the TVI extremely simple to administer. The instructions are short and uncomplicated, and should not require additional explanation. However, the manual suggests that the test administrator read through the directions on the first page with the test takers in group testing situations and with high school students or adults with low reading levels. The manual indicates that, although eighth grade students were included in initial data collection with the TVI, it is not recommended for routine use with students below the ninth grade level.

The TVI is machine scored through either a mail-in service or a local computer terminal through a teleprocessing service. Two types of report formats are available for the TVI. The first is a preprinted form reporting standard scores for each scale in a profile format, allowing the counselor to explain the results to the individual on a one-to-one basis. The other format not only reports the standard scores and places them on a scale, but also includes a printout with a computer generated narrative that explains the individual's scores in relation to norms and in terms of the content of the scale. This is useful when using the TVI in groups and in providing the individual with a written summary of the results.

The TVI provides a useful combination of both personal characteristics related to career choice and individual preferences for reinforcers in the work situation. The norm groups based on three age groups by sex are also adequate, and form the primary comparison groups for evaluating individual scores. Scores are also provided from the concurrent validation study for 68 occupations, but the numbers of respondents for these occupations are too small to be useful as reference norm groups. The manual for this inventory provides evidence of acceptable reliabilities, and indicators of sufficient validity to provide a potentially useful instrument for the practitioner, particularly in combination with vocational interest inventories and ability tests.

REFERENCES

Johansson, C. B. (1977). *Manual for the Temperament and Values Inventory*. Minneapolis: Interpretative Scoring Systems Inc.,

Schrank, F. A. (1984). Review of the Temperament and Values Inventory. In D. J. Keyser & R. C. Sweetland (Eds.). *Test Critiques, Vol. I*. (pp. 660–662), Kansas City, MO: Test Corporation of America.

Wheeler, K. G. (1985). Review of the Temperament and Values Inventory. In J. V. Mitchell (Ed.), *The Ninth Mental Measurements Yearbook*. (pp. 1535–1536) Lincoln, Neb.. Buros Institute.

Zuckerman, M. (1985). Review of the Temperament and Values Inventory. In J. V. Mitchell (Ed.), *The Ninth Mental Measurements Yearbook*. (pp. 1536–1537) Lincoln. Neb.: Buros Institute.

NOTE: Significant portions of this review were abridged from the author's original review in *The Ninth Mental Measurements Yearbook* with permission of the Buros Institute.

Instruments
For
Special
Populations

Career Evaluation Systems Series 100

Career Evaluation Systems, Inc.

Career Evaluation Systems
7788 Milwaukee Ave.
Niles, IL 60648-4794

Target Population: Age 16 through mature adult, all levels of general/potential workforce.

Statement of the Purpose of the Instrument: Integration of a battery of nationally-published/sold tests (both physical and psychometric), measuring 19 human factors and abilities, to provide an ability profile for occupations.

Titles of Subtests, and Forms and Levels with Dates of Publication: (Raw scores from tests are entered in computer systems for scale scoring.)
Abstract reasoning; (Raven Standard Progressive Matrices); Sets A,B,C,D,E; (1983)
Verbal, numerical reasoning; (SRA Verbal Form); Form A; (1984)
Spatial perception; (Rev. Minnesota Paper Form Board); Series AA; (1970)
Following directions; (PTI Oral Directions Test); (1974)
Reading level (avg/above); (Gates-MacGinnitie); Level F, Form 1; (1978)
Arithmetic level; (Jastack Wide Range Achievement Test); Rev., Form 2; (1984)
Perceptual accuracy; (IPAT CAB-Cf); (1982)
Decision speed; (IPAT CAB-Cs); (1982)
Leadership structure, consideration; (SRA Leadership Opinion Questionnaire); (1969)
Sales/people persuasion; (SRA Sales Attitude Checklist); (1960)
Finger-dexterity; (Purdue Pegboard); Except assembly; (1967)
Wrist-finger speed; (Lafayette Instrument Tapping Board) (1979)
Arm-hand steadiness and Precision aiming; (Layfayette Instrument Hole Plate); (1979)
Manual dexterity; (Minnesota Rate of Manipulation); Turning only, (1984).
Two-arm coordination; (Lafayette Instrument Two-Arm Coordination); (1979)
Two-hand coordination; (Layfayette Instrument Two-Hand Coordination); (1979)
Hand strength; (Jamar Hand Dynamometer). (1986).

Date of Most Recent Edition of Test Manual, User's Guide, Etc.: 1983 edition; revisions 1984, 1985, 1986.

Languages in Which Available: English only.

Time: Actual Test Time— approx. 190 minutes.
Total Administration Time—220 minutes.

Norm Group(s) on Which Scores Are Based: Computer-stored data from every case—general population throughout the U.S.

Manner in Which Results Are Reported for Individuals
  Types of Scores: Scale scores—rating from 6-very high to 1-very low.
  Report Format/Content
    Basic Service: Three-page computer report including (1) scale ranking for test administered, (2) scale ranking of GED, (3) scale ranking for DOT Data-People-Things worker function categories, (4) list of best match to 100 specific occupations.

Report Format/Content for Group Summaries: Not available.

Scoring
  Machine Scoring Service:
    Cost of basic service per counselee: License maintenance fee of $150/mo. covers up to 200 cases per year; $4 royalty charge per case thereafter. Plus $5 service charge (optional) per case.
    Cost of options: Overnight delivery at cost; $1.00 extra for phone-in of case data.
    Time required for scoring and returning (maximum): 24 hours, plus first class mail.

  Hand Scoring: Not available.
  Local Machine Scoring
    Provisions/conditions/equipment required: IBM-PC, PC-XT, Apple IIe, Apple II+, and D. C. Hayes 1200B SmartModem for telecommunication scoring.

Computer Software Options Available: Telecommunication scoring.

Cost of Materials
  Specimen Set: No specimen set available. Illustrated in Supply Catalog only.
  Counselee Materials: One-time license fee, training materials and physical apparatus $4700; software (incl. all future updates) $650. Consumables are ordered direct from test publishers.

Additional Comments of Interest to Users: Expanded test batteries are available for use with physically impaired (Series 200), low reader and mentally retarded (Series 300) populations. The CES(100) has been renamed CareerView, The CES(200) has been renamed Voc Scan, and the CES(300) has been renamed JobSupport.

Published Reviews
Botterbusch, K. F. (1975). Hester Evaluation System. In A. Sax (Ed.), Innovations in Vocational Evaluation and Work Adjustment. *Vocational Evaluation and Work Adjustment Bulletin, 8*(4), 62–65.
Botterbusch, K. F. (1982). Career Evaluation Systems. In *A Comparison of Commercial Vocational Evaluation Systems, (Second Edition)*. Materials Development Center, Stout Vocational Rehabilitation Institute, 25–31.
Botterbusch, K. F. (1987). Career Evaluation Systems. In *Vocational Assessment and Evaluation Systems: A Comparison*. Materials Development Center, Stout Vocational Rehabilitation Institute, 39–46.

Randall S. McDaniel
Associate Professor
Auburn University
and
Renée A. Middleton
Instructor
West Georgia College

The Career Evaluation Systems (CES) is a computerized assessment program which integrates a battery of standardized test scores to assess up to 28 vocationally relevant abilities useful for vocational evaluation and career counseling. Three different series are offered that are oriented to either the job seeking individual in business and industry (Series 100), the physically impaired job seeker (Series 200), or the competitively employable mentally retarded (Series 300). Specific test scores are required by this program and range from familiar standards such as the Raven Progressive Matrices and Purdue Pegboard to CES developed tests such as the Lafayette Multi-Choice Reaction Timer and the Lafayette Mirror Tracer. The CES is an updated and renamed version of the original Hester Evaluation System produced in the 1970s. Originator, Dr. Ed Hester (1977), claims the system was based on a number of factor-pure traits determined important to employment in work with rehabilitation clients at Chicago Goodwill Industries.

After administering up to five and one half hours of the various tests, the test scores are communicated to CES headquarters via mail, overnight courrier, phone or personal computer and modem. The CES publishers run the centralized program and return a print-out that contains scale scores on each ability and a selection of up to 165 specific feasible occupations selected form the *Dictionary of Occupational Titles*. To determine the specific occupations, the CES computer program utilizes a regression equation to establish probabilities of the client's ability to work with each level of data, people, and things. This use of probabilities rather than cut off scores differentiates the CES approach form other such systems and is one of its strengths.

Each system series manual is divided into six units. Unit I covers the general administration including test room conditions, preliminary setup, order of administration, and special instructions. Unit II provides information about the various apparatus tests, and Unit III provides similar information (purpose, administration, scoring, and data entry) about the paper and pencil tests. Unit IV provides detailed information on completing the data entry forms for computer input. Unit V deals with interpreting the result of the computer print out, and Unit VI provides sample print outs of testing results as examples. Information is provided with each print out, which explains to the client how to interpret the print-out and the manual describes how to use the report to the best advantage for different client case needs. Audio tapes are provided for training in test administration for this system and in the use of the print outs.

NORMS AND SCORES

The computer print-out from the program provides norm referenced scale scores for each ability subtest on a six point scale. A different criterion referenced scale score for each of the measured abilities is produced as they relate to the client's General Educational Development and the components of the Data, People, Things factors developed by the Department of Labor in addition to the listing of specific occupations. For the ability scales, the norm group consists of all the past individuals evaluated with this battery. The Series 100 manual reports that in 1981, 1061 individuals were in the norm group. They were predominantly under 30 years old (65%) with 10–12 years of education (66%). The average I.Q. was 100 and the group was equally split between the sexes. Caucasians made up 42% of the sample and the remainder were from various minority groups.

These test scores are used to determine the client's functioning ability on a six point scale with each of the levels of Data, People, and Things, as defined by the 1977 edition of the *Dictionary of Occupational Titles (DOT)*. For example, there are seven levels of working with data from synthesizing to comparing. The client is given a scale score for each of the seven levels. The high scores on all levels of Data, People, and Things are selected and combined to form the basis of the occupational match. Since those levels for working with Data, People, and Things were determined by the Department of Labor as a method of structuring their job analysis of jobs contained in the DOT, the test manufacturer feels this part of the ability profile is related to the criteria of actual jobs and thus the scores are criterion referenced.

RELIABILITY AND VALIDITY

Many of the tests utilized by CES are from nationally known test publishers and are widely used in the assessment field to measure single factor traits. The CES publishers therefore conclude that each individual test has accepted and published reliability and validity. While this may be true, the CES uses these scores in combination for prediction that reduces confidence in those reliability and validity figures. The manual reports an unpublished study (Hester, 1979) in which forty-four clients were retested after a period of four to six weeks with individual test-retest reliability coefficients ranging from .72 to .95. They note a tendency of client improvement on the second administration. On those two administrations, 78% of the selected job families (i.e. Worker Trait Groups or Data, People, Things levels) were the same. The manual claims a new test-retest reliability study is being undertaken, which is fortunate considering the inadequacies of the existing data.

The manual section on validity presents a discussion of the types of acceptable validity and claims a high level of user satisfaction with the system. It concludes with the statement that a formal research study on validity is in the planning stages. In short it is unknown if the system accurately measurers what it purports to measure. This shortcoming represents one of the major weaknesses of the CES.

USABILITY

The CES can be used as a stand-alone assessment battery for career counseling and guidance purposes or might best be considered the beginning point of testing in a comprehensive vocational evaluation program. Obviously, those working in general high school or college curriculum or businesses would be most interested in the Series 100, while rehabilitation providers would usually use the Series 200 or 300. Thus the system ambitiously attempts to offer testing for clients ranging from non-readers to management candidates, to provide an ability profile, and to determine where they best fit in the work force.

A potential weakness of the system is the lack of flexibility of choice of the psychometric tests utilized. Therefore, the test administrator is not able to use alternate test measures that he/she may feel more comfortable in using. However, since the system requires a number of well known tests, it is possible to save money in setting up the system if these tests are already being used by the CES purchaser.

SPECIAL CONCERNS

A certification offered to testers consists of passing an open book test, and this procedure appears to be lax and of questionable worth. Another concern is the potential cost of the system. Components for the system could cost up to $12,109 depending on the configuration of tests desired. In addition, a scoring fee of $150/month for 200 cases per year is charged with additional royalty fees for each additional case. Other charges are added for phone-in and/or overnight delivery return on print outs.

Although theoretical and statistical development procedures are briefly mentioned and possibly good, too little detail is provided on those to allow an informed opinion. The same is true of the little information on reliability on which the information provided is insufficient, and as mentioned, nothing beyond a promise is made of validity studies. It appears the publishers have spent more time on marketing than conducting ongoing dynamic research of the Career Evaluation System.

REFERENCES

Botterbusch, K. F. (1975). Hester evaluation system. In A. Sax (Ed.) Innovations in vocational evaluation and work adjustment. *Vocational Evaluations and Work Adjustment Bulletin, 8*(4), 62–65.

Botterbusch, K. F. (1987). Career evaluation systems. In *A Comparison of Commercial Evaluation Systems*. Menomonie, Wisc.: Materials Development Center, Stout Vocational Rehabilitation Institute.

Hester, E. J. (1977). Hester evaluation system, (Unpublished paper.) Presented at the Auburn Conference on Work Evaluation Systems.

Hester, E. J. (1979). Preliminary statistical report on the Hester evaluation system, Unpublished Manuscript.

McCarron-Dial System (MDS)

Lawrence T. McCarron
and
Jack G. Dial

McCarron-Dial Systems
P.O. Box 45628, Dallas, TX 75245

Target Population: The MDS can be used with special education and rehabilitation populations at any level of intellectual functioning and with disabilities in one or more of the following areas: physical, mental, emotional or functional behavior. Target disability groups include: learning disabled, emotionally disturbed, mentally retarded, cerebral palsied, closed head injured and socially handicapped or culturally disadvantaged. It can also be adapted for use with blind and deaf persons.

Statement of the Purpose of the Instrument: The MDS includes an assessment of five factors: verbal-spatial-cognitive, sensory, motor, emotional and integration-coping. Emphasis is on educational and vocational programming, development and placement. Based on significant research findings, the system predicts the level of vocational and residential functioning the individual may achieve after training. The predicted vocational level can be used to establish realistic vocational goals and/or appropriate vocational program placement. The detailed profiling of performance across five areas of behavior provides a holistic view of the individual's strengths and needs when compared to others in his/her predicted vocational range as well as the general population. Specific needs which must be remediated and/or accommodated for successful goal achievement are identified.

Titles of Subtests, Scales, Scores Provided: Peabody Picture Vocabulary Test-R (PPVT-R), Bender Visual Motor Gestalt Test (BVMGT), Behavior Rating Scale (BRS), Observational Emotional Inventory (OEI), Haptic Visual Discrimination Test (HVDT) and McCarron Assessment of Neuromuscular Development (MAND).

Forms and Levels Available with Dates of Publication/Revision of Each: Not applicable.

Date of Most Recent Edition of Test Manual, User's Guide, Etc.: April, 1986.

Languages in Which Available: In addition to English, a Spanish version of the administration instructions is available.

Time: The formal testing required for the abbreviated battery can be completed in three hours or less. The comprehensive battery requires the formal testing plus systematic observation for up to five days in a work or classroom setting.

Norm Group(s) on Which Scores Are Based: Norms for the PPVT, MAND and HVDT involve 2000 or more observations each. Norms for the OEI and BRS have been obtained on more than 500 normal and disabled adults each. The original normative sample for the entire system was 200. Additional samples have extended this number considerably. Pertinent empirical and statistical characteristics of the various norm groups are given in the manuals and in research publication.

Manner in Which Results Are Reported for Individuals

Types of Scores: The standard format for comprehensive reporting includes specific scores (raw scores and standard scores or MDS T-scores); vocational and residential placement scores; behavioral observations; case history information; lists of strengths and deficits; programming priorities; and programming recommendations.

The forms which may be used for report development are the Individual Evaluation Profile (IEP) and the Individual Program Plan (IPP). The IEP allows the user to record and profile the total score for each test administered. The IPP allows for entry of subtest scores and right/left measures. These scores are then profiled for each of the factors. Space is available to include results from others tests and work samples; strengths and weaknesses; program goals and objectives; and descriptive or narrative information. Both the IEP and IPP include profile graphs which visually summarize all scores and compare them to the general population mean, special population mean, the individual's mean, and the vocational program standard or T-score range.

Report Format/Content for Group Summaries: Not available.

Scoring

Machine Scoring Service: Optional.
Hand Scoring: Not available.
Local Machine Scoring: Not available.

Computer Software Options Available

a. Interpretation.

b. Ways in which computer version differs. Below are descriptions of various software programs available which utilize data obtained from the MDS: Computer Assessment Program (CAP)—developed as a vocational evaluation/consultive report. The CAP permits entry of up to 14 scores and profiles up to 11 variables. Six specific scores are required to generate a CAP report. Current MDS users will recognize this as the IEP level.

Individualized Trait Analysis for Program Planning (ITAPP)—developed as a resource for program planning. It provides a detailed analysis of behavioral traits at a level of specificity suitable for intervention through training and/or accommodation strategies. ITAPP permits entry of up to 123 scores and profiles up to 74 items. Current MDS users will recognize this as the IPP level.

Occupational Exploration System (OES)—The OES report includes a listing of tests administered with conversions to MDS T-scores. Occupations requiring Verbal-Spatial-Cognitive and Sensorimotor scores similar to those of the evaluee are selected from a file of over 2000 jobs. These jobs are organized for printing according to Career Area, Worker Trait Group and DOT number. If the evaluee's academic achievement level falls below the desired level for any job listed, the desired achievement level is printed. The OES program can be used alone or can access data already entered on the CAP or ITAPP program.

Remedial Motor Training (RNT)—Provides activities to remediate identified neuromotor deficits. The individual's MAND subtest scores are used to generate a detailed motor factor analysis, a profile of relative strengths and deficits and ranking of motor deficits. Remediation strategies are then presented for each deficit area. This report includes a definition of neuromotor functions and general suggestions by remediation. The training activities, materials needed and criterion of performance are specified for the individual's level of performance. The RMT program can be used alone or can access data already entered on the ITAPP program.

As an alternative to purchasing software, MDS will process these reports with 24 hour turn-around after receipt of data in our office. Prices vary as type of report.

Cost of Materials: Specimen sets are not available. The cost of the MDS is $1525.00. The only expendable items are the various test answer sheets, behavioral observation forms and report forms.

Published Reviews

Botterbusch, K. (1987). *Vocational assessment and evaluation systems: A comparison.* Menomonie, WI: University of Wisconsin-Stout.

Chan, F., Parker, H., Dial, J., Lam, C., & Carter, S. (1986). Factorial validity of the McCarron-Dial Work Evaluation System. *Vocational Evaluation and Work Adjustment Bulletin, 19*(3), 91–94.

Dial, J., & Chan, F. (1987). Diagnostic validity of the McCarron-Dial System in neuropsychological rehabilitation assessment. *International Journal of Rehabilitation, Issue 2.*

Dial, J., Freemon, L., McCarron, L., & Swearingen, S. (1979). Predictive validation of the McCarron-Dial Evaluation System. *Vocational Evaluation and Work Adjustment Bulletin, 12*(1), 11–18.

Jacobs, K. (1987). Work assessment and programming. In H. Hopkins and H. Smith (Eds.), *Willard and Spackman's occupational therapy* (7th ed.). Philadelphia: J. B. Lippincott Co.

Reviewed By

Michael Peterson
Director, Developmental Disabilities Institute
Wayne State University

The McCarron-Dial Evaluation System (MDS) is considered by the developers to be both a vocational and clinical evaluation system. The MDS was originally designed to predict the level of vocational functioning of mentally handicapped persons in sheltered workshops; however, it has since been used with other populations in a wide variety of settings. The system is intended to assess five classes of traits: (1) Verbal-spatial-cognitive; (2) sensory; (3) motor; (4) emotional; and (5) integration-coping. Each of these areas is assessed via specific assessment tools which are described below by area.

Verbal-spatial-cognitive abilities are assessed using a Wechsler or Stanford Binet Intelligence Test, the Peabody Picture Vocabulary Test (PPVT) and, in some cases, with the addition of an achievement test such as the Wide Range Achievement Test (WRAT) or the Peabody Individual Acheivement Test (PIAT).

Sensory abilities are evaluated using the Bender Visual Motor Gestalt Test (BVMGT) and the Haptic Visual Discrimination Test (HVDT). The Haptic test involves placement of articles with a variety of shapes, sizes, and textures in an individual's hand; the evaluee then selects one of five pictures that he/she believes represents the article being held. The Haptic Memory Matching Test is an adapted version that is used with blind persons.

Motor functions are measured with the McCarron Assessment of Neuromuscular Development (MAND). *Fine motor skills* are assessed via: (1) placing beads in a box; (2) placing beads on a rod; (3) finger tapping; (4) nut and bolt assembly; and (5) rod slide. *Gross motor* skills are assessed via: (6) hand strength; (7) finger-nose-finger touching; (8) standing broad jump; (9) heel-toe-walk; and (10) standing on one foot. An adaptation of the MAND is available with norms for blind and visually impaired persons.

Emotional characteristics are assessed via the Observational Emotional Inventory (OEI) which allows observation and recording of a number of problem behaviors in the following areas: neuro-psychological impulsivity; anxiety; depression-withdrawal; socialization and self-concept.

Integration-coping involves the use of traits in actual community survival situations. The Dial Behavior Rating Scale (BRS) was originally used with the system and provides a simple rating of basic community skills. The Street Survival Skill Questionnaire (SSSQ) is intended to assess a wide variety of adaptive behaviors via a formal testing process. Content includes: basic concepts; functional signs; tools; domestic management; health, safety, and first aid; public service; time; money; and measurement.

All McCarron-Dial materials are packaged in durable cases which makes transportation easy. A manual is available for the total system and separate manuals are available for the MAND, SSSQ, and the Haptic Visual Discrimination Test (HVDT). These manuals are generally well written and provide numerous case studies. Clearly, the McCarron-Dial is not one test, but a collection of tests and assessment procedures. To evaluate the McCarron-Dial, the total system must be considered as well as each component of the system.

A formal testing procedure is used for all assessment components except for the BRS and OEI which is based upon observations in a community or work setting. The formal testing process lasts approximately four to seven hours depending upon the individual and the specific tests used. Observation for a minimum of two hours per day for one week is necessary for the OEI and the Dial Behavior Rating Scale.

SCORES AND NORMS

Scores include time, quality, or a combination of these depending upon the specific test. All scores are converted into percentiles or T scores and plotted on a profile. Additionally, separate, more detailed profiles are available for the MAND, OEI and SSSQ. The SSSQ provides a criterion-referenced profile based on types of items as well as a norm-based profile.

In all cases, norms are available for mentally handicapped adults, while other norms groups are also available for some tests. The MAND provides norms for non-handicapped young adults, adult mentally disabled, and developmental norms for non-disabled children from ages 3–6 to age 18. Adult norms for deaf, blind, and older persons are available for the HVDT, HMMT, and the MAND. Normative groups range from 500 to 2,000 on components of the system.

The manuals provide a report format and several examples of actual reports. A specific manual is available that gives guidelines on using the system for report writing and individualized planning. Additionally, a number of computerized reports are available which include a general report, a prescriptive, interpretive report, an occupational exploration survey, or a combination of the above. Computerized reports can be obtained by processing via McCarron-Dial Evaluation systems or software may be purchased that facilitates on-site report development.

RELIABILITY AND VALIDITY

A number of reliability studies are presented in the manuals. Most reliability coefficients are in the high .80s and .90s and use test-retest procedures.

Both construct and predictive validity data are presented. Predictive validity is based upon the ability of the system to predict general level of vocational functioning after one year of training. Studies were conducted primarily by the authors (Dial, Freeman, McCarron, & Swearingern, 1979; Dial & Swearingen, 1976; McCarron & Dial, 1972) have yielded positive results. However, since "training" appears to relate primarily to unspecified activities in sheltered workshops, such studies may simply verify the arguments of proponents of supported employment that sheltered workshops do not provide meaningful skill development.

USABILITY OF THE SYSTEM

The McCarron-Dial Evaluation System has a variety of uses—both clinical and vocational. It was designed to assess basic abilities of persons with mental disabilities—particularly mental retardation, chronic mental illness, and related disability groups. However, components of the system appear to have wider uses.

One purpose of the system is to predict level of vocational functioning of mentally disabled persons one year after training. These levels include the normal continuum of services often available for mentally disabled persons: daycare, work activity centers, low extended sheltered workshops, high extended sheltered workshops, and transitional settings. The system was developed at a time when supported employment options were only minimally available and when intensive training using task analysis techniques was being researched. Consequently, the system has no way of predicting success under supported employment conditions. Given the reliance of the prediction process on the system of traditional service categories, a danger clearly exists that recommendations for program placement might be made that are not consistent with best practices as they are presently understood. Therefore, the prediction formula should be used cautiously as a basis for assisting in making placement decisions.

Despite the above concerns, the McCarron-Dial does appear to provide a systematic and useful analysis of basic strengths and weaknesses of an individual's trait structure—e.g., cognitive, affective, and psychomotor. The MAND appears to be an especially useful device for specific analysis of motor functioning that has both clinical and vocational implications. Excellent guides for developing individualized plans for "remedial motor training" have been developed.

Relative to analysis for vocational assessment, the McCarron-Dial must generally be interpreted clinically. The system is trait-oriented. However, the manuals do not make a direct connection between the results of the system and the worker trait profile of the Department of Labor, although a listing of DOT coded occupations is provided in the occupational exploration report. This report is tentative and appears to be based primarily upon a screening via the data, people, things hierarchy. Since the system does not assess any specific vocational skills or involve individuals in identifiable work tasks, occupational exploration and direct observation of work skills is limited.

REFERENCES

Botterbusch, K. (1982). *A Comparison of Commercial Vocational Evaluation Systems*, Menomonie, WI: Materials Development Center.

Dial, J. & Swearingen, S. (1979). The prediction of sheltered workshop performance: Special applications of the McCarron-Dial Work Evaluation System. *Vocational Evaluation and Work Adjustment Bulletin*, 9(4), 24–33.

Dial, J., Freeman, L., McCarron, L., & Swearingen, S. (1979). Predictive validation of the McCarron-Dial Evaluation System, *Vocational Evaluation and Work Adjustment Bulletin*, 12(1), 11–18.

Henke, R., & Connelly, S. (1976). Methods for diagnosing language learning disability, *Research Review*, 2(4), 1–5.

McCarron, L. (1976). *McCarron Assessment of Neuromuscular Development (MAND)*, Dallas: Common Market Press.

McCarron, L., & Dial, J. (1976). *McCarron-Dial Work Evaluation System: Evaluation of the Mentally Disabled—A systematic approach*, Dallas: Common Market Press.

McCarron, L., & Dial, J. (1972). Neuropsychological predictors of sheltered workshop performance. *American Journal of Mental Deficiency, 77*, 244–250.

Texas Rehabilitation Commission, *Vocational Rehabilitation Process for Specific Learning Disabilities*, Austin, TX: Author.

Pictorial Inventory of Careers (PIC)

Thomas F. Kosuth

Talent Assessment, Inc.
P.O. Box 5087, Jacksonville, FL 32247-5087

Target Population: Ages 13–55 mildly handicapped to regular non-handicapped.

Statement of the Purpose of the Instrument: To provide an assessment of affective vocational interest in a non-reading format.

Titles of Subtests, Scales, Scores Provided: 17 job clusters: agriculture/environmental, business-data processing, business-retailing sales, business-secretarial, communication-art/graphics, criminal justice, electrical/electronics, engineering technology, food services, health services, science and laboratory, service-barbering/cosmetology, service-fire science, service-personal, trade and industry/construction, trade and industry/mechanical, trade and industry-metal trades.

Forms and Levels Available: Level 1 Regular vocational students; Level 2 lower functioning students.

Date of Most Recent Edition of Test Manual, User's Guide, Etc.: March 1987.

Languages in Which Available: English only.

Time: Actual Test Time—22 minutes.
  Total Administration Time—22 minutes.

Norm Group(s) on Which Scores Are Based: Ages 17-55.

Manner in Which Results are Reported for Individuals
  Types of Scores: Norm values—percentile ranking with industry, positive, neutral, and negative preference.
  Report Format/Content
    Basic Service: Computer print out
    Options: Local career options, local training programs.

Report Format/Content for Group Summaries:
    Basic Service: Same.
    Options: Same.

Scoring
  Machine Scoring Service: not available.
  Hand Scoring
    Scored by: counselee; clerk; counselor.
    Time required for scoring: 2 minutes.

Local Machine Scoring
   Provisions/conditions/equipment required: Apple II series or IBM-PC Compatibles.

Cost of Materials
   Specimen Set: No cost—Preview for 10 days.
   Counselee Materials: Total package $495.00 to $695.00 depending on filmstrip or video format.

Additional Comments of Interest to Users: New program called "P.O.W.E.R." available 4/87. "P.O.W.E.R." introduces students to each cluster of careers found in PIC.

Published Reviews
   None.

Reviewed by

Linda H. Parrish
Associate Professor
Texas A&M University
and
Patricia S. Lynch
Graduate Assistant
Texas A&M University

The Pictorial Inventory of Careers (PIC) is an audio-visual instrument designed to measure vocational interests and identify areas for potential occupational exploration and training. The inventory is non-verbal and reading is not required. A series of 119 slides, depicting vocational-technical careers in 17 job clusters, is presented. There are seven slides for each career cluster, and the occupational or work environment is emphasized, rather than the individual worker.

There are two program levels in the PIC. Program 1 consists of all 119 slides plus an additional section in which examinees are presented with 11 definitions of work environments to which they express their preferences. All 130 items are responded to on a five-point scale ranging from "strongly dislike" to "strongly like" and are scored from one to five points. This program is designed for regular students. Program 2 consists only of the 119 slides to which examinees respond on a three-point scale by simply indicating "no," "?," or "yes" as to their degree of interest. Scores of one, three, or five points are assigned. The second program is designed for handicapped, disadvantaged, or limited English proficient students.

NORMS AND SCORES

The PIC (program 1) provides three types of results: 1) preference scores, 2) percentile ranks, and 3) stated interest preferences. Preference scores are determined for each career cluster by adding scores from responses to slides within each cluster. The preference scores are represented as positive (+), neutral (0), or negative (−). A raw score of 26 to 35 is positive, 17 to 25 is neutral, and 16 or below is negative.

Percentile ranks are also derived from the raw scores. No information is provided in the manual concerning the norms on which the percentile ranks are based, although one might assume they were drawn from the sample used to determine the reliability. That sample was a random group of 200 men and women enrolled in orientation courses for new students at a California community college. The group was reportedly "ethnically and socio-economically heterogeneous and ranged in age from 17 to 55."

Stated interest preference is determined by presenting eleven definitions of occupational environments and having individuals state their preference to each definition on a five-point scale. Responses of 4 or 5 are considered positive. The manual states that it is "essential" to consider all three types of results prior to counseling. This would only be possible if program 1 is used, since program 2 does not utilize the work environments section. Depending on the setting and the individual, the inventory could be self-administered and scored. No training, other than careful reading of the manual, is needed to administer the inventory.

RELIABILITY AND VALIDITY

Reliability was determined by the test-retest method over a three-week interval. Originally administered to 200 California community college students, the PIC was re-administered three weeks later to a sample (23 males and 23 females) from the original 200 students. According to the manual, this sample was "randomly selected," but it also states the 46 students "volunteered" to retake the PIC. Correlations were calculated for each of the 17 career clusters. These ranged from .61 (Food Services) to .93 (T&I Construction). The manual claims these correlations are similar to those obtained in the 30-day test-retest reliability of the Strong-Campbell, and therefore, reliability was "adequate."

The stability of scores for the three categories of positive, neutral and negative was also investigated as part of the test-retest. This resulted in no shift in preference scores 74% of the time, a shift from positive to neutral 25% of the time, and a shift from positive to negative only 1% of the time. According to the manual, these findings "reflect favorably on the instrument."

To assess validity, a sample was identified and volunteers were obtained from each career cluster. Sample sizes ranged from 30 to 49 (X = 38). The PIC was administered and, using a t-test, the group scores were compared with scores for individuals constituting those who would usually take the PIC. All t-tests were significantly different at the .01 level for the 17 occupational clusters. The authors did not compare the PIC to similar instruments, because they feel it is unique among interest inventories.

USABILITY

The PIC is simple to set up and administer; total administration time is approximately 30 minutes, whether used individually or with a group. Although the manual stresses that this instrument emphasizes jobs that do not exceed the academic capabilities of its intended examinees, it is evident that these are skilled positions that typically require training from two-year institutions, such as community or junior colleges or trade/technical schools. For example, included in Cluster 9, Food Services, are specific jobs such as baking, dietary technician, chef training, and catering arts. No jobs referencing custodial or maintenance positions or bus boys/girls are included for less academically talented populations. When using the PIC, it is important to have a trained counselor review the results with the examinee, as misinterpretation could occur.

SPECIAL CONCERNS

Although the inventory is non-reading, it does not focus on occupations that require no reading. Program 2 is designed for the handicapped and disadvantaged; however most jobs presented are not those that would be realistically suitable for many in this population. In addition, some of the occupational activities depicted are somewhat vague, and a person might express an interest in the perceived occupation rather than the actual one.

The manual claims that the instrument is sex and minority fair. Of the 119 occupational scenes, 55% show males at work (17% of these are minority) and 35% show females (21% of these are minority); in 8% of the slides, sex is indeterminable. All slides in the Service-Personal Cluster are female, and all slides in the Service-Fire Science Cluster appear to be male, although some are back views. All cosmetologists are female. The manual appears to have been written by different authors, as in Section 1, the pronoun use is consistently "he" and "his," while in Section 3, non-sexist language is carefully employed.

The manual is particularly helpful in offering counseling hints such as incorporating realistic expectations, physical requirements, employment opportunities and other considerations prior to explaining expressed occupational interests to the examinee. The manual also provides comprehensive information in such areas as cluster descriptions, job titles, *Dictionary of Occupational Titles* (DOT) numbers and U.S.O.E. instructional program codes.

A computer program is available with the PIC that creates a printout useful for counseling examinees. The program does not score the test; this must be done by the examiner or examinee, but when the raw scores are typed into the program, it produces preference scores and a graphic profile with percentile ranks. The three career clusters with the top scores are described, job titles in these clusters are listed with DOT and Guide for Occupational Exploration (GOE) references, and suggested vocational programs within these clusters are provided. The printout is very impressive visually, but the graphic profile of percentile ranks uses letters as symbols, which are not explained in the manual. In addition, the top three raw scores could theoretically all have negative preference scores, yet the printout suggests areas to explore in those clusters. The results, therefore, should be carefully reviewed by a counselor before being presented to the examinee.

The program is easy to use, and directions for its use are clearly explained in the manual. However, the manual does not state how much memory is required to run the program. If, for example, an Apple computer with 64K is used, the program will stop in the middle because of insufficient space, and the printout will not be complete. The PIC-Instant Report Summary computer printout could very well serve as a basis for further career counseling; therefore, this personalized feature is an asset.

REFERENCE

Kosuth, T. F. (1985). *The pictorial inventory of careers manual*. Jacksonville, FL: Talent Assessment.

Program for Assessing Youth Employment Skills (PAYES)

Educational Testing Service

Cambridge
888 Seventh Avenue, New York, NY 10019

Target Population: School drop outs, disadvantaged adolescents.

Statement of the Purpose of the Instrument: Provides a non-sexist measure of attitudes, cognitive skills, and vocational preference for disadvantaged or dropout youth.

Titles of Subtests, Scales, Scores Provided: Seven subtests: Job Holding Skills, Attitude toward Supervision, Self-Confidence, Job Knowledge, Job Seeking Skills, Map Reading, Zip Coding and Vocational Interest Inventory.

Forms and Levels Available with Dates of Publications/Revision of Each: Only one form—1979.

Date of Most Recent Edition of Test Manual, User's Guide, Etc.: Technical Manual—1979, User's Guide—1979, Administrator's Manual—1979.

Languages in Which Available: English only.

Time: Total Administration Time—75 minutes.

Norm Group(s) on Which Scores Are Based: 1300 students and enrollees in vocational educational special needs classes, CETA centers, skills training centers, and correctional institutions throughout the country. A total of 28 program sites participated in the field testing.

Manner in Which Results Are Reported for Individuals
  Types of Scores: Raw scores are plotted on a profile with verbal labels.
  Report Format/Content
    Basic Service: Profile (Narrative in User's Guide)

Report Format/Content for Group Summaries: Not available.

Scoring
  Machine Scoring Service: Not available.
  Hand Scoring
    Scored by: Counselor.
    Time required for scoring: 15 minutes per client.
  Local Machine Scoring: Not available.

Computer Software Options Available: Not available.

Published Reviews
White, S. A. (1985). Review of *Program for Assessing Youth Employment Skills*. In J. V. Mitchell (Ed.), *Ninth Mental Measurements Yearbook*: Volume II (p. 1223). Lincoln, NE: University of Nebraska Press.
Zakay, D. (1985). Review of *Program for Assessing Youth Employment Skills*. In J. V. Mitchell (Ed.), *Ninth Mental Measurements Yearbook*: Volume II (p. 1223). Lincoln, NE: University of Nebraska Press.

Reviewed By:

J. Paul Tonetti
New York State Education Department
Albany, New York

The Program for Assessing Youth Employment Skills (PAYES) was designed for counselors who work with "adolescents and young adults displaying low-verbal skills." It was designed to provide counselors with a structured approach for developing a profile of their clients' comprehension of the attitudes, interests, knowledge and skills needed to find, obtain, maintain and develop a job. The *User's Guide* describes the PAYES as a "tool for guidance counseling . . . useful for enrollees in CETA (now JTPA) centers, skills centers, vocational high school special needs classes, adult basic education centers and youths in correctional institutions. It is not a substitute for counseling, and . . . "is not designed to be used . . . to determine whether students should be allowed to participate in particular programs."

The PAYES is the product of a joint venture of the Department of Labor (DOL) and the Educational Testing Service (ETS) that began in 1967 and ended in 1978. Its intent was to design a test that would meet the "client assessment needs of guidance counselors in federally funded vocational training programs." Existing measures of that time were criticized for focusing on middle-class populations, and for failing to address areas pertinent to the objectives and curricula of vocationally oriented compensatory and work-training programs.

ETS began research and development in 1967 with a survey and analysis of work-training objectives, curriculum materials, and the measurement needs of counselors, administrators and other program professionals. This effort led to a PAYES of seven subtests organized into three categories: attitude, cognitive and interest. Textual material in captions, want ads and maps require a fifth grade reading level.

FORMAT AND CONTENT

The PAYES measures are contained in three separate booklets, intended to be administered in order. The booklets use line drawings to present scenes of job, school and social settings to clients. Want ads, maps and employment applications are also used. Almost all question and answer choices are read aloud by the counselor. The client is asked to respond to each situation by marking a space in the test booklet.

Booklet I—Attitudinal Measures: Items use line drawings to depict work, school and social situations. Clients indicate how they might respond to an authority figure or situation.

- *Job Holding Skills* (11 items)—Measures perceptions of appropriate employee behaviors.
- *Attitude Toward Supervisors* (13 items)—Measures compliance with demands from authority figures.
- *Self-Confidence* (15 items)—Assesses feelings of competence in social and employment situations.

Booklet II—Cognitive Measures: Line drawings, want ads, applications and maps are used to assess the client's knowledge of jobs, ability to interpret want ads, fill out applications and follow directions.

- *Job Knowledge* (30 items)—Measures six areas of job knowledge: education required, work setting, working hours, starting salaries, primary tasks, tools used.
- *Job Seeking Skills* (17 items)—Assesses ability to search for employment.
- *Practical Reasoning* (20 items)—Addresses a client's ability to follow directions.

Booklet III—Vocational Interest Measure (28 items): Clients are asked how they would feel about performing job tasks depicted by line drawings. Taps interests in seven major occupational areas: clerical, service, business, technical, aesthetic, outdoor and science.

ADMINISTRATION AND SCORING

The User's Guide advises that, ". . . Careful attention must be given to details of administration because persons with low verbal skills may have negative feelings toward multiple-choice, paper-and-pencil testing. . . . Procedures are designed to create a relaxed informal atmosphere." Although the test is not timed, about 75 minutes is suggested for administration.

Test booklets are hand scored by counselors or by clerical staff. The *User's Guide* cautions counselors to use the scores in conjunction with other observations, noting that, "Understanding of the material presented in the *PAYES* measures represents a *minimally acceptable level of knowledge and skill necessary for securing and holding an entry-level job.*" (emphasis added).

The Guide discusses the counseling implications of each subtest, interprets what a high or low score means and suggests activities that might be implemented to assist clients to acquire the knowledge and skills needed for securing and holding a job. Suggested activities include role playing and conflict resolution exercises.

TECHNICAL CHARACTERISTICS

The *Technical Manual* reports means, standard deviations and sample sizes for PAYES measures as well as for counselor, instructor, and work supervisor rating scales used as criterion measures. Reliability coefficients representing estimates of internal consistency range from .59 for *Job Holding* skills to .85 for the *Practical Reasoning* measure. As measures increase in length, they tend to have higher coefficients. The trade off between length and low reliability coefficients appears to be reasonable, given that the instrument is to be used for counseling and instruction and not for selection or prediction.

Validity of the PAYES is based on the correlation of each of the subtests (excluding the Vocational Interest Scales) with counselor, instructor, and work-site supervisor ratings. Although correlations are statistically significant, they range from very low, .10, to very modest, mid .20s. Low correlations might be explained by widely diverse projects, curricula, objectives and participants found in CETA, in-school, and corrections settings, but nevertheless, they are not high enough to lend much validity support. Intercorrelations among the six subtests cluster into two dimensions: cognitive and attitudinal.

Validation studies of the *PAYES* are dated and inadequate. There is an obvious need to validate its use with current special needs populations, particularly with special education, limited English proficient and other educationally deprived students who display low reading levels and limited world of work experiences. The recruitment of students from those groups into vocational training and work experience programs has been accelerated by the Carl Perkins Vocational Education Act and the Job Training Partnership Act, and the areas addressed by PAYES seem appropriate for the populations served by these programs. In addition, the PAYES technical manual lacks information about how valid it is in terms of its primary goal—a useful tool for guidance and counseling. It seems reasonable to expect the publishers to initiate and underwrite studies to obtain information from counselors and employers about the usefulness of PAYES.

USABILITY

The PAYES appears to this reviewer to be a useful and "counselor friendly" resource. The content is relevant to career counseling and because items are presented in an informal, non-threatening manner, the PAYES may be considered to be a structured interview—a format that should make counselors comfortable. Scoring, interpretation and follow-up activities are compatible with most counselor competencies. PAYES is the kind of tool that can help counselors understand their clients, help stimulate discussion, and result in guidance activities that help clients find and hold jobs.

SUMMARY

The PAYES has the potential to become an instrument to integrate assessment and counseling functions. However, until data are obtained to validate its use as a traditional measurement tool, the PAYES should be restricted to facilitating career guidance and instructional activities.

REFERENCES

Educational Testing Service. (1979). *Program for Assessing Youth Employment Skills, Administrator's Manual*. New York, NY: Cambridge.

Freeberg, N. E. & Vitella, P. E. (1979). *Program for Assessing Youth Employment Skills, Technical Manual*. New York, NY: Cambridge.

Educational Testing Service. (1979). *Program for Assessing Youth Employment Skills, User's Guide*. New York, NY: Cambridge.

Reading-Free Vocational Interest Inventory—Revised (R-FVII Revised)

Ralph L. Becker

Elbern Publications
P.O. Box 09497
Columbus, Ohio 43209

Target Population: All levels of MR/DD children and adults, 13 through 60; school-age LD subjects; disadvantaged adults, 21 through 61.

Statement of the Purpose of the Instrument: To determine the vocational interest of MR/DD and LD children and adults in jobs in which they are realistically able to succeed. Assesses their vocational interest in jobs in which they are proficient/productive using pictures of occupational significance.

Titles of Subtests, Scales, Scores Provided: Automotive, building trades, clerical, animal care, food service, patient care, horticulture, housekeeping, personal service, laundry, materials handling.

Forms and Levels Available, with Dates of Publication/Revision of Each: One form for males and females—1981.

Date of Most Recent Edition of Test Manual, User's Guide, Etc.: 1981, 1988.

Languages in Which Available: English, plus a Dutch version is being developed.

Time: Actual Test Time—10 minutes.
    Total Administration Time—10 minutes.

Norm Group(s) on Which Scores Are Based: Mentally retarded, learning disabled, sheltered workshop adults, environmentally disadvantaged adults.

Manner in Which Results Are Reported for Individuals
  Types of Scores: Standard scores, percentile ranks, and stanines.
  Report Format/Content
    Basic Service: Profile of vocational interests using a percentile graph showing vocational likes and dislikes.

Report Format/Content for Group Summaries: Not available.

Scoring
  Machine Scoring Service: Not available.

Hand Scoring
  Scored by: Clerk: counselor.
  Time required for scoring: 10 minutes or less.
  Local Machine Scoring: Not available.

Computer Software Options Available: Not available.

Cost of Materials
  Specimen Set: 10 test booklets and one manual $21.45.
  Counselee Materials: Manual $10.00; Occupational Title Lists $11.90.

Additional Comments of Interest to Users: R-FVII was revised in 1981. The Occupational Title Lists (©1984) is a supplement to the test for use in matching interests with jobs. The manual was updated in 1987/88.

Published Reviews
Diamond, E. E. (1982). AAMD-Becker Reading-Free Vocational Interest Inventory. In J. T. Kapes & M. M. Mastie (Eds), *A counselor's guide to vocational guidance instruments* (pp. 162–165). Falls Church, VA: National Vocational Guidance Association.
Diamond, E. E. (1978). Review of AAMD-Becker Reading-Free Vocational Interest Inventory. In O. K. Buros (Ed.), *Eighth Mental Measurements Yearbook*: Volume II (p. 1535). Highland Park, NJ: Gryphon Press.
Domino, G. (1978). Review of AAMD-Becker Reading-Free Vocational Interest Inventory. In O. K. Buros (Ed.), *Eighth Mental Measurements Yearbook*: Volume II (p.1536). Highland Park, NJ: Gryphon Press.
Holden, R. H. (1984). Review of Reading-Free Vocational Interest Inventory—Revised. In D. J. Keyser & R. C. Sweetland (Eds.), *Test Critiques*: Volume II (pp.627–630). Kansas City, MO: Test Corporation of America.

Reviewed by

George Domino
Professor of Psychology
University of Arizona

The Reading-Free Vocational Interest Inventory (R-FVII) is a non-reading vocational preference test for use with mentally retarded or learning disabled persons, aged 13 to adult, and consists of 55 pictorial triads illustrating occupational activities such as washing dishes or grooming a horse. For each triad the client selects the best liked activity. The inventory generates eleven interest area scores for both males and females: (1) automotive, (2) building trades, (3) clerical, (4) animal care, (5) food service, (6) patient care, (7) horticulture, (8) housekeeping, (9) personal service, (10) laundry service, and (11) materials handling.

The R-FVII can be administered individually or in a group and requires 20 to 45 minutes of total administration time. Both administration and scoring are basically clerical tasks, but interpretation requires professional expertise. Scoring

271

the inventory involves transcribing the 55 responses of the client onto a score sheet, with 41 of the 165 items keyed on more than one scale; this is a tedious and time-consuming task, especially if done for a group of clients.

NORMS AND SCORES

Norms are from a 1980–81 nationwide administration to samples of educable mentally retarded (EMR) and learning disabled (LD) males and females in grades 7 through 12 in public day schools, and samples of mentally retarded adults in sheltered workshops and vocational training centers.

Ten tables of norms are provided based on substantial samples: (1) Public school EMR males, ages 13 to 15-11 (N = 1080); (2) Public school EMR males, ages 16 to 22 (N = 1052); (3) Public school LD males, ages 13 to 15-11 (N = 1015); (4) Public school LD males, ages 16 to 19-11 (N = 1019); (5) Adult Sheltered Workshop Center males, no age given (N = 1121); (6) Public school EMR females, ages 13 to 15-11 (N = 1098); (7) Public school EMR females, ages 16 to 21-11 (N = 1065); (8) Public school LD females, ages 13 to 15-11 (N = 994); (9) Public school LD females, ages 10 to 19-09 (N = 973); and (10) Adult Sheltered Workshop Center females, no age given (N = 1106). Tables are clear and allow for a transformation of raw scores into T scores, percentiles, and stanines. Both raw scores and transformed scores can be placed on an individual profile sheet that allows for the plotting of percentiles into a graph, and for the designation of interest areas into "high" and "low." The profile sheet is well designed and incorporates much useful information.

RELIABILITY

Test-retest reliabilities (two-week interval) are presented in ten tables, paralleling the normative tables, but with substantially smaller samples (Ns from 48 to 92). The obtained coefficients are primarily in the high .70's and .80's showing more than adequate reliability for all scales with the possible exception of the Materials Handling scale, where seven of the ten coefficients are in the high .60s and low .70s.

Test-retest reliability tables also include the standard error of measurement, which can be more useful than the reliability coefficient, especially when dealing with a single score, and the means and standard deviations for both test and retest.

Internal consistency reliability (Kuder-Richardson #20) was also obtained, but the only statement given is that the reliabilities "ranged from a low of .61 to a high of .94 with a median of .82."

VALIDITY

Three types of validity are discussed in the manual: content, concurrent, and "occupational" validity.

Content validity, according to the author, "was built into the test when a complete search was made of jobs known to be appropriate and realistic for mentally retarded and learning disabled individuals." Thus the 11 scales were developed on the basis of logical analysis of the world of work, with items retained in a scale if their discriminating power was "sufficient," as judged by an analysis of the top and bottom 27% of a criterion category. Little information and less data are given on this, so the professional reader cannot judge the adequacy of this process. Since the obtained 11 scales do not fully match the dimensions obtained by other investigators, the content validity of the R-FVII is clearly not a closed issue.

Concurrent validity data were obtained by administering the R-FVII and the Geist Picture Interest Inventory to ten samples of subjects. The two inventories have only one scale that is identically named, the Clerical scale; these two scales correlate from a low of .21 to a high of .48, with a median r of .35. Correlations among other scales of the two inventories range from a fairly high relation between the R-FVII Building trades scale and the Geist Mechanical scale (correlation coefficients of .33 to .79, median of .46), to a low relationship between R-FVII Materials handling scale and the Geist Computational scale (.10 to .29, median of .20) although there is no strong reason why these two scales should correlate.

Occupational validity is based on a study of 619 mentally retarded males and 640 females in 11 occupational groups—presumable comparable to the 11 scales. A profile comparison indicates that occupational groups scored higher on their "own" scale rather than on the other ten scales. For the practicing counselor, this may easily be the most important type of validity data, but no statistical details are given. Thus, the available validity information represents a real weakness of this inventory, although the potentially available information could be an asset.

USABILITY FOR PRACTITIONERS

The R-FVII seems suitable for adolescent and/or adult mentally retarded or learning desabled clients where occupational planning and job placement are considered. The Manual is clearly written, and the psychometric information presented in well designed and appropriate tables. There is an accompanying *Occupational Title Lists* that offers a listing of occupational titles with respective 9-digit DOT occupational codes, as related to each of the R-FVII scales, and this can also be useful in providing concrete directions to discuss with the client. In general, the R-FVII fulfills a real need in a careful and professional manner, and it is to be hoped that future editions will improve what appears to be a potentially useful tool.

SPECIAL CONCERNS

As with any psychometric instrument, there are a number of problems with the R-FVII, some minor but irritating, and some substantial. On the minor side, is the lack of details to support the internal consistency and occupational validity. Although the manual already contains 35 tables, the additional tables needed to address these two areas would be worth the effort. The manual contains a bibliography, but none of the items is referenced in the body so the reader has to guess the degree of relevance of specific bibliographic items. The instructions on the front page of the inventory instruct the client to select the best-liked picture, but the instructions in the manual, to be read aloud by the examiner, contain the phrase "find which job you like the best and put a circle on that picture." Clearly the emphasis should be on the job liked best, and the two sets of instructions should coincide. No average ages are given for the sheltered workshop samples, nor is the issue of whether chronological age correlates with scale scores addressed.

More substantially, there is evidence that the Materials Handling scale may lack reliability and validity. In addition, a number of scales correlate substantially with one another—for example, the Automotive and the Building trades scales correlate in the high .70s in almost all samples. Are the 11 scales sufficiently independent dimensions to be of use in dealing with clients? A factor analytic approach would say no, although ultimately it must be the professional consumer who decides whether the dimensions are of practical use. A related question is whether the 11 career areas cover the world of work, at least as available in our society to EMR and LD clients; the manual indicates that it does, but more direct evidence is needed. Finally, a word of caution: for all 11 scales, a one or two point raw score difference results in rather drastically different percentile scores. For example, for EMR males a raw score of 4 on the Clerical scale equals a percentile of 50, but a raw score of 6 equals a percentile of 70. Quite clearly, extreme care must be exercised in interpretation of results.

Social and Prevocational Information Battery—Revised (SPIB-R)

Andrew Halpern, Larry Irvin and Ardan Munkres

CTB/McGraw-Hill,
2500 Garden Rd.
Monterey, CA 93940

Target Population: Grade 6 and above, including adults. Mildly to moderately retarded students.

Statement of the Purpose of the Instrument: To assess knowledge in areas that are widely regarded as important for community adjustment of adolescents and adults with mild mental retardation.

Titles of Subtests, Scales, Scores Provided: Banking, Budgeting, Purchasing, Job Search Skills, Job Related Behavior, Home Management, Health Care, Hygiene and Grooming, Functional Signs.

Forms and Levels Available, with Dates of Publication/Revision of Each: SPIB-R first published in 1975, revised in 1985. Form T for Trainable Mentally Retarded was published in 1978 (same subtests). Tests for Everyday Living (TEL), published in 1981 for L.D., has all but Functional Signs and Hygiene and Grooming subtests.

Date of Most Recent Edition of Test Manual, User's Guide, Etc.: 1985 for SPIB-R.

Languages in Which Available: English only.

Time: Actual Test Time—about 20 min per test, 3 hours total.

Norm Group(s) on Which Scores Are Based: Reference groups of mildly, moderately, and trainable retarded.

Manner in Which Results Are Reported for Individuals:
   Types of Scores: Although the original edition had reference group norms, the new (Revised) edition has only a raw score interpretation at this time. Some would call this criteron referenced.
   Report Format/Content
    Basic Service: Not available

Report Format/Content for Group Summaries: Not available.

Scoring
   Machine Scoring Service: Not available.

Hand Scoring
  Scored by: Clerk; counselor.
  Time required for scoring. 2–3 minutes per subtest.
  Local Machine Scoring: Not available.

Computer Software Options Available: Not available

Cost of Materials
  Specimen Set: $10.00.
  Counselee Materials: Manual $8.50; test booklets $32.00 per pkg. of 20.

Additional Comments of Interest to Users: A kit of instructional activities (the Skills for Independent Living Kit) is available with learning activities specified that are geared to the subtests in SPIB-T, SPIB-R, and TEL. They make a complete system when used the tests. All items are read aloud to the student.

Published Reviews
Daniels, M. H. (1985). Review of *Social of Social and Prevocational Information Battery—Revised*. In J. V. Mitchell (Ed.), *Ninth Mental Measurements Yearbook:* Volume I (p. 739). Lincoln, NE: University of Nebraska Press.
Meyers, C. E. (1978). Review of *Social and Prevocational Information Battery—Revised*. In O. K. Buros (Ed.), *Eighth Mental Measurements Yearbook*: Volume II (p. 1526). Highland Park, NJ: Gryphon Press.
Tittle, C. K. (1985), Review of *Social and Prevocational Information Battery—Revised*. In J. V. Mitchell (Ed.), *Ninth Mental Measurements Yearbook*: Volume 1 (p. 739). Lincoln, NE: University of Nebraska Press.

Reviewed By

Randall M. Parker
Professor of Special Education
University of Texas at Austin

The Social and Prevocational Information Battery—Revised (SPIB-R) (Halpern & Irwin, 1986) is a paper and pencil test designed to measure social and prevocational knowledge necessary for community adjustment of junior and senior high school students with mild mental retardation. The SPIB-R is comprised of nine subtests containing a total of 277 items representing five long-range goals. The five goals and nine subtests include: 1. Employability: Job Search Skill (32 items) and Job Related Behavior (30 items); 2. Economic Self-Sufficiency: Banking (31 items), Budgeting (33 items), and Purchasing Habits (36 items); 3. Family Living: Home Management (33 items) and Health Care (30 items); 4. Personal Habits: Hygiene and Grooming (26 items); and 5. Communication: Functional Signs (26 items).

The five goals and nine subtests (domains) listed above were selected from eight long-range goals and 54 domains identified by the authors working with

26 Oregon public school teachers of students with mild mental retardation. Content areas for each of the nine domains were identified and items were developed for each of the content areas.

The revision of the original SPIB was undertaken "to revise or replace some of the test items, . . . to update the *Administration Manual*, . . ." and to make improvements suggested in a survey of SPIB users (Halpern & Irwin, 1986, p. 77). Based on the survey data the authors revised or replaced 34 items and rewrote sections of the *User's Guide* and *Administration Manual*.

ADMINISTRATION AND SCORING

Directions for administration are clearly presented and are easy to follow. The 277 items, of which 236 are true-false and 41 are multiple choice graphics in format, are vocally administered to individuals or small groups (10 or fewer). Examinees are required to mark an "X" over the words "TRUE" or "FALSE" or in a box under the correct picture in the test booklet to indicate their answer. An example of a true-false item is, "It is safe to cross a street against a red light, because cars will stop for you." One graphics item, for example, shows four signs—HIGH VOLTAGE, CAUTION, ENTRANCE, and FOR RENT. The examinee is asked to mark an "X" under all signs that might mean danger.

Although untimed, each subtest requires from 15 to 25 minutes to complete. The authors recommend testing be divided into three sessions occurring within a period of one week. The SPIB-R is readily hand scored; however, machine scoring is also available.

SCORES AND NORMS

Raw scores are determined by counting the number of correct items for each subtest and for the total battery. Raw scores can be converted to percent correct scores or to percentile equivalents using the tables of norms provided in the manual. The original SPIB norm group, 453 junior high and 453 senior high EMR students in Oregon, was used to derive the norms. New normative data are not reported in the manual, but "are being collected . . . and will be made available to SPIB-R users at the earliest possible date" (Halpern & Irwin, 1986, p. 77). Because the normative sample was limited to Oregon, using the SPIB-R with groups in other states is questionable. It would be desirable for the authors to collect and report norms from other regions of the U.S. and for users to develop their own local norms.

RELIABILITY AND VALIDITY

Kuder-Richardson formula 20 and test-retest reliability coefficients are reported for 453 junior high and 453 senior high EMR students in Oregon schools. Both types of coefficients for the nine subtests range from the low .60s to the low .80s with median coefficients in the middle .70s. For the total battery score, a composite of the nine subscale scores, reliabilities are in the low to middle .90s. Only the reliabilities of the total battery score are high enough for use with individuals; the subtest reliabilities, however, are adequate for research and group program planning.

The test manual reports two validity studies (one predictive and one concurrent). The predictive validity study involved obtaining rehabilitation counselor ratings of community integration, economic self-sufficiency, communication, family living, and personal habits for 105 students who had been tested with an experimental version of the SPIB one year earlier. Correlations between the ratings and the SPIB scores, which represent predictive validity coefficients, ranged from .13 to .35. The canonical correlation between the set of counselor ratings and the set of test scores was .58.

The concurrent validity study involved correlating three SPIB subtests, Banking, Purchasing, and Job Search Skills, with behavior performance tests administered to students from 36 classrooms in seven states. The three SPIB subtests correlated in the middle to upper .70s with the behavior performance tests.

Additional validity studies, particularly studies of the validity of the test in its recommended usage—assessing student instructional needs and evaluating instructional outcomes, are necessary before users can have confidence in making decisions based on SPIB-R scores.

USABILITY

The SPIB-R manual suggests the test is particularly useful to special education teachers attempting to develop and evaluate curricula for their classes. To this end the authors recommend teachers use the Program-Related Assessment (PRA) model. The PRA model consists of four stages: 1. Assessing student needs, 2. Program planning, 3. Program implementation and monitoring, and 4. Program evaluation. The use of the SPIB-R and *Skills for Independent Living* materials (Halpern & Irwin, 1982) to accomplish the aims of the PRA model are summarized in the test manual. This test would also be useful in planning job training and evaluating the outcomes of the training for groups of students.

SPECIAL CONCERNS

Compared to other tests of this general type, the SPIB-R is technically among the best (for an objective review see Halpern, Lehmann, Irwin, and Heiry, 1982). However, because the authors did not report new reliability, validity, and normative data upon revision, Meyers' (1978, 1982) comments regarding the original SPIB are still relevant. Meyers (1982, p. 175) stated that although the test "has sufficient total battery reliability for use in selection and placement of individuals, . . . some of the scale scores have insufficient reliability for individual use." Meyers noted that scale scores, nonetheless, have adequate reliability "for group use in evaluation of programs, description of a dependent population, accountability reporting, and the like (1982, p. 175)." Additionally, Meyers (1978) suggested further validity study and regretted the restriction of the construction and normative samples to Oregon and Caucasion groups. In short, the SPIB-R needs further reliability, validity, and normative work for one to have confidence in using it to assess individual needs. As it now stands, the SPIB-R appears adequate for use with groups in curriculum development and evaluation.

REFERENCES

Halpern, A., & Irwin, L. (1986). *Examiner's manual: Social and Prevocational Information Battery—Revised*. Monterey, CA: CTB/McGraw-Hill.

Halpern, A., Leymann, J., Irwin, L., & Heiry, T. (1982). *Contemporary assessment for functionally mentally retarded adolescents and adults*. Austin, TX: PRO-ED.

Irwin, L., Halpern, A., & Becklund, J. (1981). *Skills for independent living: Teacher's manual*. Monterey, CA: CTB/McGraw-Hill.

Meyers, C. E. (1978). Review of the Social and Prevocational Information Battery. In O. K. Buros (Ed.)., *The Eighth Mental Measurements Yearbook* (pp. 1526-1527). Highland Park, NJ: The Gryphon Press.

Meyers, C. E. (1982). Social and Prevocational Information Battery. In J. T. Kapes & M. M. Mastie (Eds.), *A counselor's guide to vocational guidance instruments* Falls Church, VA: National Vocational Guidance Association.

Valpar-17—Pre-Vocational Readiness Battery (PVRB)

Valpar International Corporation

VALPAR International Corporation
P.O. Box 5767, Tucson, AZ 85703-5767

Target Population: Special Needs populations, including Learning Disabled and Trainable Mentally Retarded, ranging from junior high school students to adult populations.

Statement of the Purpose of the Instrument: PVRB is designed both as an assessment and training tool related to the functional skills and abilities of individuals in educational and vocational settings. The instrument is designed to assist users in the development of Individual Educational/Vocational Plans.

Titles of Subtests, Scales, Scores Provided: PVRB has four subtests: 1) Developmental Assesssment, 2) Workshop Evaluation, 3) Interpersonal/Social Skills, 4) Money-Handling Skills. Subtests provide time scores, error scores, time/error scores, point scores.

Forms and Levels Available, with Dates of Publication/Revision of Each: Revised form, October 1986.

Date of Most Recent Edition of Test Manual, User's Guide, Etc.: October 1986.

Languages in Which Available: English and Spanish.

Time: Actual Test Time—Power Test/No time limits.
Total Administration Time—Approx. 3 hours.

Norm Group(s) on Which Scores Are Based: 1) MTM Standards, 2) Research Norms (Sheltered-Independent Living Groups), 3) School for Exceptional Children.

Manner in Which Results Are Reported for Individuals
  Types of Scores: Percentile ranks, MTM standards, DOT Worker Qualifications Profile Factor Scores.
  Report Format/Content
    Basic Service: Individual Exit Profile Form on which are recorded the percentiles and/or MTM standards for each subtest.
    Options: Narrative report based on Individual Exit Profile results and information presented in the Report Writing section in Manual.

Report Format/Content For Group Summaries: Not available.

Scoring
  Machine Scoring Service: Not Available.
  Hand Scoring
    Scored by: Clerk; counselor.
    Time required for scoring: Approximately 30 minutes.

Local Machine Scoring: Not available.

Computer Software Options Available: Not available.

Cost of Materials
Counselee Materials: Materials for all subtests are reusable. Score sheets and Individual Exit Profile Forms are purchased in pads of 100 @ $13.75 each.

Published Reviews
Botterbusch, K. F. (1980). *A Comparison of Commercial Vocational Evaluation Systems*, Menomonie, WI: University of Wisconsin—Stout, Materials Development Center.

Reviewed By

John R. Nicholson
Program Developer
The Helping Hand of Goodwill Industries
Prairie Village, KS

The Pre-Vocational Readiness Battery (Valpar 17), developed and marketed by the Valpar Corporation, has been available since 1978. It has been used extensively in a wide range of vocational evaluation settings to assess clients' strengths and weaknesses relevant to vocational placement.

The Valpar 17 can be best viewed as a series of screening tests. Unlike diagnostic instruments, which are generally more accurate in assessing the nature and extent of a problem, the main function of a screening test is to easily and quickly separate individuals who may have a problem or deficit from those who probably do not. A screening test shows the evaluator areas of possible weaknesses that can be more fully assessed by diagnostic instruments. During 1986 extensive modifications were made to the Valpar 17 that resulted in the removal of several subtests and the lowering of its price.

DESCRIPTION

The Valpar 17 consists of four distinct subtests: Developmental Assessment, Workshop Evaluation, Interpersonal and Social Skills, and Independent Living Skills. All of these subtests may be administered to a client, or any combination of subtests may be given. Throughout the evaluation, the evaluator is encouraged to give instructions at three levels of difficulty: verbal only; verbal plus a demonstration of the task; and verbal, demonstration of the task, and a sample to duplicate.

Developmental Assessment: This subtest consists of four parts: Patterning/ Color Discrimination/Manipulation; Manual Coordination, Work Range/Dynamic Strength/Walking; and Matching/Vocational Knowledge/Measurement.

Several simple, functional, non-medical measures of physical and mental abilities are accomplished. These segments begin at a very simple level and progress to more complicated tasks. An excellent test of fine motor skills is included using a copper maze with a ¼″ plastic path. A counter keeps track of the number of times the client touches the copper during the test. The client is evaluated by the time taken to complete the maze, and the number of errors made while tracing the path. This subtest, depending on the functional level of the client, will take from 10–45 minutes to complete.

Workshop Evaluation: Three or four clients can be evaluated at one time with this segment. The object is to complete as many assemblies as possible during a twelve minute period. By using parts for assembly that have different textures, a unit has been designed to enable visually impaired clients to complete the assemblies in three of the four positions. Including setup, practice, testing, and clean-up, this segment takes about 30 minutes to complete.

Interpersonal/Social Skills: This test is also referred to as the Critical Barriers Inventory (CBI). It is a questionnaire that must be filled out by the supervisor of the client. It takes about 10 minutes to complete, once the supervisor becomes familiar with the form. Sixteen questions are asked about Practical Skills, 13 concerning Socialization Skills, 15 about Aggravating Behaviors, and 16 on Work Related Skills. Each question is scored as 0, 2, or 4 with the higher score indicating a greater degree of client problems.

Independent Living Skills: Because a majority of this section has been eliminated as part of recent modifications, it might more appropriately be named Money Handling Skills. The client is assessed on abilities to count money, make change, and solve simple word problems. Depending on the functional level of the client, this subtest could take five to 20 minutes to administer.

ADMINISTRATION AND USE

The Valpar 17 can be administered by anyone with a testing background, and requires only a few hours of preparation to administer. However, the scores on this test are not nearly as important as interpreting behaviors observed during the evaluation. It may take 50 or more administrations before the evaluator becomes accomplished enough to differentiate "normal" responses to questions from "abnormal" responses. For this reason, beginning evaluators should work under the supervision of an experienced administrator of the Valpar 17.

The Valpar manual states that the Valpar 17 "is specifically designed as an evaluation battery and doubles as a training program for mentally retarded persons." (Valpar, 1980). Most evaluators find that the work sample is best used on clients who are in work activity centers or sheltered workshops.

TECHNICAL QUALITIES

The original, and apparently only, norming study for the Valpar 17 was completed at the Madonna School for Exceptional Children in Omaha, Nebraska. The subjects were 20 clients at the school, ages 11 to 20 years. All of the subjects lived at home with either parents or guardians and had I.Q. scores ranging from a low of 40 (Stanford-Binet) to a high of 68 (WISC-R). No other demographic information is presented in the study (Table, undated).

In preparing the norm summary, Valpar presents a table for each part of the test. Ranges of scores are not included. It must be assumed that all 20 subjects were able to complete all parts of the test, since sample size is not reported. Also, scores are not presented for standing work range or walking (Nicholson, Nailen, and Tobaben-Wyssnan, 1984). The norm book that accompanies the Valpar 17 indicates norms for 10 groups which range from institutionalized, non-working to competitively employed (Valpar, 1978). These norms have been extrapolated from the scores of the Madonna population, and, based on the scores of over 200 work activity and sheltered clients, are *very inaccurate* (Nicholson, et al. 1984).

Studies have not been undertaken to determine content, concurrent, predictive, or construct validity. Test-retest or other types of reliability estimates are unavailable. This lack of information is a major deficit of the Valpar 17.

SPECIAL CONCERNS

As with all Valpar work samples, the equipment is interesting to view, and motivates most clients to become involved in the assessment. Face validity is high, and an experienced evaluator can obtain a general idea of the functional level of the client. Since this is a screening test, scores should not be used to determine eligibility for services, but instead should guide the evaluator toward areas of appropriate diagnostic testing.

This assessment works especially well in settings where an evaluator wants to obtain an overview of the client's functional level (e.g. prior to task assignment in a work activity center). The Valpar manual states that the work sample can also be used as a training program for the mentally retarded. If the evaluator is planning to utilize scores on the test to measure advancement, training must not be done on any of the test items. This would be similar to teaching the answers to an intelligence test in order to increase the client's IQ.

The major weaknesses of the Valpar 17 are its poor norms, and its total lack of reliability and validity data. Given the instrument's cost and the recent effort to make revisions, it would be reasonable to expect the developers to undertake more intensive studies of its technical qualities. Since technical information is unavailable, users should undertake technical studies with their own clients.

Despite its limitations, the Valpar 17 yields substantial information relevant to vocational evaluation and planning. In addition to indicating the weaknesses of the individuals being tested, the test also indicates areas of strength that may not have been previously identified.

Given the price of almost $3,000, it would be difficult for other than very large workshops to purchase a Valpar 17. Although it is expensive, this work sample is recommended for evaluation centers that deal with mentally retarded clients on a regular basis. To alleviate part of the cost, perhaps several workshops can arrange to share a unit.

REFERENCES

Nicholson, J. R., Nailen, P. M., & Tobaben-Wyssmann, S. (1984). Valpar 17 prevocational readiness battery: A question of norms. *Vocational Evaluation and Work Adjustment Bulletin, 17*(3), 83–84.

Table of Statistical Data for VCWS 17 (undated). Tucson: Valpar Corporation. Unpublished manuscript.

Valpar (1980). *Pre-vocational readiness battery: Developmental assessment.* Tucson: Valpar Corporation.

Valpar (1978). *Pre-vocational readiness battery: Norm manual.* Tucson: Valpar Corporation.

NOTE: Significant portions of this review were abridged from the author's original review in *Vocational Evaluation and Work Adjustment Bulletin, 17* (3), 83–84, 1984, with permission.

CHAPTER VII

Additional Career Assessment Instruments

Additional Career Assessment Instruments

Nanciann Frazier
Certified Psychological Associate
Longview Counseling Services
Longview, Texas

In addition to the 43 widely-used instruments described and reviewed earlier in this book, there is a multitude of instruments designed for use in career guidance and counseling available on the market today. Sifting through the various publishers' catalogues to obtain the information necessary to choose an appropriate instrument is a burdensome task. Hence this chapter provides a brief description of 126 career guidance instruments presently available. Although every effort was made to be comprehensive, instruments may have been inadvertently excluded.

To facilitate the use of the information in this chapter, it is provided under the following headings:

- *Type of Instrument*. Each instrument has been placed in the most appropriate category. However, counselors may find that some tests have several uses. For example, some interest inventories may also be appropriate for some special populations even though they were not categorized as a special populations' instrument.

- *Name*. The name of the instrument is contained in boldface print. Common acronyms, when available, are provided in parentheses immediately following the name.

- *Publisher*. Only the name of the publisher is provided. The addresses of the publishers are listed in Appendix B. Additional information about the instruments can be obtained by writing to the publishers.

- *Date*. The date given refers to either the initial date the instrument was developed and/or a recent revision. A range of dates (e.g. 1951-1984) signifies ongoing development and revision of the instrument during that time span. "No Date" indicates that the publishing date was unavailable.

- *Population*. The population refers to the group of individuals for whom the publisher indicates the test is appropriate.

- *Reference*. Several of the major sources for test reviews are cited here in an abbreviated form. An annotated bibliography of each source is presented in Appendix A. The significance of the abbreviations is as follows.

  — MMY refers to the *Mental Measurements Yearbook*. The number immediately following denotes the volume number (Volume 6, 7, 8, or 9). The numbers following the colon refers to the test number.
  —TC is the abbreviation for *Test Critiques*. The number which follows the dash indicates the volume number (Volume 1, 2, 3, or 4).
  —CG refers to *A Counselor's Guide to Vocational Guidance Instruments* (First Edition). The number following the dash refers to the page number on which the review is found.
  —MEG and MECD refer to *Measurement and Evaluation in Guidance* and *Measurement and Evaluation in Counseling and Development* respectively. The numbers following the dash refer to the month and year of the issue in which the review is found (e.g. 10/85 denotes October, 1985).
  — Bott., 1980, 1985 and 1987 refer to three publications, authored by Karl Botterbusch and published by the Materials Development Center at the University of Wisconsin-Stout. The 1980 reference is for *A Comparison of Commercial Vocational Evaluation Systems*, the 1985 reference is for *Testing and Test Modification in Vocational Evaluation*, and the 1987 reference is for the most recent revision of the 1980 reference under a new title *Vocational Assessment and Evaluation Systems: A Comparison*.

- *Brief Description*. This section provides an overview of what is measured and includes the titles of some of the scales associated with each instrument. Additional comments are included for some instrument (e.g. to indicate a major use, special reports or profiles, and the need for special training in administration).

A. MULTIPLE APTITUDE AND OCCUPATIONAL ACHIEVEMENT BATTERIES

Name of Test/Publisher/Date/Population	Reference(s)	Brief Description
Adult Basic Learning Exam (ABLE) The Psychological Corporation 1967–86 Adults	MMY8:2 MMY7:3	Measures the achievement in basic learning of adults who have/have not completed high school. Three levels yield grade scores 1 to 12 for vocabulary, reading, spelling, and arithmetic (computation, problem solving, total). Often used in evaluating job applicants.
Aptitude Based Career Decision Test (ABCD) Prep 1986 Adults		Provides a measure of the following 7 aptitudes: numerical reasoning, analytical reasoning, inductive reasoning, numerical computation, spatial visualization, vocabulary, and clerical perception. Identifies potential for success in 66 occupational families.
Aptitude Tests for Occupations PRO-ED No Date Grades 10–Adult		Designed to measure aptitudes and potential; related to occupations and careers. Consists of the following 6 tests: Personal/Social, Mechanical, General Sales, Clerical Routine, Computation and Scientific. Tests may be administered independently.
Aptitudes Bennett & McKnight 1986 High School Students		This self-report measure allows students to estimate their aptitudes as outlined in the GATB. First, students view a filmstrip on aptitudes, and then they complete a 10-item checklist. Includes directions for correlating scores with the 66 Worker Trait Groups.
Ball Aptitude Battery Ball Foundation 1986 High School Seniors		Designed to measure the following aptitudes on paper and pencil or on computer: clerical, vocabulary, numerical computation, numerical reasoning, inductive reasoning, paper folding, and analytical reasoning. Additional subtests are available in paper and pencil or in apparatus form only.
Career Ability Placement Survey (CAPS) Educational and Industrial Testing Service (Ed ITS) 1976 Grade 7–College		Designed to measure the following occupational abilities keyed to entry requirements for most jobs in the 14 COPSystem Career Clusters: mechanical reasoning, spatial relations, verbal reasoning, numerical ability, language usage, word knowledge, perceptual speed and accuracy, and mechanical speed and dexterity.

Name of Test/Publisher/Date/Population	Reference(s)	Brief Description
Comprehensive Ability Battery (CAB) Institute for Personality and Ability Testing 1975–77 Grade 10–Adult	MMY8:484	Consists of four test booklets containing 20 subtests, each designed to measure a primary ability factor related to performance in industrial settings. Examples of scores reported are: verbal and numerical ability, clerical speed and accuracy, memory span, and organization and production of ideas.
Tests of Adult Basic Education (TABE) CTB/McGraw Hill 1976–87 Adults	MMY8:33	Provides information on an adult's proficiency in the basic skills of reading, mathematics, and language. Identifies weaknesses and establishes level of instruction for adults seeking vocational-technical training or general literacy and self-improvement study.
Word and Number Assessment Inventory (WNAI) NCS Interpretive Scoring Systems 1976–77 Grade 9–Adult		Yields three scores, verbal, mathematical, and total, and compares these scores with those of individuals at various educational levels and in a number of occupations. Provides career information relevant to the scores and offers suggestions for improving word and number skills.

B. INTEREST INVENTORIES

Name of Test/Publisher/Date/Population	Reference(s)	Brief Description
Applied Biological and Agribusiness Interest Inventory The Interstate Printers and Publishers 1965–71 Grade 8	MMY8:990	This inventory is designed to measure a student's interests in biological and agribusiness occupations. Contains 100 items that assess specific interests, such as: animals, plants, mechanics, and business.
Canadian Occupational Interest Inventory Nelson Canada Limited 1981–82 Adult	MMY9:188	Measures adults' attitudes toward occupationally related activities. The following dichotomous factors are included: things vs. people, business contact vs. scientific, routine vs. creative, social vs. solitary, and prestige vs. production.
Career Area Interest Checklist Bennett & McKnight 1986 High School Students		This abbreviated version of the Career Interest Survey determines students' preferences for 12 career area interests, such as: artistic, plant and animals, mechanical, industrial, selling, humanitarian, leading/influencing. Students respond to 144 work activities.
Career Directions Inventory (CDI) Research Psychologists Press, Inc. No Date High School to Adult		Designed to assist high school and college students and adults in educational and career planning. Consists of 100 triads of job-related activities, and is scored for 15 basic interest scales. Individual's pattern of interests is compared to patterns of individuals in a wide variety of occupations.
Career Exploration Series CFKR Career Materials, Inc. 1979–81 Grades 9–College, & Adults	MMY9:196	Designed to help students identify specific jobs that match their educational goals and interest areas. Focuses on 6 occupational areas, such as: agriculture-conservation-forestry, business-sales-management-clerical, consumer/home economics-related fields, and design-performing arts-communication.
Career Guidance Inventory Educational Guidance, Inc. 1972–79 Grades 7–13	MMY9:197 MMY8:996	Measures comparative strength of students' interests in trades, services, and technologies. Scores are reported for 14 engineering-related trades (e.g. carpentry, masonry, mechanical engineering technology), and 11 non-engineering-related trades (e.g. business management, communications, medical technology).

Name of Test/Publisher/Date/Population	Reference(s)	Brief Description
Career Guidance Inventory for Trades, Services, and Technologies (CGI) CTB/McGraw Hill 1972 Grade 9 and Above		This interest inventory is designed for students who are not college-bound. Responses to 250 forced-choice items provide scores for 25 occupational scales such as: masonry, sheet metal and welding, chemical and laboratory technology, sales, food service, transportation service, business management.
Career Interests Strategic Career Services No Date Adults		This questionnaire identifies on individual's interests and compares them to over 1,500 traditional and non-traditional, existing and emerging occupational fields. Also useful in exploring the possibilities of home-based businesses, independent consulting services, franchises.
Career Interest Survey Bennett & McKnight 1986 High School Students		Designed to measure students' likes and dislikes for 180 common work activities. Provides scores for 12 interest areas such as: scientific, protective, industrial, selling, accommodating, physical performing, etc. Accompanied by Career Goal Worksheet to stimulate further career exploration.
Career Interest Test (CIT) Educational and Industrial Test Services Ltd. 1971–83 Adolescent–Adult	MMY9:198	Measures vocational interests in the following 6 areas: outdoor-physical, scientific-theoretical, social service, aesthetic-literary, commercial-clerical, and practical-technical.
Computerized Career Assessment and Planning Program (CCAPP) Cambridge Career Products No Date High School Students		Provides students with career knowledge and teaches them decision-making skills via 4 modules: career assessment, selecting alternatives, career planning, and career exploration. Printouts contain information such as: interest and skill summary, list of occupational clusters, and job hunting plan.
Gordon Occupational Checklist II The Psychological Corporation 1961–81 Grades 8–12, & Adult	MMY9:443 MMY7:1019	Designed to measure areas of job interests for individuals seeking education and job training below the college level. Includes 6 broad vocational interest categories: business, arts, outdoors, technical-mechanical, technical-industrial and service.

Test	Reference	Description
Hackman-Gaither Interest Inventory Psychological Service Center of Philadelphia 1968 Grades 7 to Adult		Assesses an individual's vocational interests and preferences in the following areas: business, sales, scientific and technical artistic, health and welfare, business clerical, mechanical, service, and outdoor activities.
How Well Do You Know Your Interests? Psychologists and Educators Inc. 1974 Grade 10–Adult		Designed to measure attitudes towards jobs, activities, things, and people in 10 vocational areas: business, mechanical, outdoor, service, research, visual art, amusement, literacy, music, and general work attitudes.
Inventory of Interests Guidance Testing Associates 1971 Adolescent–Adult	MMY9:525	Provides ratings for 136 occupations in 14 areas that parallel the 1965 edition of the Dictionary of Occupational Titles. Also contains information on 56 majors commonly found in college guides. Designed primarily for use as a counseling aid.
Judgement of Occupational Behavior—Orientation (JOB-O) CFKR Career Materials, Inc. 1981 Grade 6–Adult	MMY9:560 CG-69	This 9-item questionnaire contains 9 scales: education, interest, inclusion, control, affection, physical activity, hands/tool machinery, problem solving, and creating ideas. Scores are compared to 120 job titles. Designed to emphasize job awareness and promote job exploration.
Milwaukee Academic Interest Inventory Western Psychological Services No Date Grades 12–14		Designed to aid college-bound seniors and college freshmen and sophmores in selecting a major. Assesses academic study interests in 6 major areas: physical science, healing occupations, behavioral science, economics, humanities-social studies, and elementary education.
UNIACT IV American College Testing Program 1973–84 High-School–Young Adulthood	MMY9:43 TC-1	This unisex interest inventory is designed to eliminate sex-role stereotyping, and is a component of the ACT Career Planning Program. Students respond to 90 activities grouped into 6 areas: science, creative arts, social service, business contact, business detail, and technical.
USES Interest Checklist U.S. Department of Labor 1979 Adults	Bott., 1985	Contains 210 work activity statements for which client checks "like," "dislike," or "uncertain." Designed for individuals with no stated work interests or who are unaware of the variety of available jobs/occupational fields. ICL is a counseling tool, and is not scored.

293

Name of Test/Publisher/Date/Population	Reference(s)	Brief Description
Vocational Interest Profile Report Cambridge Career Products No Date High School Students		This micro-computer program analyzes students' choices of preferred work activities and ranks them according to 12 broad work categories. Provides a detailed report of 12 occupational categories and their descriptions, examples of jobs within each category, and references to G.O.E. and D.O.T. Available for Apple and IBM.
Vocational Preference Inventory, 1985 Revision Psycological Assessment Resources 1953–78, 1985 High School–Adult	MMY9:1342 MMY8:1028	This interest and personality inventory consists of 160 occupational titles used to assess vocational and occupational interests. Scores are provided for 11 dimensions related to interpersonal relationships, interests, and values, such as: realistic, enterprising, self control, and acquiescence.
Vocational Research Interest Inventory (VRII) Vocational Research Institute No Date High School–Adult		This interest inventory is available in two versions: paper and pencil form and software compatible with Apple/IBM personal computers. Measures 12 interest areas tied to DOT, and provides individuals with a profile analysis. Contains separate pre-vocational and vocational norms.
What I Like To Do Science Research Associates 1954–75 Grades 4–7	MMY8:709	This inventory is designed to identify the interests, and curricular and career preferences of children in the intermediate grades. Scores are provided for the following 4 broad areas: play, academic, arts, and occupations.
Work Activities Checklist Bennett & McKnight 1986 High School Students		First, students view the "Work Activities" filmstrip, which describes 10 basic types of work activities. Then, they complete a 10-item checklist to identify their preferences for work activities. Provides correlations between activities and Worker Trait Groups.
Work Activities Inventory Cambridge Career Products No Date High School Students		This micro-computer program is designed to aid students in their selection of an area of study related to their interests and goals. Contains a total of 30 areas from 6 work activity categories: doers, investigators, creators, organizers, influencers, and helpers.

C. MEASURES OF WORK VALUES AND JOB SATISFACTION

Name of Test/Publisher/Date/Population	*Reference(s)*	*Brief Description*
Career Orientation Placement and Evaluation Survey (COPES) Educational and Industrial Testing Service (EdITS) 1978 Grade 8–Adult	MECD 10/85	Measures the following 8 dimensions of personal values related to career evaluation and selection: investigative, practical, independent, leadership, orderliness, recognition, aesthetic, and social. Designed to increase self-awareness. Component of the COPSystem.
Employment Readiness Scale Anthony M. Alfano 1973 High School & Adults		Measures work values to determine an individual's readiness for employment. Especially applicable for high school students planning to work in an unskilled, semi-skilled employment setting upon graduation.
Hall Occupational Orientation Inventory (HALL) Scholastic Testing Service, Inc. 1968–76 Grades 3–Adult, & Literate Adults	MMY8:1003 TC-1 CG-102 MEG-1/79	Measures psychological needs that are correlated to personality traits and job characteristics identified by the U.S. Dpt. of Labor. Provides 22 scores such as: self-actualization, creativity and location concern. Useful in broadening the individual's perceptions of potential and priorities.
Job Descriptive Index (JDI) Bowling Green State University 1975 Employees	MMY9:550	Provides an assessment of job satisfaction in any occupational field. Measures the following 5 components of satisfaction: work on present job, present pay, opportunities for promotion, supervision on present job, and people on present job.
Minnesota Satisfaction Questionnaire (MSQ) Vocational Psychology Research, University of Minnesota 1963–67 Adults in business and industry	MMY8:1052	Assesses an employee's job satisfaction in 20 areas, such as: ability utilization, company policies and practices, independence, moral values, responsibility, supervision-human relations, variety, and working conditions. Designed for use in occupational and social research.
Ohio Work Values Inventory Bradford J. Fenner 1971–74 Grace 3–Adult	MMY8:1017 MECD-10/85	This inventory is designed to measure work values in the following 11 areas: altruism, object orientation, security, control, self-realization, independence, money, task satisfaction, solitude, ideas or data orientation, and prestige.

Name of Test/Publisher/Date/Population	Reference(s)	Brief Description
Study of Values Riverside Publishing Company 1931–70 Grade 10–Adult	MMY8:686 TC-1	Measures the relative prominence of 6 basic interests or personality motives: theoretical, economic, aesthetic, social, political, and religiuos. Useful for student educational and vocational planning, guidance, personnel selection and research.
Work Values Inventory (WVI) Houghton Mifflin Co. 1968–70 Grade 7–Adult	MMY8:1030 TC-2 CG-170	Assesses 15 values related to an individual's vocational satisfaction and success, such as: altruism, esthetics, intellectual stimulation, economic returns, security, supervisory relations, variety, and a way of life. Designed for use in academic and vocational counseling.

D. CAREER DEVELOPMENT/MATURITY INSTRUMENTS

Name of Test/Publisher/Date/Population	Reference(s)	Brief Description
Career Awareness Inventory Scholastic Testing Service, Inc. 1974–80 Grades 3–12	MMY8:994 CG-115 MEG-7/80	Assesses students' occupational awareness in 7 areas: related occupations, contact with occupations, job characteristics, functions of occupations, grouping of occupations, work locations of occupations, and self-assessment of career awareness. Can be used to evaluate the effectiveness of career education programs.
Career Education Readiness Test Career Education Readiness Measurement and Research 1975 Grades K–3, 4–6		Measures students' attitudes and knowledge in the following 6 areas: sex role stereotyping, intrinsic and extrinsic reasons for working, occupational esteem, awareness of vocational concepts, occupational responsibilities, and world of work vocabulary.
Career Path Strategy Wilmington Press No Date Age 16 to Adult		Evaluates an individual's career potential by measuring the following factors: mental ability, vocational interest, personality, ideal career and lifestyle, personal background data, cultural geographic and economic opportunities and limitations, preliminary career decision and strategy for achieving goals.
Career Skills Assessment Program The College Board 1978 Grades 9–14 and Adult	CG-126 MEG-10/80	Designed to measure the progress of groups or individuals in reaching career development goals, developing specific skills, and evaluating a career education program. Contains 6 subtests such as: self-evaluation, and development skills, career awareness and employment seeking skills.
Comprehensive Career Assessment Scale Learning Concepts 1974 Grades 3–7, 8–12, and Teachers	MMY8:999	Provides familiarity and interest scores for 15 areas, such as: business and office, construction, manufacturing, public service, etc. Helpful in assessing needs, planning curriculum for and/or evaluating career education programs.
Knowledge of Occupations Test Edupac, Inc. 1974 High School	MMY8:1008	Assesses student's career knowledge in terms of earnings, licensing and certification, job description, employment trends, training, terminology, graphs and tools. Designed for use in individual counseling and in planning group career education programs.

Name of Test/Publisher/Date/Population	Reference(s)	Brief Description
New Mexico Career Education Test Series Monitor 1973 Grades 9–12	MMY8:1013	Designed to assess specific learner objectives in career education. Contains the following components: Attitude Toward Work, Career Planning Test, Career Oriented Activities Checklist, Knowledge of Occupations, Job Application Procedures, and Career Development Test.
Occupations and Career Information BOXSCORE Chronicle Guidance Publications, Inc. 1973 Grades 7–12	MMY8:1015	Designed to measure basic knowledge of occupational information. Test questions deal with the following type of information: work performed, entry requirements (e.g., schooling), licensing requirements, rewards (earnings), occupational outlook, and general information on the world of work.

E. COMBINED ASSESSMENT PROGRAMS

Name of Test/Publisher/Date/Population	Reference(s)	Brief Description
Experience Exploration Chronicle Guidance Publications, Inc. 1981 Grades 8–Adult		Identifies potential occupations by assessing a persons's work experiences and interests in 10 occupational areas: outdoor, mechanical, computation, scientific, persuasive, artistic, literary, musical social service, and clerical.
Individual Career Exploration (ICE) Scholastic Testing Service 1976 Grades 3–7, 8–12	MMY8:1581	Measure interests, experiences, abilities, and ambitions of students and relates to them to future occupations in 8 areas: service, business contact, organization, technology, outdoor, general science, culture, and arts and entertainment. Picture and verbal forms.
JOBTAP II Educational Testing Service (ETS) 1985 High School–Adult		This microcomputer-based job training assessment program measures a wide range of basic work skills. A profile of these skills is combined with background information, work experience, and interest to form a career development plan identifying job training programs which suit the individual's needs.
Kuder Career Development Inventory Science Research Associates, Inc. 1975–77 Grades 9 & 10, Adult & Out of School Youth	MMY9:995 CG-136	Consists of Personal Data Form and Kuder Career Interest Survey. Provides scores for 6 broad interest areas (e.g., technical/mechanical/skilled) at 3 early levels (early, delayed, and late). Also reports an Academic Level of Interest score.
Major-Minor-Finder (M-M-F) CFKR Career Materials, Inc. 1978–83 Grades 11–12, College Bound Students	MMY9:643	Designed to aid college-bound students in choosing a major. Matches students' aptitudes and interests with job outlook predictions and numbers of colleges offering various majors. Covers 9 broad interest areas and contains information for 99 majors.

F. CARD SORTS

Name of Test/Publisher/Date/Population	Reference(s)	Brief Description
Career Values Card Sort Kit Career Research and Testing No Date Adults		Contains 41 cards which describe the variables of work satisfaction, such as: time freedom, precision work, power, technical competence and public contact. Useful with job seekers, career changers, and those wishing to improve their present jobs. Includes guidelines for counselors and group facilitators.
College Major Card Sort College Major Card Sort 1980 Junior High–College Students		Provides students with an overall picture of common college majors, including information on background skilled courses required in college and several occupational outlets for each major. Helpful in establishing a starting place for career exploration.
Missouri Occupational Card Sort (MOCS) Career Planning and Placement Service 1980 College–Adults, College-bound 11th and 12th Graders	CG-148 MEG-10/81	Designed to broaden knowledge of self and of specific occupations. Encourages further self and career exploration by increasing the number of occupations under consideration. Contains 90 occupations divided into Holland's code: realistic, investigative, artistic, social, enterprising, and conventional.
Missouri Occupational Preference Inventory (MOPI) Human Systems Consultants, Inc. 1980 High School & College Students, Employment Training Clients	CG-149	Designed to assist individuals in exploring potential careers, understand reasons for occupation choices, and in planning further exploration. Consists of 180 occupations subdivided by educational requirements: high school, beyond high school, and college.
Motivated Skills Card Sort (MSCS) Career Research and Testing 1981 Any Individual Seeking Career Guidance Assistance		Provides assessment of proficiency in, and motivation to use 48 skills. Primarily used to identify skills important to individual's career satisfaction and success. Contains 48 skill cards and 8 category cards.

Name of Test/Publisher/Date/Population	Reference(s)	Brief Description
Non-Sexist Vocational Card Sort NSVCS 1974 High School–Adult	CG-150 MEG-10/81	Examines the following areas that can limit perceived vocational options: feelings, values, needs, interests, fears, fantasies, life style preferences and the internalized sex, race, and class stereotypes. Contains 76 occupations.
Occupational Interest Card Sort (OICS) Career Research and Testing 1981 Anyone Seeking Career Guidance Assistance		Designed to assist individuals in identifying and clarifying preferred occupations. Contains 113 occupation cards, 5 category cards, and 9 supplementary activities designed to stimulate career exploration.
Occ-U-Sort CTB/McGraw Hill 1981 Grades 11–12, College & Adults	MMY9:853 CG-151 MECD-10/82 MEG-10/81	Contains 180 occupations based on Holland's RIASEC typology. Designed to: stimulate career exploration, aid in the career decision making process, stimulate individual thinking about motives for occupational choice, increase self-awareness, broaden options, and increase awareness of the world of work.
Vocational Insight and Exploration Kit (VIEK) Consulting Psychologists Press, Inc. 1970–80 High School & College Students & Adults	MMY9:1337 MEG-10/81	Focuses on eliminating career indecision by broadening self awareness and self exploration, increasing the range of vocational options, and clarifying pros and cons of vocational alternatives.
Vo-Tech Major Card Sort College Major Card Sort 1982 Junior High–College Students		Provides students with an overview of common vo-tech majors, including information on the background courses and skills required of them, training opportunities, and occupational outlets for their chosen majors. Helpful in establishing a starting point for career exploration.

Name of Test/Publisher/Date/Population	Reference(s)	Brief Description
Birkman Method—Needs at a Glance Birkman and Associates 1951–1984 Personnel in Business/Industrial Settings		Consists of a computer-scored questionnaire that measures self and social perception and occupational interests. Scores are combined to identify the following: attitudes, value systems, motivational characteristics, etc. Individual scores are compared to an expansive data base, and a printout is provided.
Exploring Career Options (ECO) NCS Professional Assessment Services 1987 Adults Considering Career Change or Re-Entering the Job Market		Measures work related personality characteristics, verbal and numerical abilities, personal style, and temperament and values that affect career interests and satisfaction. Recommends 10 to 15 career paths from a pool of 1,000 potential occupations.
Forer Vocational Survey: Men–Women Western Psychological Services No Date Adolescent–Adult		Designed to evaluate interpersonal behavior, attitudes towards people, work, and supervision and work dynamics. Subject completes sentence stems that measure reactions to specified situations, causes of feelings and actions, and vocational goals.
Measures of Occupational Stress, Strain, and Coping Marathon Consulting and Press 1983 Adults		Consists of: Occupational Environmental Scales, which measure 6 potentially stressful aspects of work environment; Personal Strain Questionnaire, which measures 4 dimensions of occupational stress; and Personal Resources Questionnaire, which measures potential for dealing effectively with stress.
Orientation Inventory Consulting Psychologists Press, Inc. No Date Grades 10–Adult		Assesses three types of orientation toward satisfaction and rewards: self-orientation, interaction orientation, and task orientation. Designed to predict success and performance in various types of work.
Self Description Inventory NCS Interpretive Scoring Systems 1975–77 Grades 9 & Up	MMY9:1096	Assesses normal personality functioning and vocationally-oriented dimensions of personality. Reports 22 scores: 11 personal description (e.g. caution-adventurous, impatient-patient,), 6 vocationally oriented scales (RIASEC), and 5 administrative indexes (e.g. response percentage).

Vocational Implications of Personality (VIP) Talent Assessment Inc. 1986 Jr. and Sr. High School & Adults	This computerized personality assessment gathers information on four factors, (self-awareness, centeredness, perceptions, and decision making) and then identifies individuals as having one of eight work styles such as: forecaster, enthusiast, organizer, precisionist, designer, caretaker, purist, etc.
Work Attitudes Questionnaire Marathon Consulting and Press No Date Adults	Designed to differentiate "workaholic" individuals from other committed workers. Consists of two scales. The first assesses the level of work commitment. The second assesses the psychological healthiness or unhealthiness of work attitudes.
Work Situations Bennett & McKnight 1985 High School Students	First, students view a filmstrip which describes the major work situations. Then, they complete a 10-item checklist to identify their temperments and adaptive skills. Also includes a listing of Worker Trait Groups by Work Situations, which promotes further career exploration.

H. INSTRUMENTS FOR SPECIAL POPULATIONS

Name of Test/Publisher/Date/Population	Reference(s)	Brief Description
Adaptability Test Science Research Associates, Inc. 1943, 1954, 1967 Applicants or Employees Limited in Adaptability	Bott., 1985	Contains 35 items including word definitions, analogies, arithmetic computation, and series designed to differentiate between those who would perform better in routine jobs and those who could be placed in jobs that demanded more learning ability.
Comprehensive Occupational Assessment and Training System (COATS) Prep, Inc. 1975–81 High School and Adults in Manpower and Training Programs	Bott., 1980	Designed for self-interpretation and provides activities to change behavior. Contains 4 components that can be used independently: job matching, employability attitudes, work samples (contains 26 work samples such as masonry, real estate, and nutrition), and living skills (literacy and knowledge).
Geist Picture Interest Inventory Western Psychological Services 1959–71 Grades 8–Adult, Non-readers or Limited Readers	MMY6:1054	Provides scores for 11 or 12 interest areas such as: persuasive, clerical mechanical, scientific, outdoor, computational, artistic, social service, etc. Also provides scores for 7 motivational areas such as: family, prestige, financial, and environmental. Contains male and female versions.
Hester Evaluation System (HESTER) Hester Evaluation Systems, Inc. 1973–81, 1986 Physically and Mentally Handicapped, High School–College	Bott. 1980	Combines performance and 9 paper/pencil tests to assess 19 ability factors. Hands-on tests measure such skills as finger dexterity, reaction time, arm-hand steadiness, etc. Paper/pencil tests measure abilities such as numerical and verbal reasoning, perceptual accuracy, sales and leadership ability, etc.
Jewish Employment Vocational Service Work Sample System (JEVS) Vocational Research Institute 1973 Un/Under Employed, Physically and Mentally handicapped, and High Functioning EMR	MMY8:982 CG-166 Bott., 1987	Consists of 28 work samples related to 10 Worker Trait Group Arrangements in the DOT (3rd ed.) and 12 Work Groups of three work areas in the DOT (4th ed.). Useful in evaluating disadvantaged youth and adults for vocational placement and training, and in rehabilitation and school settings. Requires training to administer.

Key Educational Vocational Assessment System (KEVAS) Key Education Inc. 1985 Handicapped and Non-Handicapped High School–Adult	Bott., 1985 Bott., 1987	Consists of 20 apparatus, achievement, interest and personality tests that must be administered by two trained examiners. Measures such variables as: hearing, visual and color acuity, auditory and visual reaction time, abstract reasoning ability, response to stress, vocational interest, etc.
Microcomputer Evaluation and Screening Assessment (MESA) Valpar International Corporation 1984 High School–Adult; Vocational Rehabilitation Applicants, Vocational Technology Students, Prisoners and Manpower Trainees	Bott., 1985 Bott., 1987	Consists of 9 work samples: Hardware screening, physical capacities and mobility evaluation, vocational interest and awareness screening, independent perceptual screening assessment, taking/persuasive screening, working conditions, specific vocational preparation and computer screening. Provides individual with Worker Trait Profile.
Microcomputer Evaluation of Career Areas (MECA) The Conover Company No Date Junior and Senior High School Students, Disadvantaged and Special Needs	Bott., 1985 Bott., 1987	Designed for vocational exploration via 15 work samples containing 3 tasks each, such as: automotive, building maintenance, cosmetology, graphic design, custodial housekeeping, electronics, small engines, food service, health care, business and office, manufacturing, distribution, and computers.
Micro-Tower Institute for Crippled and Disabled 1977 Special Needs Populations	Bott., 1987	Contains 13 work samples: electronic connector assembly, bottle capping and packing, lamp assembly, blue print reading, graphic illustration, filing, mail sorting, zip coding, recording, checking, making change, payroll computation, want ad comprehension, and message taking.
Personnel Tests for Industry—Oral Directions Test (PTI-ODT) The Psychological Corporation 1946, 1954, 1974 Bilingual Persons with English As a Second Language	Bott., 1985	This wide-range test of general mental abilities also assesses an individual's comprehension of oral directions. This instrument can be used as a screening device for vocational trainees and industrial personnel.

Name of Test/Publisher/Date/Population	Reference(s)	Brief Description
Picture Interest Exploration Survey (PIES) Education Achievement Corporation 1974 Grades 7–12, Non-readers or Limited Readers	MMY8:1018	This career interest survey employs 156 slides. Each slide depicts a worker's hands performing a task that represents a particular occupation. Scores are provided for 13 occupational areas, such as: office, sales, construction, mechanics and repairmen, and agriculture.
Prep Work Samples Prep, Inc. 1977 Special Needs Populations	Bott., 1985 Bott., 1987	Consists of 27 independent work samples, such as: drafting, wood construction, food preparation, travel services, small engine, police science, electronics, commercial art, fire science, refrigeration, solar technology, machine trades, etc. One of the four components of COATS.
San Francisco Vocational Competency Scale The Psychological Corporation 1968 Mentally Retarded Adults	MMY7:1073	Rates mentally retarded adults for participation in sheltered workshops and other work shop programs. Focuses on the following four areas: motor skills, cognition, responsibility, and social emotional behavior.
Skills Assessment Module (SAM) Piney Mountain Press No Date Ages 13–18 Who Are Mildly Handicapped (LD, ED, Mildly Retarded), and/or Disadvantaged	Bott., 1985 Bott., 1987	Assesses general aptitude, specific work behavior, and learning styles via 3 paper and pencil tests and 12 work samples: mail sort, payroll, computation, patient information memo, pipe assembly, block design, small parts, color sort, circuit board, etc.
Social and Prevocational Information Battery—Form T CTB/McGraw Hill 1978 Mild to Moderately Retarded Students		Consists of 9 tests that measure knowledge of skills and competencies necessary for community adjustment of TMR students. Responses are either yes-no or picture selection so that reading deficiencies are not penalized. SPIB-T can be used for screening, diagnosis, and program evaluation.
Talent Assessment Program System (TAPS) Talent Assessment, Inc. 1980–81 Age 13 & Up, TMR & Above, & Disadvantaged	Bott., 1987 CG-177	This performance battery consists of 10 tests designed to assess functional level of career-related attributes that correspond to worker trait factors described in the DOT. Tests include: structural and mechanical dexterity with small tools, visualization, discrimination by size and shape of objects, etc.

Instrument	Reference	Description
Testing, Orientation, and Work Evaluation in Rehabilitation (TOWER) Institute for Crippled and Disabled 1974 Disabled Persons	Bott., 1987	Assesses vocational potential of disabled individuals in 14 areas of work: clerical, drafting, drawing, electronics assembly, jewelry, leather goods, lettering, machine shop, mail clerk, optical mechanics, pantograph engraving, sewing, workshop assembly, and welding.
Test Orientation Procedure Psychological Corporation No Date Undereducated Adults: Spanish Speaking Adults		This exercise is designed to prepare for evaluation of undereducated and/or Spanish speaking applicants. Consists of simulated job application and 5 test familiarization samples: speed and accuracy, spelling, vocabulary, arithmetic, and information.
USES Basic Occupational Literacy Test (BOLT) United States Employment Service 1974 Grades 1–11 School Dropouts	MMY8:491	Designed to measure basic reading and arithmetic skills of school dropouts who are referred for occupational training or remedial education. Provides scores for reading vocabulary, reading comprehension, arithmetic computation, and arithmetic reasoning.
USES Non-reading Aptitude Test Battery (NATB) United States Employment Service 1965–82 Disadvantaged Grades 9–12, & Adults	MMY9:1305 TC-3 CG-181	Non-reading adaptation of the GATB that includes 7 or 8 pencil and paper tests and 4 performance tests. Provides 9 scores: intelligence, verbal, numerical, spatial, form perception, clerical perception, motor coordination, finger dexterity, and manual dexterity.
Valpar Component Work Sample System Valpar Corporation 1974–81 General Population and Industrially Injured Persons	Bott., 1987 CG-184	Consists of 19 work samples, each designed to measure broad worker traits, such as: small tools, upper extremity range of motion, and simulated assembly. Provides both scores and clinical observations that can be used for job training and placement, and for constructing educational and rehabilitation programs.
Vocational Adaptation Rating Scales Western Psychological Services 1980 Mentally Retarded Persons Aged 13–50	MMY9:1334	Uses parents', teachers', and professionals' ratings to measure maladaptive behaviors likely to hinder vocational adjustment. Provides frequency and severity scores in 17 areas, such as: verbal manners, communication skills, respect for property, rules and regulations, and grooming and personal hygiene.
Vocational Evaluation Systems (by Singer) New Concepts Corporation 1971 Special Needs Populations	Bott., 1985 Bott., 1987	Gathers a wide variety of occupational information via 28 independent and versatile work samples such as: bench assembly, electrical wiring, plumbing and pipe fitting, needle trades, cook and baker, cosmetology, office services, information processing, and machine trades, etc.

Name of Test/Publisher/Date/Population	Reference(s)	Brief Description
Vocational Information and Evaluation Work Samples (VIEWS) Vocational Research Institute 1977 Moderate and Severely Mentally Retarded Adults	Bott., 1985 Bott., 1987 CG-167	Consists of 16 work samples grouped into four levels of Data, People, Things typology. Samples include: bolts and washers sorting, stamping, mail sort, machine feeding, paper cutting, drill press, and circuit board assembly. Training required to administer.
Vocational Interest and Sophistication Assessment (VISA) O.S.U. Nisonger Center 1968 Mildly Retarded Adolescents and Young Adults	Bott., 1980 CG-189	This reading-free instrument provides a measure of an individual's interest in and knowledge about a series of job alternatives. Activities depicted are in the unskilled and semi-skilled job areas.
Vocational Interest Temperament and Aptitude System (VITAS) Vocational Research Institue 1979 Educationally and/or Culturally Disadvantaged	Bott., 1985 Bott., 1987 CG-168	Contains 21 independent work samples based on 16 Work Groups. Samples include: laboratory, engineering, and craft technology, production work, quality control, financial detail, and oral communications. Requires training to administer.
Vocational Opinion Index ARBOR, Inc. 1973–76 Disadvantaged Trainees in Vocational Skills Programs	MMY9:1340 MMY8:1056	Designed to measure attitudes, perceptions, and motivations that affect an individual's ability to get and/or hold a job. Provides 13 scores for 3 broad areas: attraction to work, losses associated with work, and barriers to employment.
Vocational Skills Assessment and Development Program Brodhead-Garrett Company No Date Handicapped and Disadvantaged, Ages 12–Adult	Bott., 1985 Bott., 1980	Program consists of three phases. The first is comprised of 18 work samples in 3 main areas: sorting, assembly, and salvage. The second provides occupational information and develops entry level skills in areas such as: health and basic tools. The third develops basic skills for specific occupations.

Test	References	Description
Wide Range Employability Sample Test (WREST) Jastak Associates Inc. 1980 Age 16–54, General Population, Sheltered Work-shops, and Industrial Settings	MMY9:1365 MMY8:987 CG-192 Bott., 1987	Measures work productivity in terms of quantity and quality of performance on 10 tasks: folding, stapling, packaging, measuring, stringing, gluing, collating, color matching, pattern matching, and assembly.
Wide Range Intelligence and Personality Test (WRIPT) Jastak Associates. Inc. 1958–74 Ages 9½ and Over	MMY8:492	Provides a measure of students' abilities in 10 areas, such as: vocabulary, coding, verbal reasoning, spelling, etc. Also derives scores for intelligence, capacity, motivation, and language.
Wide Range Interest-Opinion Test (WRIOT) Jastak Associates. Inc. 1979 Age 5–Adult	MMY9:1366 MMY8:1029 TC-4 CG-196	This pictorial instrument provides scores for 18 occupational interests, such as: art, sales, personal service, and biological science; and for 8 vocational attitudes, such as; sedentariness, ambition, sex stereotype, and negative bias.
Work Skills Development Package (WSD) Attainment Company No Date Severely Mentally Retarded, Mentally Ill and/or Physically Disabled	Bott., 1985	This prevocational training program contains 20 work samples, grouped into 4 difficulty levels, that assess 3 pre-vocational skills: discrimination between objects, manipulation of small objects, and application of basic concepts. Examples of work samples are: snap box packaging, and tactile discrimination.

I. OCCUPATIONAL APTITUDE, ACHIEVEMENT, AND MANUAL PERFORMANCE MEASURES IN SPECIFIC AREAS

Name of Test/Publisher/Date/Population	Reference(s)	Brief Description
Bennett Hand Tool Dexterity Test The Psychological Corporation 1981 High School & Adults		Designed to measure manual dexterity and gross motor coordination. Subject removes 12 bolts from one vertical board and replaces them on another. Task requires the use of four tools: two open end wrenches, one adjustable wrench, and one screwdriver.
Computer Operator Aptitude Battery (COAB) Science Research Associates, Inc. 1974 Computer Operator Applicants and Trainees	Bott., 1985	Consists of 3 subtests: sequence recognition, format checking, and logical thinking. Scores from subtests combine to predict job performance of computer operators and to identify those applicants with the potential to succeed as a computer operator.
Computer Programmer Aptitude Battery (CPAB) Science Research Associates, Inc. 1967, 1974 Computer Programmer Trainees	Bott., 1985	Designed to assess an individual's potential to succeed as a computer programmer. Consists of 5 subtests: verbal meaning, reasoning, letter series, number ability, and diagramming.
Crawford Small Parts Dexterity Test (CSPDT) The Psychological Corporation 1946–56 High School & Adult		Measures eye-hand coordination and fine finger dexterity in two parts. Part I-Subject uses tweezers to insert pins in close-fitting holes, and then places collars on the pins. Part II-Subject places small screws in holes by hand, and then uses a screwdriver to screw them down.
Flanagan Aptitude Classification Test (FACT) Science Research Associates, Inc. 1953 Students or Prospective Employees	Bott., 1985	Designed to predict success in various occupational fields via composite occupational scores. Consists of 16 subtests such as: inspection, coding, memory, precision, assembly, scales, coordination, judgement and comprehension, arithmetic, patterns, components, tables, mechanics, reasoning, etc.
Manipulative Aptitudes Test Western Psychological Services 1967 Grades 9–12, & Adults	MMY8:1040	Uses rectangular plexiglass board with sockets and a T-bar to measure eye-hand coordination and manual dexterity. Requires movement of hands, arms, and fingers in thrusting and twisting motions during two tasks: one using preferred hand and one with both hands.

Test	Reference	Description
Minnesota Clerical Test (MCT) The Psychological Corporation 1933–59 Clerical Applicants	MMY9:713 MMY6:1040	Designed to measure clerical aptitude. Focus is on perceptual speed and accuracy in two tasks: name comparison and number comparison. Each part consists of 100 pairs that subject must identify as identical or dissimilar.
Minnesota Rate of Manipulation Test, 1969 Edition American Guidance Service, Inc. 1931–69 Grade 7–Adult	MMY7:1046	Measures arm-hand dexterity using a form board with 60 round holes and 60 cylinders that fit into the holes. Consists of five different manipulative activities: placing, turning, displacing, one-hand turning, and two-hand turning. Also provides norms and instructions for the blind.
O'Conner Finger Dexterity Test Stoelting Company 1920–26 Ages 14 & Over	MMY6:1078	Designed to measure motor coordination and finger and manual dexterity. Consists of plate containing 100 holes arranged in ten rows. Subject's task is to insert small metal pins, in groups of three, as rapidly as possible.
O'Conner Tweezer Dexterity Test Stoelting Company 1920–28 Ages 14 & Over	MMY6:1079	Designed to measure motor coordination and finger and manual dexterity. Consists of plate containing 100 holes arranged in ten rows. Subject's task is to insert small metal pins, one by one, into each of the holes, using metal tweezers.
Office Skills Test Science Research Associates—Business Program Division 1977 Entry Level Applicants in the Business Field	Bott., 1985	Designed to measure clerical ability of entry level job applicants via 12 subtests: checking, coding, filing, form completion, grammar, numerical, oral directions, punctuation, reading comprehension, spelling, typing, and vocabulary.
Pennsylvania Bi-Manual Worksample American Guidance Service, Inc. 1943–45 Age 16–39		Measures manual dexterity and eye-hand coordination in two parts: Assembly-requires manually assembling bolts and nuts, and then placing them in a hole in the board; and Disassembly-requires removing the assemblies from the hole, taking them apart, and returning the parts to their bins.
Purdue Pegboard Science Research Associates, Inc. 1941–68 Grades 9–16, & Adults		Measures gross movement of hands, fingers, and arms, and tip of finger dexterity. Consists of pegboard containing two rows of 25 holes into which pins are inserted individually with the right hand, left hand, and both hands

Name of Test/Publisher/Date/Population	Reference(s)	Brief Description
Sales Attitude Checklist Science Research Associates, Inc. 1960 Individuals Interested in Sales Positions	Bott., 1985	Designed to assess sales attitudes and habits via 31 self-descriptive, forced-choice items. Specifically intended for use in identifying potentially successful salespeople.
Short Employment Tests (SET) The Psychological Corporation 1972–1978 Applicants for Clerical Positions	Bott., 1985	Designed to measure verbal, numerical, and clerical aptitudes via 3 tasks: recognize synonyms, perform arithmetic computations, and locate proper names in an alphabetical list and assign codes to the amount associated with each name.
Short Tests of Clerical Ability (STCA) Science Research Associates, Inc. 1959–73 Applicants for Office Positions	MMY8:1039	Measures 7 clerical aptitudes and abilities: arithmetic, business vocabulary, checking, coding, directions-oral and written, filing, and language. Useful for selection and placement in various office jobs, such as: secretary, stenographer, office clerk, etc.
SRA Pictorial Reasoning Test (PRT) Science Research Associates 1967, 1973 Ages 14 & Up with Some High School Education	Bott., 1985	Provides a general measure of the learning potential of individuals from diverse backgrounds with reading difficulties. Helpful in identifying an individual's potential for training and employment.
SRA Test of Mechanical Concepts Science Research Associates, Inc. 1976 Grades 8–12, & Adults	MMY8:1045 Bott., 1985	Measures an individual's ability to visualize and comprehend basic mechanical and spatial interrelationships. Reports four scores: mechanical interrelationships, mechanical tools and devices, spatial relations, and total.
Stromberg Dexterity Test (SDT) The Psychological Corporation 1945–51 Trade School & Adults	MMY4:774	Designed to aid in choosing workers for jobs requiring speed and accuracy of arm and hand movement. Test consist of 54 red, blue, and yellow discs and a durable board containing 54 holes on one side. Subject is timed while sorting the discs by color, and while placing them in the holes.
Work Content Skills Inventory Strategic Career Services No Date Adults		Contains 300 specific work-content skills in several occupational areas, such as: general management, human resources, leadership and motivation, communications, corporate law, public relations, banking, finance, and accounting, etc. Useful in understanding an individual's performance capabilities.

APPENDIX A

Sources of Information About Tests and Testing

Sources of Information About Tests And Testing

Robert P. Jordan
Librarian
Iowa Testing Programs
University of Iowa

and

David A. Jepsen
Counselor Education
University of Iowa

INTRODUCTION

The following textbooks, reference books, and monographs were chosen for this bibliography because of their timeliness and usefulness in the field of career guidance assessment. The fact that several of the psychometric texts have undergone multiple revisions indicates their continued value. Since the first edition of *A Counselor's Guide* was published, the stalwart *Mental Measurements Yearbook* and *Tests in Print* have been fortified by several other reference books containing test bibliographies and reviews. And because of the growing interest in career development for persons with special needs, a section of materials for assessment in that area has been added. As a final addition, there is a section listing periodicals which publish test reviews and/or research on tests.

The following list is not exhaustive. The reader should find here a basic core of books, monographs, and journals from which most questions concerning testing can be answered.

STANDARDS FOR PUBLISHERS AND USERS OF TESTS

American Personnel and Guidance Association. (1982). APGA policy statement: Responsibilities of users of standardized tests. In J.T. Kapes & M.M. Mastie (Ed.). *A counselor's guide to vocational guidance instruments* (pp.225–244). Falls Church, VA: Author.

Eight sections comprise this APGA statement: Introduction, decision rules (i.e., whether to test), test selection, qualifications of test users, test administration, scoring of tests, test interpretation, and communication (i.e., the legal and/or ethical issues considered in the reporting of test data to the client or others). The target audience for this policy statement is the professional membership of APGA (AACD). It is designed to address the necessity to establish guidelines against the misuse of tests.

American Psychological Association. (1985). Standards for educational and psychological testing. Washington, DC: American Psychological Association.

Co-sponsored by the APA, American Educational Research Association, and the National Council on Measurement in Education, these standards address technical problems, ethics, and applicability of tests in both research and clinical settings.

PSYCHOMETRIC TEXTS AND MONOGRAPHS

Aiken, L.R. (1985). *Psychological testing and assessment* (5th ed.). Boston: Allyn & Bacon.

Besides covering the usual historical and psychometric background information most measurement texts do, Aiken also has a chapter on testing special abilities and one on the assessment of interests, attitudes, and values. Discussion of the Kuder and Strong inventories makes up most of the latter chapter.

Anastasi, A. (1981). *Psychological testing* (5th ed.). New York: Macmillan.

A chapter on the "Measures of Interests, Values, and Personal Orientation" includes discussions on the major vocational interest inventories although recent revisions of the SCII manual and newer inventories, e.g. the OASIS, are not covered. Other assessment techniques, such as projective instruments, tests of self-concept, and observation instruments, are included in the following chapters.

Cronbach, L.J. (1984). *Essentials of psychological testing* (4th ed.). New York: Harper & Row.

Included are specific chapters on personnel selection, interest inventories, and personality assessment including occupational prediction. Cronbach states that this book was written not only for testing specialists, but also for other professionals, i.e. lawyers, doctors, et al., who sometimes must deal with tests in their work.

Goldman, L. (1971). *Using tests in counseling* (2nd ed.). New York: Appleton-Century-Crofts.

Much of the information about specific measurement devices is now dated. Tests such as the Brainerd Occupational Preference Inventory and the Cleeton Interest Inventory are cited but are long out of print. However, Goldman's introduction to the purposes of testing, the selection of tests, and his "Potpourri of Interpretive Problems" are still relevant. His chapter, "Statistical Bridges," gives a good overview of classical test theory. Another chapter, "Clinical Bridges," deals mainly with the practical clinical applications of assessment.

Hopkins, K.D., & Stanley, J.C. (1981). *Educational and psychological measurement and evaluation* (6th ed.). Englewood Cliffs, NJ: Prentice-Hall.

What separates this text from other measurement books is its chapter on "Standard Interest, Personality, and Social Measures." Major interest inventories are described and briefly critiqued. Some facsimiles of the instruments are included.

Lyman, H.B. (1986). *Test scores and what they mean* (4th ed.). Englewood Cliffs, NJ: Prentice-Hall.

This book was written for those with very little background in testing. In this new edition, Lyman has added material covering latent trait theory, competency testing, computer-assisted testing, adaptive and performance testing.

Nunnally, J.C. (1978). *Psychometric theory* (2nd ed.). New York: McGraw-Hill.

Nunnally succeeds in covering the technical side of testing in a not-so-technical manner. The material is understandable and usable by all behavioral scientists in both basic and applied research. Thus, the information is general in nature.

Shertzer, B., & Linden, J.D. (1979). *Fundamentals of individual appraisal: Assessment techniques for counselors*. Boston: Houghton Mifflin.

This textbook is written for measurement courses with the student of counseling in mind. The authors try to familiarize counseling students with the major assessment tools, to explain how to select the appropriate one in a given situation, and to introduce the technical aspects involved. The history of assessment instruments and the social, ethical, and legal ramifications of their use are also presented.

TEST BIBLIOGRAPHIES AND REVIEWS

Andrulis, R.S. (1971). *Adult assessment: A source book of tests and measures of human behavior*. Springfield, IL:Thomas.

Over 150 assessment devices are described in detail. Interest and vocational measures (pp.206–235) as well as aptitude, achievement, attitude, and personality instruments outlined in other chapters will be of interest to counselors. Introductory remarks on the purposes of tests and measures, what to consider in choosing among the instruments, and background information in psychometrics preface the rest of the book. Also included is a list of other resources, such as ERIC, which may be helpful to practitioners.

Association for Measurement and Evaluation in Counseling and Development. Committee to Screen Career Guidance Instruments. (1986). Reports. Alexandria, VA: Author. (ERIC Document Reproduction Service No. ED 273 664)

The Committee has compiled a series of test reviews that were published in the Association's AMECD Newsnotes from the Spring 1980 to the November 1985 issues. Each entry has information on the instrument's purpose; availability of norms, validity, and reliability data; format; and scoring. Cost information is now probably out-of-date for most of the instruments. Some instruments, such as the Self-Directed Search, have been revised since the reviews appeared in *AMECD Newsnotes*. The critical part of each review is concerned with the acceptability of using the instrument for individual counseling, group counseling, group screening, research, and classroom groups by teachers.

Educational Testing Service. *Test Collection*. (1987). The ETS Test Collection catalog, volume 2: Vocational tests and measurement devices. Phoenix, AZ: Oryx.

Among the measures described in this second volume from ETS's Test Collection are vocational interest and aptitude tests, work samples, attitude measures, measures of career development, certification tests, measures for use with handicapped, and instruments to measure organizational climate and managerial styles. Entries include pertinent bibliographical and ordering information.

Educational Testing Service. *Test Collection*. (1985). Measures of vocational choice-perception and development: Annotated bibliography of tests. Princeton, NJ: ETS.

Both commercially published and unpublished instruments are found in this bibliography. Those included are part of the Test Collection department at ETS. These instruments are described as helping individuals match their interest to appropriate vocations or courses of study. These annotated bibliographies from ETS are computer-generated and are updated periodically.

Educational Testing Service. *Test Collection*. (1986). Vocational interests: Annotated bibliography of tests. Princeton, NJ: ETS.

This is also a bibliography of both commercially published tests and unpublished experimental measures which are purported to assess vocational interests, abilities, and work-related experiences. Included are instruments for use at the sixth grade through adult levels. Bibliographic information is in machine-readable format, and each entry is followed by an abstract.

Kapes, J. T., & Mastie, M. M. (Eds.). (1982) *A counselor's guide to vocational guidance instruments*. Falls Church, VA: National Vocational Guidance Association. Reviews of forty tests divided into appropriate categories comprise the primary emphasis of this volume. Over 70 additional tests and inventories are briefly described. A summary of the principles of choosing a test, a checklist of testing competencies and a bibliography of testing references are also included.

Keyser, D.J., & Sweetland, R.C. (Eds.). (1984–87). *Test critiques*. (Vols. 1–6). Kansas City, MO: Test Corporation of America.

This six volume work (to date) is comprised of original reviews of measurement devices which the editorial staff determined are the most frequently used in the areas of psychological, educational, and business testing. These instruments include most of those used in vocational guidance. Coverage overlaps with the Mental Measurements Yearbook series.

Krug, S.E. (Ed.). (1987). *Psychware yearbook: A reference guide to computer-based products for behavioral assessment in psychology, education, and business*. Kansas City, MO: Test Corporation of America.

This comprehensive reference contains 339 entries for computer-based assessment packages, ranging from vocational guidance to behavioral medicine. Information on each instrument includes: Product name, supplier, category, application, sales restrictions, type and cost of service, product descriptions, and sample printouts. The yearbook uses five indexes to organize and find the instruments including: product title, category, application, service listing, and supplier.

Mitchell, J.V. (Ed.). (1985). *The Ninth mental measurements yearbook*. Lincoln, NE: Buros Institute of Mental Measurements.

This is the most well-known source of test reviews. The ninth edition has included a score index from which a test can be identified by the variables it claims to measure. There are broadly based scores, such as "vocational ac-

318

tivity" or "career interest," as well as rather specific scores, e.g., the "fire-fighter aptitude" or "flight attendant" in the Strong-Campbell Interest Inventory. The information included is also available on-line through BRS.

Mitchell, J.V. (Ed.). (1983). *Tests in print III: An index to tests, test reviews, and the literature of specific tests.* Lincoln, NE: Buros Institute of Mental Measurements.

Nearly all commercially published tests in the English language are listed here. The major format change from TIP II is its alphabetical arrangement by test title rather that alphabetically within broad subject categories. This reference work essentially acts as an index to the more recent editions of the *Mental Measurement Yearbook* series.

Sweetland, R.C., & Keyser, D.J. (Eds.). (1986) *Tests: A comprehensive reference for assessments in psychology, education and business* (2nd ed.). Kansas City, MO: Test Corporation of America.

This second edition of *Tests* follows close on the heels of the first edition (1983) and its supplement (1984). Obviously, more recent tests or newer editions of established tests published since 1983 will be included here rather than in *Tests in Print III* (1983). *Tests* is narrower in coverage than TIP III, but there is quite an overlap with Mitchell's book. Unlike TIP III, however, each test's entry includes the purpose(s) for as well as a description of the instrument. There is no mention of publication date(s) in the entry from which the user may help discern the age of the test described. Those career counselors serving handicapped clientele may find the hearing-impaired, physically-impaired, and visually-impaired indexes to *Tests* very handy.

MATERIALS SPECIFIC TO CAREER GUIDANCE

Herr, E.L. & Cramer, S.H. (1988). *Career guidance and counseling through the life span: Systematic approaches* (3rd ed.). Boston, MA: Little, Brown & Co.

Herr and Cramer have written a standard textbook in the field of career counseling. Chapter 16, "Assessment in Career Guidance and Counseling," gives an overview of the use of tests in career guidance. The authors cover the predictive uses of tests followed by a discussion of different tests and interest inventories for discrimination ("discrimination" being the discovering of what occupational or educational groups a client resembles). Monitoring, the process of choosing a career, and evaluation of the counselor's intervention are the two other functions of assessment. In all four functions, examples of appropriate instruments are given.

Krumboltz, J.D. & Hamel, D.A. (Eds.). (1982). *Assessing career development.* Palo Alto, CA: Mayfield Publishing Co.

This book of edited articles brings together the views of recognized professionals in the area of career assessment especially as it relates to career education. Topics include practical difficulties encountered, alternative ways of assessing, major research issues and measurement problems in assessing outcomes.

Montross, D.H. & Shinkman, C.J. (Eds.). (1981). *Career development in the 1980's: Theory and practice.* Springfield, IL: Thomas.

Two chapters by J.O. Crites address the issue of counselors becoming disenchanted with tests. In "Career Counseling: A Comprehensive Approach" (pp. 67–89), Crites focuses on the questionable status of the predictive validity of occupational tests. Even with some reservations, Crites believes there is a place in counseling for tests. This refrain continues in his other chapter, "Integrative Test Interpretation" (pp. 161–168), where he encourages the counselor to use tests as a means to establish and continue communication between client and counselor. In the chapter, "Applications of Vocational Interest Inventories" (pp. 169–181), J.C. Hansen makes scale-by-scale comparisons among four major interest inventories (Strong-Campbell Interest Inventory, Kuder DD, Jackson Vocational Interest Inventory, and the Self-Directed Search).

Rodgers, R.C. (Ed.). (1983). *Measurement trends in career and vocational education*. San Francisco, CA: Jossey-Bass.

Career counseling, according to Rodgers, is a field of ever-widening complexity. Four state-of-the-art chapters cover guidance and assessment instruments for the handicapped, work adjustment measurement, and a chapter on the use of assessment instruments which can link job-seekers to appropriate occupations. This book is no. 20 in the publisher's series, *New Directions in Testing and Measurement*.

Seligman, L. (1980). *Assessment in developmental career counseling*. Cranston, RI: Carrol.

Chapters 2 and 3 of Seligman's book cover "The Use of Assessment in Career Counseling" and "Types of Assessment" available for counselors. Chapter 2 is nontechnical theory, and chapter 3 is application of different instruments in career counseling.

Super, D.E. (Ed.). (1974). *Measuring vocational maturity for counseling and evaluation*. Washington, DC: National Vocational Guidance Association.

Chapters by such notables as Crites, Super, Harris, Passow, et al., highlight this collection of readings in the assessment of career development in counseling.

Tittle, C.K., & Zytowski, D.G. (Eds.). (1978). *Sexfair interest measurement: Research and implications*. Washington, DC: U.S. Government Printing Office.

This work is a collection of papers addressing the problem of sex bias in such well-known interest inventories as the Strong-Campbell Interest Inventory and the Vocational Preference Inventory. Since this publication came out, newer editions of the inventories or their manuals have appeared so that some of the criticisms in Tittle and Zytowski may be dated.

Zunker, V.G. (1982). *Using assessment results in career counseling*. Monterey, CA: Brooks/Cole.

After three introductory chapters on assessment concepts and the rationale behind using assessment results in counseling, Zunker covers individual varieties of tests and inventories in the following chapters. Reviews of specific instruments are found within each category. For example, Zunker reviews, among others, the Armed Services Vocational Aptitude Battery under "Using Ability Tests" (pp. 28–41). In the chapter titled "Combining Assessment Results" (pp. 125–138), the ACT Career Planning Program is reviewed. Case studies are included to illustrate interpretations for some of the instruments.

MATERIALS FOR SPECIAL POPULATIONS

Biller, E.R. (1985). *Understanding and guiding the career development of adolescents and young adults with learning disabilities*. Springfield, IL: Thomas.

Dealing with the learning disabled counselee not only requires the knowledge of the association between normal "adolescent behavior and adult career outcomes," but also the very special behaviors of the LD adolescent. There is a chapter covering career assessment for LD adolescents and another which explores a developmental career curriculum.

Bolton, B. (Ed.). (1986). *Handbook of measurement and evaluation in rehabilitation* (2nd Edition). University Park, MD: University Park Press.

This text is divided into three major sections. "Fundamentals of Measurement" covers the introduction to psychometric theory. The second section, "Review of Instruments," has a chapter which reviews vocational inventories. The bulk of the book is taken up by Section III, "Applications for Rehabilitation." Chapters within this section address the issues of applying test results in the development of individualized rehabilitative programming with various special populations.

Botterbusch, K.F. & Michael, N. (1985). *Testing and test modification in vocational evaluation*. Menomonie, WI: Materials Development Center, Stout Vocational Rehabilitation Institute, University of Wisconsin-Stout.

This publication is a guide to the selection, use, and modification of psychological tests when used with three disability groups: visually disabled, hearing impaired, and mentally retarded. This guide is comprised of three sections which 1) give general psychometric information and explain the use of tests in evaluation programs, 2) describe the modification of tests for the special populations stated above, and 3) review the tests used in evaluation programs. The reviews in section 3 are further divided into categories of tests (achievement, aptitude, intelligence, interest, work attitude, etc.). An alphabetical list of reviewed tests and a publisher's directory are in appendices.

Botterbusch, K.F. (1987). *Vocational assessment and evaluation systems: A comparison*. Menomonie, WI: Materials Development Center, Stout Vocational Rehabilitation Institute, University of Wisconsin-Stout.

This is the latest in a series of Materials Development Center publications which describe and critique available vocational evaluation and assessment systems applicable to special populations. The previous (1980) edition was entitled *A Comparison of Commercial Vocational Evaluation Systems*. Several of the newer systems covered are dependent on computers for either scoring or administration. And in the preface, the author explains the reasons behind the trend toward assessment systems which test isolated work samples and utilize psychometric instruments rather than use a long-term observation of a person's ability to function at a job. Each system critique follows a detailed formal outline.

Peterson, M. (1986). *Vocational assessment for vocational education: Competency analysis and work sample development*. Starkville, MS: Author.

The author reviews the problems in using work sample systems with special students. In a detailed approach to work sample development, a procedure is given for analyzing special student competencies needed for success in vocational education programs. In addition, there is a step-by-step description of how to develop a work sample using the aforementioned analysis of student competencies. A criterion-referenced approach is advocated so that a clear picture of a student's strengths and weaknesses relative to success in a vocational education program can be obtained.

Peterson, M. (1986). *Vocational assessment of special students: A procedural manual.* Starkville, MS: Author.

This is a comprehensive manual to help develop a model of vocational assessment of special students in public schools. The three-stage model described includes: 1) a curriculum-based vocational assessment where existing personnel and resources are used to obtain informal information about students, 2) specific assessment questions (e.g., whether a student may enter into a particular vocational education program), and 3) vocational evaluation—an intensive time-limited process of vocational assessment and exploration. Included in appendices are not only names and addresses of resources for further information on specific testing techniques, but also reviews of tests and work sample systems.

Power, P.W. (1984). *A Guide to vocational assessment.* Austin, TX: PRO-ED.

Written for anyone who counsels clients with disabilities, the book addresses both the intellectual and emotional needs in regard to vocational evaluation and rehabilitation. Specific vocational interest, intelligence, and educational achievement instruments are discussed in reference to people with disabilities. An achievement test by John O. Willis is included in one of the book's appendices.

Scholl, G., & Schnur, R. (1976). *Measures of psychological, vocational, and educational functioning in the blind and visually handicapped.* New York: American Foundation for the Blind.

Because of the mainstreaming of children with handicaps in the last two decades, counselors have been faced with assisting students with visual handicaps. This book is a compendium of information on tests which can be administered to those with such handicaps.

PERIODICALS WHICH PUBLISH TEST RESEARCH AND REVIEWS

Listed below are those periodicals which, over the last few years, have published in this country a large portion of reviews and research articles using career guidance tests as well as evaluations of career development programs. *News on Tests* deserves a special note. A newsletter published ten times each year by the Test Collection division of ETS, *News on Tests* has bibliographic data and abstracts of the new tests acquired by the Test Collection including those of interest to counselors. Test reviews in the journals listed below are cited as well as new ERIC documents and published monographs in the field of assessment. As with the ETS annotated bibliographies listed above, the materials cited reflect what ETS has acquired. But its research library and test collection are the most extensive on assessment in the United States, and very little escapes their notice.

AMECD Newsnotes. Association for Measurement and Evaluation in Counseling and Development, 5999 Stevenson Ave., Alexandria, VA 22304 (4/yr.). (Formerly: *AMEG Newsnotes*)

Applied Psychological Measurement. Applied Psychological Measurement, Inc., N658 Elliott Hall, University of Minnesota, Minneapolis, MN 55455 (4/yr.).

Career Development Quarterly. National Career Development Association, 5999 Stevenson Ave., Alexandria, VA 22304 (4/yr.). (Formerly: *The Vocational Guidance Quarterly*)

Contemporary Education Review. American Educational Research Association, 1230 17th St. NW, Washington, D.C. 20036 (2/yr.).

The Counseling Psychologist. Counseling Center, University of California-Irvine, Irvine, CA 92717 (4/yr.).

Counselor Education and Supervision. American Association for Counseling and Development, 5999 Stevenson Ave., Alexandria, VA 22304 (4/yr.).

Elementary School Guidance and Counseling. American Association for Counseling and Development, 5999 Stevenson Ave., Alexandria, VA 22304 (4/yr.).

Journal of Applied Psychology. American Psychological Association. 1200 17th St. NW, Washington, D.C. 20036 (4/yr.).

Journal of Career Development. Human Sciences Press, 72 Fifth Ave., New York, New York 10011 (4/yr.). (Formerly: *Journal of Career Education*)

Journal of Counseling and Development. American Counseling for Counseling and Development, 5999 Stevenson Ave., Alexandria, VA 22304 (4/yr.).

Journal of Counseling Psychology. American Psychological Association. 1200 17th St. NW, Washington, D.C. 22304 (6/yr.).

Journal of Educational Measurement. National Council of Measurement in Education, 1230 17th St. NW, Washington, D.C. (4/yr.).

Journal of Personality Assessment. Society for Personality Assessment, Inc., 1070 E. Angeleno Ave., Burbank, CA 91501 (6/yr.).

Journal of Psychoeducational Assessment. Grune & Stratton, Inc., 6277 Sea Harbor Dr., Orlando, FL 32821 (4/yr.).

Journal of Vocational Behavior. Academic Press, 111 5th Ave., New York, NY 10003 (6/yr.).

Learning Disability Quarterly. University of Kansas Medical Center, Dept. of Special Education, Kansas City, KS 66103 (4/yr.).

Measurement and Evaluation in Counseling and Development. American Association for Counseling and Development, 5999 Stevenson Ave., Alexandria, VA 22304 (4/yr.).

News On Tests. Test Collection, Educational Testing Service, Rosedale Road, Princeton, NJ 08541 (10/yr.). (Formerly: *Test Collection Bulletin*)

Personnel Journal. Personnel Journal, Inc. 929 Harrison Ave., Suite 100, Columbus, OH 43215 (4/yr.).

Psychology in the Schools. Psychology Press, Inc., 4 Conant Sq., Brandon, VT 05733 (4/yr.).

School Psychology Review. National Association of School Psychologists, P.O. Box 184, Kent OH 44240 (4/yr.).

APPENDIX B

Addresses of Publishers

Addresses of Publishers*

Alfano, Anthony M.
6263 Twilight Avenue
Kalamazoo, MI 49004

American College Testing Program
2201 North Dodge Street
P.O. Box 168
Iowa City, Iowa 52243

American Guidance Service
Publishers' Building
Circle Pines, MN 55014

American Testronics
P.O. Box 2270
Iowa City, Iowa 52244

ARBOR, Inc.
The Science Center
34th and Market Streets
Philadelphia, PA 19104

Attainment Company
P.O. Box 103
Oregon, WI 53575

Bowling Green State University
Bowling Green, OH 43403

Birkman & Associates, Inc.
3040 Post Oak Boulevard/Suite 1425
Houston, TX 77056

Brodhead-Garrett Company
4560 East 71st Street
Cleveland, OH 44105

Cambridge Book Company
88 Seventh Avenue
New York, NY 10106

Cambridge Career Products
#2 Players Club Drive
Charleston, WV 25311

Career Education Readiness
 Measurement and Research
Southern Illinois University
Box 123
Edwardsville, IL 62025

Career Planning and Placement
 Service
100 Noyes Hall
University of Missouri
Columbia, MO 65211

Career Research and Testing
2005 Hamilton Avenue Suite 250
San Jose, CA 95125

Career Research and Testing
1190 Bascom Avenue
San Jose, CA 95128

CFKR Career Materials, Inc.
110 Glenn Way
P.O. Box 5096
Belmont, CA 94002

Chronicle Guidance Publications,
 Inc.
Moravia, NY 13188

*Includes all publishers of instruments either described and reviewed in the main body
of this work or listed in compilation of additional instruments.

The College Board
888 Seventh Avenue
New York, NY 10019

College Major Card Sort
208 West, 100 South
Orea, UT 84057

The Conover Company
P.O. Box 155
Omro, WI 54963

Consulting Psychologists Press, Inc.
577 College Avenue
P.O. Box 11636
Palo Alto, CA 94306

CTB/McGraw Hill
Del Monte Research Park
Monterey, CA 93940

Ed ITS
P.O. Box 7234
San Diego, CA 92107

Educational Achievement
  Corporation
P.O. Box 7310
Waco, TX 76710

Educational and Industrial Test
  Services Ltd.
83 High Street
Hemel Hempstead, Harts.
HP13AH, England

Educational Guidance, Inc.
P.O. Box 511
Dearborn, MI 48121

Educators Assistance Institute
2500 Colorado Avenue
Santa Monica, CA 90406

Edupac, Inc.
231 Norfolk Street
Walpole, MA 02081

Elbert Publications
P.O. Box 09497
Columbus, Ohio 43209

Evaluation Systems, Inc.
7788 Milwaukee Avenue
Niles, IL 60648

Fenner, Bradford J.
29 075 Avondale Lane
Lombard, IL 60148

Guidance Testing Associates
St. Mary's University
One Camino Santa Maria
San Antonio, TX 78284

Hester Evaluation Systems, Inc.
2709 W. 29th Street
Topeka, KS 66614

Houghton Mifflin Company
1 Beacon Street
Boston, MA 02107

Human Systems Consultants, Inc.
110 North Tenth Street, Suite 7
Columbia, MO 65201

Institute for Crippled and Disabled
400 First Avenue
New York, NY 10009

Institute for Personality and Ability
  Testing, Inc.
1801 Woodfield Drive
Savoy, IL 61874

The Interstate Printers and Publishers
P.O. Box 594
Jackson at Van Buren
Danville, IL 61832

Key Education, Inc.
673 Broad Street
Shrewsbury, NJ 07701

Life Skills Center
1201 Second Street
Corpus Christi, TX 78404

Marathon Consulting and Press
585 Anfield Road
Columbus, OH 43209

McCarron Dial Systems
P.O. Box 45628
Dallas, TX 75245

NCS Professional Assessment Services
P.O. Box 1416
Minneapolis, MN 55440

Nelson Canadian Limited
1120 Birchmount Road
Scarborough, Ontario,
Canada MIK564

New Concepts Corporation
1802 N. Division Street
Morris, IL 60450

NSVCS
Route 4, Box 217
Gainesville, FL 32601

OSU Nisonger Center
1580 Cannon Drive
Columbus, OH 43206

Piney Mountain Press
P.O. Box 333
Cleveland, GA 30528

Prep, Inc.
1007 Whitehead Road Extension
Trenton, NJ 08628

PRO-ED
5341 Industrial Oaks Boulevard
Austin, TX 78735

Psychological Assessment Resources
P.O. Box 998
Odessa, FL 33556

Psychological Corporation
555 Academic Court
San Antonio, TX 78204

Psychological Service Center of
   Philadelphia
Suite 904
1422 Chestnut Street
Philadelphia, PA 19102

Psychologists and Educators, Inc.
211 West State Street
Jacksonville, IL 62650

Publishers Test Service
2500 Garden Road
Monterey, CA 93940

Research Psychologists Press, Inc.
P.O. Box 984
Port Huron, MI 48060

Riverside Publishing Company
P.O. Box 1970
Iowa City, IA 52244

Scholastic Testing Service, Inc.
480 Meyer
P.O. Box 1056
Bensenville, IL 60106

Science Research Associates, Inc.
155 North Wacker Drive
Chicago, IL 60606

Stoelting
1350 South Kostner Avenue
Chicago, IL 60623

Strategic Career Services
3704 Mt. Diablo Boulevard
Suite 313
La Fayette, CA 95549

Talent Assessment, Inc.
P.O. Box 5087
Jacksonville, FL 32207

Train-Ease Corporation
47 Marble Avenue
Pleasantville, NY 10570

United States Department of Defense
Testing Directorate, Headquarters
Military Enlistment Processing
   Command
Attn: MEPCT
Fort Sheridan, IL 60037

329

United States Department of Labor
Division of Testing
Employment and Training
  Administration
Washington, D.C. 20213

United States Employment Service
Employment and Training
  Administration
200 Constitution Avenue N.W.
Washington, D.C. 20210

Valpar Corporation
3801 East 34th Street, Suite 105
Tucson, AZ 85713

Vocational Psychology Research
University of Minnesota
Elliot Hall
75 East River Road
Minneapolis, MN 55455

Vocational Research Institute
Jewish Employment and Vocational
  Service
2100 Arch Street, 6th Floor
Philadelphia, PA 19103

Western Psychological Services
12031 Wilshire Boulevard
Los Angeles, CA 90025

The Wilmington Press
13315 Wilmington Drive
Dallas, TX 75234

Wintergreen Software
1010 Sherman Avenue
P.O. Box 1229
Madison, WI 53701-1229

World of Work, Inc.
2923 N. 67th Place
Scottsdale, AZ 85251

APPENDIX C

Users Matrix

User's Matrix of Career Assessment Instruments

This User's Matrix provides a convenient method to locate quickly instruments covered in the *Counselor's Guide*. It will be most useful, for example, for those wishing to scan down a listing of all instruments for elementary grades, or all instruments for special populations, or all work values measures. Using the Matrix in combination with the Index, the reader can locate the page of the *Counselor's Guide* on which any specific instrument is reviewed or described. The 43 instruments for which complete reviews are contained in this book (Chapter VI) are printed in bold face type. The others are briefly described in Chapter VII, "Additional Career Assessment Instruments." A "P" indicates the *primary* category or use for the instrument while an "S" suggests a *secondary* or other category addressed by a particular instrument. An "X" is used to designate *level(s)* of use.

The **Category** corresponds to those used in Chapter VI. **Level** refers to the suggested grade or age use. **Elementary** includes pre-school through grade five; **Middle/Junior High School** includes grades six through nine; **High School** grades ten through twelve; and **Post-High School/Adult** refers to technical/trade school, college/university, and/or adults who are 18 years of age or older. In adhering to these levels please note that instruments appropriate for use at ninth grade are always included in the junior high school level. For example, if an instrument is suggested for use at grades 9–12 it is included in both the junior high and high school level.

A total of 169 instruments are included in the User's Matrix. Most of the reviews in Chapter VI and descriptions in Chapter VII provide sources of addition reviews or information concerning each of the 169 instruments. The reader is encouraged to utilize these sources to increase his/her knowledge and understanding of instruments corresponding to an identified type and level of need.

Compiled by: Edwin A. Whitfield, Ohio Department of Education; Jerome T. Kapes, Texas A & M University; and Marjorie Moran Mastic, Washtenaw Intermediate School District, Michigan.

Alphabetical Listing of Career Assessment Instruments By Category and Level of Use

LEGEND

P—Primary Category of Use
S—Secondary Category of Use
X—Level of Use

INSTRUMENTS	Aptitudes	Interests	Values	Career Development	Combined Measures	Personality	Special Populations	Elementary School	Junior High/Middle School	High School	Post-High School/Adult
ACT Career Planning Program (CPP)	S	S			P				X	X	X
Adaptability Test	S						P			X	X
Adult Basic Learning Exam (ABLE)	P										X
Adult Career Concerns Inventory (ACCI)				P							X
Applied Biological and Agribusiness Interest Inventory		P							X		
Apticom	S	S			P		S			X	X
Aptitude Based Career Decision Test (ABCD)	P										X
Aptitude Tests for Occupations	P									X	X
Aptitudes	P									X	

Instrument													
Armed Services Vocational Aptitude Battery (ASVAB)	P											X	X
Assessment of Career Decision Making (ACDM)						P					X	X	X
Ball Aptitude Battery	P										X		X
Bennett Hand Tool Dexterity Test	P							S			X		X
Birkman Method–Needs at a Glance				S	S		P						X
Canadian Occupational Interest Inventory		P									X		X
Career Ability Placement Survey (CAPS)	P								X		X	X	X
Career Area Interest Checklist		P									X		X
Career Assessment Inventory—The Enhanced Version (CAI)	P				P				X		X	X	X
Career Awareness Inventory					P			X	X	X	X		X
Career Decision Scale (CDS)					P						X	X	X
Career Development Inventory (CDI)		P			P				X		X	X	X
Career Directions Inventory		P			P			X	X		X		X
Career Education Readiness Test								X	X				
Career Exploration Series		P							X		X	X	X
Career Evaluation System Series 100	S					S	P					X	X
Career Guidance Inventory		P							X		X		X
Career Guidance Inventory for Trades, Services, and Technologies		P							X		X	X	X
Career Interests		P											X
Career Interest Survey		P									X		

LEGEND

P—Primary Category of Use
S—Secondary Category of Use
X—Level of Use

INSTRUMENTS

Instrument	Aptitudes	Interests	Values	Career Development	Combined Measures	Personality	Special Populations	Elementary School	Junior High/Middle School	High School	Post-High School/Adult
Career Interest Tests (CIT)		P							X	X	X
Career Maturity Inventory (CMI)				P					X	X	X
Career Occupational Preference System Interest Inventory (COPS)		P							X	X	X
Career Orientation Placement and Evaluation Survey (COPES)			P						X	X	X
Career Path Strategy				P						X	X
Career Skills Assessment Program (CSAP)				P					X	X	X
Career Survey	S	S			P				X	X	X
Career Values Card Sort Kit			P								X
College Major Card Sort					P				X	X	X
Comprehensive Ability Battery (CAB)	P								X	X	X
Comprehensive Career Assessment Scale		S		P				X	X	X	

336

Instrument	1	2	3	4	5	6	7	8	9
Comprehensive Occupational Assessment and Training System	S	S		S	F			X	X
Computerized Career Assessment and Planning Program (CCAPP)	S	P						X	
Computer Operator Aptitude Battery (COAB)	P								X
Computer Programmer Aptitude Battery (CPAB)	P								X
Crawford Small Parts Dexterity Test	P				S			X	X
Differential Aptitude Tests (DAT)	P		P				X	X	X
Employment Readiness Scale		S		P				X	X
Experience Exploration	S						X	X	X
Exploring Career Options (ECO)	S	S	S	P					X
Flanagan Aptitude Classification Test (FACT)	P				S			X	X
Forer Vocational Survey: Men-Women				P				X	X
Geist Picture Interest Inventory	S	S			P		X	X	X
Gordon Occupational Checklist II	P	P					X	X	X
Hackman-Gaither Interest Inventory	P	P					X	X	X
Hall Occupational Orientation Inventory (HALL)			P			X	X	X	X
Harrington O'Shea Career Decision-Making System (CDM)	P	P					X	X	X
Hester Evaluation System (HESTER)	S				P			X	X
How Well Do You Know Your Interests?	?	S					X	X	X
Individual Career Exploration (ICE)	S	S	S	P		X	X	X	

337

INSTRUMENTS

Instrument	Aptitudes	Interests	Values	Career Development	Combined Measures	Personality	Special Populations	Elementary School	Junior High/Middle School	High School	Post-High School/Adult
Interest, Determination, Exploration and Assessment Section (IDEAS)		P							X	X	
Inventory of Interests		P							X	X	X
Jackson Vocational Interest Survey (JVIS)		P								X	X
Jewish Employment Vocational Services Work Sample System (JEVS)	S						P				X
Job Descriptive Index (JDI)			P								X
Judgement of Occupational Behavior-Orientation (JOB-O)		P							X	X	X
Jobtap II					P					X	X
Key Educational Vocational Assessment System (KEVAS)	S	S			S	S	P		X	X	X
Knowledge of Occupations Test				P						X	
Kuder Career Development Inventory		S			P				X	X	X
Kuder General Interest Survey, Form E (KUDER-E)		P							X	X	X

338

Instrument									
Kuder Occupational Interest Survey, Form DD (KUDER-DD)	P							X	X
Major-Minor-Finder (M-M-F)					P			X	X
Manipulative Aptitudes Test	P					S	X	X	X
McCarron-Dial System (MDS)	S				S	P	X	X	X
Measures of Occupational Stress, Strain, and Coping				P					
Microcomputer Evaluation and Screening Assessment (MESA)	S				S	P		X	X
Microcomputer Evaluation of Career Areas (MECA)	S				S	P	X	X	X
Micro-Tower	S					P			X
Milwaukee Academic Interest Inventory	P							X	X
Minnesota Clerical Test (MCI)	P							X	X
Minnesota Importance Questionnaire (MIQ)			P					X	X
Minnesota Rate of Manipulation Test, 1969 Edition (MRMT)	P					S	X	X	X
Minnesota Satisfaction Questionnaire (MSQ)			P						X
Missouri Occupational Card Sort (MOCS)	P							X	X
Missouri Occupational Preference Inventory (MOPI)	P							X	X
Motivated Skills Card Sort (MSCS)		P						X	X
Myers-Briggs Type Indicator (M-BTI)		P					X	X	X
My Vocational Situation (MVS)		P						X	X
New Mexico Career Education Test Series							X	X	
Non-Sexist Vocational Card Sort	P							X	X

INSTRUMENTS

INSTRUMENTS	CATEGORY							LEVEL			
	Aptitudes	Interests	Values	Career Development	Combined Measures	Personality	Special Populations	Elementary School	Junior High/Middle School	High School	Post-High School/Adult
Occupational Aptitude Survey and Interest Schedule (OASIS)	S	S			P				X	X	
Occupations and Career Information BOXSCORE				P					X	X	X
Occupational Interest Card Sort (OICS)		P								X	X
Occ-U-Sort		P								X	X
O'Conner Finger Dexterity Test	P						S		X	X	X
O'Conner Tweezer Dexterity Test	P						S		X	X	X
Office Skills Test	P						S			X	X
Ohio Vocational Interest Survey, Second Edition (OVIS)		P							X	X	X
Ohio Work Values Inventory			P					X	X	X	X
Orientation Inventory			S			P				X	X
Pennsylvania Bi-Manual Worksample	P						S			X	X

Instrument									
Personal Skills Map						P	X	X	X
Personnel Tests for Industry-Oral Directions Test (PTI-ODT)	S					P		X	X
Pictorial Inventory of Careers (PIC)		S				P	X	X	X
Picture Interest Exploration Survey (PIES)		S				P	X	X	
Planning Career Goals (PCG)	S	S	S		P			X	X
Prep Work Samples	S							X	X
Program for Assessing Youth Employment Skills (PAYES)	S	S	S	S		P	X	X	X
Purdue Pegboard	P					S	X	X	X
Reading Free Vocational Interest Inventory—Revised (RFVII)		S				P	X	X	X
System for Assessment and Group Evaluation/Compute-A-Match	S	S		P				X	X
Sales Attitude Checklist			P			P		X	X
Salience Inventory (SI)							X	X	X
San Francisco Vocational Competency Scale	S			S		P			X
Self Description Inventory						P	X	X	X
Self-Directed Search (SDS)		P					X	X	X
Short Employment Tests (SET)	P					S		X	X
Short Tests of Clerical Ability (STCA)	P					S		X	X
Sixteen PF Personal Career Development Profile (PCDP)					P		X	X	X
Skills Assessment Module (SAM)	S						X	X	
Social and Prevocational Informational Battery—Form T (SPIB-T)	S		S			P	X	X	X

INSTRUMENTS

INSTRUMENTS	CATEGORY							LEVEL			
	Aptitudes	Interests	Values	Career Development	Combined Measures	Personality	Special Populations	Elementary School	Junior High/Middle School	High School	Post-High School/Adult
Social and Prevocational Information Battery—Revised (SPIB)	S			S			P		X	X	X
SRA Pictorial Reasoning Test (PRT)	P						S		X	X	X
SRA Test of Mechanical Concepts	P						S		X	X	X
Strong-Campbell Interest Inventory (SCII)		P							X	X	X
Stromberg Dexterity Test (SDT)	P						S			X	X
Study of Values (SOV)			P							X	X
Talent Assessment Program System (TAPS)	S						P		X	X	X
Temperament and Values Inventory (TVI)			S			P			X	X	X
Test Orientation Procedure	S						P				X
Testing, Orientation, and Work Evaluation in Rehabilitation (TOWER)	S						P			X	X
Tests of Adult Basic Education (TABE)	P										X

UNIACT IV	S	P							X	X
USES Basic Occupational Literacy Test (BOLT)	P						P	X	X	X
USES General Aptitude Test Battery (GATB)		P							X	X
USES Interest Checklist		P								X
USES Interest Inventory (USESII)		P							X	X
USES Non-Reading Aptitude Test Battery (NATB)	S						P	X	X	X
Valpar Component Work Sample System (VALPAR)	S						P		X	X
Valpar-17 Pre-Vocational Readiness Battery	S				S	S	P	X	X	X
Values Scale (VS)			P		S	S		X	X	X
Vocational Adaptation Rating Scales	S				S	S	P	X	X	X
Vocational Exploration and Insight Kit (VEIK)		P			S				X	X
Vocational Evaluation Systems by Singer (VES)	S	S				S	P	X	X	X
Vocational Implications of Personality (VIP)						P		X	X	X
Vocational Information and Evaluation Work Samples (VIEWS)	S						P		X	X
Vocational Interest and Sophistication Assessment (VISA)		S			S		P	X	X	X
Vocational Interest, Experience, and Skill Assessment (VIESA)	S	P				S		X	X	X
Vocational Interest Inventory (VII)		P						X	X	X
Vocational Interest Profile Report		P							X	
Vocational Interest Temperament and Aptitude System (VITAS)	S						P		X	X
Vocational Opinion Index						S	P	X	X	X

INSTRUMENTS

INSTRUMENTS	CATEGORY							LEVEL			
	Aptitudes	Interests	Values	Career Development	Combined Measures	Personality	Special Populations	Elementary School	Junior High/Middle School	High School	Post-High School/Adult
Vocational Preference Inventory, 1985 Revision (VPI)		P				S				X	X
Vocational Research Interest Inventory (VRII)		P								X	X
Vocational Skills Assessment and Development Program	S						P		X	X	X
Vo-Tech Major Card Sort		P							X	X	X
What I Like To Do		P						S	X		
Wide Range Employability Sample Test (WREST)	S						P	X		X	X
Wide Range Intelligence and Personality Test (WRIPT)	S					S	P	X	X	X	X
Wide Range Interest-Opinion Test (WRIOT)		S					P	X	X	X	X
Word and Number Assessment Inventory (WNAI)	P								X	X	X
Work Activities Checklist		P								X	
Work Activities Inventory		P								X	

Work Attitudes Questionnaire					P				X
Work Content Skills Inventory	P								X
Work Situations					P			X	
Work Skills Assessment Package	S					P	X	X	
Work Values Inventory (WVI)			P				X	X	
World of Work Inventory (WOWI)	S	S		P			X	X	

INDEX